Edward F. Beale
and the American West

Edward Fitzgerald Beale was a midshipman at the time this miniature was painted in about 1842. (*Courtesy National Trust for Historic Preservation.*)

Edward F. Beale

&

The American West

GERALD THOMPSON

University of New Mexico Press
Albuquerque

JH

Library of Congress Cataloging in Publication Data

Thompson, Gerald.
    Edward F. Beale and the American West.

    Bibliography: p.
    Includes index.
    1. Beale, Edward Fitzgerald, 1822–1893. 2. South-
west, New—Description and travel. 3. United States—
Exploring expeditions. 4. California—Gold discoveries.
5. Indians of North America—California. 6. Explorers—
Southwest, New—Biography. 7. Pioneers—California—
Biography. 8. Soldiers—United States—Biography.
9. Politicians—United States—Biography. I. Title.
F786.B362T48   1983   979'.02'0924 [B]   83–1323
ISBN 0–8263–0663–2

Design: Cyd Riley.

For My Mother

CONTENTS

ILLUSTRATIONS

M A P S

Our measures of time are all false and absurd together, we might find a thousand better clocks than any that have ever been carried up into the sky by a church steeple. Thoughts, feelings, passions and events— these are the real moral timekeepers. What is it to me the mere ticking of a pendulum?

—Edward F. Beale, Journal (ca. 1842)

P R E F A C E

Edward Fitzgerald Beale (1822–93) was a major figure in the history of the American West. Few Americans have gained distinction in so many different fields—naval officer, explorer, bureaucrat, rancher, politician, and promoter. During his lifetime, Beale was regarded as "Mr. California," and numbered among his friends such preeminent men as Robert F. Stockton, Kit Carson, Thomas Hart Benton, Bayard Taylor, U.S. Grant, and many others. A study of Beale's life offers important insights into many of the events and personalities that dominated post-1845 America. A colorful and interesting man, Beale successfully pursued a personal El Dorado of adventure, status, and wealth. In so doing, he mirrored the dreams of countless Americans of his day.

Despite his achievements and importance, Beale has been largely forgotten. He is remembered, if at all, as a quixotic man who presided over a strange experiment to introduce camels into the Southwest. The intended purpose of this biography is to portray him as a human being—complex, with qualities of greatness and weakness—and to fix his position more precisely within the historical landscape.

Beale's accomplishments can be readily cataloged. He emerged from the Mexican War as the most prominent American hero of the fighting in California. In 1848, on his own initiative, Beale carried the first samples of gold from the new El Dorado to the East Coast. There, his avid promotion of California helped spark one of the greatest mass migrations of the nineteenth century. In 1852, as a disciple of Thomas Hart Benton, Beale gained the appointment to serve as California's first superintendent of Indian affairs, and helped charter a new, humanitarian policy toward Native Americans. Following his controversial removal from office, Beale next plunged into San Francisco politics and led the Law and Order forces in opposition to the revolutionary tactics of the Vigilantes. His family connections with President James Buchanan earned Beale another government post in 1857 as superintendent of a transcontinental wagon road project. For two and one-half years, he explored and constructed a road across the Southwest, and experimented with the use of camels. On the eve of the Civil War, Beale joined the Republican Party. In 1861 Lincoln appointed him surveyor general of California, an important position which Beale neglected. Lincoln dismissed him from office, but not before Beale had used his position to secure title to Rancho El Tejon, one of the largest ranches in the American West. His financial future was bright.

After 1864, Beale began to divide his time between California and

Pennsylvania. He dabbled in Pennsylvania politics, and gained the distinction of being one of the first politicians to urge that Negroes be granted the right to vote. To increase his status and power, Beale purchased the Decatur House in 1872 and moved to Washington, D.C. For the next two decades, his home served as social center of the nation's capital, while Beale rose to an important position within the Republican Party. Soon, Beale became President Grant's closest personal friend. In addition to his social activities, Beale maintained a lifelong interest for business affairs, and during the 1870s and 1880s he spearheaded the movement for an interoceanic canal across Central America. By the time of his death in 1893, Beale was a recognized figure on the national scene.

Almost anyone who ever met Beale described him as a remarkable man—witty, intelligent, and energetic. Despite his many interests, he still found time for service as a diplomat and for a happy family life. He was a handsome man, slightly below medium stature with a thin, wiry build. An abundance of nervous energy seemed to keep him constantly in motion. Beale was generally sensitive, occasionally violent, and frequently outspoken. His frankness probably prevented him from ever holding a high elective post.

Throughout his life, two primary forces motivated Beale: a desire for adventure and a drive to achieve wealth and status. The Far West afforded the opportunity to fulfill these ambitions, as Beale endeavored to profit from the government positions he held. But Beale's career did not fit the classic mold of the self-made man. Almost invariably, he sought and leaned heavily on family connections, political friendships, and simple luck for advancement. In this regard, Beale was perhaps typical of many American success stories in the nineteenth century.

In the course of researching this book, I have consulted over three hundred libraries, archives, and historical societies. Three types of primary historical material proved most valuable: Beale's private papers (Decatur House Papers), National Archives' materials, and newspapers. The Decatur House Papers, located in the Library of Congress, are very important and revealing. As a public servant, Beale generated a large body of correspondence, all of which is located in the National Archives. Finally, the tedious process of combing local newspapers divulged crucial information which could not have been obtained elsewhere. Other Beale material surfaced in a surprising number of collections in various repositories around the country. Legal records also proved important, particularly in following Beale's investments and business activities.

A large number of individuals and institutions have earned my thanks and gratitude for the help they provided during the course of this book. Professor Harwood P. Hinton provided key research suggestions, constant encouragement, and sound editorial advice. I am very grateful to him. Professors Paul A. Carter and Roger L. Nichols both read the manuscript and made many helpful criticisms. Among the other individuals to whom I owe a "thank you" are Henry P. Walker, Paul W. Gates, Harland Boyd, Richard Bailey, Duncan V. Patty, Andrew Rolle, W. N. Davis, David Williams, Lee Scott Theisen, Gerald Stanley, Mary Lee Spence, Jack Smith, Dennis Alward, and Nina Caspari.

I would also like to thank the staffs of the following institutions: California State Archives, California Historical Society, Society of California Pioneers, California State Library, Bakersfield Public Library, Los Angeles County Archives and Records, UCLA Special Collections, San Diego Historical Society, Delaware County Historical Society, Historical Society of Dauphin County, Arizona Historical Society, Historical Society of Pennsylvania, Cornell University Special Collections, Harvard University Special Collections, Princeton University Special Collections, Eleutherian Mills Historical Library, Huntington Library, the Library of Congress, and the National Archives. The Interlibrary Loan Department of the University of Arizona deserves my special thanks, as does the Tejon Ranch Company, which generously provided the photographs of Beale's ranch.

I also wish to thank my mother and father for their tolerance over many years. To Margaret, my wife, I wish to express my loving gratitude for her continued patience and encouragement. At times during the last four years, she felt as though Edward Beale had joined our family, as I become totally preoccupied with reconstructing Beale's eventful life and career.

G.T.
Toledo, Ohio

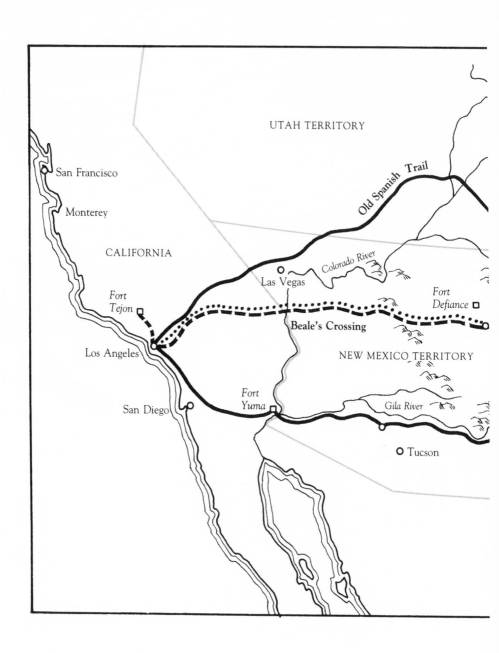

UTAH TERRITORY

San Francisco

Monterey

CALIFORNIA

Old Spanish Trail

Colorado River

Las Vegas

Fort
Defiance

Fort
Tejon

Beale's Crossing

Los Angeles

NEW MEXICO TERRITORY

San Diego

Fort
Yuma

Gila River

Tucson

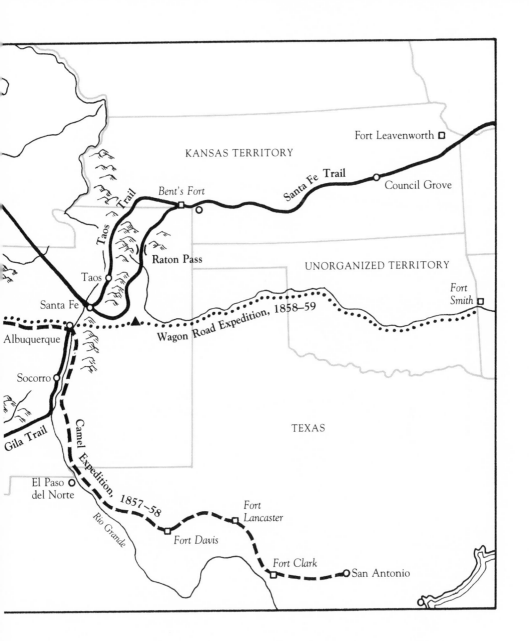

Chapter 1

A MIDSHIPMAN'S LIFE

All was now hurry & hustle. The meeting of friends—the greeting of acquaintances—the consultations of men of business. I alone was solitary and idle. I had no friend to meet, no cheering to receive. I stept upon the land but felt that I was a stranger in that land.

In endeavoring to form for myself a just estimate of human nature—to learn for the sake of comparing them the effects produced on the minds of man by every station of life and every earthly pursuit, I have visited the haunts of the low and guilty, and mingled for a brief season with the profligate, the criminal and the base in many of the countries my feet have trod. . . .

—Beale Journal 1842

Before daylight on a chilly spring morning in 1892, two men mounted horses at Rancho El Tejon headquarters and rode slowly east. Edward F. Beale, well-known California pioneer was the older man; his companion was a young San Francisco reporter. They passed the bubbling Paso Creek, covered by thick wild grapevines and followed a trail which climbed into the Tehachapi Mountains. Seventy years old and bothered by gout, Beale felt this might be his last opportunity to overlook his immense domain. As the sunrise crowned the peaks with a "halo of glory," the two men reined up their mounts. Beale indicated that from the top of a nearby ridge one could see a magnificent scene of woods, peaks, canyons, and streams.

Upon reaching the summit the two riders sat in their saddles for a long time, taking in the grand panorama of nature—"sublime and

1

beautiful." All the land they could see, stretching for miles in every direction, Beale owned, more than 270,000 acres. The reporter said that Beale was overcome as "a flood of early recollections rolled over him."[1]

According to family tradition, Beale's Scotch-Irish forebears emigrated to Virginia from the West Indies, where they had been wealthy plantation owners. In the 1660s, Captain Thomas Beale, a Royalist Knight of Malta, settled in Richmond County, and the Virginia Beales were his descendants. The Beales were very proud of their ancestors: one had died at the side of George Washington in western Pennsylvania following Braddock's defeat in 1755, while yet another lost his life serving under John Paul Jones's command. By 1790, a branch of the Beale family had settled at Mill Town Plantation, near Hampton, Virginia, where George M. Beale, Jr., the father of Edward, was born in 1791.[2]

Equally prominent during these years were the Truxtuns, Edward F. Beale's matrilineal ancestors. Commodore Thomas Truxtun played a prominent part in the naval operations of the Revolution, and in 1794, President Washington appointed him a captain in the fledgling American navy. Truxtun's greatest victories came against the French in the undeclared naval warfare of 1798–1800, when, as captain of the *Constellation*, he commanded a squadron in the West Indies. Congress awarded Truxtun a medal and a vote of thanks. Lloyd's of London presented him a superb silver service valued at $3,000. Prior to his death in 1822 at the age of sixty-seven, Truxtun sired a large family—two boys and eleven daughters. Aaron Burr described the collective Truxtun ladies as the "handsomest women of the period." The youngest daughter, Emily (Edward's mother), was born in Perth Amboy, New Jersey on September 30, 1798.[3]

George Beale also selected a naval career. In 1812, he received a commission as a purser or navy paymaster and served with distinction. During a crucial battle on Lake Champlain, Beale's "gallantry and good conduct and services" earned him a silver medal from the U.S. Congress. After the war ended, Purser Beale remained in the navy, and during a three-year period in Washington, he won the affections of the comely Emily Truxtun. They were married in Philadelphia on May 4, 1819, with Bishop William White, an Episcopalian, performing the service. The young couple took up residence at Bloomingdale, an estate of some fifty acres, located a mile and a half north of the Capitol Building, just beyond the boundary line of the city of Washington.[4]

Bloomingdale provided a comfortable home for the George Beales. The estate was a gathering place and occasionally the temporary residence for young naval officers on duty or leave in Washington. Beale regarded himself as a southern gentleman, and his home always reflected the graciousness and hospitality of the southern gentry. George Beale loved the outdoors—especially to hunt, fish, or ride. Abundant small game could be found in the woods near Bloomingdale, within eyesight of Capitol Hill; or if Beale desired to fowl, he could ride down to the Tiber River marsh lands and join absentee congressmen hunting birds only a few hundred yards south of James Monroe's rear porch.[5]

In January of 1821, George and Emily Beale's first child was born, and they named the baby "Truxtun" honoring Emily's father. Some months after Truxtun's birth, Beale received orders to join the frigate *United States,* and his long, happy sojourn in the Washington vicinity abruptly ended. Leaving his twenty-three-year-old wife in charge of Bloomingdale and its household of slaves, he reported for sea duty. For much of the next nine years, he would be home only on temporary leave.

The winter of 1821–22 again found Emily Beale "lying-in" at Bloomingdale. On February 3, 1822, she bore another boy and christened him Edward Fitzgerald Beale. Nicknamed "Ned" by his family and friends, the boy's early years were dominated by his mother. Ned saw his father infrequently, but when George Beale came home, he took the boys hunting, fishing, and riding. Before many birthdays passed, Ned Beale acquired his father's deep love for horses and regarded himself as an excellent judge of equine stock. George Beale believed in education, and everywhere he went his young son observed him reading. In later years, Edward F. Beale recalled that he never saw his father "without a book in his hand, even when he went fishing or on a hunt."[6]

Despite his father's studious example, young Ned failed to take his schooling seriously. He was a "bad boy, much given to playing truant," he later told historian Hubert H. Bancroft. Beale spent many of his youthful days roaming the Washington area with a small black lad, probably a Beale slave. One of their greatest pleasures was swimming in the cool waters of the Potomac River during the sweltering months of July and August. Ned excelled at the sport and boasted that he could swim the Potomac at a point near the Long Bridge to Arlington, where the river was nearly a mile wide. Ned Beale possessed a volatile personality and early acquired something of a reputation as a scrapper. On one occasion, probably in 1829 or 1830, Beale and a friend started to fight close to the president's house. A tall, white-haired old man intervened, separated the battling boys, and demanded to know the cause of the altercation. Beale replied that he was "hurrahing for Jackson," but that his opponent refused to do so (probably a Clay supporter). The old man revealed himself to be Andrew Jackson and promised the boy that if he ever desired anything in the future to come visit him at the White House.[7]

In the fall of 1832, Beale's parents enrolled the two brothers in Georgetown College. The Jesuit institution enjoyed a reputation for strictness and academic excellence, and many prominent southern families sent sons there to be educated. Many of the students, like the Beale boys, were not Catholics.

At Georgetown College Beale earned the rudiments of a classical education. He liked his studies and quickly surpassed his older brother. The young boy's facile mind seemed ideally suited for the memorization which the Jesuits emphasized. Latin writers such as Cicero, Horace, Virgil, and Ovid were learned "by heart," as were such Greek luminaries as Xenophon, Theocritus, and Homer. Beale's teachers also considered mathematics and foreign languages to be valuable, and Beale may have started on the road to mastering several foreign languages at this time.

In April of 1835, when they were approximately halfway through their studies toward a degree, Ned and Truxtun received tragic news from Bloomingdale—their father had suddenly died. On April 8, Emily Beale quickly withdrew her sons from Georgetown College.[8]

Emily found herself in a difficult position. George Beale's estate carried financial encumbrances, and relatives urged her to sell the property rather than try to manage it herself. Her husband had speculated in real estate, and owned five unimproved lots in Washington and a piece of property in Georgetown. More importantly, Beale had acquired three Washington houses, presumably rentals. The young widow felt burdened by her new responsibility, but she decided to manage the estate and pay off the indebtedness. The increased size of her family also compounded the difficulties. Two daughters, Elizabeth and Emily, and a third son, George, Jr., had been born between 1823 and 1838.[9]

Ned Beale soon expressed a strong interest in a naval career. She and her son called on President Jackson to request a midshipman's appointment. Upon meeting Jackson, Mrs. Beale recited the contribution to the American Navy made by her father, Commodore Truxtun, as well as George Beale's heroics at Lake Champlain. Then the young Ned stepped forward and reminded the President that several years before Jackson had promised a scuffling youngster "anything," when he heard he had been willing to fight for the president. Obviously enjoying Ned's recital, Jackson penned a brief note, handed it to young Beale, and stated that he should take the paper to Secretary of the Navy Mahlon Dickerson. The note read "give this boy an immediate warrant."[10]

Beale desired a naval career for several reasons. First, his family had long been associated with the sea. Second, he possessed a true romantic spirit and doubtless envisioned himself performing heroic and patriotic deeds in exotic parts of the world. Finally, a naval officer's commission could open the path to the upper echelons of American society. Although an officer's pay was relatively low, his commission automatically labelled him a gentleman, and hence socially acceptable. Consequently, on December 15, 1836, when official notification came of his appointment as "Acting Midshipman," he was jubilant. "I accept the appointment with pleasure," Beale wrote Secretary Dickerson, "and trust, Sir, that my conduct in the service will be the best evidence I can give, how highly I estimate the kindness shown me in the selection you have made."[11]

In February of 1837, Beale received orders to report for duty on the *Independence* at Boston. Constructed in 1814, the ship was a recently razeed (repaired) frigate of sixty guns, under the command of Commodore John L. Nicolson. Soon after boarding, Beale was harassed by other midshipmen who scoffed at his elaborate homemade uniform, embellished with Commodore Truxtun's large, old-fashioned buttons. Beale fought a fist fight to defend his family honor and was victorious, gaining the respect of his comrades. When the *Independence* set sail, it carried George M. Dallas to his new assignment as minister to the court of Nicholas I, Czar of Russia. The old frigate left Boston on May 20.[12]

Beale found life on shipboard strange and demanding. The salty, nautical language posed a seemingly insurmountable barrier. To a fifteen-year-old boy the names of the innumerable ropes and the commands of the deck officers seemed exasperating. The few romantic notions he had about seafaring vanished dramatically one day, as young Beale stood on deck. Suddenly, without warning, a common sailor slipped from a top yardarm, and struck headfirst the oaken deck near Beale's feet. The man's skull was smashed to a "disgusting mass." The tragic death, a routine accident, affected the sensitive boy greatly. He cried quietly for a long time that night, while his hammock rocked gently with the ship's motion.[13]

On July 29, 1837, the *Independence* reached its destination of Kronstadt, the Russian port on the Gulf of Finland. After taking on supplies, the ship sailed for its assigned station off the Brazilian coast. Commodore Nicolson took up the command of the Brazilian squadron, which consisted of his flagship, the *Independence*, the *Fairfield*, and the *Dolphin*. During the months of South American duty, Beale acquired the necessary skills of seamanship and leadership. In July of 1839, he received his coveted warrant as a full midshipman, issued only after his superiors' letters of recommendation had been forwarded to the Navy Department for study.[14]

In Brazilian ports, Beale grew acquainted with different types of people, and acquired a tolerant attitude toward foreign customs. He earnestly endeavored to experience as much of life as possible. While on shore leave, he "visited the haunts of the low and the guilty and mingled for a brief season with the profligate, the criminal, and the base," he recorded in a diary. Like many of his companions, Beale succumbed to the dual temptations of liquor and fallen women, and in his journal he carefully penned a hangover cure: mix half a gill of brandy and an equal amount of water, add sugar, then blend in three fresh eggs. Beale was now eighteen years old, of average height, thinly built, with moderately long, brown hair. He was a handsome young man, and he was vain about both his personal appearance and his dress.[15]

Beale spent more than twenty-four months on the *Independence* and did not receive a leave until April of 1840, when the frigate returned to the United States for extensive repairs. In Washington, Beale's family discerned a remarkable change in Ned, for he had grown to adulthood during the three years of absence. Late in summer, Ned received orders for his next assignment. He traveled to Norfolk to join his new ship, the sloop-of-war *Levant*, bound for the West Indies.[16]

Beale spent only eight months in the West Indies Squadron. On May 10, 1841, he received a three-month leave and returned home. While at Bloomingdale, Beale realized that an important career hurdle lay just ahead; it was time for the 1837 midshipmen to prepare for their officers' examinations, and he needed orders to go to the naval school. On August 31, he explained to George E. Badger, secretary of the navy, that his date of entry was next to come before the naval examining board, and received orders to study at the Naval Asylum in Philadelphia.[17]

At the school midshipmen received detailed instruction, approximately six months in duration, to intensify and broaden the knowledge they had gained at sea. The course of study included higher mathematics, navigation, foreign languages, and moral philosophy.

The Asylum was located on a twenty-acre tract on Gray's Ferry Road near Philadelphia. One wing of the building housed the midshipmen, while the other quartered pensioners, for whom the Asylum had originally been designed. The midshipmen's tiny rooms, replete with barred windows, strongly resembled prison cells. One night in mid-September of 1841, Beale wrote his brother Truxtun that in his new quarters, he looked just like a monk but felt like the Devil. A charcoal likeness of that "respectable gentleman" gazed down at Ned from where an earlier reefer had drawn it on the wall of "Cell No. 2, Ward No. 1." Ned grew depressed in the cramped, darkened room (he had forgotten to purchase a lamp) and recorded that he felt "as low spirited as an absence from those we love must ever occasion in a man's feelings."[18]

Beale and his friends frequently managed to escape the tedious confines of naval studies. The reefers spent their leaves, legitimate or "french," strutting about Philadelphia in their fancy dress uniforms, smoking fine cigars. The Schuylkill Rangers, a Philadelphia juvenile gang, was the great town foe of the Asylum "mids." On one occasion, Beale represented the midshipmen in a pugilistic encounter with the best battler of the Rangers. Despite his slight build, Ned's quickness and tenacity won the "freedom of the neighborhood" for himself and his companions. Othertimes, Beale spent his leaves visiting his cousins—the Porters, a well-known naval family, residing in the nearby town of Chester.[19]

During the winter of 1841, smallpox broke out in Philadelphia. At the naval school, the cadets were vaccinated, but unfortunately for some, the vaccine had been improperly prepared and the serum failed to take. Beale's friend, Daniel Ammen, a twenty-three-year-old midshipman from Ohio, contracted the disease but managed to survive. Professor David McClure avoided smallpox but died in April from pneumonia, a frequent killer in the nineteenth century. After the head professor's death, the governing board of the asylum closed the school for six weeks, and those midshipmen not confined to hospitals quickly fled the city.[20]

After the school reopened in May, Beale's class was notified that a board of examination would convene on June 13, 1842 to review the candidates. The board included Commodores James Barron (president), James Biddle, and George C. Read; Captains Daniel Turner and Isaac McKeever; and Professor William Chauvenet, mathematics examiner. The board called midshipmen at random, and not until the prior evening did they know their turn was at hand. On June 23, Edward F. Beale nervously climbed the stairs to the room where the board was meeting. Beale displayed his journal, a requirement of all the candidates, then presented letters of support from his commanding officers. Commodore Barron posed important questions in seamanship. All midshipmen stood in awe of Barron, for twenty years earlier he had killed in a duel Commodore Stephen Decatur, the naval hero. Beale's responses to the questions fell below average, but they were more than adequate to pass. The board's favorable decision on Beale's performance surprised the young man, and he termed it "the most extraordinary event of my life."[21]

As a passed midshipman, Beale sailed on the *Columbus*, commanded by Captain William C. Spencer, on August 29, 1842, to join the Mediterranean squadron. His new position gave him greater freedom and additional responsibilities, but he was not a commissioned officer. The passed midshipmen as a group were discontented, as they frequently waited from three to eight years before obtaining a commission. All too often the prized lieutenant's epaulets were bestowed on individuals who possessed high political connections, regardless of their actual abilities. He passed the next two years engaged in uneventful duty in Europe and South America.[22]

Beale was an appropriate representative of America overseas, for like the young nation which he served, he contained within himself abundant contradictions. Close friends admired his constant cheerfulness, but others noted his eccentric ideas and volatile temper. Beale attempted to hide his tendency toward moodniess and melancholia. "If we could draw back the veil from the hearts of the most cheerful scene," he wrote in his private journal, "there would be much weeping among us for the *sorrows of others, or our own!*" He condemned false friendships and insincere actions but occasionally acted in the same manner himself. Next to his cure for a hangover, for instance, Beale penned a quotation that seemed to represent a working model: "He who has never committed a crime cannot appreciate virtue."[23]

Beale recorded his reflections about life. He discovered religion, of sorts, and wrote of the "infinitely superior wisdom of the Creator," versus the "littleness of men." He looked back with anguish and horror on his earlier life, when he had mingled with the lowly. He expressed compassion for society's unfortunates and condemned the universal apathy for allowing sin, sorrow, and destruction to possess fellow men—"beings like ourselves!" The solution, he felt, demanded all persons to distinguish right from wrong in their hearts in a type of religious awakening, for only then could a man truly taste the "excellence of the one and the hatefulness of the other."

Writing in his diary, Beale despaired a man's ability to improve himself or his society through the exercise of reason. Beale angrily penned that "men are very fond of proving their steadfast adherence to nonsense." He pointed to the feuding sects of Christianity for especial condemnation. Each denomination stood ready to cut another's throat or banish a rival to "eternal hell fire, hot lead, and brimstone" for trivial, unimportant differences. Beale had read the *Koran* and recommended a verse in Chapter 5 to Christians which urged all men to "excel each other in good works" and leave doctrinal quibbles to Allah. Forgetful of Islam's historic intolerance, Beale stated that although he was not a Mohammedan, should his portrait ever be taken he feared it would be in "slippers and turban." Despite his professed interest in Islam, Beale never took to heart the *Koran*'s injunctions against alcohol, pork, or gambling.

Beale frequently read romantic poetry of Keats and Shelley. He liked their descriptive imagery and attempted to emulate Shelley's style in his own rough verses. Beale dissented from European romantic emphasis on the "wonderous charm" of antiquity. He postulated that in ancient times men undoubtedly criticized themselves for being "flat, jejeune, *modern!*" —just as they were doing at present. Consequently, Beale's view of history was tempered with pragmatism and a faith in the present. What then constituted the value of the romantic school? Beale felt that William Wordsworth's poetry, for instance, inspired an inner awareness of "Truth" that should be directed toward the future.[24]

Beale was prized for his camaraderie. On a page of his journal he again urged himself to avoid "revelling & feasting" and then proceeded to describe his shameful conduct of the previous evening. Following his sizeable consumption of port wine, Beale's friends cajoled him into dancing a madrille, a sport which he usually did not enjoy. In a sulky mood he performed the mazy revolution of the dance, much after the manner of a "bear led round a ring by a female monkey." Despite a hangover the next morning, Beale remembered his dance partner clearly—too clearly. She possessed the complexion of a new cent, and Beale "wished she'd have had a new scent for a perfume, and a face less like a musk rat."

During these years Beale joined the numerous confraternity of those individuals wounded by love or false friendship. "Love is the fickliest of the things of life," he morosely wrote, probably after losing a lady's affections. It was best "never to confide in any man, much less *woman*" and to avoid all close links with other people. "Let not any being control you through your dependence on him for a portion of your happiness," he gloomed. He learned this truth from "bitter experience." Despite these youthful musings, Beale prized true friendship throughout his life.

In these years of voyaging to distant lands, Beale also formed his conception of the nature of society. Influenced by a conservative family and his naval career, Beale believed that society was an organic entity with each grade contributing to the whole and required to show deference to the other classes. His views coincided in this regard with Edmund Burke, the noted English conservative, whom Beale may have read. Beale despised individuals who bred discontent by pitting one class against another and felt that history would leave these villains "naked and disgraced." From his own observations and reflections, Beale concluded that the "man of rank" in dealing with society and with his God, afforded the "most wonderful subject for contemplation this world can furnish." The young midshipman vowed that he would become such a "man of rank."[25]

Upon returning home from a voyage in early 1845, Beale spent several months on leave at Bloomingdale, then was assigned to the naval squadron commanded by Captain Robert F. Stockton. The commander had orders to sail for the Mediterranean and display to European countries the peculiar construction of the *Princeton*, Stockton's ingenious steam-powered, screw-propelled warship. A wealthy New Jersey capitalist and inventor, as well as a career naval officer, Stockton was an intimate of presidents, especially Andrew Jackson. A deeply religious man, Stockton was known to take the ship's pulpit and preach to officers and men on God, duty, and the special manifest destiny of America. Beale regarded Stockton as a genius and looked forward to the upcoming cruise.[26]

With the inauguration of James K. Polk as the new president in March, Beale learned that the Navy Department had cancelled the Mediterranean cruise. New orders came several weeks later and Beale reported at Norfolk on March 25 for duty aboard the *Porpoise*. Stockton had been instructed by Polk to sail for the Texas coast with his squadron and there acquaint himself "with the dispositions of the people of Texas, and their relations with Mexico." Beale summarized the orders more succinctly: the squadron had sailed to Texas to investigate the "annexation of Mexico."[27]

Stockton's squadron entered Galveston harbor on May 13, with the *Porpoise* leading. The warships fired a customary salute. Later that week, town officials entertained the officers of the squadron at a "Great Ball." On June 23, 1845, Stockton departed for Washington, bearing the news that the Texas Congress had unanimously accepted the United States offer of annexation.[28]

While at home, Beale sought to remain under Stockton's command, especially after he heard that Stockton would soon sail for the Pacific. When orders came transferring Beale, his mother Emily came to the rescue. Mrs. Beale asked Secretary James Buchanan to use his influence to alter her son's orders, and the bureaucrat wrote a letter of introduction for Emily to Naval Secretary George Bancroft and asked him to honor Mrs. Beale's desires regarding her son. One month later, Ned Beale received orders for duty aboard the frigate *Congress*, assigned to Stockton's squadron. Once again, Beale tightly packed his sea chest, journeyed to New York City, and reported for duty on September 2, 1845, at the Gosport Navy Yard.[29]

Strained foreign relations menaced Stockton's upcoming Pacific cruise. An American offer to settle the disputed Oregon boundary at the forty-ninth parallel had been spurned by Britain, and President Polk angrily adopted a hard line on future negotiations. The United States boldly asserted a claim to all of Oregon as far north as fifty-four degrees, forty minutes. Relations with Mexico were also tense, and if hostilities broke out, the Pacific Squadron would be severed from Washington, virtually an independent command. Few American naval officers feared the helpless Mexican navy, but the British fleet was a dreadful subject for contemplation. Stockton and others, such as James Buchanan, hoped to avoid, if at all possible, a clash with Her Majesty's celebrated warships.[30]

Shortly after reporting to the *Congress*, Midshipman Beale received a promotion, to the rank of acting master. A ship's master was one of the most important officers on board and ranked in importance just below the first lieutenant. He generally handled the shipping and stowing of stores, inspected rigging, spars, sails and hold, and supervised preparations for anchoring. The master also kept the ship's log and daily reported the reckoning or location to the captain. With the promotion Beale received additional duty—that of a private secretary to Stockton himself![31]

Commanded by Captain Samuel F. Du Pont, the *Congress* sailed to Norfolk, where Secretary Bancroft visited the ship. By October 25, the *Congress* stood ready to sail, but at the scheduled departure time another delay occurred. Commodore Stockton suddenly disembarked and caught the steamer for Washington for a last-minute conference. Beale also left the ship for a short trip to Philadelphia, presumably on ship's business. On October 28, he wrote Mrs. Samuel F. Du Pont, who resided in Wilmington, that he would be returning to Norfolk the next day and would be happy to take her husband any packages. Stockton returned to the *Congress* on October 29, 1845 and gave instructions to sail.[32]

Shortly after the *Congress* reached the open sea, Commodore Stockton spoke to the assembled crew and officers. He praised Captain Du Pont and the other officers. The flag of their country, he told the men, was entrusted to them, and he counted on their patriotism, honor, and undaunted valor. The success of the voyage depended upon them. Stockton concluded his exhortation with the cryptic statement that their ship now sailed "for California and Oregon, and then where it may please Heaven." Walter Colton, the ship's chaplain, offered a prayer for the cruise, and the officers and seamen sang the traditional song, "Hail Columbia, Gem of the Ocean." Stockton and the ship's officers then retired to the commodore's cabin for an elaborate meal.[33]

Amidst the daily routine, Chaplain Colton confided to his diary that the *Congress*, a fast ship, was the "highest triumph of human skill—the noblest representative of art." Beale agreed. Built by Yankee craftsmen in Portsmouth, New Hampshire in 1842, the *Congress* was a sleek-lined vessel, almost new. The ship carried a crew of 480 men. After a fortnight of sailing, the ship had traversed 1,800 miles of ocean and reached the choppy seas off the French islands of Guadaloupe and Martinique.

On November 20, the ship's lookout sighted a brig, standing down, waiting for the *Congress*. The brig hoisted Danish colors, and the American frigate "hove to" at cable length. A Danish officer of the *Mariah* stated that his ship was forty days out from Rio Grande, Brazil, bound for Hamburg. He dsesired to correct his reckoning. Aided by an American officer, it was found that the *Mariah* was seven degrees out of longitude, a sizeable error. The American sailors asked for fruit, but the Danes lacked that valuable commodity.[34]

Stockton took advantage of the chance encounter with the *Mariah* to implement a daring scheme. He summoned Beale to his cabin and discussed with him the need to learn about British fleet movements. He instructed Beale to ship aboard the Danish vessel and sail to England; there Beale would disguise his identity and attempt to learn if British warships were about to sail for the Pacific. The young naval officer also would seek information on British feelings on the question of Oregon boundary. Once he completed the assignment, Beale would take passage for the United States and report in person to President Polk and Navy Secretary Bancroft. He hoped to rejoin Stockton several months hence at Callao, Peru, with dispatches from the Navy Department.

Beale hastily packed his belongings for his mission as a spy. Climbing over the railing into the ship's dinghy, bouncing madly in the choppy waters, he fumbled with several packages and spilled them into the turbulent sea. Beale reached the *Mariah* and the two vessels parted for their different destinations.[35]

Beale discovered the *Mariah* was 480 miles off course, and, more alarming, she had lost both her captain and first officer. Beale volunteered his services and navigated the ship for the remainder of the voyage to England. There, in line with Stockton's orders, he attempted to acquire information on the British fleet and official government feelings regarding Oregon.

By late February of 1846, Beale was again in Washington and reported to President Polk and Secretary Bancroft. The officer told his superiors that the British navy had been making warlike preparations (a conclusion the American minister in London had already reached). On February 23, President Polk recorded in his diary that Britain was indeed engaged in making "warlike preparations." Polk then proceeded to clarify the American position on Oregon. The door was not closed to further negotiations and the United States might accept a compromise.[36]

On March 7, Bancroft handed Beale packages for Commodore Stockton. As instructed, Beale boarded the frigate *Potomac* at Norfolk and sailed for Panama. He crossed the isthmus by boat and mule and arrived at the settlement of Panama on the Pacific. There he found a letter from Stockton ordering him to catch the next steamer for Callao, Peru.

On May 8, Beale reported to Stockton on the *Congress*. In addition to official letters for Stockton, Beale brought personal letters for the officers; he even carried newspapers. Relaying the latest news from home, Beale was an extremely popular man for the next few days.

12

The *Congress* left Callao on May 9 and began the long voyage across the Pacific. The passage had a calm monotony to it. On June 9, the *Congress* arrived in Honolulu, exactly one month after leaving Callao. She had averaged 235 miles per day, one of the fastest crossings ever recorded.[37]

The *Congress* rested at anchor in Honolulu Bay for two weeks. The natives proved a constant source of diversion, with the officers pointing to them as examples of degenerate non-Christians. The sight of Hawaiian women swimming naked in view of the Americans shocked Reverend Colton, but he duly recorded in his diary that they looked just like "mermaids." The Americans also found the *Brooklyn* at Hawaii, loaded with Mormon settlers, led by the bubbling Irishman, Samuel Brannan, a recent convert. They hoped to found a colony in California.

Stockton sailed on June 23, having received news the preceding day that American and Mexican troops had clashed on the Texas border. War seemed imminent. A tense excitement prevailed as the ship headed for California. Stockton ordered his gun crews to drill, firing the cannon shot out across the ocean. The Fourth of July passed in discussion of a possible Mexican war. Both men and officers appeared eager to engage in battle. Reverend Colton noted how the young men seemed to think they could "hew their way with cutlass and a pound of pork to the halls of Montezuma."

On July 15, the lookout sighted the California coast. Beale viewed the rugged shoreline at daybreak as the sunlight reddened the pines atop the cliffs south of Monterey. But the sight quickly vanished, when a thick summer morning's fog enshrouded the *Congress* and prevented movement in unknown waters. Shortly after noon, the fog lifted and the *Congress* rounded a point and entered the large, crescent-shaped expanse of Monterey Bay.[38]

Edward F. Beale was now twenty-four years old and held a responsible position in the United States Navy. He possessed a vigorous, attractive personality and seemed gifted with all the qualities necessary to become a successful naval officer. He was intelligent, obedient, loyal, and courageous. Nevertheless, his quixotic nature often contradicted his attributes. Frequently, Beale appeared more interested in adventures and exotic experiences than in the purposeful pursuit of a career. The possibility of fighting Mexicans in California strongly appealed to the restless young man.

Chapter 2

HERO OF SAN PASQUAL

We, your friends and brother officers, have ordered from England a pair of epaulets and sword, . . . in testimony of our admiration of your gallant conduct in the bold and hazardous enterprise of leaving Gen. Kearny's encampment after the battles of "San Pascual" and "San Bernardino" of the 6th of December, 1846, for the purpose of bringing information to the garrison of San Diego, and obtaining relief for the suffering troops. . . .

—Lieutenant J. W. Revere,
et al. to Beale,
December 21, 1846

I was carried, a very-much crippled young man, to the home of a Mexican family. I was treated with such care and tenderness that when I was restored to health I desired to know more of the people of my hospitable hosts, and what I saw of them turned the current of my life, for I determined to live among the Mexicans of California.

—Edward F. Beale

In Monterey, Stockton met with Commodore John D. Sloat, commander of the Pacific Squadron, and learned that fighting had flared in California between American and Mexican forces. Stockton held orders to replace Sloat as the Pacific Squadron's commander, which now included the overall direction of naval and land operations against the Mexicans. As he prepared for his new command, Stockton listened intently as Sloat, a sickly man, recited in detail the dramatic events of recent months.[1]

During the late spring of 1846, American settlers in the Napa and Sacramento valleys had rebelled against Mexican authorities, who earlier had threatened to expel unauthorized American immigrants. On June 6, Captain John C. Fremont, who had been in California for several months, supposedly engaged in scientific exploration for the United States, joined the rebellious settlers. With Fremont's encouragement, the settlers proclaimed themselves independent, and on July 4, at Sonoma, they hoisted a banner carrying the image of a California grizzly bear. At Monterey, Sloat learned of Fremont's action and ordered his squadron to seize Monterey and San Francisco. The commodore later became unnerved when he learned that Fremont had acted without orders, solely on his own initiative. Consequently, Sloat was delighted when Commodore Stockton arrived in California in late July.[2]

Upon taking command of American naval and land forces in California, Stockton vowed to drive out all hostile Mexicans. Promoted to acting lieutenant by Stockton, Beale described the commodore's battle plan as "the greatest enterprise ever proposed by a maritime commander." Stockton immediately organized the ship's company into an infantry battalion and ordered it to march into "unknown country" and engage the enemy. The sailor forces departed in August for southern California where the Mexican forces were concentrated. On the eleventh, the Americans landed at San Pedro and marched to Los Angeles without opposition. Stockton believed that the men under General Jose Maria Castro had fled to Mexico. On August 22, he wrote Navy Secretary Bancroft that during the month he assumed command, he had "ended the war, restored peace and harmony among the people and put a Civil Government into successful operation." Stockton now contemplated an invasion of Acapulco, Mexico, perhaps followed by an overland march to the Mexican capital![3]

Stockton appointed Beale to become military governor of San Jose, a small community sixty miles south of San Francisco, but the expedition to Acapulco was never launched. On September 31, the dismal news arrived that Captain Archibald Gillespie, the American commander at Los Angeles, had been driven from that settlement by Mexican troops. Beale blamed Gillespie for the Los Angeles "uprising" believing he had been negligent and failed to respect the customs of the Mexican inhabitants. Ordered by Stockton to proceed to Sonoma and bring Fremont and his men to San Francisco, Beale on October 3 left the *Congress*, anchored in San Francisco Bay, and sailed at the head of a small group of boats.[4]

Beale informed Fremont of the recent events at Los Angeles. Assembling some 160 volunteers, Fremont placed his men aboard Beale's boats, and they sailed for San Francisco. Fremont and Beale took the lead boat, the fastest, and quickly outdistanced the others. At nightfall, the boat landed on an island, and Beale gathered branches to prepare a signal fire for the other boats. After supper, he realized that he had forgotten to provide himself with blankets, but Fremont generously offered to share his large grizzly bearskin.[5]

Shortly after retiring, Beale began to itch furiously and told Fremont that his bearskin was infested with fleas. To his great discomfort, however, he discovered that he had built the signal fire with poison oak branches. By the time the boats reached San Francisco Bay, Beale was swollen and cursing his misfortune. The surgeon on the *Congress* provided no relief. He treated Beale by dousing him with arnica, an irritant used to increase circulation for sprains and bruises. Beale fumed, stated that the doctor had received his diploma in a Sioux medicine lodge, and angrily swore to give the medical man a vitriol bath if he ever caught him ashore. Despite Beale's discomfort, the expedition to Sonoma was a success. Fremont's men boarded the *Sterling,* a merchantman, and on October 13, both the *Congress* and the *Sterling* sailed for the south.[6]

Along the California coast, the two ships became separated in heavy fog. The *Sterling* encountered the *Vandalia,* which reported that an attempt to recapture Los Angeles had failed. Fremont decided to stop at Monterey and equip his forces before moving south to Los Angeles. Stockton took the *Congress* to San Pedro, then sailed on to San Diego, believing that it offered a better base for operations against the Mexican forces. At San Diego, he sent marines and forty Bear Flaggers ashore to join the small garrison of Americans. Stockton now began active preparations for an overland march on Los Angeles. He drilled the men as infantry and assigned his officers to command infantry, cavalry, and artillery units.[7]

Because of his knowledge of horses, Beale became a cavalry officer. He was ordered to collect all cattle, horses, and mules in the countryside and help improvise from rawhides necessary items, such as harness. While on this duty he acquired an intimate knowledge of the topography of the region, met with many Mexicans, and improved his Spanish. On an expedition in late November, Beale and his cavalrymen rode to Warner's Rancho to confiscate cattle and horses, only to learn that the Mexican rebels had driven all livestock to the interior. After collecting assorted animals, Beale's party started back to San Diego, but Mexican lancers attacked them. Although the Mexicans roughly handled his force, the Americans managed to keep the "valuable loot." William R. Manchester, an American, received a severe lance wound and subsequently died.[8]

On December 3, Commodore Stockton received a communication from Brigadier General Stephen W. Kearny, announcing that he had crossed the Southwest from Santa Fe and was entering California with a contingent of dragoons. Kearny requested Stockton to send a force to meet his party and escort it through the enemy-held countryside east of San Diego. Stockton questioned the bearer of the communication, Edward Stokes, an Englishman who owned a nearby ranch, about the size of Kearny's force. When Stokes estimated the column at approximately 350 men, Stockton decided to dispatch a small force of forty men under Captain Archibald Gillespie and Lieutenant Beale to join Kearny. The two officers were to march to Kearny's camp, provide information on the local scene, and then guide him to San Diego. Stockton advised Kearny by letter that the Mexican forces in the vicinity of San Diego consisted of some 150 mounted lancers. Perhaps contemplating Kearny's 350 dragoons, he suggested that the general might try to surprise the Mexicans. At eight o'clock that night (December 3), Gillespie and Beale left San Diego with their detachment and a small cannon.[9]

The Americans took the road east past the old Spanish mission and then turned northeast into the coastal mountains. The party consisted of twenty-four members of the California Battalion, ten carbineers from the *Congress,* and four officers. Two civilians—Edward Stokes and Raphael Machado, a recent defector—also accompanied the troops. The Mexicans in San Diego watched the force leave, and Andres Pico, who commanded the Mexican forces, soon learned of the Americans' movement. The road to Kearny's camp passed through rugged, steep countryside, and the march was difficult. Nevertheless, at noon on December 5, Gillespie's party contacted Kearny near Warner's Rancho.[10]

Kearny now started for San Diego. The column halted for the night at Stokes's Santa Maria Rancho, with the two groups camping some two miles apart. After supper, Gillespie sent Beale and Alexis Godey of the California Battalion over to Kearny's camps to ascertain the general's plans for the next day. Kearny had been impressed by Stockton's suggestion to surprise the enemy, although unaware that the commodore believed his force to be four times its actual strength. Kearny and his officers wanted to fight. Captain Henry S. Turner, the adjutant, confided to his diary that unless they were "fortunate enough to get into a fight" and emerge victorious, the long overland march from Fort Leavenworth would seem a hollow enterprise.

Kearny questioned Beale closely about the road to San Diego and the probable location of enemy troops. Beale replied that two roads led to San Diego. The road to the left, which he and Gillespie had just traveled, ran via El Cajon and Mission San Diego and presented no problems.

The other road led to San Pasqual, where the Mexican forces had camped. If the general took that route, the Mexicans would fight at San Pasqual. Beale strongly urged Kearny not to attack. The Americans were tired, poorly equipped, and poorly mounted (some rode emaciated mules), while the Mexicans were fine horsemen who kept their animals in excellent condition. Despite Beale's advice, Kearny decided to attack. Beale hurriedly rode back to camp and groomed the Sutter cannon, a four-pounder, for the battle that was expected the next morning.[11]

Kearny sent out scouts to reconnoiter and locate the Mexican position. This act alerted Pico's forces, as the American party made a great deal of noise, and one dragoon even dropped a blanket or jacket, marked with the distinctive "U.S." emblem. The element of surprise was lost, but Kearny decided to continue the assault. At one o'clock on the morning of December 6, Kearny ordered Gillespie to prepare his men for action. An hour later, in cold, rainy weather, the American column slowly began to move toward the small Indian village of San Pasqual. On entering a high pass, the men felt a freezing wind swept down from higher elevations of the snow-covered mountains. In the long column, Beale rode close to General Kearny. Several miles from San Pasqual, while still in the pass, Kearny halted the troops, delivered a brief speech of encouragement, then ordered the cannon to the rear.[12]

Kearny's advance followed a narrow rail down the steep mountainside into the valley. Gradually, the column stretched out to over a mile in length. According to Beale, Kearny ordered his men to "trot" as they neared the valley, but Captain Abraham Johnston misunderstood the command and shouted "Charge!" Johnston galloped down the hill toward the distant enemy campfire. Kearny was flustered and exclaimed: "Oh Heavens! I did not mean that!" Twelve men followed Johnston's wild charge. Mexican lancers struck, killed Captain Johnston and a private, then rode away.[13]

Captain Benjamin Moore then led a second charge by forty of the best mounted troops. Mexican lancers met the dragoons, turned, and charged the ranks. The Americans found themselves at a terrible disadvantage. Their powder was damp from the rain, and cavalry sabers and navy cutlasses proved no match for the long enemy lances. In the predawn darkness, Beale saw a Mexican rider, fired his pistol, and the man fell. Captain Moore was killed and Gillespie suffered fearful wounds as the disorganized battle swirled across the valley. Eventually, Gillespie got the Sutter gun into action, but after firing the cannon he collapsed from wounds. Beale now took command of the naval-marine forces. By the time the main body of Kearny's dragoons arrived, the Mexican lancers had departed the field. Nineteen Americans lay dead and an equal number severely wounded. General Kearny had been pierced by three lance thrusts. The Mexicans suffered no fatalities, although a number were wounded, including the man Beale shot.[14]

Captain Henry S. Turner temporarily replaced Kearny in command of the Americans. He quickly dispatched a messenger with a request to Commodore Stockton to send a "considerable force," together with carts for transportation of the wounded. Lieutenant Godey raced through the countryside with the important communication. At San Diego, Stockton received the news with surprise and began to organize a large party for the field. Godey hurried back to San Pasqual but was captured by the Mexicans.[15]

Immediately after the battle, the Americans resumed the march to San Diego. Pico closely followed their movements and had his lancers outflank Kearny's column, preventing the Americans from reaching an important spring. Beale and Kit Carson led a force to drive a small group of Mexicans from a hill that commanded the American position. The column then straggled up the hill, losing their cattle herd in the process. Camped on San Bernardino Hill, they saw Mexican lancers surround their position. The situation was desperate. Lacking adequate food and water, they resorted to frontier expediency and butchered their mules. The camp was renamed Mule Hill. The soldiers also erected a low stone breastworks for protection and waited for Stockton to send aid from San Diego.[16]

Meanwhile, in the Mexican camp, Andres Pico questioned Godey about the American wounded. Pico expressed concern for his friend Gillespie. Godey told Pico that Gillespie still lived, although dangerously wounded. Pico proceeded to send Gillespie food under a flag of truce and offered to exchange prisoners. Kearny felt that the white flag was a ruse, but Beale volunteered to meet the Mexicans and report on the proposed prisoner exchange.[17]

Beale rode down the hill toward the Mexican camp. Under his coat, he carried a concealed revolver, capped and charged, ready to fire. Speaking fluent Spanish, he told a Mexican picket that he came to discuss the proposed exchange of prisoners, and a sergeant hurried to Pico's tent. In a few minutes, three Californians rode up. Andres Pico dismounted, advanced toward Beale on foot, and unbuckled his sword, throwing it twenty feet to his right. Beale did the same with his sword. Then as the two men advanced toward each other, Beale threw aside his concealed pistol. Pico generously ignored Beale's hidden weapon.

The two men discussed the prisoner exchange. The Americans held a weak bargaining position—Kearny had captured only one Mexican while Pico held three Americans. Beale was especially anxious to secure Godey's release, believing him the most valuable man. In an attempt to outwit

Pico, Beale described the man he wanted but did not name him. Pico was not fooled and told Beale to describe another man because the Mexicans would not release Godey. Thinking that Pico would again refuse, Beale described a man named Burgess, the individual he least wanted. Pico was smart, however, immediately agreed, and the exchange took place.[18]

When Beale and Burgess returned to the American camp on Mule Hill, Pico's astuteness in releasing the man became apparent. Burgess knew nothing of Stockton's preparations to send aid, while the released Mexican knew the desperate situation faced by the Americans. A sense of despair fell over Kearny's soldiers. One sailor stated that they faced the "gloomy prospect of starving . . . or going down to be shot and lanced like dogs."[19]

On the afternoon of December 8, Kearny again attempted to move his troops. Burning their military baggage to prevent delay, the soldiers mounted up and prepared to move—only to see Pico redeploy his lancers. A battle would ensue if the Americans left the hill. Beale went to Kearny and volunteered to carry another message to Stockton. Kearny agreed, and the American column fell back into position on the hillside.

When Kearny asked whom Beale wished to have accompany him, he quickly answered: "Carson and my Indian servant." Kearny did not wish to spare Carson but finally permitted the scout to go. Carson and Beale then prepared for the assignment. Each man secured a rifle, a revolver, a knife, and a blanket.

After nightfall, the three men sneaked down the hill toward the Mexican lines. A double ring of sentries encircled the American position. Beale pulled off his boots to prevent noise, and the three men repeatedly crawled on their stomachs. Once they came so close to some Mexicans they could hear low Spanish voices and smell cigarrillo smoke. Evading Pico's guards, they started across the countryside. Beale had lost his boots, and the jagged rocks and prickly pear cactus tore at his bare feet. The next morning at dawn, they concealed themselves and rested for the day. After dark on December 9, the trio resumed their trek. Twelve miles from San Diego, the three men separated, and each headed toward town by a different route. They hoped at least one of them would reach Stockton.[20]

That night the Indian messenger reached San Diego first and gave Stockton an account of Kearny's plight. Stockton had failed to hurry to Kearny's relief after Godey's arrival, because Captain Turner's letter had not indicated Kearny's defeat, nor the desperate situation on Mule Hill. At ten o'clock, Beale arrived in a state of absolute exhaustion, his feet brutally lacerated from the cross-country trek. Beale stated that Kearny's situation was so desperate that if not immediately reinforced the entire command would be forced to surrender or face annihilation. In describing the battle of San Pasqual, he stated firmly that Kearny had been defeated. At this point, Beale collapsed and was placed in the ship's hospital where he remained for several weeks. Complete recovery from his injuries—both physical and mental—would take nearly a year. Stockton's relief force of 125 men left for Mule Hill. Knowing that the Americans outnumbered his lancers, Pico abandoned the siege and returned to Los Angeles.[21]

When he was able to leave the ship's hospital, Beale took up residence in a Mexican home in San Diego. This family treated him with such care and tenderness that Beale was deeply impressed. He found himself strongly attracted to the free life-style of the Californios, particularly their pleasures of horsemanship, music, and dancing, tempered by strong familial and religious ties. At San Pasqual, he was struck by the honor and courage of these people; in San Diego he found the Californios a patient people who stressed personal friendship above all else. Beale later stated that this period "turned the current of my life, for I determined to live among the Mexicans of California."[22]

Stockton, meanwhile, proceeded with his plans to subdue California. Kearny placed his men under Stockton's command, and the combined force marched north to Los Angeles. Battles were fought at San Gabriel and La Mesa, near Los Angeles, and the Americans handily defeated the Mexicans. Pico was ready to surrender. In early January of 1847, John C. Fremont and his men arrived in the Los Angeles area, and Pico surrendered to him, believing Fremont would give more lenient terms than either Stockton or Kearny. The Capitulation of Cahuenga was signed on January 12, 1847, and shortly afterward Fremont notified Stockton and Kearny that he had accepted Pico's surrender.[23]

Soon after the defeat of the Mexicans, a dispute broke out between Stockton, Fremont, and Kearny over the control of the civil government in California. Earlier, in the autumn of 1846, Stockton had established the beginnings of civil government, and he believed he held an a priori right to control by virtue of his conquest. Stockton and Fremont ignored Kearny's orders from President Polk and argued that they applied to a nonexistent situation. Stockton then named Fremont as governor over the strong objections of Kearny. The commodore even went so far as to tell Kearny he would ask for his recall. Often impetuous, Stockton had misjudged the situation. A new commander for the Pacific Squadron arrived carrying instructions from President Polk which directed that the civil government should be under the senior army officer—Kearny.[24]

As early as January 27, 1847, Beale had been drawn into the bickering between Stockton, Kearny, and Fremont. In this dispute the battle of San Pasqual loomed increasingly important. Kearny had made a number of serious misjudgments, and if these actions became widely known, he would appear incompetent. Such incomptency would provide Stockton with a justification for appointing Fremont governor and stripping Kearny of authority. On January 27, just for the record, Stockton ordered Beale to write an account of the Battle of San Pasqual and to render it as favorable as possible to Kearny. Beale and Stockton knew that it would be impossible to show Kearny in a favorable light. The commodore also wished to get his side of the California story to Washington as soon as possible. Army couriers had already gone east with Kearny's reports. Despite Beale's ill health, Stockton felt that his young subordinate was the best candidate to carry important dispatches east. Beale was known in Washington, and he also had been at San Pasqual and witnessed the general's incompetence.[25]

Navy officers in California regarded Beale as a true hero of the fighting. On December 21, 1846, a group of twenty officers presented Beale with a testimonial gift in honor of his valor. The gift consisted of lieutenant's epaulets and a sword. An accompanying letter spoke of Beale's "cold determination" in obtaining relief for the suffering troops at Mule Hill. The navy officers hoped the president would recognize Beale's gallant conduct and commission him a full naval lieutenant. Beale responded that such a testimonial would serve in the future "as a noble incentive to merit all the distinction your partiality had conferred upon me."[26]

On Feburary 15, 1847, Stockton ordered Beale to proceed to Washington with dispatches for the Navy Department. He had selected him for the assignment in consequence of his "heroic conduct" in volunteering to travel through enemy lines from Kearny's camp to San Diego for assistance. Beale would accompany Kit Carson who was preparing to leave for the East. Stockton instructed Beale to present his packages to John Y. Mason, secretary of the navy.[27]

Carson's party left California for Santa Fe, New Mexico, on February 25. Besides Carson, the group included R. Eugene Russell (son of Colonel William "Owl" Russell, California's secretary of state under Fremont), Theodore Talbot, a California Battalion officer, Beale, and several packers with mules and supplies. The party followed a route across the Mojave Desert (in later years Beale would state that he had crossed Death Valley with Carson) to the Colorado River, then traveled along the Gila River in Arizona. Beale was so weak from his injuries that for the first twenty days of the journey, Carson had to help him on and off his horse. Near the Colorado River, the party exhausted their water supply and suffered from thirst for several days; while in Arizona they were attacked by Apache Indians.[28]

On April 9, 1847, Carson's group reached Taos, New Mexico. A rebellion had swept Taos in January, and Charles Bent, New Mexico's governor and close friend of Carson, had been killed by the Indian and Mexican rebels who had hoped vainly to throw off American rule. Carson's wife, Josefa, barely managed to escape with her life. The recent arrivals from California witnessed the first hangings of rebels. Carson and Beale soon pushed east, following the Santa Fe Trail.[29]

In late April, at Mann's Fort in southwestern Kansas, Carson found two other parties, headed by William G. Peck and John McKnight, who had been attacked by Indians, probably Comanches, east of the fort. The three parties joined and started east. Some ninety miles east of Mann's Fort, at the Great Bend of the Arkansas River, the enlarged party was attacked by Pawnees, who stole two horses. Carson's men boarded the steamboat *John J. Hardin* at Westport, Missouri (Kansas City) and reached St. Louis on May 16. Carson and Beale stayed several days at the home of United States Senator Thomas Hart Benton, to whom Carson delivered several letters from Fremont.[30]

In late May, Carson and Beale reached Washington. Beale delivered his packages at the Navy Department on May 31 with the accompanying instructions. Secretary Mason read Stockton's letters, wrote on the package that he hoped the dispute was ended, and forwarded the papers to President Polk. With the delivery made, Beale went to his family's home, Bloomingdale, and sought a rest. His weight had dropped to around 111 pounds and he looked cadaverous. He blamed his condition on a constant diet of mule meat, without bread or salt, plus the rigors of the trail.

Within a week, Beale learned that he would accompany Carson on a return trip to California. On June 7, Carson delivered to Polk a letter that Fremont had written Benton, giving Fremont's and Stockton's side of the controversy. Mrs. Fremont accompanied him and attempted to elicit some expression of approval of her husband's conduct from Polk, but he politely declined. As early as April 30, Kearny's dispatches had arrived, and Polk recorded in his diary that he believed Colonel Fremont had refused to obey Kearny and in "this he was wrong." Fremont's case was not helped by his father-in-law Benton, lately a critic of the administration, due to Polk's failure to appoint him supreme American commander in Mexico. Polk had a long discussion with Carson about the state of affairs in California, and the next day, the cabinet agreed that Fremont and Stockton had acted improperly. Polk decided to send Carson back to California with messages for the principal military and naval commanders there. Instructions also went to Beale to accompany Carson.[31]

Beale and Carson departed for California in mid-June. The journey was arduous, and one hundred miles west of Fort Leavenworth, near Council Grove, Beale collapsed. Colonel William H. Russell, traveling east from California, encountered the Carson party, and took Beale back to Leavenworth.

Beale again returned to his home in Washington to recuperate. He felt that he had been "headstrong and foolish" to attempt a difficult cross-country journey while still in ill health, and he harbored a deep sense of failure. In late August, probably at Beale's request, Senator Benton wrote to Navy Secretary Mason and requested that Beale be appointed dispatch carrier to California. In his letter, Benton described Beale's heroism at length. Secretary Mason replied on August 27, stating that the Navy Department appreciated Beale's services and assured Benton that Beale would be given another opportunity to carry messages when he had recovered his health. Mason suggested that there might be an assignment for Beale by early fall.[32]

On September 20, 1847, Beale received a friendly letter from Mrs. Fremont, requesting that he remain in Washington for the pending trial of her husband, who had been charged with repeated acts of disobedience. Fremont and Benton believed that Beale could testify that Kearny had acted improperly and incompetently at San Pasqual. If Fremont's defense could raise the issue of Kearny's conduct, the move would divert attention from Fremont's actions and tend to justify Stockton's excluding of Kearny from a commanding role in California. More than anyone else, Beale was prepared to point an accusing finger at Kearny.[33]

The Fremont court martial began in November. Early in the trial the question of the relevancy of Kearny's conduct had been raised, but the court rejected the issue. On December 22, Beale took the witness stand. Fremont, serving as his own counsel, asked Beale about an incident which took place aboard the *Congress* in July of 1846, shortly after the frigate had arrived in Monterey. Beale related that when Admiral Seymour's flagship of the British Squadron had entered Monterey Bay, the Americans feared the British might take action against them. Stockton ordered the deck of the *Congress* cleared and prepared for battle. The British visit, fortunately, turned out to be peaceful, and the English maintained a strictly neutral stance. In questioning Beale about the incident, Fremont hoped to establish that throughout California, there existed a widely held belief that England would soon move against the United States in the area. He hoped to place his own decision to join the Bear Flag Rebellion on a similar ground.[34]

Fremont then asked Beale if Kearny was acquainted with Kit Carson. Previously, Kearny had stated that he never saw Carson before he delivered a letter from Fremont, after the battle of San Pasqual. Beale replied that the two men were intimately acquainted. At San Pasqual, Kearny had even stated that he could not spare Carson to accompany Beale to San Diego. Fremont questioned Beale about his trip to San Diego with Carson; it was clear that he had moved the questioning directly into the realm of Kearny's conduct at San Pasqual. Then he quickly and dramatically asked if Kearny had burned public property on Mule Hill. Before Beale could respond, the judge advocate asked Fremont to submit to the court an explanation as to the relevancy of the present testimony and his line of questioning.

On December 23, the next day, Fremont declared that since the early days of the trial his questions had been ruled inadmissable, and he would not pursue them any further. Fremont then turned to Beale, the witness, and asked his first question of the day: who accompanied him from Mule Hill to San Diego? Again the question was challenged on the grounds of relevancy, and the court declared that the "military details of General Kearny's march from Santa Fe to San Diego are not material to this trial." Consequently, Beale's testimony was of little use in Fremont's defense.[35]

Beale received orders the same day to rejoin the Pacific Squadron. On January 7, 1848, he sailed from New York for Jamaica. Upon arrival in Kingston, he discovered that the steamer schedule had been changed and was forced to spend a month on the island.[36]

While awaiting the departure of a ship for Panama Beale wrote a lengthy letter to the Navy Department concerning the political scene in Central America. He stated that Great Britain was on the verge of invading Nicaragua in order to control the important transit route across Nicaragua. Before leaving the United States, Beale had talked with John M. Clayton, a prominent Delaware politician very interested in Central America. Perhaps influenced by Clayton's views, Beale told the Navy Department that Britain might soon control the best pathway for a transisthmian canal and pointed out that the route via the St. Johns River was "obviously the shortest and most feasible." The river could be navigated by flat-bottomed, light draft vessels into Lake Nicaragua. The distance from the lake to the Pacific Ocean required a canal, but the span appeared only "trifling." The letter coincided with Clayton's ideas concerning Central America and marked the beginning of Beale's lifelong interest in an interoceanic canal.[37]

Beale disliked serving aboard the *Ohio*, under Commodore Thomas Jones, and found the ship to be far from a "marine paradise," despite the prayers ordered up twice a day. He felt disgusted with the state of affairs in Washington. Fremont had been found guilty and eventually resigned his commission, which Beale considered a great injustice. With unusual candor, Beale admitted that he seemed to lack any special zeal for the service, but that since the battle of San Pasqual, he had been plagued by a "restless uneasiness" that kept him in constant motion. Beale had heard nothing from Kit Carson in over eight months and feared that the scout had lost his life somewhere on the plains. It was clear that Beale was suffering from mental depression.[38]

By the time the *Ohio* reached Mazatlan, Mexico, on May 6, 1848, the war with Mexico had ended. Beale had still not received his lieutenant's commission, despite his gallant service, and kept his rank of "acting" lieutenant. Promotions came slowly in the navy and were generally speeded or delayed by one's political supporters. Unfortunately, Beale's sympathies were with the enemies of Polk's administration. Also, another side existed to Beale's personality. Officers who served with him during the Mexican War remembered that when he became drunk, he grew quarrelsome and vicious. During the spring of 1848, Beale apparently sought "an escape" through heavy drinking. At a departure parade in Mazatlan, he appeared on horseback undressed and in a state of reeling intoxication. He made a memorable display of horsemanship and refused an order to return to his ship. Beale also managed to alienate his commander, Commodore Jones. Unlike Stockton, Jones was older and a personally distant man. Many younger officers regarded him as a fussy relic from a bygone era. On one occasion, aboard the *Ohio*, Beale drew a cartoon of Jones, which poked fun at a well-known episode in Jones's career. The drawing was widely circulated and the old commodore took a dislike to Beale's artistry as well as his personality traits of wit and exuberance, which captivated most people. By the summer of 1848, Ned Beale's career appeared becalmed, if not actually sinking.[39]

Chapter 3

PASSAGE TO EL DORADO

The arrival of Lieutenant Beale, . . . *with a lump of gold weighing eight pounds,* threw Wall street into a state of the greatest excitement and delight. Mr. Aspinwall, of the house of Howland & Aspinwall, was surrounded with crowds of eager brokers and merchants, all curious to catch a glimpse of the eight pound lump. There was no mistake about it. There was the pure gold fresh from *El Dorado* . . . Lieut. Beale assures us that he has seen a lump actually weighing 25 pounds. He says that everybody is getting rich in California—that common laborers can almost make a fortune.

—New York *Herald*
May 30, 1849, page one

Beale's change of luck came from an unlikely source. In July of 1848, Acting Lieutenant Beale and the naval officers stationed at La Paz in Baja California, heard the astounding news of a large gold discovery near Sacramento in newly acquired California. The strike had occurred six months earlier, on January 24, when James Marshall spotted some golden flakes in a millrace on the American River. An attempt by Marshall and rancher John A. Sutter to keep the strike a secret failed, and when word reached the streets of San Francisco, American sailors deserted their ships and started for the Sierra foothills. A mass of people followed on their heels. "The whole country from San Franciso to Los Angeles and from the seashore to the base of the Sierra," proclaimed the editor of the San Francisco *Californian*, "resounds with the sordid cry of 'gold! Gold!! GOLD!!!' "[1]

Beale was captivated by the spectacle of the gold rush, and the possibility of overnight wealth. He knew the importance of the news of the gold discovery to the residents of the United States and desired to be the messenger who carried back the important information to the East. When Commodore Jones drafted several lengthy letters to the Navy Department, Beale volunteered to cross Mexico with the dispatches—at his own expense. Jones agreed to the proposition. On July 29, Beale left La Paz on the *Congress* for Mazatlan, on the mainland, carrying three letters and a small quantity of gold. At Mazatlan he took passage in a small Mexican *goleta* (schooner) and sailed for the harbor at San Blas, arriving there by mid-August. [2]

Everyone he encountered, including the Mexican governor, warned him against the overland trip. Numerous bands of *ladrones* (robbers) prowled the roads and preyed on travelers. Beale felt that safety lay in a disguise, so he outfitted himself as a Mexican. He dressed in leather breeches, red flannel shirt, rawhide boots and topped out his costume with a large, glazed sombrero. On his person he carried four revolvers and a bowie knife. Beale left San Blas alone on horseback on August 12 with high expectations for a dangerous trip.

Before he reached Tepic, some fifty miles from San Blas, Beale was stopped by several men who claimed to be local police. When they demanded to see his passport, he drew his revolver and requested one of them come forward and examine his passport. The man approached, looked at the document, and apologized for stopping an American officer. Beale ordered them to depart down the road in the direction from which he had just come. Once they passed out of pistol range, Beale spurred his horse and galloped toward Tepic. Believing that he might be killed on the journey, Beale opened the dispatches at Tepic, copied them, and placed the originals in the Mexican mail.

In Mexico City Beale reported to Nathan Clifford, U.S. minister to Mexico. Here Beale rested for three days while Clifford composed messages to James Buchanan, secretary of state. Like everyone else that Beale encountered, Clifford was impressed with the California gold discovery and wrote Buchanan on August 21 that Beale would fully confirm the extent and value of the gold mines. He also suggested to Buchanan that a dependable means of communication be opened between Mexico City and Washington, such as a regular steamer plying between Vera Cruz and the United States. [3]

Beale rode out of Mexico City at midnight with a Mexican guide, heading for Vera Cruz. At the end of the first day, Beale met a horseman carrying a carbine who, upon being questioned, stated that he was hunting for his mule. Beale replied that he needed a lasso, not a carbine, to hunt for a mule. The hombre, as Beale called him, then changed his story and said he was really looking for game. Beale believed the man intended to waylay him, and he and the guide spurred their horses and fled into the darkness. Shots rang out as they sped away. Forty-eight hours after leaving Mexico City, Beale reached Vera Cruz. Here he hired a rowboat and went to Anton Lizardo, an anchorage for the American squadron but could not locate a vessel bound for the United States. Four days after reaching Vera Cruz, Beale finally found passage in the sloop-of-war *Germantown*, bound for Mobile, Alabama. On September 14, 1848—forty-seven days from La Paz—he reached Washington.[4]

Newspaper columns soon were filled with Beale's version of the American El Dorado. In Washington he told Secretaries Buchanan and Mason about California and on September 18 had a conference with President Polk. The president regarded Beale as a member of the Benton faction, his opponents, and may even have doubted Beale's veracity. On the night of Beale's visit, Polk reflected on the day's events and recorded in his diary that "nothing of importance occurred" that day.[5]

On September 21, the Washington Daily National *Intelligencer* published Beale's article on California. The naval lieutenant, proclaimed the newspaper, had brought the "most extraordinary intelligence about the real El Dorado, the Gold region in California." An intense state of excitement existed there among all classes of people. Entire towns had been abandoned, their populations drawn to the hills to search for gold. Beale's descriptions were confirmed by letters of Commodore Jones and Thomas O. Larkin, which Beale had carried with him from La Paz. In a lengthy letter to Jones, Larkin described a tour of the mines he had made that June. Larkin's letter made a deep impression in Washington for he was known to have a conservative nature. Eastern newspapers soon were carrying California stories, sparked by Beale's arrival. Beale displayed his small sample to many newspaper reporters, one of which described the gold as "resembling the scales of a small fish," with the largest flake not weighing more than one ounce.[6]

A week later the Washington *Intelligencer* published a second article about Beale, entitled "A Ride Across Mexico" written by William Carey Jones, Fremont's brother-in-law. The story related Beale's hazardous journey from La Paz. Jones must have spent considerable time with Beale in order to obtain the details of the ride, and he may have added a few literary embellishments. Curiously, the article followed a printing of Senator Benton's July speech concerning Beale's bravery at San Pasqual. "A Ride Across Mexico" made Beale a national celebrity. Newspapers throughout the country carried the story either in its entirety or abridged. Even *Littell's Living Age*, a highly regarded Boston literary magazine, published the complete text.[7]

In early October of 1848 Beale received orders to return to California and was handed dispatches to deliver to certain military authorities en route. He now possessed a confidence in himself he had never known before. Several months earlier, his career seemed to be stalled, but now, everywhere he went, his name (if not his face) was instantly recognized. He traveled west by stagecoach to St. Louis, and in late October reached Fort Leavenworth, Kansas. In Leavenworth, he took time to write a letter to Captain Du Pont, his old commander of the *Congress*. Beale always played the role of a proper sycophant to his superiors. He speculated about his upcoming crossing of the Southwest, adding that to some degree it was insane to undertake "this terrible journey in mid winter." Beale stated that if indeed he were crazy, then like a certain "very great man of our acquaintance," he possessed a "good deal of method in my madness." The unexplained allusion seemed to refer to Fremont.[8]

Beale stated that next fall, he would return east to commence "life in earnest." While in the East he had spent time in Chester, Pennsylvania, where he had met Mary Edwards, the daughter of wealthy Samuel Edwards of Chester, Pennsylvania. Edwards was a prominent Democrat, who had been highly influential during Andrew Jackson's presidency. Ned Beale and Mary had become engaged before he started west.[9]

In Mid-November of 1848 Beale left Fort Leavenworth for California. The weather was extremely cold. Riding with him was a cavalry guard of seventeen mounted recruits and a few "adventurers." Fortunately, the group included experienced mountain men Andrew W. Sublette and Baptiste Perrot. Between Council Grove and Big Timbers, Colorado, the party clashed twice with hostile Indians. the recruits gave Beale numerous difficulties, and he called them "utterly worthless!" Every day, he found it necessary to punish two or three for some incompetence. Beale's party reached Big Timbers on the Arkansas on December 3. Here in a large grove of cottonwoods trappers and thousands of Indians were in winter camps. The weather grew cold, with snow and freezing temperatures.[10]

At Big Timbers, Beale wrote Harry Edwards, brother of Mary Edwards. He told Harry that the cold was so severe that a trader lost ninety mules in a snowstorm some sixty miles to the south. On the route to Big Timbers, he had counted seventy-two animals dead or dying from the freezing temperatures. In order to build a fire at night, the party occasionally had to wade across the icy Arkansas at a shallow point to collect driftwood. Beale chided his friend, saying "with no disparagement to your manhood, Harry, but I do not really think you could stand what I am doing." Beale said that he had been warned that the Raton Mountains in southern Colorado would be impassable with the deep snow but he had "passed *impassable* places before." The Indians also were very hostile and several men, whom he knew quite well, had been killed. In conclusion Beale asked Harry Edwards to give his warmest love to his sister Mary. He signed off with the statement: "A snow storm is no place for letter writing."[11]

The passage through the Raton Mountains was indeed difficult. The depth of the fresh snow forced the men to dismount and walk ahead of their animals in order to break a trail for the poor creatures. Several in Beale's party suffered severe cases of frostbite. Francis X. Aubry, a trader in the area, lost sixty mules during one night. His favorite saddle mule froze to death inside a tent, despite two blankets Aubry had thrown over the animal for warmth. Beale estimated that the snow depth exceeded twenty feet in places. Finally, on Christmas Day of 1848, the crippled party straggled into Santa Fe. Several men required amputations of feet and hands.

In Santa Fe Beale delivered a set of letters to Colonel John M. Washington, commanding in New Mexico, and requested Washington's assistance in equipping the party for the remainder of the trip. Washington assigned a sergeant and seven privates to go with Beale. The naval officer announced that any recruit could stay in Santa Fe, and several indicated they wished to do so.[12]

Beale inquired as to the fate of John C. Fremont's railroad survey party which had headed west before he did. Fremont had doggedly climbed into the heart of the mountains to search for a railroad route and met near distaster in the deep snow. By the time the Fremont party reached Taos, ten men had died, charges of cannibalism surfaced, and critics were quick to speculate that Fremont's leadership qualities failed.[13]

Beale rode out of Santa Fe on January 11, 1849, without learning of Fremont's fate. His little party followed the Rio Grande south to the small town of Socorro, and some fifty miles beyond they took the western trail toward the Mimbres Mountains. They soon found themselves in a raging snowstorm. As they toiled through snow-blocked passes, the sergeant and seven men deserted, heading east to the settlements on the Rio Grande. Beale declared that if they survived the weather, the Apaches surely would get them. Eventually, the party reached the Gila River, and hit Kearny's old trail to California.[14]

The Gila trail was not a regular road; it wound in a zigzag fashion around precipices, plunged abruptly into great gorges, and climbed steep cliffs. The countryside was desolate—a vast region of rugged, inaccessible mountains, covered with snow. One evening while encamped along the Gila River in central Arizona, Beale decided to go hunting for game. He saddled his horse and rode off alone. About six miles from camp, he shot and killed a deer. While he dressed the carcass, he saw a small Apache band riding rapidly toward him. They heard the rifle shot which killed the deer. Beale knew an unpleasant death awaited him if captured. He abandoned the deer, mounted his horse, and galloped toward camp with the Indians in hot pursuit. Three miles from his camp, Beale topped a hill and saw one of his men approaching on foot. The man had walked away from camp to help in the hunt. He cried out for Beale to save him, shrieking that he was the "father of six helpless children!" Beale quickly decided to give the man his horse and stay behind himself. He told the man to ride back to camp and "give my body a decent burial!" Beale drew his revolver and waited for the Indians to discover him. When the Indians came over the hill, they saw the rider and raced after him. In their haste they overlooked Beale, who walked back to camp along a circuitous route.[15]

Beale's party continued west along the Gila River to the Colorado River. West of the Colorado in the barren Mojave Desert, they lacked water and were forced to bore holes in the sand. The temperature on the desert was hot as the Sahara. On April 1, 1849, Beale reached San Francisco.

The city had changed dramatically since Beale's previous visit. A sea of frame shanties and tents stretched along dozens of narrow streets. The rage for gold swallowed up all other passions. Discoveries had been made throughout the Sierra Nevada foothills. Men had become rich, almost overnight, and gold fever burned unabated among San Francisco's residents. Beale shared in the excitement but determined to return East as quickly as possible to tell the world that the gold strike was far larger than anticipated.[16]

On April 12 Beale sailed on the *Oregon*, a Pacific Mail Company steamer, for Panama and passed through the channel entrance to San Francisco recently dubbed the "Golden Gate." As usual, he carried dispatches to Washington from Commodore Jones. Beale had secured a sizeable amount of gold himself, including an eight-pound lump, which he exhibited to whomever he met. At Panama City, Beale found a state near chaos. Two thousand argonauts were stranded, trying desperately to find passage to California. Beale soon left for Charges, the Caribbean port of Panama, where he sailed on the bark *Florida* for New Orleans. Later, in Mobile, Alabama he gave a lengthy story to the *Mobile Register* of his winter crossing to California and the wealth of the new gold regions. The *Register's* article was reproduced throughout the East.[17]

Edward F. Beale arrived in New York City on May 29, 1849, after a record passage of forty-four days. Disembarking from the steamer, he rushed to the Wall Street offices of William H. Aspinwall, president of Pacific Mail Steamship Company and a man whose fortunes already were linked to California's commercial development. After a hurried conference, Beale and the financier appeared on the street, where an immense crowd of brokers, merchants, and speculators waited to hear Beale's news. In an excited voice, Beale told stories of overnight fortunes being made in the foothills of the Sierra Nevada. With his own eyes, he had seen a lump of virgin gold that weighed twenty-five pounds. Then Beale held above his head the proof of his words—a shining eight-pound golden nugget, valued in excess of $2,000. "There was no mistake about it," exclaimed a New York *Herald* reporter, "it was pure gold fresh from *El Dorado.*" Everyone was "getting rich in California," Beale told the crowd, and "common laborers can almost make a fortune."[18]

P. T. Barnum, who recognized a kindred spirit, asked Beale if he would sell his eight-pound lump, or at least allow Barnum to exhibit it for the public's gratification. Beale temporarily declined Barnum's offer, believing that he could display the gold more effectively himself. He enjoyed the excitement and purposely fueled the gold frenzy with his glittering descriptions—and his own appearance. He wore a watch, totally encased in pure California gold—"one of the ugliest looking, and richest, and most valuable watches in existence," a newspaperman observed. From the links of the watch chain dangled a number of large gold nuggets. It was the type of uniform guaranteed to attract attention.[19]

The New York *Herald* called Beale's report the "most extraordinary and astounding intelligence" yet received from the California gold region. The naval officer had arrived ahead of the mails, and carried the earliest valid (i.e., government) intelligence on the fabled region. The newspaper declared that the wealth of California far exceeded earlier estimates. Beale was quoted as saying that some 100,000 men would be working the gold fields by midsummer. The *Herald* speculated that roughly 300 million dollars in gold would be produced during the next season and that this money would spark a commercial revolution deeper and more intense than any before experienced in man's history.[20]

On May 30, Beale left New York for Washington. Two days later, he presented correspondence from Jones to the Navy Department. The official information concerned the movements of the Pacific Squadron and was of little public interest. Beale also visited the White House and discussed California gold with President Zachary Taylor. Washington received Beale as a hometown boy who had achieved success and fame. Beale's uncle, Robert Beale, sergeant at arms for the U.S. Senate, held a dinner in honor of the young acting lieutenant. The influential *National Intelligencer* declared that the naval officer had truly seen the elephant and that the reporter had been permitted to see its image in the eight-pound chunk of virgin gold that Beale carried.[21]

On June 5, Beale conversed at length with George W. Crawford, secretary of war, on the subject of California. Beale told Crawford that Californians disliked military government and desired to have a regular civil government established. He doubted, however, that California could move quickly toward statehood because most of its population was at work in the gold fields. Beale seemed to suggest that the federal government aid in creating civil government in California. One of the persons standing to gain from California statehood was John C. Fremont, who harbored ambitions to serve in the U.S. Senate.[22]

Beale took the opportunity to describe for the newspapers the best overland route to California. He ranked the Panama route first but advised that if shipping became uncertain argonauts should follow the route from Vera Cruz across central Mexico to Mazatlan. Beale criticized the so-called Gila route with strong language. The Gila River was navigable for only a short distance and should not be considered as a water route across the Southwest. Perhaps thinking of Benton and Fremont's plans for a railroad over a central route he added that the Gila transit was "impracticable for all time to come for a railroad." On the other hand, the Colorado might prove navigable, but little was known about the river. It was possible that gold placers would be found along its banks, as well as on the Gila River.[23]

In anticipation of another assignment, Ned Beale and Mary Edwards were married on June 20, 1849. They were united in a small, private ceremony at the Edwards's home in Chester, Pennsylvania, by Reverent Mortimer R. Talbot, a U.S. Navy chaplain. Mary Edwards Beale was a small, attractive young woman and a fitting consort for her adventurous husband. The newly married couple had no time for a honeymoon. The day after the wedding, Beale made plans to sail for California. He had received orders to carry dispatches to military authorities on the Pacific Coast. On June 30, Beale sailed from New York on the *Cresent City* with 200 passengers aboard.[24]

While waiting on the Pacific coast of Panama for a steamer to San Francisco, Beale met Bayard Taylor, the robust poet and journalist of the New York *Tribune*. The two men quickly became friends and found they shared many common interests. Taylor was going to California to report the gold rush for the *Tribune*, but he harbored a greater personal ambition. Taylor hoped to produce a true literary work that would capture for posterity the astounding event taking place on the Pacific slope. He felt Beale could serve as a guide in California. The idea intrigued the naval officer, who appreciated literature and regarded poetry as one of the highest callings to which a man could aspire. He also was aware that Taylor's writings on California might add luster to his own reputation.[25]

The voyage proved mostly uneventful. When the vessel entered the harbor at Acapulco, the Mexican authorities, fearing cholera, ordered the ship to sea or they would open fire. On approximately August 10, the cry, "There is California!" was heard as the *Panama* passed the southern tip of Baja California.[26]

On August 14, the *Panama* anchored at San Diego. John Weller boarded the steamer to travel north to Monterey. He headed the Boundary Commission, attempting to survey the line between the United States and Mexico, and hoped to obtain additional funds from General Bennett Riley, military commander, to continue his work. Beale carried official dispatches from Secretary of State John M. Clayton to Fremont, offering him the position of boundary commissioner. President Taylor had decided to remove Weller and with some justification; he was accused of misuse of funds and incompetence. Beale knew the contents of his dispatches, but he revealed nothing when he met Weller.[27]

On August 23, the vessel reached San Francisco. The community presented the novel spectacle of an "instant" city. Upwards of 50,000 gold seekers crowded into thousands of tents and wood-frame shanties thrown up haphazardly along the waterfront and in nearby hills. The sleepy Mexican village of 1847 now bustled with an international population, with large numbers of Mexican, Chinese, and Irish emigrants. The harbor sprouted a forest of masts, as hundreds of vessels lay anchored or beached by their owners. Beale and Taylor considered themselves lucky to obtain a room at the City Hotel at twenty-five dollars per week. Taylor discovered that rumpled newspapers which filled the spaces of his trunk could be sold for four thousand times their actual cost. Nearby, the city's most active gambling establishment, a large tent called "El Dorado," rented for $40,000—an astonishing sum. According to Taylor, gamblers and gold dust could be seen everywhere, and the poet even noticed men digging at the street in front of the United States Hotel in search of gold dust, spilled or leaked from miner's pouches.[28]

Beale and Taylor quickly prepared for a trip to San Jose, residence of John C. Fremont. They outfitted themselves Californio style: flannel shirts, serapes, and Chilian spurs. Colonel Lyons of Louisiana joined them. Beale rode a California sorrel, while his companions were mounted on mules. The party traveled for two days and reached San Jose at evening. Beale left Taylor and Lyons at the Miner's Home, a hotel, and went to visit Fremont, who resided with his friend Grove Cook.[29]

Beale delivered Clayton's letters to Fremont. Fremont said that he would accept the boundary commission appointment—the president had left him no choice—but he proposed to resign as quickly as possible. Nevertheless, the appointment pleased Fremont greatly. It indicated that much of his trouble with the Polk administration had been politically inspired. He already was determined to secure a senatorship from California, once statehood was achieved. Fremont also told Beale that he had obtained a large Mexican land grant, Las Mariposas (Butterflies), in the Sierra foothills, and his men were engaged in gold mining.[30]

Once in the foothills, at the Mokelumne Diggings, Beale and Taylor saw the true nature of El Dorado. Indeed, a man could make a large sum of money by strenuous labor, but mining operations already had organized into companies which employed cheap Mexican labor. All was not happiness in the diggings. Mexican and white laborers had clashed when the Americans attempted to drive foreigners from the gold field. For a time, whites even tried to force out Andres Pico, Beale's friend and one of the most respected Californios.[31]

Returning to San Francisco, Beale and Taylor parted company. The reporter left on a walking trip to Monterey, while Beale set out for the same destination by more conventional means. A constitutional convention was meeting in Monterey, preparing the document for California's statehood. Many of Beale's friends were there, including Fremont. Beale mixed with the delegates at the convention and kept up with the deliberations. When the convention ended, Beale left Monterey with the Fremont family. Fremont had played a behind the scenes role at the convention, which had debated many important topics. Slavery, for instance, had been excluded from California, but Negroes and Indians, (including Indian descendants) had been denied the right to vote. Mexican representatives were especially chaffed by this provision, since many of them claimed Indian ancestors. The convention settled the eastern boundary question, excluding from projected state boundaries the Mormon communities on the Sierra's eastern slope.[32]

In late October Beale obtained from his friend Bayard Taylor a set of letters of introduction to literary friends back east. In his request for these, he told Taylor that he planned one quick trip to the Mokelumne Diggings before leaving and would check on Taylor's interests in the mines. Apparently Beale and even Taylor had made some investments. Taylor wrote several glowing letters for Beale. He told Thomas Buchanan Read, a writer, that Ned Beale was a true friend, a rare commodity who possessed a "soul to reverence that divine art of poetry we are striving to master." Taylor wrote R. H. Stoddard, his closest friend, that Beale appreciated poetry and esteemed poets, and he must show the naval officer his poem "Castle in the Air." Taylor already had shown him "some of the figures on the frieze."[33]

Beale carried important documents east. Commodore Jones sent letters to the State Department, and a treaty recently concluded between the Sandwich Island commissioner and the king of the islands. Jones also handed Beale a printed copy of the new California Constitution, in the process of being ratified by the people of California. The man who had carried to the East the first news of the gold discovery, now carried the first state constitution of California for consideration by Congress. Beale left San Francisco on November 1 and reached New York harbor on December 7 aboard the *Crescent City*. The eastern states soon knew that a new state had organized on the West Coast and demanded admission to the Union.[34]

Beale delivered his packages in Washington and hurried to the Edwards home in Chester to rejoin his wife. He found that his warrant as a ship's master (dated August 6) had arrived, but he still had not received his lieutenant's commission. But there was also good news at Chester. Mary Beale was expecting their first child. In March of 1850, the Beales became the parents of a baby girl, and they named her Mary, after her mother. During the winter months Beale attempted with little success to write out an account of his overland journey of the previous year. He also made a trip to New York City on business, probably to see William H. Aspinwall, who had hired Beale around this time to look after his California mining interests. While in New York, Beale saw Horace Greeley, editor of the *Tribune,* and asked about Bayard Taylor and was told his friend was not in the city.[35]

On March 28, Beale received a letter from Taylor, saying that he had finished *Eldorado,* his book on California, and wished to dedicate it to him. Taylor thanked Beale for his help in California and for being a true friend and companion. Beale answered that he was so proud of the dedication that he could not adequately express his feelings. Beale also asked Taylor to visit him. He was attempting to reconstruct his winter journey (1848–49) to California, but his "laboring mountain of brain" had produced only the head and shoulders of a "foolscap mouse." Beale seemed determined to be a writer, and his poetry, letters, speeches and diaries showed his inherent ability. Yet he found writing even simple letters to be a tremendous chore. Beale told Taylor that he may have lost an appointment because of his writing inabilities. The Interior Department had requested his services on the Boundary Commission, but the secretary of the navy sent instead the chief astronomer, arguing that the astronomer would "do or write something creditable to the Department."

Beale was happy with his home environment in Chester. He urged both Taylor and Stoddard to visit and insisted that they bring the "Castle in the Air." The poetic image of the fountain, described by Stoddard, haunted him "like the memory of an old sweetheart." Beale was also a proud father and desired to present baby Mary to Taylor. "There was never known such a baby before," he proclaimed. Not surprisingly, he applied for and received a long furlough.[36]

At the end of April of 1850, Beale reported to the Navy Department in Washington—then returned to Chester to spend a few more hours with his wife and young daughter, who was ill. Upon his arrival at home, he found a telegram awaiting him—orders to proceed immediately to New York and take the *Crescent City*, the steamer, to California. In the middle of the night, Beale awakened his wife, looked at the sick baby, and said a hurried, tearful goodbye. He later said that the departure almost broke his heart.[37]

Beale possessed a true luxury on this trip—a private room. He also had the companionship of a few friends: Harry B. Edwards, his brother-in-law; Gwin Harris Heap, a cousin; and William Carey Jones, Fremont's brother-in-law and a good friend. Beale actually was traveling to California in two capacities: naval officer and employee of William H. Aspinwall and Robert Stockton. In April the two men had leased quartz property on Fremont's Mariposa Grant and intended to commence hardrock mining operations. The ship carried ore-crushing machinery destined for the Mariposa. Beale supervised the unloading of the machinery on the isthmus and transported it safely to the west coast of Panama. Here over 2,000 Americans were awaiting passage to California. Although a riot broke out before the departure of the *Tennessee*, he had the machinery placed aboard and carefully avoided the fighting. When Beale arrived in San Francisco, the *Herald* on June 20 declared his quartz machinery to be the first of its kind to reach the gold fields.[38]

The machinery was hauled to the Stockton-Aspinwall lease, an outcropping about one mile east of the Mariposa vein and near Stockton Creek. Stockton was considered knowledgeable about gold mining. For several years, he operated gold mines in Virginia and even developed a quartz mining mill based on his invention of the Stockton battery. The battery consisted of a single stamp with its own mortar and individual openings for conveying and discharging ore. It could be used independently as a mill or in combinations. Probably, Beale brought one of his employers' mills to San Francisco. The Stockton-Aspinwall mine commenced operations in August or September of 1850. John Barnett served as foreman of the actual operation, while J. R. Norris held a dual capacity as business agent and manager.[39]

In Washington, while Beale jockeyed quartz-crushing machinery to California, Fremont and Benton sought to secure a federal position for their friend and supporter. First, Fremont wrote Secretary Clayton on June 10 and asked him to appoint Beale as United States marshal for California. He told Clayton, who knew Beale, that the appointment would be a natural one. Beale was known for his courage and energy and was well liked by the people. His laborious services and heroic conduct in California and the Indian country entitled him to the consideration of the government. Finally, Beale's appointment would be good for California and would gratify his friends. In a postscript, Fremont added that Senator Benton joined in the recommendation. Fremont sent a similar letter to President Zachary Taylor. But Beale failed to receive the appointment, possibly due to the untimely death of the president in early July.[40]

In mid-September, a reporter from the Sacramento *Transcript* visited the Mariposa neighborhood and exclaimed, "All is quartz! quartz!" Other companies were also starting hardrock mining. The Mariposa Mining Company, owned by Palmer, Cooke and Company of San Francisco, also held a lease from Fremont and located a thirty-two stamp mill, powered by two steam engines, on their property. Prospects appeared bright for both the Mariposa Mining Company and the Stockton-Aspinwall operation. Stockton had been especially glad to enter the quartz enterprise because the large influx of California gold had wiped out his Virginia mining operation. Some practical miners, however, dissented from the rosy forecast of the quartz advocates. Edmund Booth, residing near Sonora, stated that "quartz mining, as understood at the east, is humbug." In his opinion the proper machinery had not yet been invented.[41]

After obtaining dispatches for Washington, Beale returned to the East. At Chester he found that his commission as a lieutenant in the United States Navy had been delivered. The promotion was granted on October 3, and predated to take effect from the previous February. Beale also received a well-deserved furlough of a year. Yet, Beale also suffered several disappointments. Mary, his wife, was experiencing great difficulty with her eyesight, prohibiting her from reading or writing. Fremont had again failed to gain the U.S. Marshal's position for Beale. On September 3, both Benton and Fremont had written Daniel Webster, the new secretary of state, and repeated their praises of Beale. Fremont's recommendation now carried additional weight because California reportedly would be admitted to the Union within the week. Fremont confidently wrote Mrs. Mary A. Edwards, Beale's mother-in-law, describing his efforts to obtain for Beale an "honorable and lucrative" office in California. He promised to hand him his revolver when he himself departed for the West Coast. But the appointment was never confirmed.[42]

Beale had not been long at Chester, when Samuel Edwards, his father-in-law, became ill and died. The whole family mourned and were "perfectly heartbroken." Edwards had wielded power in Pennsylvania politics for many years; consequently, Beale contacted many of Edwards's old political friends to attend the funeral. He telegraphed the sad news to James Buchanan, who failed to receive the message and thereby missed the services. Buchanan apologized and stated that for the last thirty-five years his friendship with Samuel Edwards had not been "interrupted for a single moment."[43]

With a year's furlough from the navy, Beale decided to devote his time to the Aspinwall-Stockton interest in California. Recently, the two men had learned that their quartz-mining operation had lasted only a month. Expenses had gone far beyond a profitable level. As a result, Aspinwall and Stockton asked Beale to go directly to the mines at Mariposa and consult with Norris, Rube, and Hart. If the situation was unpromising, he would shut down the mining operation, discharge Norris and the other men, and sell the mining equipment. Aspinwall and Stockton instructed Beale to investigate some other form of business investment on the Pacific Coast.[44]

Beale sailed for California in mid-January of 1851. At Gorgona, Panama, he found that every building in town, except for Miller's Hotel, had burned in a fire on January 22, which engulfed the bamboo structures. His employer, William H. Aspinwall, was in the process of constructing a railroad across Panama, and a portion of the roadbed was completed. Beale estimated that within four months the railcars would be operating. On February 2, he left Panama on the *Columbia,* a new steamship of Aspinwall's Pacific Mail line. As they moved north the captain apparently became ill, and Beale volunteered to command the ship. Off Cape Blanco, Beale observed a vessel showing distress signals. It was the *Trident,* a sailing ship, out of San Francisco and bound for Panama. The commander of the *Trident* indicated that his ship's supply of food was dangerously low. Beale generously supplied them with flour. The *Columbia* touched at Acapulco, San Blas, and San Diego. On February 25, the ship arrived at San Francisco, and Beale found himself surrounded with old friends. Local newspapers received him as a hometown celebrity.[45]

Beale found San Francisco in a state of turmoil. An outbreak of unprecedented violence had led to the organization of a vigilance committee which took upon itself the task of maintaining law and order in the sprawling town. Beale proceeded directly to the Mariposa property and quickly determined that the situation there was hopeless. But Beale saw an opportunity in California that Aspinwall had not considered. Once the Panama Railroad was completed, Aspinwall would control nearly all transportation from the East Coast to California by his steamers and railroad. Believing that Aspinwall could also control land transportation and freighting to the mines in the interior, Beale invested his employer's money in local freighting from San Francisco. In short order, Beale achieved a dominant position and for a time was regarded as king of the transportation to the northern mines.[46]

Beale made important friends during these days. He met John Nugent, publisher of the San Francisco *Herald*, a Democratic newspaper, and Nugent and possibly others soon pushed Beale's name before the public as a candidate for Congress from the southern portion of the state. Three Democrats sought the nomination: Beale, Edward Marshall, and David Terry. In May the state convention would meet at Benecia, and Nugent believed that Beale held the best chance for winning. Nugent reasoned that the Marshall and Terry forces would cancel each other out, leaving the nomination open for Beale.

But at the Benicia State Democratic Convention in May of 1851, Beale failed to receive his party's nomination. Edward Marshall, a Kentucky lawyer from the mining camp of Sonora, garnered the nomination and went on to win the general election.[47]

Despite his setback in California politics, Beale was pleased with his career thus far. As the leading promoter of the great gold rush, twenty-nine-year-old Beale had become one of the best-known Americans connected with the new state. He had arduously cultivated "men of rank" in all fields of endeavor, from politics to belles lettres, and won their trust and friendship. Benton and Fremont especially desired to give him a position in the federal government, and before long, Beale would be rewarded for his loyalty and assistance.

Chapter 4

A PLAN FOR CALIFORNIA'S INDIANS

Surely that which was attempted and accomplished by a few poor priests, is not too great a task for the mighty republic of the United States. . . . Every useful mechanic art, all necessary knowledge of agricultural pursuits was here taught under a system of discipline at once mild, firm, and paternal. It is this system, modified and adapted to the present time, which I propose for your consideration. . . .

—Beale to Luke Lea, Commissioner
of Indian Affairs
November 22, 1852

In 1852, Ned Beale was appointed as California's first superintendent of Indian affairs. From firsthand experience, he was aware of the suffering the Gold Rush had inflicted upon California's Indian population. Hordes of settlers and miners had evicted entire tribes from their ancestral homes. Unlike the fierce warriors of the Plains, California Indians tended to passivity and only occasionally resisted white encroachments. If a tribe decided to fight the Americans, or if depredations against livestock occurred, a war of extermination frequently resulted. Only a few northern tribes managed to conduct effective warfare. Throughout California, but especially in the Sierra foothills and the great central valleys, the Indian population had been decimated, and thousands faced starvation. In 1850 the federal government became aware of the tragedy taking place in California and sent an Indian Peace Commission to investigate the situation.[1]

45

Early in 1851, three federal commissioners—Redick McKee, Oliver Wozencraft, and George W. Barbour—arrived in California and began to make treaties and allocate lands to more than one hundred and thirty tribes. The commisioners promised the Indians beef, blankets, and other sorely needed supplies. They also set aside large tracts of land, designated for reservations. For their part, the Indians agreed to reside on the reservations and refrain from stealing produce or livestock belonging to settlers. To supply the Indians' needs, the commissioners entered into large contracts for beef and other foodstuffs. Beef contracts were especially attractive, for the market was tight, and the government agreed to pay twice the going rate for beef.[2]

Fremont and Beale quickly became involved in the beef contract business. Fremont signed contracts to furnish $183,825 in beef to the Indians and allowed Beale a 25 percent interest, probably in return for money he loaned Fremont to make the purchases. When he had worked for Aspinwall and Stockton, Beale had served as cattle buyer, and he likely now advised Fremont in making purchases. In July of 1851 the two men left San Francisco and traveled to southern California, the principal cattle-raising area, and began to purchase cattle. They hired Mexican vaqueros and accompanied the drove of animals to a distribution point on the San Joaquin River, some two hundred and twenty miles north of Los Angeles. Fremont's contract called for nineteen hundred beeves, and he received roughly ninety-six dollars per head, double or triple the actual market price.[3]

Opposition to treaties and proposed reservations quickly arose in California. Critics charged that the treaties gave away one-half of the mineral and agricultural lands of the state. Moreover, doubts existed about the commissioners' authority to enter into contracts for the federal government. By the fall of 1851, the antitreaty sentiment had grown so large that it seemed unlikely that the United States Senate would ratify the commissioners' work.

Believing that Indian affairs in California needed close attention and firm direction, Senator Thomas Hart Benton on November 12 wrote Alexander H. Stuart, secretary of the interior, and recommended the creation of the position of superintendent of Indian affairs for California. He also knew the best man for the post—Edward F. Beale of California. Beale enjoyed the confidence of most Americans in California, Benton said, and was sensitive to the political winds. Certainly the naval officer equalled "Fremont and Carson in his knowledge of western Indians." Furthermore, Beale had performed extensive service for the nation and had received no reward from the government.[4]

Beale's supporters in Washington lobbied hard to secure the California appointment for him. Fremont wrote Senator William M. Gwin and Congressman George W. Wright of California, urging Beale's appointment, and asked Wright to work diligently on the matter. By late December of 1851, the entire California delegation joined to support Beale. Senator Gwin and Congressman Joseph W. McCorkle and Edward Marshall sent a letter to President Millard Fillmore and "sincerely & cheerfully" recommended Beale for Indian superintendent of California. The naval officer was closely identified with the early history of the state, they said, and possessed a "thorough knowledge of the *whole* state & of Indian character," making him particularly well suited for the job. They all concluded that Beale's appointment would be satisfactory to all the parties with California.[5]

Beale also asked old acquaintances to support his appointment. On January 30, 1852, he wrote Senator John M. Clayton of Delaware, former secretary of state, and reminded him of a promise. "Some years ago at New Castle on the occasion of my saving the life of young (William) Janvier," Beale began, "you told me if I ever stood in need of your assistance to claim it as a promise. I wish to be appointed the '*Indian Superintendent*' in California." Would Clayton write Interior Secretary Stuart, and assure him of Beale's fitness, character, and integrity? "A strong letter from you would make the matter quite sure . . . ," he added.[6]

While Beale lobbied for himself, he also tried to help Fremont sort out his case before the Indian Department regarding payment of his beef claim for $183,825. In late January, both Beale and his brother-in-law, Harry B. Edwards, appeared before a Washington notary and certified to Fremont's honesty in buying cattle for the government during the summer of 1851. Edwards stated that the price was fair, although high, due to circumstances, but added that as the cattle buyer for Fremont's Mariposa Rancho he never paid less than 25¢ per pound for beef. The cattle Fremont delivered to Commissioner Barbour on the San Joaquin averaged 500 pounds (estimated) and at 25¢ per pound his herd would have been worth about $125 per head, or nearly $250,000 for approximately 2,000 animals. Beale agreed with Edwards. He had purchased cattle for Aspinwall and Stockton at prices that varied from twenty to thirty cents per pound. Beale mentioned that Fremont had negotiated part of the government drafts he had received from Commissioner Barbour in payment for the cattle, believing that the drafts would be honored. Beale, who had accepted some of the drafts, stood to lose a large amount of money if Fremont failed to obtain the government endorsement.[7]

If Beale received the post of Indian Superintendent in California, he would be required to resign from the navy. This did not distress him greatly for he felt somewhat bitter about the eight years he served as a passed midshipman and acting lieutenant before receiving his commission. In January of 1852, he had joined a host of young naval officers in sending to Congress a "Memorial of Passed Midshipmen" which criticized at length the unfairness of this system. The Washington *National Intelligencer* published on January 24, 1852 this petition signed by 250 men, which included Edward F. Beale, Daniel Ammen, David D. Porter, James M. Duncan, and many other friends.

During these days Beale also thought of his friend Bayard Taylor, whom he had not seen in over a year. The previous March he had heard that Taylor's young wife had died from tuberculosis, only three months after their marriage, but he had postponed writing him. In a letter dated February 3, 1852, Beale said he heard that Taylor was considering dropping his work with poetry. Beale hoped this was not the case and thanked Taylor for eulogizing his Mexican War exploits in a passage of "Summer Camp."

> O Friend, whose history is writ in deeds
> That make your life a marvel, come no gleams
> Of past adventure, echoes of old storms,
> And Battle's tingling hum of flying shot,
> To touch your easy blood and temp you o'er
> The round of yon blue plain? Or have they lost,
> Heroic days, the virtue which the heart
> That did their best rejoicing, proved so high?
> Back through the long, long cycles of our rest
> Your memory travels: through this hush you hear
> The Gila's dashing, feel the yawning jaws
> Of black volcanic gorges close you in
> On waste and awful tracts of wilderness,
> Which other than the eagle's cry, or bleat
> Of mountain-goat, hear not: the scorching sand
> Eddies around the tracks your fainting mules
> Leave in the desert: thorn and cactus pierce
> your bleeding limbs, and stiff with raging thirst
> Your tongue forgets its office. Leave untried
> That cruel trail, and leave the wintry hills
> And leave the tossing sea! The Summer here
> Builds us a tent of everlasting calm.

But Beale expected no calm, however, and said in conclusion that he planned to return to California.[8]

On March 4, as expected in many quarters, Fillmore sent to the Senate the name of his nominee for the position—Edward F. Beale. Opposition to Beale's appointment developed quickly. Foes of Benton and Fremont told Fillmore that Beale had been involved in the controversial cattle contracts for Indians in California. On March 8, Beale secured an authorization from Fremont to state upon all occasions that Fremont had been the "sole responsible contracting party." Beale had never been a partner in any transactions, Fremont wrote, and added that he was leaving for England, and if anyone contradicted him, Beale should produce the letter. The firm denial by Fremont helped stifle the charges.[9]

Whig opponents also raised the charge that Beale, a Democrat, should be denied the post because he was personally unfit—a drunkard and a quarrelsome man. During a social gathering in Washington, Lieutenant Fabius Stanley, a naval officer and friend of Beale's, had made a number of remarks while inebriated. Stanley said that if the president ever saw Beale under the influence of liquor, he would have pondered the appointment for a long time. When inebriated, Beale turned into a "quarrelsome and dangerous man." Stanley had personally seen Beale drunk on one occasion and had heard about his famous drinking episode in Mazatlan in 1848.

Word of Beale's being a "common drunkard & c" reached President Fillmore. Stanley learned of the problems his gossip had caused and immediately tried to right the situation. He contacted his brother, Congressman Edward Stanley of North Carolina, who took the problem to Senator Gwin. Several persons then visited the president, probably Stanley and Gwin, and Fillmore declared himself satisfied that Beale was not a drunkard and was, in fact, the right man for the job. Lieutenant Stanley offered profuse apologies to Beale and said that he uttered the statements at an "unguarded" moment, and hoped Beale was still his friend. On March 11, 1852, Ned Beale received his commission as superintendent of Indian affairs for California.[10]

Within a week, Beale submitted to Indian Commissioner Luke Lea a budget for the California superintendency for the fiscal year beginning July 1, 1852. He made his estimates on the basis of his own judgment and the advice of longtime residents of California. Some items might appear extravagant, Beale stated, but all estimates must quadruple eastern prices due to local conditions. In contrast to his predecessors—McKee, Barbour, and Wozencraft—Beale vowed to practice the most rigid economy. Still, he planned to "temper economy with judgment" in laying the foundation for the California superintendency. His itemized budget, slightly modified by Congress, totalled $42,150.[11]

As Beale prepared for his assignment, Indian conditions in California continued to deteriorate. The California state legislature adopted a resolution which opposed the commissioners' treaties. Then, word came that the settlers in the vicinity of Humboldt Bay had massacred Indians and gained the support of local politicians for their act. Commissioner McKee had tangled with Governor John Bigler over the question of Indian policy and responsibility for the massacres. Most California newspapers condemned the treaties and the plans for reservations.[12]

In mid-May, California's reaction to Beale's appointment reached the East. The San Francisco *Herald* stated that the new bureaucrat would permanently remove the wandering Indian tribes from the white community and place them on reserves in the Colorado River area or the country east of the Sierra Nevada range. The San Francisco *Picayune* doubted Beale's appointment for he was a Democrat and possessed no special fitness for the office. He might be a good mountaineer or woodsman but still a "very indifferent negotiator of treaties." The *Picayune* raised the standard for a Whig candidate for the post and declared Indian Agent Redick McKee's knowledge of Indian matters in the state exceeded that of any other man in California.[13]

McKee intensely disliked the appointment of Beale. He wrote Indian Commissioner Lea on May 1 that he hoped Beale's appointment would serve the public interest but added that the Whig State Central Committee and other influential Whigs in California disapproved of the selection. He also personally disliked the choice but promised to subordinate his own feelings and render all possible assistance to the new superintendent. McKee urged that the treaties be ratified and carried out in good faith. The commissioners in California could envision no solution to the Indian problem unless Congress adopted their expensive plan. "The Indians must be *fed* for awhile, or *killed off,*" McKee wrote to President Fillmore.[14]

In Washington, Beale spent many hours examining the California treaties. On May 11, at the request of Indian Commissioner Lea, he drafted a lengthy defense of the treaties. The California commissioners, Beale stated, had acted with caution and deliberation in setting aside reservations and making promises for food. He said that Indians were extremely suspicious once a confidence had been broken. If the Senate failed to ratify the agreements, the Indians of California would continue to roam, and the settlers would exterminate them. The federal government, unlike the state, should recognize that Indians held a possessory right to the land and were, therefore, entitled to a reservation.

The charge that the Indian commissioners had given away the best agricultural land in the state was utterly false. As a rule, the land provided the Indians under the treaties was "such as only a half-starved and defenceless people would have consented to receive. . . ." The reservations laid out in southern California were "composed of the most barren and sterile lands" to be found in the state and totally unfit for agricultural purposes.

Several points in the treaties drew criticism. The gifts of agricultural implements at this time were pointless, Beale stated, as most California Indians lived at too primitive a level to learn their use. But if an agent considered a given tribe capable of farming with modern equipment, the government should make the implements available. A proposal to establish Indian schools also seemed too far advanced for most tribes. Many persons criticized the treaties for promising food subsistence. Under the agreements, the government pledged to supply Indians with cattle for several years to prevent starvation and to provide the basis for tribal herds. Beale recognized that the practice might prove initially expensive, but critics should remember that it would terminate in a few years, and other Indian tribes in the nation were receiving annuity payments in perpetuity. Beale concluded that strict frugality at present might be ill timed. If the government failed to establish an effective reservation system in California, the result would be expensive Indian war, the cost of which could not be estimated.[15]

Heavy opposition from the California delegation doomed the treaties in spite of Beale's support. In secret session on June 1 and 8, the Senate rejected all eighteen treaties. The large sums of money necessary to fulfill the commissioners' promises and the large size of the reservations led the lists of reasons for rejection.

With the treaties rejected, Indian Commissioner Lea handed Beale the distasteful task of examining accounts and contracts of the three California commissioners. Beale immediately asked Lea to have someone else from California carry out this investigative assignment. One of the contractors was John C. Fremont, his "intimate friend and companion." Beale did not want to investigate Fremont. Although certain the procedure would be beneficial to Fremont, Beale said he would find the task "exceedingly delicate, unpleasant, and embarrassing." The assignment was shelved for the time being.[16]

Beale now reviewed his budget for the California superintendency, making minor changes owing to the rejected treaties. He wrote Lea that the Indians would be "restless and suspicious" from disappointment over the broken promises. Consequently, he proposed the sum of $5,000 for provisions and gifts be increased. He felt the various California tribes should send delegates to him, and he would distribute presents as a way of placating hurt feelings. He intended to give American flags to all tribal leaders, stating that Indians regarded the Stars and Stripes as "big medicine." Beale's budget for Indian presents was small, but the Indian Department hoped to obtain a special appropriation of $100,000 to ease the transition of the California Indians from their seminomadic state to reservation life.[17]

On July 26, Interior Secretary Stuart asked Commissioner Lea to issue Beale his instructions and send him to California. On the thirty-first Lea complied. Beale would supervise official conduct and investigate the accounts of the Indian agents within his jurisdiction. He would examine all claims, accounts, vouchers, and disbursements connected with California Indian affairs. Lea urged proper record keeping and told Beale that no claim should be forwarded to Washington without his own personal investigation. Finally, Beale would try to develop a plan for the future. "You will adopt every means in your power to acquaint yourself thoroughly with the condition of the various tribes within your Superintendency," wrote Lea, "and keep this Department fully advised of all the facts connected therewith, together with your views as to the measures proper to be adopted for their future management and control."[18]

As a heated debate raged in the U.S. Senate, Beale sailed from New York by steamer for California on August 5, 1852. He was accompanied by Harry Edwards, Fred Kerlin, his wife's cousin who would serve as superintendency clerk, and his personal servant. Mary chose to remain at home in Chester. On September 5, 1852, Beale reached San Francisco aboard the steamer *Oregon* from Panama. The *Alta California* stated that his appointment to the arduous and important duties of this new office satisfied everyone.[19]

After eleven busy days, Superintendent Beale sent his first report to Commissioner Lea on September 16. Indian affairs in California were in a dismal state. Instances of the "grossest mismanagement or ignorance" had come to his attention, and the Indian agents (former commissioners) had been negligent and reckless. A rigid investigation was in order. McKee and Wozencraft had both shipped their accounts to Washington, but Beale intended to examine their accounts since those transmittals. Bringing California Indian affairs into shape would be a difficult and toilsome business, Beale warned. Due to the treaties' rejection, the whole policy would have to be changed.

Beale's call for an official investigation had been prompted in part by a conference with Agent Wozencraft concerning beef contracts. When he asked Wozencraft for proof that the Indians actually received cattle under contracts, the agent said that he always took the word of the traders appointed to make the deliveries. Wozencraft added that he generally accompanied the cattle to the delivery but upon questioning admitted that he ordered 1,500 head of cattle delivered to the Four Creeks region, on the upper San Joaquin River, without having been there himself. Beale also discovered that in some instances the contractors who supplied the cattle and the traders who delivered the animals were the same people.[20]

On September 21, Joel H. Brooks, formerly employed by Major James Savage, Indian trader on the Fresno, told Beale about illegal activities in cattle dealings. Savage had instructed Brooks to deliver cattle to Indians on the upper San Joaquin, King's River, and other southern spots. He was directed to take receipts for double the delivered amount, then make no second delivery. Savage planned to sell the remaining cattle to hungry miners. The herd which Brooks described contained 1,900 head of cattle which had belonged to John C. Fremont. Brooks implicated Fremont's faithful friend, Alex Godey. Following Savage's instructions, Brooks turned over the second herd of cattle to Godey, who proceeded to sell the animals to miners. Trader James Savage was apparently the key figure in the dubious transaction, but he had been killed in August. The exact truth of the matter might never surface. One thing was certain— Agent Wozencraft did little to see that the Indians received their livestock.

Beale also obtained a written statement from H. C. Logan, who described the cattle speculations of Indian Agent Redick McKee. Logan stated that a year earlier, General James Estell, McKee and McKee's son drove cattle north under a contract awarded by McKee. Logan delivered the cattle to George P. Armstrong, but few beeves ever reached the Indians. McKee told Logan that his partnership with Armstrong reaped a handsome profit from the animals. General Hitchcock agreed with Logan's assessment of McKee and stated that he did not want the agent to accompany troops into the field. But Agent McKee did more than traffic in cattle. Captain John H. Lindrum, Third Artillery, remembered an instance when the army quartermaster transported Indian goods for the agent. Several times during the trip, McKee sold Indian supplies—tobacco, pipes, blankets, and other items—to the soldiers in the escort party.[21]

By the end of September, Beale wrote Commissioner Lea about California Indian matters. Nearly 1,000 head of cattle supplied to agents McKee, Wozencraft, and Barbour remained unissued to the Indians. If the cattle were reclaimed from the traders, as Logan suggested, this might place the government under an obligation to pay the contractors. Beale could not pay for cattle without additional funds, for Congress had cut the contingency appropriation. Beale told Lea that the California agents had clearly acted improperly. They knew little about local Indian affairs, and neither Wozencraft nor McKee had visited the tribes within the last six months. Due to their negligence, government funds had been squandered in every direction.[22]

A break soon occurred in the impasse. On October 1, Agent Wozencraft resigned, and word of Benjamin D. Wilson's appointment as agent reached Beale. Wilson, a longtime resident of Los Angeles, had married into a rich Mexican family and knew a great deal about southern California Indians. Above all, he was an honest man.

Throughout October, Beale spent long hours at work in his office at 123 Montgomery Street in San Francisco. While he investigated the accounts of the three agents, he sent Harry Edwards into the interior to meet with tribal leaders to assure them of the government's good intentions. Later, Beale himself visited the tribes living along the Russian River and near Clear Lake, some one hundred twenty miles north of the city. The Indians of the region were quiet and peaceable, but whites were rapidly filling the countryside. Permanent arrangements were needed for the Indians. In the Clear Lake country, Beale learned that several prominent Mexican families had raided Indian settlements to procure slaves. The practice was far from uncommon. Peter Campbell, a government investigator, wrote from Sonoma on October 28, stating that California was populated by many "sordid base and unchristian beings, who value the dollar gained no matter how dishonorably, more than the tranquility and happiness of a nation."[23]

Despite his varied tasks, Beale drew up a plan for the conduct of Indian affairs in California. His policy required the close cooperation of the military. "I propose a system of 'military posts' to be established on reservations for the convenience and protection of the Indians," Beale wrote to Commissioner Lea, with the reservations "to be regarded as military or government reservations." At each reserve, an Indian agent would instruct the Indians in useful subjects, particularly farming. Beale hoped that the farms would produce enough food for both the Indians and the attached military garrison. In sum, the proposed reservation system would involve little expense to the government once in operation. Under Beale's proposal, Indians would never obtain "title" to reservations; ownership remained with the federal government. After studying the plan, General Hitchcock on October 31 endorsed it as the "only one calculated to prevent the extermination of the Indians." A practical man, Beale had taken into account the "actual condition of things in this country."[24]

In Washington, Congress had voted $100,000 for the aid of California's Indians. The Indian Bureau decided that $25,000 should be spent in the East on presents, while the remaining $75,000 would be spent by Beale in California, largely for food. A special agent, Pearson B. Reading, was appointed to supervise the eastern purchases. Reading made the expenditures in New York City: small white porcelain beads ($4,500), small black beads ($2,000), small red beads ($3,000), large glass beads, assorted ($2,000), turkey red prints ($2,000), and gray-colored shawls

($1,500). The remainder of the money would be spent to transport the two hundred pounds of trade goods to California.

In early November, Reading arrived in San Francisco by steamer with one hundred pounds of trinkets. Beale disapproved of the purchases, feeling that the money could have been more wisely spent. He sent an itemized list of Reading's purchases to Agent B. D. Wilson for his opinion. Most of the goods were "entirely useless," responded Wilson on November 11. California Indians never used such things. Admittedly, they could use the cloth, prints, and shawls in some fashion, but overall the purchase was "a bad one." In many places, Indians faced starvation; they needed food not clothing![25]

Beale continued to refine his basic plan for Indian reservations. On November 22, he wrote Commissioner Lea about the possibility of spending all of the $100,000 appropriation on the development of his experiment in one section of the country—southern California. If he attempted to spread the money to all the tribes of the state, each Indian in California would receive the sum of one dollar. To be effective, the expenditure should be concentrated. Beale listed his reasons for choosing the south. First, northern California was mining country and heavily populated. The Indians presented no problems. Miners went about well armed and owned few cattle to tempt Indian thefts. Second, the central part of the state presented the same conditions. The Indians of the region tended to be harmless and docile.

But southern California offered a different picture. Most of the population lived on ranches, located at great distances from each other. These ranches would be at the mercy of the tribes in event of a general uprising. But why protect the least populous part of the state? Beale answered his own question stating: "because it is from this quarter we draw our supplies of beef cattle entirely." An Indian war in southern California could cut off the San Francisco market, and within one week the price of beef would double. After six months, beef would be almost nonexistent in both city and mines.

The Indians who lived in Los Angeles County posed no threat. Formerly under the control of the old mission system, they generally lived on ranchos, and worked as servants or vaqueros. But north of Los Angeles lived several tribes: Tejones, Cowillas, Cowchillas, and Freznales. These tribes, numbering some 5,000 "bold and enterprising" Indians, had existed for years by depredating on the Los Angeles area. All cattle drives from Los Angeles to San Francisco went through the Tejones' country. In the winter months, the Indians would descend on Los Angeles through the Tejon Pass and raid the surrounding ranches. Beale proposed spending the entire appropriation on keeping these tribes peaceful.

By ignoring other tribes in the state, Beale realized that suffering might occur in certain districts. He knew many Indians in the northern and middle districts had been "driven from their fishing and hunting grounds, hunted themselves like wild beasts, lassoed, and torn from homes made miserable by want, and forced into slavery." Nevertheless, they posed no threat to Americans and therefore must be neglected temporarily. Beale mentioned that a single drydock or public building might cost a million dollars, but a sum of only half that amount would prevent the deaths of 75,000 human beings. For the remainder of California's Indians, Beale requested a Congressional appropriation of $500,000.

Once again, Beale described to Lea his plan to use Indian labor to feed themselves and the military forces of California. He would draw upon the experiences of the old mission establishments of the Spaniards in this effort. "Surely that which was attempted and accomplished by a few poor priests," he wrote, "is not too great a task for the mighty republic of the United States." The priests had taught every mechanical and agricultural art to the Indians under a "system of discipline at once mild, firm, and paternal." Beale wanted the government to adopt the Mission system, substituting Indian agents for priests. No other way would "preserve this unforunately people from total extinction, and our government from everlasting disgrace."[26]

General Hitchcock supported Beale's reservation plans. He reported to the adjutant general that if the current settlement trends continued in California the Indians would be driven soon beyond the Sierra Nevada. If that occurred, they would spread a "leaven of bitterness" among the tribes of the Great Basin, which as yet had had few dealings with Americans. The California Indians would take with them a knowledge of firearms and an "instructive spirit of war" which would make the "pacific transit over the Continent" next to impossible for years to come. Beale's plan gave the government great leeway and could prevent needless bloodshed. He urged the War Department's support not only for the plan but for Beale's continuance in office (Democrat Franklin Pierce had recently won the presidential election). Beale understood Indians better than any man in the West, according to Hitchcock, and he brought to the performance of his duties "earnest zeal, a humane spirit, and untiring perseverance and an honest independence."[27]

On December 1, 1852, the *Herald* published a long article, written by John Nugent, which described Beale's military reservation system with its self-sufficient farmers. "Adopt this sytem, and all fear of collision between the whites and the Indians would be at once removed," stated the writer.[28]

In early December, Beale toured the San Joaquin Valley, looking for an appropriate site for a reservation. From Fresno River, on the fourteenth he wrote to Lea that he had selected a tract of land lying between San Joaquin and the Fresno rivers. The proposed reservation boundaries measured twelve miles wide and forty miles long, with the only valuable part being the narrow strip of arable land along the river banks. Natural barriers and an adjacent Spanish land grant would prevent contact with white settlers in the future.[29]

On his trip, Beale also learned that most of the Indians had deserted rancherias and fled to the mountains. A general belief existed that the Indians intended to depredate against the whites. Beale asked an old acquaintance, "Niague," a celebrated Indian chief, to send runners to invite the bands to a council meeting. In a few days, a delegation assembled on the Fresno. Beale had known many of the leaders for several years, and he spoke to them plainly. He declared that if they would work for their own support, the government would assist them. Those who were lazy or refused to work would not profit from the work of the industrious. Anyone caught stealing or in any other act of "rascality" would receive a severe punishment. Beale cemented the agreement with presents.

The Indians believed Beale was a truthful man, and they returned to their families in the hills. Within a matter of days, men, women, and children began to arrive at the Fresno, expressing their desire to go to work and "raise food for their own subsistence." One observer, who had spent considerable time in the West among Indians, said he had never witnessed such a dramatic turnaround in so short a period of time.[30]

Beale next planned a trip to the Colorado River, but he received an urgent letter from Commissioner Lea, which ordered his immediate return to Washington. Leaving the Fresno reserve in charge of his subordinates, Beale hurried back to San Francisco.[31]

On January 15, 1853, Beale sailed for Panama aboard the *Golden Gate*. The San Francisco *Herald* praised his accomplishments. The superintendent had "laid the foundation for the establishment of a sound policy with regard to the Indians of California." It was hoped he would gain the necessary backing in Washington to carry out his program. Arriving in Washington in late February, he reported to Commissioner Lea on California affairs. To Beale's satisfaction he learned that the government favored his proposals. The president, the commissioner of Indian affairs, and the Senate's Committee on Indian Affairs all favored his program.

On February 25 to support further his plan for a new departure in Indian-white relations in California, Beale submitted a report which described shocking massacres of Indians by white citizens. California Indians lived under the threat of extermination, Beale asserted. At the Trinity River, local militia attacked an Indian village at daybreak. Only a woman and child managed to escape. The attackers returned from the foray with a bag containing one hundred and thirty scalps. Similar massacres had occured at Happy Valley, Humboldt Bay, and other locations in the state. The story was the same: "It was a massacre of helpless and defence-less beings, perhaps mostly women and children." Slave hunters preyed upon the natives in northern California. Juan Berryessa and other large landowners enslaved many Indians from the Clear Lake region and forced them to work as laborers. Indian slaves were also sold for profit to white settlers. As the government had an obligation to protect the Indians from such injustices, Beale asked Congress to appropriate $500,000 for the "immediate subsistence and support" of the California tribes. He also called for the speedy adoption of measures to enable him to begin an experimental reservation system.

Beale realized there was a strong possibility that President Pierce, soon to be inaugurated, would remove him from office and acted accordingly. To counter such an event, he appended to his statement a letter from John Bigler and Samuel Purdy, California's governor and lieutenant governor respectively. They strongly urged Beale's retention in office and stated that the prosperity of the state depended to a large measure on the successful implementation of Beale's Indian policy.[32]

On March 3, 1853, Commissioner Luke Lea sent Beale's report to William K. Sebastian, chairman of the Senate Committee on Indian Affairs. Lee urged that the Congress act immediately on the proposed legislation before adjournment. Congress wasted little time in approving the measure. The Indian appropriation which related to California authorized the president to select five military reservations from the public domain in California, Utah, or New Mexico for the purposes of Beale's experiment. The reservations should not contain more than 25,000 acres, and they must be located on uninhabited lands. Congress also approved $250,000 for the cost of subsisting and removing the Indians. With an eye toward the incoming chief executive, a proviso was inserted which gave the president the right to alter, discard, or accept the plan. If he approved it, the three agencies in California would be abolished. Fillmore quickly signed the measure into law, but Franklin Pierce would determine the nature and direction of Beale's plan.[33]

At the White House, President Pierce examined and approved Beale's plan for California's Indians. On March 25, he instructed Robert McClelland, newly appointed secretary of the interior, to take the necessary steps to put the plan into operation. McClelland directed Beale to meet with the president at 7:30 A.M. on March 29, presumably to discuss the proposed California reservations. The day before his meeting with the president, Secretary McClelland ordered Beale to "report without delay" to California. The government granted him wide latitude in his instructions and told him to adopt whatever measures in his judgment would accomplish the desired objective. Beale was directed to treat the Indians with humanity and kindness and ensure that the public funds were "legally, judiciously, and economically expended." Under no circumstances would his expenditures exceed the amount of the appropriation.[34]

For the moment, Beale found that his accounts were not in order. On March 24, he wrote Commissioner Lea that he had discovered that several important vouchers were missing from the last quarter and consequently his accounts would be delayed until his return to the West Coast. On March 31, George P. Manypenny, who succeeded Lea as commissioner, stated that Beale's explanation was satisfactory. On the same day, Beale took pleasure in addressing a letter to Redick McKee, informing the agent that his agency had been abolished by an act of Congress and his services would no longer be required.[35]

Beale's report on the plight of the California Indians was made public while he was in Washington, and many people were shocked by the revelations. Throughout the country, newspapers reproduced sections of the report. On April 13, Samuel F. Du Pont, Beale's former commander, wrote a letter to his former subordinate. Du Pont expressed shock at the horrid details brought to light by Beale, but he felt proud that a former naval officer had been the instrument of their disclosure. The editors of the New York Times were especially angered by the treatment of the California Indians. The white trespassers upon Indian territory had committed barbarities without precedence in the history of Christendom. To call such men "savages and brutes," stated the Times, "would be a libel upon the animal kingdom." The newspaper praised Beale's proposed establishment of a mission system for the Indians and lauded his courage in revealing such a shocking tale of massacre and fraud.[36]

While riding high in public esteem, Beale was again drawn into the schemes of Benton and Fremont. During the recent session of Congress much debate had swirled around the question of the route of the proposed railroad to California. The day before the California superintendency was funded, Congress authorized the secretary of war, Jefferson Davis, to send out survey parties over the several contending routes. Thomas Hart Benton proposed to Davis that Fremont and Beale lead an expedition across the Rocky Mountains on the central route. Benton and Beale both pointed out that the superintendent could select sites for Indian reservations in New Mexico and Utah while making the journey, thereby fulfilling the stipulations of the Indian appropriation.

When Davis indicated that he did not know when the appropriations for the survey would be available, Benton suggested to Beale the idea of his supervising a private surveying party while traveling west to California. Beale accepted the offer.[37]

Benton already was promoting settlement on land in Nebraska Territory where Indian titles had not yet been extinguished. Perhaps this tactic would gain support for his central route railroad. Indian Commissioner Manypenny had advised Benton that no part of Nebraska was open to settlement until the Indian titles had been cleared. But Benton ignored the commissioner and published an "official" map, showing areas of Nebraska marked as open for settlement. Benton angered not only Manypenny but Senator David Rice Atchison of Missouri, an important member of the Senate's Indian Affairs Committee. Atchison wanted settlers kept out of Nebraska at present, for he advocated the expansion of slavery. By his involvement with Benton, Beale gained the displeasure of both Manypenny and Atchison.[38]

On April 13, Secretary McClelland gave Beale his final instructions. He should proceed immediately to California by the most "expeditious route." All reservation sites selected must be made in conjunction with the military commander in California. McClelland was aware of Benton and Beale's plan for a private railroad surveying expedition to California. Consequently, he emphasized that in traveling there, Beale must not allow any subject other than the Indian reservation plan to engage his attention.

At Benton's direction, Beale ignored the subtle warning implied in his instructions. By early May, the private exploring party, without surveyors, assembled in St. Louis. In addition to Beale the party contained Gwin H. Heap, Beale's cousin; Antoine Leroux, a guide; Elisha Riggs, a Washington banker; Henry Rodgers, an associate from the navy; and servants. Senator Benton accompanied the party to the railhead at Westport, where he delivered a speech benefitting the historic occasion. After describing to the crowd Beale's prior accomplishments, Benton focused his attention on Gwin H. Heap. The latter was thirty-six years old, well traveled, and had lived in Africa. Benton joked that Heap wished he had a camel so he could ride quickly over the plains and spoke emphatically about Beale's strict economy in marked contrast to the elaborate government surveys. After itemizing their expenses, Benton concluded that a total amount of $86.30 would be spent for the important project. Unnamed political foes, Benton thundered, had desired to make

Beale return to California by steamer, to prevent him exploring the central route to the Pacific. They had failed, and now Beale would prove that the "American road to India" should follow the central path.[39]

In St. Louis Beale had drawn upon the Indian Department for $2,600 and contracted with Henry E. Young to convey the party from Westport to Walker's Pass in California for $1,825.00. Young agreed to furnish the expedition with all necessary stores, provisions, arms, and ammunition, as well as animals for the journey. Young would also personally accompany the party to California. When Commissioner Manypenny saw the $2,600 draft, he became angry and contacted Secretary McClelland. On May 9, he ordered Beale to make no further drafts until he reached California. In the future Beale's drafts must always include an exhibit of the liabilities they were designed to meet.[40]

On May 10, Beale's party left Westport for Council Grove. A few miles outside of town, a group of ladies drank a "stirrup cup" of champagne to Beale's success, and the railroad exploring party headed west along the Santa Fe Trail. A dedicated sportsman, Beale enjoyed immensely the excellent hunting which abounded on the plains. Heap recorded in his diary that the party frequently feasted on buffalo hump and tongue. West of Bent's Fort, the group followed the Huerfano River into the Sangre de Cristo Mountains and reached Fort Massachusetts on June 5 in southern Colorado. As the nearest supplies were at Taos and Santa Fe, more than one hundred miles away, Beale set out for the settlements. Several days before he reached Taos, the local residents had assembled and endorsed the Benton route for a transcontinental railroad and drafted a petition to Congress. Beale's role as head of Benton's survey party was known, and he received an enthusiastic welcome when he arrived.[41]

With fresh supplies, the party pushed on and on June 18 reached the Cochatope Pass in south-central Colorado. The Cochatope summit, the lowest pass on the continental divide along the central route, was an important spot on the proposed railroad line. Fortunately, for Benton's plans, Beale found the pass a "natural GATE." Heap recorded that as he approached the pass, the grade was so gentle that a traveler had difficulty in knowing whether he was climbing or descending.

The party finally reached the Colorado River. It was swollen by newly melted snow. A pirogue (dugout canoe) was used to cross the river, but in ferrying the supplies, the pirogue tipped over, and nearly all supplies were lost.[42]

Beale sent Gwin H. Heap and several members of the expedition to return to New Mexico for supplies and began to worry about lost time. He was sick with dysentery, and icy baths in a nearby, snow-fed stream failed to help. Commissioner Manypenny had opposed the overland trek and now would appear right, once word of Beale's troubles got back East. Certainly, he had not taken the "most expeditious" route to California. Finally, on July 17, the united party resumed its western journey.[43]

In California, government officials and friends began to worry about Beale. General Hitchcock sent a detachment of soldiers to Walker's Pass to wait for Beale, but after spending quite some time there, they returned to Fort Miller on July 6. Harry Edwards and Alex Godey, who had also gone to the pass, likewise gave up the long vigil. Edwards returned to San Francisco on August 6.[44]

Beale's party, however, began to make good progress. They crossed western Utah, passed the Mormon settlement at the Vegas, and then fought the blazing heat of the Mojave Desert. On August 22, the party arrived in Los Angeles, some two months late.

As Californians read about Beale's safe arrival, Senator Benton in Washington published Heap's diary in several issues of the *National Intelligencer* and showed President Pierce letters from Beale, which Heap had sent East from Santa Fe shortly after the canoe accident. Beale described the level pass and the ease and practicality of the central railroad route. "We are victorious in the public estimation . . . ," Benton wrote Beale and added that the president was well pleased with his accomplishments.[45]

In his eighteen months as Indian superintendent, Beale had displayed imagination, intelligence, and an ability to temper his idealism with reality. He convinced the government to reinstitute the old mission system in California, a radical departure in government-Indian relations. Yet, once Congress and the president had approved his plan for self-sufficient reservations, Beale allowed Thomas Hart Benton and personal ambition to divert his attention momentarily away from his official responsibilities. En route west he conducted an "unofficial" railroad survey to California along the central route and thereby jeopardized his career and the fate of many California Indians. The months ahead would prove crucial in determining the success or failure of Beale's reservation system.

Chapter 5

FEUD WITH
THE INDIAN OFFICE

Beale . . . (said) that Mr. Manypenny had been stabbing him in
back all winter, and he now slapt him in the face for it.
—Thomas Hart Benton to the public,
Washington *National Intelligencer*
May 15, 1855

Upon his arrival in Los Angeles on August 22, 1853, Beale sent Commissioner Manypenny a hurried assessment of the Indian situation. The
Congressional act which established the California superintendency abolished the old Indian agencies but failed to substitute new ones or provide for agents. Beale hesitated to set up agencies, even though President
Pierce had sanctioned his doing so in a conversation before he left
Washington. The same problem existed with regard to hiring farmers,
blacksmiths, carpenters, and other necessary skilled labor. The congressional appropriation was strictly for "subsistence," and if that designa-
tion meant only food, Beale faced grave problems. Regarding the location
of reservations, he originally hoped to establish two of the five authorized on land along the Mojave River, south of Walker's Pass. But an
examination of that country revealed no suitable sites. During the next
few days, he planned to inspect a spot near the head of the Tulare Valley
and hoped for better luck.

Beale asked Manypenny to show patience and consideration. He envisioned almost constant travel around the state and predicted that it
would be difficult to keep his accounts in order and forward them to

Washington on time. He felt confident he could fulfill the goals and implement the new policy, but it would require time, at least five years. If the Indian Office would grant him that time without interference, Beale said, the Indians would emerge not only self-sufficient but producing enough surplus foodstuffs to pay the expenses of everyone employed by the Indian Office in California.[1]

Placing his letter in the mail, Beale turned next to the question of a location for his experimental reservation. Accompanied by Wilson, he rode to the Tulare Valley to council with the Indians who resided on the watershed of the upper San Joaquin. During Beale's absence in the East, Harry Edwards and Alex Godey had visited among the tribes in an effort to keep them peaceful and receptive to Beale's reservation plan. At Tejon Pass, some sixty miles north of Los Angeles, Beale fortuitously met a team of three topographical engineers engaged in surveying railroad routes in south-central California. Lieutenants John G. Parke, George Stoneman, and Robert S. Williamson had expert knowledge of the state from their surveys, and Beale questioned them closely as to the best location for an Indian reserve in the area lying between the Sacramento River and the Tejon Pass.[2]

The remarks of Parke and his associates confirmed a decision that Beale had reached earlier. Influenced by his talks with Wilson and his own knowledge of California, Beale had favored for some time a reservation at the Tejon. The government surveyors bolstered that decision. A year before, he had told Commissioner Lea that the Tejon Pass was a key gateway to San Francisco for Los Angeles stockmen, and hostile Indians could effectively cripple the state by closing that avenue of commerce. Also, Tejon Indians frequently raided the Los Angeles vicinity. By establishing a reserve in the area, he could not only prevent depredations but turn the Tejones into peaceful farmers. Still, Beale's plan would succeed only if the Indians agreed to try it. Couriers were dispatched from Tejon Valley, to ask the tribes to come in for a council so Beale might tell them about the government's intentions.[3]

On September 12, Beale opened the council meeting at Tejon Pass. Over one thousand Indians were assembled, and Beale addressed the Indians through Wilson, who interpreted into Spanish, a language that many Indian leaders understood. He told them that he was their friend, desired them to be happy, and was prepared to use every available means to make them content. On the proposed reservation, the Indians would live free from the encroachments of the white man. Farming would be the key, and Beale reminded his listeners that they already knew something about agriculture. But the reservation he proposed was not like

64

the mission establishments, where in former times Indians had labored for the benefit of the government and the church. On Beale's reservation, the Indians would labor solely for their own benefit. A system of rewards and punishments would be arranged by the Indians themselves, and their leaders would be chosen by the tribe, not appointed by white men. Beale swore he would gain nothing personally from their labor, but that the Indians should regard him as chief. He promised to work to promote their interests.

The council at the Tejon lasted two days. Beale warned the Indians that the alternative to his humane plan was "extermination by disease and mixture with the white race." Ploughs, agricultural implements, and stock would be furnished the Indians when they moved to the reservation. Interpreter Wilson, a man the Indians respected, also spoke. He said Beale would fulfill his promises, despite the failure of other white men on former occasions. The Indians accepted Beale's word and agreed to move to the new reservation and commence a new life.[4]

Beale's plan received widespread endorsement. The *Alta* stated that it would be impossible to devise any other plan which would "so effectually protect the whites from the predatory incursions of the Indians, or shield the Indians against the injustice and oppression of the whites." The editor noted that hungry Indians always stole from whites, and frequent clashes occurred. The experiment of feeding the Indians at government expense, supposedly the plan of Commissioners McKee, Barbour, and Wozencraft, was so outrageously expensive that it would never be tried again. The public had only two options on the Indian question: either "the whole Indian race in California must be exterminated by the unsparing ravages of hunger and civilized agression, or they must be brought together, organized into a community, made to support themselves by their own labor; and be elevated above the degraded position they now occupy." Within five years, the *Alta* forecasted, the Indians of California would cease to be an expense of the federal government, and all the hostilities would be over. The editor lyrically declared that the Indians would be "transformed from a state of semi-barbarism, indolence, mental imbecility and moral debasement, to a condition of civilization, Christianity, industry, virtue, frugality, social and domestic happiness, and public usefulness."[5]

One possible problem loomed regarding the proposed reservation at Tejon—the site was supposedly covered by a Spanish land grant. Beale wrote Manypenny at the end of September and explained that the Tejon area contained no settlers. Congress, like himself, had believed that sufficient land existed in the public domain. Unfortunately, almost all arable land had been taken up by preemption claims of white settlers. Despite the Spanish grant, Beale told Manypenny that he would start the farm at Tejon and leave the problem of land title to Congress. If the title proved legitimate, the government could either buy the property or the Indians could be removed. Poor quality land was available elsewhere, but the experiment required the "best quality" of tillable soil. If the Indian farm failed to produce a good first crop, it might discourage the Indians so greatly as to make additional farming ventures useless.

Beale's plans were grandiose. In time, he hoped to remove all Indians from northern California and locate them on reservations in the southern part of the state. The Indians in the extreme north, such as Modocs, however, were different, and Beale speculated that those tribes—"bolder, more warlike, and less disposed to agricultural pursuits"—would require a different approach. Beale predicted that the total number of Indians involved in his experiment might reach 75,000 or even 100,000. If so, he would require an additional appropriation of $500,000 to provide for them.[6]

Beale visited the small reserve on the Fresno and was happy with the report which his brother-in-law Edwards furnished him. Beginning in March, Edwards had supervised the ploughing and sowing of 350 acres. Indian youths from twelve to twenty years old, none of whom had ever before used a plow, performed the work. Indians also dug a two-mile ditch which completely encircled the field. Four feet wide and four feet deep, the ditch served to prevent wild horses, cattle, or other animals from entering the fields. Edwards also constructed a corral in a similar fashion, surrounding the one-hundred-yard-wide-corral with a ditch that measured seven feet wide and six feet deep. According to observers, the ditch was the most extensive ever dug in California during a single day. The Indians seemed "delighted" at the work they had accomplished and at the prospects of a rich harvest of wheat, corn, pumpkins, and melons. Sadly, however, bugs invaded the wheat field and destroyed most of the crop.

Edwards stated that the Tejon region was an excellent location for a reservation. The Indians had engaged in farming there during the last season and produced abundant harvests, which permitted many feasts. They were ready to conduct more extensive farming operations during the coming season. Edwards had visited most of the tribes in the valleys and mountains south of Stockton, and all expressed a willingness to move to the Tejon, preferring it over other places.[7]

Well satisfied, Beale returned to San Francisco. He asked the members of the California congressional delegation for their opinion on the project. Senators Gwin and Milton S. Latham approved the idea of Beale making conditional arrangements subject to approval of Congress. Weller also gave his support but added that the congressional act still appropriated too much land for Indian use, hurting California's white citizens. J. A. McDougall also concurred with Beale's proposals. With the backing of leading California politicians, Beale felt safe to move ahead with the reservation. He forwarded all the opinions to Washington, confident that Commissioner Manypenny would support him.[8]

During the fall of 1853, Beale's Montgomery Street office bustled with activity. He assigned Gwin Harris Heap to investigate the accounts of the former commissioners—McKee, Barbour, and Wozencraft—and devoted his time and efforts to the reservations. In early October, Beale left San Francisco and went to Grass Valley to visit the tribal leaders of the region. He held a council with twenty headmen and tried to persuade them to move onto the reservation being created at the Tejon. The conference was held at Storms Ranch, some six miles outside the community. Storms spoke the Indian language with fluency and acted as Beale's interpreter. Weimah, chief of the Bear River Indians, agreed to take his people to the Tejon, but several of the other chiefs showed doubt. It would be hard for their people to believe the government's promises after the lies of the past. Beale understood and suggested they send a few young men to the Tejon to observe the reservation and spend some time there. Next year, based on their reports, the chiefs could determine if Beale had spoken the truth. The Indians consented to send fifty emissaries. In mid-October, the young men from the Grass Valley area, accompanied by N. Blackstone, a reporter for the *Alta California*, arrived in San Francisco and took a steamer to Los Angeles where B. D. Wilson met and escorted them to the Tejon.[9]

Expenditures for the new reservation soon soared to $125,000. Beale contracted for 1,000 head of cattle at $65,000, spent $10,000 on agricultural implements, $20,000 for mules and horses, and $10,000 on freighting costs. Then there were wages, plus incidental expenses—$20,000. The costs appeared extravagant, but Beale actually had established two reservations at Tejon, encompassing some 50,000 acres, rather than one of 25,000 acres. When B. D. Wilson admonished him about expenses, Beale reminded him that many Indians from the Four Creeks area would go to the Tejon, adding greatly to the Tejones own population. Beale had grown quite fond of Wilson and gave Wilson charge of the purchase of five hundred head of cattle. He additionally contracted with Andrew Sublette, an old friend, for 100,000 pounds of wheat, a sizeable quantity.[10]

The reservation was located in a long valley, forty miles in length by twelve miles in width. The entire area was "finely watered" by mountain springs and creeks, and a lake graced the northern end. Beale told his friends that the reservation could support 50,000 Indians. At the Tejon, the Indians were actively working on their winter quarters, and Beale said he intended to build a large adobe building, bigger than Mission San Fernando, to provide permanent homes for the Indians.[11]

On December 16, Beale held a great feast. Tribes from throughout the southern San Joaquin attended, some even came from beyond the Sierras. Beale presented the celebration to reward the Tejon Indians for their efforts and to convince other tribes to move onto the reservation. The feast lasted all night, and the Indians consumed prodigious quantities of beef, rice, and other foods. A dance then lasted far into the early morning hours. Beale talked at length to the assembled Indians and explained his plans. The emissaries from some of the distant tribes appeared pleased with the prospect of having farms of their own and volunteers assistance in the labor currently going on at the Tejon. Beale distributed presents, and the Indians returned to their homes to report on the new reservation.[12]

Shortly before the feast at the Tejon, Beale received a letter from Ignacio del Valle of Los Angeles, who claimed to be a part owner of the Spanish grant covering the reservation area. Del Valle had heard astonishing rumors that Beale had established a reservation for Indians on his land. If these rumors were indeed true, Beale must have been ignorant that he and Jose Antonio Aquirre jointly owned the land. Aguirre had received the grant from Manuel Micheltorena, Governor of California, on November 22, 1843, and on June 30, 1845, the Mexican government issued a patent. Neither man wanted to offer an "unreasonable or unjust obstacle" to the Indian policy of the United States government and stood ready to consider any fair proposition for the purchase of their rights.

Beale delayed answering the letter until December 28. On that date he wrote Del Valle that if the United States Land Commission, created to investigate all problems with Mexican titles, approved Del Valle's title, the government would vacate the property. In the meantime, his Indian reservations would do no harm to the land and would remain.[13]

By late December Beale could report to Commissioner Manypenny that his reservation plan submitted to Congress during the last session was now in "full and successful operation." He now proposed to locate three of the five reservations in the vicinity of the Tejon. One military post should provide ample protection for three reservations and would work a substantial savings. Beale hoped to establish another reservation near Fort Yuma, and the last one near Warner's Pass, possibly at Rancho Temecula.

Beale described the progress made at the Tejon. He now had thirty to forty plows in the fields each day. Behind every plow were Indian boys, handling the blades "with as much dexterity and skill, as though they had done nothing else during their whole lives." One square mile at the Tejon had been plowed and planted, and by March 1, an additional 2,500 acres would be planted in wheat. If the Indian farm produced 35 bushels per acre of wheat, Beale predicted a harvest worth $437,500, figuring 10 cents per pound. In the future, he planned to plant tobacco, sugar cane, rice, corn, and vegetables in the same proportion as the wheat.

Since his return to California, Beale had worked hard and hoped that his efforts would meet with approval from the Interior Department. He described himself as "weary of the anxiety, and continual care," which the work brought. "Jealousy, envy, and detraction," he wrote, "is the fate of anyone who attempts an innovation, on any old established custom, and I am not vain enough to suppose I may escape this inevitable fate."[14]

Then Beale received an angry letter from the commissioner. Manypenny reiterated that no part of $250,000 appropriation might be used for any purpose other than the removal and subsistence of the Indians. If Beale wished to locate a suitable reservation on land reported part of a Spanish grant, Manypenny said, it would be prudent to postpone all action for present on the implementation of the plan. Beale should wait for congressional approval before proceeding. Under no circumstances would the Interior Department sanction the purchase of any land or claims to land. Finally, Manypenny warned that Beale's actions must conform "in all respects to the requirements of the law." Beale ignored the letter.[15]

The reservation continued to expand. By February, the Indians had finished planting wheat and were sowing five hundred acres in barley and one hundred fifty acres in corn. They had clearly shown their willingness to labor long and hard. Only occasionally did Beale have to discipline a "lazy" Indian. The entire reservation system had been established with the assistance of only twelve white employees. Although a military force had not been sent to the Tejon, Beale said he felt perfectly safe in the midst of 2,500 Indians. Perhaps his proudest accomplishment was the irrigation ditch, six feet wide and eight feet deep, running for nine miles around the fields.

By spring, Beale hoped to develop a governing body for the reservation. He proposed that six chiefs, plus himself, sit as a council to decide upon the laws for the reservation. The council would determine the disposition of the surplus produce, which promised to be large. The council should meet on the first of every month and discuss matters which concerned or interested the Indian population. By degrees, Beale hoped "to raise these people to believe that God has not created them to live and die as the wolves and beasts of their mountains."[16]

In March of 1854, Beale learned that his wife had finally made up her mind to join him in California. She planned to meet him at Panama. Beale placed the reservation in the hands of his assistant, Samuel A. Bishop, informed the San Francisco office of his plans, and caught the steamer for Panama. Upon arriving at the isthmus, Beale found a letter which indicated that Mary would not be going to Panama; in fact, she was critically ill. Ignoring possible charges that he had deserted his post, Beale hurried to secure passage for New York.

Beale spent four days in Chester. He saw that Mary was recovering and booked tickets for their return to California. Beale avoided Washington because he had heard that Manypenny had questioned his 1853 accounts and might detain him. He also was unsure just how the commissioner would regard his return East without authorization.[17]

Indeed, Commissioner Manypenny had become quite irritated by Beale's independent conduct. He had examined accounts closely—and was shocked. The expenditures were enormous. The superintendent had paid far too much for most items listed. In January, he had sent Beale's accounts to Interior Secretary McClelland, saying they were far in arrears. Manypenny appended a long list of objections to the expenses. McClelland looked over the accounts and returned them to Manypenny, stating the costs were too high, but perhaps there was an explanation. He urged Manypenny to consult with the members of the California delegation. If the delegation supported Beale, he would be retained in office. Without their support, Manypenny could proceed as he desired.[18]

In early April, Manypenny wrote Beale that the Indian Office had not received a communication from him since late December. Without information he had not way to determine the "judiciousness or otherwise" of the Tejon reservation. He repeated his view on the undesirability and illegality of locating the reservation on private property. He also chided Beale for suggesting that a reservation be located at the junction of the Gila and Colorado River in "Utah"; surely, Beale knew the spot was in New Mexico. In conclusion, Manypenny asked Beale to make an estimate for the California superintendency's expenses for the next fiscal years.[19]

On April 13, 1854, Manypenny transmitted Beale's accounts, complete with itemized comments, to the California delegation. With the sole exception of Congressman Milton S. Latham, the delegation refused to support Beale. Senator Weller had already stated that too much money had been spent on Indians, and the reservations were too large.

His opposition was expected. But Gwin's disapproval came as a surprise. A year earlier, Gwin had visited the Tejon and reported favorably on Beale's work. Manypenny then consulted with Secretary McClelland and the California politicians about Beale's successor.

Thomas Hart Benton told Beale not to worry. Pierce's administration would not dare remove him from office; he had a grip on the public mind. Beale's successful railroad expedition and his successful colonization of Indians showed his indispensability. Benton urged him to write up full accounts of his labors with the Indians and have them published in the newspapers for added insurance. Benton admitted that the commissioner was a "low fellow," who hated a successful man like Beale. The old senator promised to take care of Manypenny: "I have him on the anvil and will hammer him." Unforunately, Benton was aging and out of touch with Washington politics.[20]

Soon after disembarking, Beale conferred with Major General John E. Wool, who had replaced E. A. Hitchcock as commander of the Pacific Department. Wool endorsed his decision to locate two of the five reservations at the Tejon. In a letter to Commissioner Manypenny the next day, Beale referred to the bureaucrat's April letter which he had just read. He mentioned Wool's approval of the two reservations at Tejon, which Beale had ordered surveyed, and touched the subject of his possible violations of the law in placing the reservation on private property. While he may have overstepped the letter of the law, he always acted within the "spirit of the law" and had never taken a step without consulting with the "most intelligent and prominent" governmental officers in the state.[21]

Beale tried all available means to gain political support for his program and keep himself in office. He had the Tejon reservation officially named the Sebastian Reservation, in honor of Senator William Sebastian, chairman of the Indian Affairs Committee. He later proposed a reservation in northern California to be called the "Wool" Reservation honoring the Pacific Department's commander.[22]

On May 15 Beale sent to Washington his estimated budget for the next fiscal year. It came to an astronomical sum of $617,350. The largest single item was ticketed for subsistence, Indian removal, and buying breeding stock for the reservations. Beale followed Benton's advice and began publishing articles on his experiment in the local newspapers. Successive issues of the Los Angeles *Weekly Star* (June 17 and 24) carried long articles which extolled Beale and the Tejon reserve. The newspaper's editor visited the reservation and described his findings. Several Indian rancherias, governed by chiefs and subchiefs, were situated on the Tejon. Juan Viejo, regarded as chief of the whole valley, expected to have five hundred of his people there shortly. Vicente, a native of the Tejon, lived with one hundred of his band, while Jose's rancheria contained another hundred Indians. At the Old Adobe, Beale's headquarters, Zapetero resided with three hundred Indians, while two hundred additional persons resided at two other rancherias.

Wallace, the editor of the Los Angeles *Star,* found the farm in excellent condition. The harvest was taking place, and Wallace said he had never seen a finer crop of wheat. He predicted thirty-five bushels of wheat per acre and roughly calculated a production of 8,000 barrels of flour. The irrigation system at Tejon drew praise, and Indian laborers had even cut a road up Tejon Canyon to obtain lumber. The editor seemed to sense Beale's removal and pleaded for a fair trial for the young superintendent. He acknowledged that Beale was ambitious, but his ambition ran "in a road which few have the capacity or taste to travel." Within a very short time, Beale had worked a remarkable change in the Indians. Writing a letter to Senator Sebastian, Wallace said that "too much praise cannot be awarded Lt. Beale, for his success and his devotion to his work."[23]

The date of his dismissal was May 31. In informing the editor of the Washington *Evening Star* that Beale had been removed from office by President Pierce, Manypenny gave the reasons for the action: (1) contradicting his official instructions, Beale had not taken the nearest and quickest route to California but went overland, exploring a central railroad route for a private party; (2) Beale's accounts were late, thoroughly confused, and showed "great extravagance"; (3) Beale never advised the Indian Department about his trip to Chester either before or after the fact; (4) Beale had been directed to deposit with the subtreasurer at San Francisco the $250,000 appropriation and make withdrawals of only $20,000 at a time; within three days of deposit, Beale withdrew half the amount; and (5) Beale communicated only infrequently with the Indian Department. The government learned more from Beale's letters to Benton, published in the *National Intelligencer,* than from his official correspondence. In assessing Beale's work in California, the Indian Bureau believed it would "prove to be worse than failure."

A full investigation would be made into Beale's affairs, including the "now celebrated beef contract" of Fremont, which Beale was believed "mightily mixed up" in. The *Star* added that Beale was recently seen in Philadelphia and Washington, while absent without leave from California. Beale's successor was Thomas J. Henley, postmaster of San Francisco and a loyal Democrat.[24]

In late June Beale received official word of his dismissal. On June 20, he wrote to Henley, his designated successor, describing the harvest at the Sebastian Reservation. The season had been especially cold during the winter and dry in the late spring and summer, and only 42,000 bushels of wheat and 10,000 bushels of barley had been produced. With ordinary conditions the harvest could have been twice that amount. Beale told Henley that he did not think the surplus food should be distributed to starving Indians outside the reservation. Instead, it should be used as a magnet to draw those Indians into the reservation system. He hoped that Commissioner Manypenny might come to California and see the experiment's success.

Beale offered Henley suggestions for the future. The sick Indians needed a hospital. Houses should be constructed along with a granary, store houses, and sheds. Schools should also be established. Beale recommended mandatory attendance for young Indians, not trusting to the whims of Indian parents. All Indians must be required to labor, unless sick or infirm. Whether Henley would take Beale's advice would soon be seen.[25]

In early July of 1854 San Francisco newspapers printed stories about Beale's removal. The *Alta* copied the charges from eastern papers, stating that the superintendent could not account for $250,000, but added that he undoubtedly could explain his conduct. John Nugent of the *Herald* expressed his bitterness stating that the action of Pierce's administration would render it "odious and unpopular." Beale had authorized him to state that the charges of defalcation were no more than a "wretched fabrication." Beale could account for the expenditure of every dollar with government vouchers. Nugent reminded readers of Beale's past services to the nation and stated that to dismiss Beale for paying a "flying visit" to his home at Chester was simply a convenient pretext.

On July 10, 1854, the coast steamer the *Southerner* docked at San Francisco. Among the passengers up from Los Angeles were Beale, Mary, and their servant. On July 15, Henley resigned from his postmaster position, and on July 26, he relieved Beale of the superintendent's duties. Beale kept a cordial attitude toward Henley, perhaps hoping that the new superintendent might support him when Beale's accounts underwent examination.[26]

In San Francisco Beale met J. Ross Browne, the government's special investigator. Beale knew that Browne eventually would review his accounts—if he had not already been asigned the task. Before leaving Washington, Browne had discussed Beale's accounts with Secretary McClelland but had received no precise instructions. Meanwhile, Beale and his wife used their social talents to charm the "confidential" agent. Browne later wrote his wife that he had "fallen in love with Mrs. Beale."

He described Mary as the most amiable and accomplished lady he had met in California. With Browne's friendship seemingly secure, Beale urged that both Henley and Browne thoroughly investigate his accounts.[27]

Beale made a great show of attempting to assist Henley in his new position. In late July, he accompanied Henley on a trip to southern California, hoping to quiet Indians who had grown restless upon hearing of Beale's dismissal. At the Sebastian a large number of Indians had fled into the mountains, supposedly due to Beale's removal. When Beale and Henley reached the Tejon, they spent some time accounting for government property in Beale's possession. Livestock presented a difficult problem because Beale and associates owned part of the livestock on the reservation. Eventually, Beale and Henley reached an understanding, and Henley gave Beale an itemized receipt for all property, including the estimated harvests from several crops. Henley supported Beale's plan for the self-sufficient reservations and endorsed the Tejon experiment. He announced publicly that he would continue Beale's program.[28]

By late August, Henley began to suspect that some of Beale's great achievements at the Tejon reservation were exaggerations—if not outright lies. One of the employees related the history of the Tejon Indians prior to Beale's arrival. Some three hundred Indians had always resided in the vicinity of the valley. They had hunted and roamed frequently, but they also grew corn and wheat the "same as at present." The Indians prized peace and had never committed depredations on the whites. Only when the commissioners' treaties were rejected did they talk of violence, and only then after rumors that the whites intended to kill them. Actually, no more than eight hundred Indians resided at the Tejon during the time Beale estimated the reservation's population at 2,500. Henley forwarded the statements to Manypenny and asserted they could be "relied upon as strictly true."[29]

Both Beale and Browne urged an investigation of Beale's conduct as superintendent, and authorization soon came. Manypenny directed Henley and Browne to investigate Beale's accounts, particularly the prices paid for cattle, transportation, and other items. Beale had grossly overcharged the government, and Manypenny hoped that Browne's investigation would prove it.

Browne asked Beale to provide written testimony covering questionable items in his accounts. The cattle contracts proved most embarrassing. Beale had paid twice the going rate for cattle, but he explained to Browne that the high prices had been caused by the lateness of the season, plus ranchers added an extra fee for driving the cattle to the Tejon. Following this testing, Browne left San Francisco to interview residents in the Los Angeles area, particularly B. D. Wilson.[30]

Beale hurriedly wrote Wilson and told him to expect a visit from Browne. He enclosed a copy of the statements he had made concerning the cattle contract Wilson had negotiated. Beale coached Wilson's replies to Browne. He should stress his own personal experience in buying cattle, the recent reduction in cattle prices, the need to drive cattle quickly to the Tejon, and that more hands than usual had been employed. Wilson should invite Browne into his home and treat him kindly, and Beale said that he wished he could spend just ten minutes in person with Wilson to impress upon him the importance of convincing Browne.[31]

By October 15 Henley and Browne submitted a report that partially exonerated Beale from wrong-doing. They both agreed the plan for the self-sufficient reservation was a good one, but the problem of high prices for livestock and supplies still remained. Circumstances determined to a large extent the price of a commodity. It would be up to the Interior Department in Washington, stated Browne and Henley, to decide whether or not Beale had acted wisely in his purchases. They planned to continue to examine the prices and the conditions which existed at the time the contracts were made.

Three days later, Beale and his wife sailed for the East. The San Francisco *Herald* commented on the ex-superintendent's accounts and said that Beale carried proof of his fidelity to Washington and would extract from the government the admission that he had been removed without cause. When he finished in Washington, he would return to California "now forever hereafter his home."

Browne addressed a letter to his wife in time for the *Golden Gate's* departure. He stated that Beale had not acted in bad faith toward the government, but his negligence was "quite sufficient to justify the administration in his removal."[32]

The Beales reached New York on November 9 and proceeded to Chester. Six days later, they went to Washington and were lodged at Brown's Hotel. Beale prepared for a quick closing of his accounts. But Commissioner Manypenny did not plan for Beale's accounts to pass without protest. He raised objections to almost every item Beale purchased during his tenure as superintendent. He also requested that Beale respond in writing and explain the circumstances relating to every government voucher. The statements must be sworn before a magistrate. Beale resented the "orders" to make an affidavit but would comply.[33]

Throughout November and December, Manypenny sent Beale countless lists of "objections to vouchers." Beale held his temper and responded, explaining the circumstances surrounding the purchase. Fred Kerlin, his clerk, helped with these statements. Manypenny then discovered a flaw in Beale's system for the issuance of cattle to the Indians and demanded a precise record of the number of cattle slaughtered each day on the Tejon reservation and at the Fresno farm. Beale responded that the records did not exist for the Fresno farm. At the Tejon, Beale had personally directed the issuance of beeves; the number butchered depended upon the number of Indians present. The records were available only on a monthly basis.[34]

Beale realized that he would have to spend a long time in Washington before his accounts cleared. He moved from Brown's Hotel to a house on C Street and invited Bayard Taylor to come and visit. Beale described his business in Washington as "the most harassing character," amounting to little more than "Bull baiting." He had been removed for reasons of politics, but now Manypenny and others sought "to justify the act by a system of persecution the most contemptible and vexatious." Beale vowed to bide his time: "With sense of unforgotten wrong; And the hate that waits and watches long." Beale declared "a word or two" would pass between some of them and himself before he left Washington "which they will never inscribe on their family plate."[35]

At the end of December the examination of Beale's accounts entered a new phase. Manypenny forwarded the accounts to the second auditor, with objections to a large portion of the money due. If his objections were upheld by the Treasury Department, it would mean the end of Beale's career as a public servant. J. Ross Browne arrived in Washington early in January of 1855, and Beale hoped Browne's statements would support his case.[36]

Browne submitted a 131-page report on Beale's accounts. He concluded that Beale had not committed any criminal acts while holding the office of superintendent of Indian affairs, but he had been careless about his responsibilities and fully deserved removal. The lengthy report described the men who surrounded Beale as using their offices and connections to secure advantages for themselves and their friends. A general feeling existed in California that to charge the government an exorbitant rate was simply good business. Frequently, Beale, or his subordinates, paid prices which far exceeded the going rates, but Brown attributed these occurrences to Beale's ignorance of prices, rather than an attempt to defraud the government.

When Beale learned of the report, he became furious and concluded that both Browne and Henley had deceived him with false friendship. Beale wrote Wilson that "meanness, spite and malice" stood allied in opposition against him. He felt nothing but contempt for both Browne and Henley. The two men had changed their attitude toward him since the preliminary report of October 15, and appearances suggested that Browne's final report conformed to what Manypenny had desired.[37]

The long fight over his accounts began to show. Inwardly, Beale boiled, and his agitation threatened to end in violence. In early February, William H. Russell of Missouri visited President Pierce and pleaded Beale's case. He was accompanied by Beale's old naval friend, Lieutenant John Guest. Russell told of Beale's honesty and dedicated service. Pierce replied that he still held the "highest regard" for Beale. If the ex-superintendent would just remain calm, he would receive a favorable adjustment.

Beale sought to support his accounts with whatever documents he could secure. He asked John C. Fremont to write a description of their 1851 cattle drive. On April 3, Fremont sent a short letter and told how they had lost five hundred head of cattle on the drive. Fremont's simple statement helped bolster Beale's contention that several hundred of cattle in Alex Godey's possession were strays, and not stolen government property. On drives from Los Angeles to San Francisco, a number of cattle were always lost. Manypenny had no reason to object to purchase of cattle from Godey on the grounds that they might have been stolen.[38]

President Pierce proved a man of his word. In early April, the Treasury Department approved Beale's vouchers, and at last, he could breathe freely. J. M. Brodhead, second comptroller, on April 9 wrote to James Guthrie, secretary of the treasury, that Beale had fully cooperated with the government in the examination of his accounts. Beale had always responded to queries with "commendable promptness and candor," delivering "ready and unembarrassed replies." Brodhead stated that he had known Beale from their boyhood days in Washington, and the examination of accounts confirmed his belief in Beale's honesty and uprightness. The Washington *Evening Star*, the first newspaper to call attention to Beale's case, printed an article which announced "a complete triumph for Mr. B."; all of his disbursements had been allowed.[39]

With his accounts cleared, Beale decided to confront Manypenny, the cause of his recent misfortunes. He asked two friends to visit E. Wallach, editor of the *Evening Star*, to learn the source of Wallach's information for the anonymous charges which the newspaper had printed the previous July. Richard H. Weightman was one of the men who called at the newspaper office. He was particularly qualified for the errand. Weightman was widely known as the man who had killed Francis X. Aubry with a bowie knife in a saloon brawl in New Mexico. Only a foolish man would lie to Weightman about such an important matter. In a friendly manner, Weightman made the inquiries of Wallach, who showed a willingness to supply the requested information. He admitted that all the information printed in the *Evening Star* had been personally supplied by Indian Commissioner Manypenny. Beale had suspected the commissioner and prepared to obtain satisfaction.[40]

The commissioner generally ate lunch at Willard's Hotel, and Beale went there to await his arrival. When Manypenny walked through the hotel door, Beale quickly confronted him. In a loud voice so onlookers could hear, he charged that the bureaucrat "had been stabbing him in the back all winter," then stepped up to the surprised man, and slapped him hard across the face with his open hand. When Manypenny ignored the challenge to his personal honor, Beale slapped him again. Manypenny then grabbed Beale by his fancy cravat and, to the amazement of Willard's clientele, the two men commenced to wrestle on the floor. When friends separated them the commissioner turned and attempted to smash Beale with a hotel chair.

Once again, in a loud, firm voice, Beale said he stood prepared to give Manypenny a gentleman's satisfaction. The commissioner failed to answer the challenge, but Beale said his friends would inform Manypenny where he could be found. Beale quickly went to the train depot and departed for Chester, in order to avoid possible prosecution under the District of Columbia's antidueling laws, which included issuing challenges. Manypenny, who knew that Beale was an expert with almost any weapon, refused to duel.[41]

Beale sent President Pierce the letters written by the men who had interviewed Wallach. The letters showed Manypenny's conduct in an unfavorable light; he had passed judgment on Beale activities before his accounts reached Washington. He urged the president take action against Manypenny and punish him. Beale also filed legal proceedings against the commissioner.[42]

The altercation between Beale and Manypenny was reported in many newspapers. In Washington, the long-running dispute between Benton and Manypenny was renewed in the public press, as Benton attacked Manypenny's attempt to villify Beale. Charges also flew back and forth between Manypenny and Wallach, editor of the *Star*. Benton, noted for his ability to continue a debate *ad nauseam*, addressed the Senate on Beale's virtues. He attacked the government for dismissing men like Beale, Carson, and Fremont, who could do so much to rectify the relations with the Indians, which now seemed heading toward war.[43]

In mid-May of 1855 San Francisco learned that Beale's accounts had been settled. The *Alta* gave the news a brief note, but the *Herald* gloated with triumph. "Beale, as we always predicted, has gained a most signal triumph over his traducers," stated Nugent. The settlement of his accounts should satisfy everyone who did not personally know Beale. His

friends "never for a moment believed him to be capable of an act unworthy of an honorable man, or of the reputation he had earned by long,
faithful, and successful service to his country."[44]

Beale wasted little time in the East and returned to California with
his wife, daughter Mary, and two servants on May 30. He faced an uncertain future in California, but he possessed enough capital to enter
into business. Ranching especially appealed to him. He had been in government service without interruption since he first joined the navy at
age fourteen, and the possibility always existed that another government
position might come his way in the future. In the summer of 1855, Beale
felt certain of one thing: his future lay in California, not in the East.[45]

In his years as superintendent of Indian affairs for California, Ned
Beale had played a key role in the formulation of a new Indian policy,
based on the Spanish mission system. His self-sufficient reservation system captured the imagination of prominent men in Fillmore's administration. Although Beale never used the word, he had suggested and placed
into operation at the Tejon a program leading to "acculturation." He
saw the reservation as easing the transition from a traditional native society into an American melting pot. But Beale made many mistakes.
Foremost, he neglected to oversee closely the distribution of the large
appropriations entrusted to his care. With a greater attention to detail,
the Tejon experiment might have been far more successful for less money.
After Beale was removed from office, Henley allowed the experiment to
die. The Tejon reservation was one of the first such experimental reservations in the Far West, but it would not be the last. In time, the government would adopt the Beale concept of the reservation, a vehicle for
the transformation of Indian culture and life-style. But in the summer of
1855, Beale's thoughts had turned away from Indian affairs.

Edward F. Beale as surveyor
general of California, 1862.
(*Courtesy California Historical
Society.*)

Beale in 1876 upon being appointed minister to Austria-Hungary. (*Courtesy California
State Library.*)

Thomas Hart Benton greatly
helped Beale's early career.
(*From* Thomas H. Benton *by*
Theodore Roosevelt.)

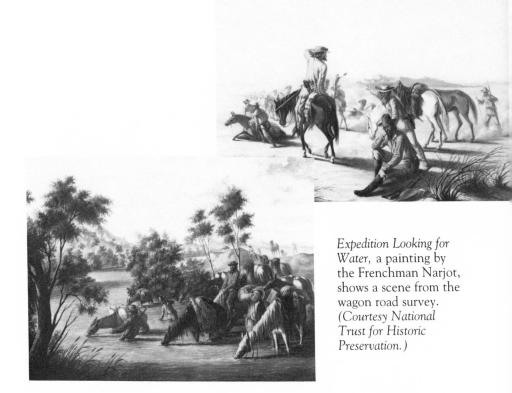

*Expedition Looking for
Water,* a painting by
the Frenchman Narjot,
shows a scene from the
wagon road survey.
(*Courtesy National
Trust for Historic
Preservation.*)

This painting by Narjot emphasizes the thirst experienced by men and horses, while the camels look on with disdain. Beale commissioned both of these oil paintings to document the camel experiment. (*Courtesy National Trust for Historic Preservation.*)

Star Oil Works at Pico Springs in
the 1870s. Beale was among its
several owners, and he had
recognized the potential for oil
revenue on his own holdings at El
Tejon Ranch since the late 1860s.
(Courtesy Society of California
Pioneers.)

Benjamin D. Wilson contributed to
the organization of the California
Indian superintendency. (Courtesy
California Historical Society.)

Commodore Thomas Truxtun, grandfather of Edward F. Beale. *(Courtesy Long Island Historical Society.)*

Battle of San Pasqual. *(Courtesy Library of Congress.)*

Beale's award case contains the presentation sword and epaulets that he was given for his heroism at the Battle of San Pasqual. Also included are a pair of matched dueling pistols and a Bowie knife with grizzly bear handle. *(Courtesy National Trust for Historic Preservation.)*

Mary Edwards Beale, wife of Edward F. Beale. (*Courtesy National Trust for Historic Preservation.*)

Truxtun Beale, son of Edward and Mary, in 1890. (*Courtesy National Trust for Historic Preservation.*)

Mary Beale Bahkmeteff, their eldest daughter, about 1880. (*Courtesy National Trust for Historic Preservation.*)

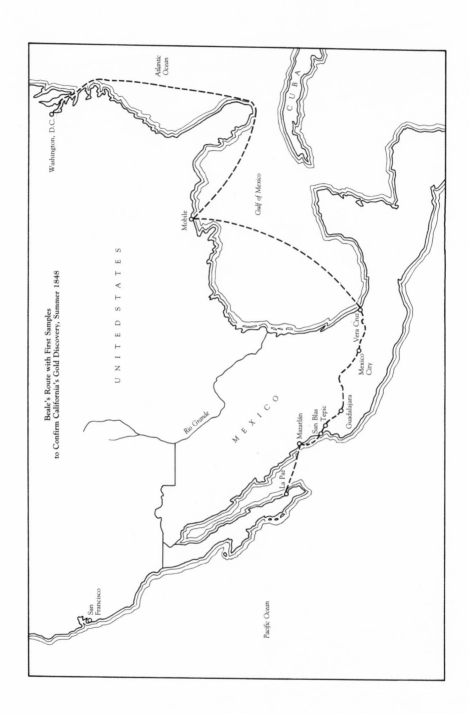

Beale's Route with First Samples
to Confirm California's Gold Discovery, Summer 1848

Atlantic
Ocean

CUBA

Washington, D.C.

Gulf of Mexico

Mobile

UNITED STATES

Vera Cruz

Rio Grande

Mexico
City

MEXICO

Guadalajara

Mazatlán

Tepic

San Blas

La Paz

San
Francisco

Pacific Ocean

Chapter 6
"LAW & ORDER" VERSUS THE VIGILANTES

The only party you can rely upon here [San Francisco] for support hereafter is the "law and order party" those who have stood by you during these perilous times at any personal risk or hazard, these are the only men entitled to consideration and in this view of the case there is no doubt but what Beale's appointment as Sheriff of this County would do more for the success of law and order than any act which could be done.

—William C. Kibbee to
Governor J. Neely Johnson
August 8, 1856

I, Edward F. Beale, do solemnly swear that I will support the Constitution of the United States of America and the Constitution of the State of California, and that I will faithfully discharge the duties of the sheriff of the City and County of San Francisco to the best of my ability.

—Sworn before Judge D. O. Shattuck,
August 13, 1856

Ever since his first visit to California during the Mexican War, Beale had been attracted to the life of the rancheros. The opportunity now presented itself for him to buy a large Mexican land grant in southern California, ideal for stockraising. On August 8, 1855, he purchased Rancho La Liebre (The Hare) from William C. Walker. The Mexican grant contained eleven square leagues of land, some 49,000 acres, and was located ten miles southwest of the Tejon reservation. Beale paid Walker

$1,500 for the land. Only five days earlier, Walker had purchased La Liebre from José María Flores, and it appeared that Walker had acted as a front man for Beale in the purchase. Beale knew that Flores had failed to get the title confirmed by the U.S. Board of Land Commissioners in 1854, which accounted for the low price. Beale either believed he stood a good chance to have the Board's decision reversed by the federal district court or desired to secure the property's use for the several years which the lengthy appeal process would require. In any event, La Liebre would provide pasturage for the livestock jointly owned by Beale and his partner, Samuel A. Bishop.[1]

In mid-1855, Beale found his financial status shaky. His wife was pregnant again, and he had no constant income. John C. Fremont, who enjoyed a national reputation, owed Beale a sizeable sum of money from the 1851 cattle contract and the debt was long overdue. On October 1, Beale filed a suit against Fremont in the Twelfth District Court in San Francisco. As a legal basis for the action, he submitted a statement signed by Fremont on September 18, 1851, which specified that Beale should receive 25 percent of Fremont's proceeds from the cattle contracts, amounting to $183,825 (after a reduction of $57,130 and a 5 percent discount). Beale's share would be $29,376. Beale alleged that James King of William and Company, a defunct banking firm, had paid Fremont the money when he presented a government check on August 1, 1854. Since the government had paid Fremont, he must pay Beale. Beale's timing was impeccable. Fremont contemplated the nation's highest office as the Republican standard bearer, but he was vulnerable. In March of 1852, Fremont had publicly denied Beale's involvement in cattle contracts at the time of Beale's nomination for Indian superintendent. Both men had lied about the relationship and would suffer a severe loss of public confidence if the Beale-Fremont agreement turned into an open court battle. But Beale needed money. The threat of a lawsuit was enough, and an out-of-court settlement was reached.[2]

While a resident of San Francisco, Beale sought to play an active role in local politics. In the late summer of 1855, he considered running for sheriff of San Francisco County, one of the most lucrative offices on the West Coast, but he decided it was too late to enter the contest. One of Beale's supporters, however, failed to get the word about his withdrawal and placed his name in nomination at the party caucus. Beale was embarrassed when his supporter cast the only vote for him.[3]

San Francisco politics was unusually rough. The Democrats held an unsavory reputation for employing a small army of "shoulder-strikers," or toughs, to manipulate the election balloting. The extent of illegal voting practices, however, was never learned. Other parties may have been equally guilty. On August 21, 1855, when the city elections were held, an acquaintance of Beale's named James P. Casey became embroiled in a fight at a polling place on Kearny and Pine streets. A former county supervisor, Casey published a minor newspaper and was a favorite of the growing population of Irish Democrats, who crowded the city in search of work. Casey and the political machine of David C. Broderick had provided jobs by letting large municipal contracts for improvements such as street construction and paving.[4]

At his ward's polling place, Casey was attacked by several armed men. Instead of fleeing, the feisty Irishman grabbed one of his assailants, and while shots were being fired wildly at him, Casey wrestled a knife away from one attacker and began to defend himself. Although grazed by several shots, Casey managed to give his enemy, Bob Cushing, a severe knife wound; then he picked up a dropped pistol and commenced firing, wounding another attacker, J. W. Bagley. The "riot," as the newspaper termed the incident, ended when a policeman escorted Casey to jail. Most Democrats were outraged when they heard about the assault and Casey's subsequent arrest.[5]

On the evening of the brawl, Beale, Bailie Peyton, and Joseph P. Hoge visited Casey in his jail cell. Casey, his clothing in shreds, accepted the congratulations of the three men for his display of bravery. Peyton and Hoge both volunteered to act as his counsel. Several days later, the court discharged Casey and stated that no grounds existed for charges against him. Actually, Casey had been attacked by Democratic thugs: he had fallen out with the Broderick machine and aligned with the Know-Nothing Party; however, he soon reconciled his difference with Broderick. Beale also may have flirted with the Know-Nothing Party at this time, for the most enthusiastic support for his Indian policies had come from a Know-Nothing paper, the Los Angeles *Southern Californian.*[6]

Violence flared repeatedly in San Francisco during these months. On November 17, Beale's friend, William H. Richardson, U.S. marshal and quartermaster general of the California State Militia, was killed by Charles Cora, a gambler. James King of William, former banker and now editor of the San Francisco *Bulletin,* used the murder of Richardson to dramatize the city's need for law and order. The outspoken editor feared that Cora would somehow manage to escape justice; it had happened often enough before. Richardson was a well-known, popular man. Several of the most important men in San Francisco served as his pallbearers, including Beale and John Nugent. Reverend William A. Scott presided over the funeral services, and Beale accompanied his friend's body to the Lone Mountain Cemetery, perched on a hillside south of the city. Beale was appointed to the grand jury which met on December 14 to consider a number of cases, including the one concerning Charles Cora. The jury wasted little time in indicting Cora for the murder of Richardson.[7]

In January of 1856, Cora was brought to trial and pleaded "innocent" by virtue of self-defense. Throughout the city, Richardson was known as a man with a violent temper, and the gambler's defense seemed plausible to many San Franciscans. On January 12, Beale interrupted his grand jury duties and testified at Cora's trial. As a prosecution witness, he described Richardson as a close friend, who was exceedingly generous, liberal, and "very amiable and peaceable." Beale said that Richardson never carried a gun, nor was he ever excited by liquor. His testimony carried little weight with several jurors, as that group split and could not reach a verdict. Apparently several members of the jury believed Cora's defense and felt that he had shot Richardson in a lover's quarrel involving Belle Cora, the gambler's attractive companion. In the columns of the San Francisco *Bulletin*, King berated the hung jury and pointed to it as yet another example that the city needed a thorough sweep of criminals, who not only roamed the streets, but infested local government and justice.[8]

Meanwhile, the grand jury, which had been meeting for weeks in a cramped, filthy room, concluded its deliberations. The laws recommended in its final report showed the remarkable changes which had taken place in the city in a few short years. One of the main recommendations called for strict enforcement of the antidueling laws. Another prohibited the carrying of concealed weapons. Even peace officers should carry their weapons in plain sight. The jury urged that gambling establishments and "houses of ill 'fame' " receive the full attention of the public authorities. Drinking houses also constituted a "prominent evil" in the community and only individuals of good character should be granted licenses for such establishments. Other items in the report dealt with improvements in the public schools, the county hospital, and the alms house. Public nuisances, such as pestilential slaughter houses, fast driving, and discharging firearms within the city limits, also were called to the attention of the authorities.[9]

A major point in the report seemed directly related to the *Bulletin's* charges. The grand jury recommended a sweeping change in the jury system. A large majority vote (two-thirds or three-quarters) should constitute conviction, rather than the unanimous verdict which had produced so many hung juries. This proviso seemed tailored to fit Cora's case, which would be tried again in the future. But in spite of all the suggestions, the grand jury's report had not made the basic reforms in government that James King of William and the San Francisco business community desired. Tension within the city continued to mount.

With his services as a grand juror ended, Beale momentarily forgot about city affairs. He worried about Mary who was pregnant and in less-than-robust health. On March 6, 1856, she gave birth to a boy. The overjoyed parents named the child Truxtun in honor of Beale's famous grandfather. Beale's short period of domestic happiness, however, was soon shattered by explosive events in the city.[10]

James King of William was not the only journalist engaged in the exposure of evil. James Casey's *Sunday Times* published a series of articles on "Banks and Bankers," which touched a sensitive nerve in James King of William's background, particularly his earlier activities as a banker. A friend of Casey, John C. Cremony, published an anonymous card in the *Sunday Times* which asked why the San Francisco Customs House had not merited the *Bulletin's* criticism. Was it because Thomas Sim King, the editor's brother, held a lucrative position there? Shortly thereafter, the *Bulletin* attacked Casey and described how he had served time in Sing Sing prison. Casey responded with a personal challenge to the *Bulletin's* editor, and King declared he was armed and always ready. On May 14, Casey accosted King on the street, gave a warning, then drew and fired his pistol. King staggered into a nearby building, suffering from a grave wound. Casey quickly surrendered to the sheriff. Almost immediately, a Committee of Vigilance was organized, led by William T. Coleman, a local businessman who had headed a similar group in 1851. If King died, the residents of San Francisco knew that the committee would attempt to take Casey from jail and execute him.[11]

Sheriff David Scannell summoned prominent citizens to maintain law and order in the city. His request brought forth a large number of citizens, from various backgrounds, who enlisted in opposition to the committee. Heading the list of the law and order forces were the names of William T. Sherman, the banker; Hall McAllister, judge; Eugene Casserly (later U.S. Senator); Fred Kerlin; and Beale. Somewhat friendly toward Casey, Beale may have felt the shooting was justified. Sherman personally disliked Casey for his attack on San Francisco bankers but believed he must be defended against a lynch mob. Upon examining the jail, Sherman doubted that Casey was secure there. John Nugent, editor of the *Herald*, refused to support the committee, despite his involvement with the 1851 organization. The city was divided over the need for the Committee of Vigilance, and some men, like Beale, suspected that its aims did not correspond to its stated goals.[12]

On the morning of May 18, the officers of the committee, backed by an impressive display of force, removed Casey and Cora from the county jail and took the men to their headquarters on Sacramento Street, dubbed Fort Gunny Bags. Two days later James King of William succumbed to his wounds. On May 22, while an enormous funeral procession snaked through the streets, the committee executed both Casey and Cora. Sherman, Beale, and other supporters of law and order suddenly found themselves in an increasingly uneasy position, as both the federal and state government refused to act to restore constitutional government to the city.[13]

San Francisco's coroner bravely summoned a jury to examine the deaths of Casey and Cora. Beale, Redick McKee, and five other men made up the coroner's jury. The inquest was short in duration, but the jury spent a long time in consultation over the verdict, perhaps worried about the implications of their decision, now that the Vigilance Committee controlled the city. Nevertheless, the jury returned and stated that Casey and Cora "came to their deaths by hanging, which hanging was committed by a body of men styling themselves a Vigilance Committee of San Francisco."[14]

As he watched the unfolding drama in San Francisco, Beale's attention suddenly turned to Indian affairs. The Indians of the southern San Joaquin Valley were committing depredations—particularly stealing livestock. Settlers in the area had organized into an armed group, attacked a local Indian rancheria, and killed five innocent Indians. With the tribe vowing revenge, the entire southern San Joaquin Valley threatened to erupt into a tragic war. General Wool learned that the settlers planned to exterminate the Indians and immediately contacted Governor J. Neely Johnson. Wool urged that Beale be appointed a brigadier general in the state militia and charged with preventing the whites from getting out of control. Certainly, Beale was known and trusted by the Indians of the region. Finally, at the repeated insistence of Wool, Beale accepted the militia commission and prepared to go to the scene of the incident.[15]

On May 26, Governor Johnson ordered General Beale to proceed with "celerity" to the San Joaquin Valley and restore peace. Johnson told him that regular troops already had clashed with the hostiles and killed eight Indians, who had fought bravely inside earthen breastworks they had constructed. On two previous occasions the Indians had defeated volunteer forces. Johnson said that the state government was short of money, but the current budget would allow five hundred dollars for negotiations. He urged Beale to incur whatever expenses were necessary to quiet the Indians, however, and the legislature would fund the money at its next session.[16]

Beale left San Francisco on May 26, and reached King's River on June 5. There he conferred with the Indian subagent, a Mr. Campbell, and learned that the whites at the towns of Woodville and Visalia had greatly scared the Indians, whereupon the natives had fled into the mountains. The next day, Beale sent Campbell with five steers to seek out the Indians and inform them that he desired to hold a council. Beale himself went to Elbow Creek, where he found Lieutenant LaRhett L. Livingston, Third Artillery, encamped with thirty men. Ten miles south of Elbow Creek, he met Benjamin Allston, First Dragoons, with ten men. The two officers confirmed the story that the whites at Visalia and Woodville planned a campaign of extermination against the Indians.[17]

Beale returned to Visalia and Woodville and met with several prominent residents and called for a combined town meeting. At first, the citizens refused to listen to Beale's plea for conciliation with the Indians; they demanded stern punishment for the depredation. Beale carefully explained that he was empowered by the state government to negotiate with the Indians to settle the disputes, and he asked leading residents to accompany him to the Indian council. They agreed to do so. The next morning, Beale asked Allston and Livingston, plus their men, to accompany him as an escort.[18]

On June 8, Beale opened a council with some sixty to seventy Indians, representing twelve tribes. His object was peace, Beale told the Indians, but if they did not heed his words, he was prepared to chastise them severely. It would be foolish for the Indians to war with the whites; they would all be destroyed. After two hours, the conference adjourned. When it resumed, Beale informed the Indians that they must return to the reservation on King's River. Those who lived south of that stream must go to the Tocole Valley. The Indians consented, persuaded as much by Beale's presents as by his words.

Three days later, on June 11, Beale rode to the Couilla Valley near Woodville and met with some three hundred Indians. Coming from several different tribes, the Indians declared their willingness to do anything to preserve peace. Beale then distributed gifts. The total handed out previously and here included: 2,500 pounds of beef, 3,300 pounds of flour, 1,000 pounds of wheat, 43 shirts, 24 jumpers, 147 yards of sheeting, 10 needles, 119 spools of thread, 224 yards of calico, 6 bolts of calico, 206 yards of thread, 10 pounds of tobacco, and one coffee pot. Beale next drew up an estimate of the destruction the Indians had caused: seven dwellings @ $500 each; one sawmill and 100,000 feet of lumber @ $15,000; seven horses @ $100 each; and 75 to 100 head of cattle @ $50 each. Beale may have expected that the citizens would be reimbursed later by either the state or federal government.[19]

Having completed the Indian assignment, Beale turned back to the chaos in San Francisco. With the Vigilantes in firm control of the city, he decided to offer himself as candidate for the important office of sheriff of San Francisco County. He had the backing of most of the Law and Order Party, as well as Governor Johnson. Beale resigned his commission as brigadier general, but he liked the sound of the title, and for the remainder of his life he went by "General" Beale, causing widespread confusion among reporters and others who knew that he had spent sixteen years in the navy.[20]

Sheriff David Scannell was unpopular with the Vigilance Committee, and the leaders of that organization sought a way to remove him from office without resorting to violence. Under a recent act for reorganizing San Francisco's government, the sheriff, the coroner, and the assessor were required to post bonds before a board of bond commissioners. Under Vigilante influence, the commissioners had found Scannell's bond unacceptable and declared the office vacant. Scannell ignored the decision and continued to claim the sheriff's office, although the real function of the office lay with the Vigilance Committee during this period. But the committee could not remain in the open defiance of the United States government for long, so plans were made to convert the vigilante organization into a political machine.[21]

On July 13, the Vigilance Committee issued an open letter concerning the sheriff's office. Printed in the Alta California, the letter stated that the fees received by the sheriff of San Francisco County were probably the highest in the entire United States. As a result, his influence and patronage were great. The executive committee of the Vigilantes asserted that Sheriff Scannell was a man of the "lowest character" and totally unfit for the office. He was charged with: (1) inattention to duty; (2) packing juries during important cases; (3) submitting bills to the Board of Supervisors listing exorbitant fees, frequently double the standard rates, and in some cases, even illegal fees. On the night of July 14, a large gathering of citizens sympathetic to the Vigilantes assembled in front of the Montgomery Block and urged the resignation of county officials. But Scannell and other officers refused to resign.[22]

The County Board of Supervisors met on July 17, declared the offices of sheriff, coroner, and assessor vacant, and then balloted to fill the positions. The board quickly elected a coroner and assessor, but the contest for the sheriff's post was heated. Beale led the list of candidates. Several inconclusive ballots were taken when Judge Thomas W. Freelon entered the room and protested the proceedings. Freelon said the selection of the sheriff was vested in the Court of Sessions, over which he presided, and he would not recognize any man chosen by the board. On the following day, Judge Freelon appointed Charles L. Strong to the position of sheriff. The San Francisco Herald of July 19 pointed out that

Freelon's Court of Sessions could no longer fill vacancies because the state legislature on March 20, 1855 had vested the power in the county boards. But the legislative act excluded San Francisco County from the new law.[23]

On several occasions during late July and early August of 1856, the board of supervisors attempted unsuccessfully to elect a sheriff. Finally, on August 7, Beale obtained the necessary votes and was declared the duly elected sheriff. William C. Kibbe, quartermaster and adjutant general of the California militia, informed Governor Johnson of Beale's election and urged the governor to issue instructions to Beale similar to those they had issued to Scannell, authorizing him to call upon the military if necessary to carry out the laws. Kibbe told Johnson that Judge Freelon had decided that only the governor could determine the issue of the sheriff's appointment. Kibbe urged Johnson to endorse Beale: "Beale's appointment as Sheriff of this County would do more for the success of law and order than any act which could be done."[24]

Although Beale had the votes of the county board, he still did not have the office. Scannell declared that he would swear out warrants against anyone who interfered with the duties of his office. Charles L. Strong, Freelon's sheriff, continued to claim the office. Both Beale and Strong sought out men to serve their bondsmen. On August 11, prior to the examination of Beale's bonds, Judge Freelon declared that he felt the question could only be decided by the state supreme court. Beale's bondsmen included several old friends such as Sanford Lyons and Robert C. Page. The board found problems with Beale's sureties, so he returned the next day with additional bondsmen and easily made the $100,000 requirement. On August 13, before Judge D. O. Shattuck, Beale took an oath of office and swore to "faithfully discharge the duties of the Sheriff of the City and County of San Francisco." Two days later Charles L. Strong posted his bonds to be sheriff. Kibbe pleaded with Governor Johnson to recognize Beale, but it became clear that the matter would remain unsettled until the fall election.[25]

As Beale's hopes to become sheriff faded, the Vigilance Committee on August 18 conducted a grand parade through the streets of San Francisco and disbanded. Its members, however, quickly metamorphosed into the People's Party, running a full slate of local candidates in the fall election. Charles Doane, commander of the Vigilante military, stood as candidate for sheriff, while the Democrats threw their support to David Scannell, still a popular man, in his fight to retain office. If the sheriff's office was not vacant, the Democrats reasoned, Doane would not be able to fill it. Beale went along with the party's plan.[26]

Early in the summer, Beale had identified himself with the group supporting Democrat James Buchanan for the presidency. This developed naturally from the Edwards family's long friendship with Buchanan. Beale hoped to gain a federal appointment from Buchanan's election; he wanted very much to regain his former office as Indian superintendent in California. On July 16, at a Democratic rally in Portsmouth Square, Beale was elected as one of several honorary presidents of the gathering. Shortly thereafter, the Buchanan Democrats organized the Keystone Club, which became an important political tool for the local Democratic Party. C. A. McNulty was elected the club's president, and Beale served as vice-president.[27]

From early August until the fall election, the Keystone Club aired its views in the San Francisco *Herald.* The club attacked the prevailing "political fanaticism" as reflected by Fremont's running as the Republican presidential candidate and the recent activities of the Vigilance Committee. The Keystone Club's policy statement touched on the construction of a transcontinental railroad and assured everyone that only the Democratic Party could build it. Sectional issues had no place in national politics, which again was a reference to the Republican discussion of slavery. The Republican Party was labeled as sectional and hence divisive. The nation's hopes lay with Buchanan, and not with Fremont's "piratical crew which would strand the ship of State upon the breakers of Sectionalism."[28]

The People's Party of San Francisco, formerly the Committee of Vigilance, loomed increasingly strong with each passing week. Prominent Democrats found themselves reduced to the status of common ward leaders in order to fight the new threat. Earlier, California's Democrats had split into two factions: David C. Brockerick's Irish-dominated city machine and William M. Gwin's Southern-oriented "Chivalry" forces. Now the combined threat of the People's Party and the Republicans drove the Democrats together.

In the Eleventh District, on the city's southside near Mission Dolores, Beale took the lead in organizing the local Democrats. He was elected president of the Young Hickory Club, as the ward's Democrats called themselves, and concentrated on turning out the voters of the district. The Hickory Club adopted a number of resolutions, duly printed by Nugent's *Herald,* which accepted and endorsed the national Democratic Party platform as adopted in Cincinnati. The platform contained the "time-honored and Union-saving principles of that party, as created by Jefferson, and sustained by Jackson, and their patriotic successors." Every week, the Young Hickory Club met at the Nightingale Hotel, a well-known drinking spot near the mission.[29]

On September 5, Beale wrote presidential candidate James Buchanan and urged him to speak out on behalf of the Pacific railroad. In California the railroad was *the* issue, and the Republicans were making consistent gains on that subject. If the Democrats could but "stop the mouths of our opponents" on that subject, said Beale, the party would be assured of a great victory in that state. California Democrats anxiously awaited Buchanan's word on "this important question," and Beale said that everyone was working hard for a Democratic victory.

Two weeks later, in response to other entreaties, Buchanan addressed a letter on the railroad to B. F. Washington, chairman of the Democratic State Central Committee of California. Buchanan said he unequivocally supported the construction of a Pacific railroad. The government should aid in the project, and he did not feel it would be unconstitutional to do so. Congress could appropriate money for the Pacific railroad just the same as it did for harbor defenses. Newspapers throughout the state reproduced the letter.[30]

Beale also received a letter from Thomas Hart Benton, ex-senator of Missouri. Benton had run for the office of governor of Missouri and lost. Sectional feelings in that state had become so pronounced that a man like himself could not win an election. "Of that canvass you will have heard the result, and that sectional feeling was too strong to admit of electing a man who would not represent that feeling against the north," Benton stated. He added that "the two halves of the Union are now pitted against each other, and every public man must join the section he lives in, or be left behind. I will not become sectional. . . . " The Benton family opposed Fremont's candidacy, and the senator was distressed with his son-in-law, whom Benton believed somewhat responsible for the growing sectionalism of the United States. Even Kit Carson openly opposed his former commander.

Several newspapers went so far as to attack Fremont's courage in a sarcastic piece of doggerel that compared Fremont unfavorably to Beale, and reminded readers of the disastrous Fourth Expedition:

> When government dispatches, John,
> Were given you and Beale,
> To cross the Rocky Mountains, John,
> You were true as steel.
> You started both together John—
> Found snow drifts in your way—
> Beale foolishly went through, John,
> But you did wisely stay.[31]

In California the election of 1856 caused an outpouring of speeches, parades, barbecues, and other public displays. The Democrats fielded a slate of local candidates far superior to the fare that was generally dished up for the lesser offices in an effort to avoid political disaster. Beale made himself visible in the cause of the Democracy. On one occasion, the ladies of the Young Hickory Club presented an elaborate flag to General James A. McDougal, who in turn presented the banner to Beale. Upon receiving the flag, Beale made one of his first political speeches.[32]

The coming election, Beale predicted would stand as a "monument for the rebuke of fanaticism." At no time since the revolution had there been such an alarming moment for the nation as during the present campaign. The Republican Party threatened to destroy the Union with its "incendiary torch of fanaticism." Beale reminded his listeners that America offered the only hope in the entire world for many a "solitary serf" in Europe. A vote for the opposition counted as an effort to extinguish the "feeble ray of hope in the breast of the oppressed wherever the oppressor's iron heel has left its stamp." He called upon the residents of the "glorious old Eighth Ward to turn the tide of battle and save the Union." Beale pointed to the flag he had just been given ("wrought by hands dear to every gallant heart") and urged his audience to join him in the great fight in November. "They must leave the "flag unstained by defeat, unsullied, triumphant."

After the meeting ended, Beale provided a local newspaper with a copy of his speech and forwarded his remarks to James Buchanan. The presidential candidate replied that Beale's speech upon the presentation of the flag from the ladies ("God Bless them!") was highly admirable. He also told Beale the election was now a sure thing.[33]

On October 25, 1856, all the Democratic clubs in San Francisco gathered for an impressive Saturday night rally before the election. An immense torchlight parade wound through the city streets. The entire route seemed "one brilliant blaze . . . the greatest political demonstration ever made in California," according to a local newspaper. Amidst the grand display of fireworks, enjoyed by spectators who crowded the nearby hills, prominent Democrats delivered their final speeches. One theme remained constant: a transcontinental railroad could never be built by a sectional party, and the Republicans were surely sectional.[34]

On election eve, November 3, the Republicans paraded and advertised their candidates with great fanfare, although their demonstrations were smaller than the Democratic performance. Illuminated transparencies in the torchlight parades attracted much attention, with one device satirizing the recent Democratic-backed plan to open the reaches of arid West by the use of camels. The transparency of a "mongrel herd of badly painted dromedaries" was entitled by the Republicans: "The First Train for California."[35]

The election results were predictable. Buchanan carried California, but the People's Party thoroughly defeated the Democratic organization in San Francisco. The "Businessmen's Revolution" had succeeded, despite the united efforts of the various factions of the Democratic Party. The Republicans fared poorly, although Fremont managed to carry Beale's district by eleven votes. Charles Doane was the only candidate for sheriff because the Democrats agreed that David Scannell had never vacated the office and was, therefore, still sheriff. At the state level, the Democrats maintained their power, with the exception of the legislators from San Francisco who, almost to a man, now represented the People's Party. Beale doubtless was satisfied with the election: Buchanan had won, and he looked forward to a federal job.[36]

Before Beale left San Francisco to go to Washington and lobby for a position, he sought out General Wool and asked him to write a letter of recommendation in his behalf to James Buchanan. Beale had decided to try to regain his post as superintendent of Indian affairs. In this letter Wool related that if Beale had been permitted to continue as superintendent in 1854, he would have succeeded in carrying out the government's plan for self-sufficient Indian reservations. Henley "has significantly failed in executing the plan," Wool stated. For himself, the general had no other motivation in recommending Beale for the office other than "an anxious desire to see the humane policy of the United States Government honestly and fairly carried out towards the Indians."[37]

Beale left San Francisco on January 20, 1857, and sailed for Panama with his family. On the *Golden Gate* with Beale were two United States senators, newly elected David C. Broderick and reelected William M. Gwin, along with a large number of pilgrims "making their hegira from California to the great political Mecca, Washington."[38]

Chapter 7

WAGONS, RAILROADS & CAMELS

No one who has not commanded an expedition of this kind, where everything ahead is dim, uncertain, and unknown, except the dangers, can imagine the anxiety with which I start upon this journey. Not only responsible for the lives of my men, but my reputation and the highest wrought expectations of my friends, and the still more highly wrought expectations of envious enemies— all these dependent on the next sixty days' good or evil fortune.

—Journal of E. F. Beale
August 27, 1857

A year in the wilderness ended! During this time I have conducted my party from the Gulf of Mexico to the shores of the Pacific Ocean, and back again to the eastern terminus of the road, through a country for a great part entirely unknown, and inhabited by hostile Indians, without the loss of a man. I have tested the value of the camels, marked a new road to the Pacific, and travelled 4,000 miles without an accident.

—Journal of E. F. Beale
February 21, 1858

When Beale reached Washington, he learned that he would not be reappointed Indian superintendent of California. J. Ross Browne's lengthy report had exonerated him from charges of wrongdoing, but the investigation showed that he had been careless with government funds. But as a family friend of Buchanan's, he deserved a reward. When the position of superintendent of a government survey for a military wagon road from

New Mexico to California was offered to him, Beale took it. The survey also involved a plan to test camels in the southwestern deserts as an aid to transportation. The exotic beasts assured Beale of public visibility, and once again he would have the opportunity to point the way for the Pacific railroad by constructing a road to California. [1]

For many years, Californians had demanded a wagon road from the eastern states. In April of 1856, some 60,000 residents signed a memorial to Congress which urged the construction of such a highway. Following Buchanan's election in the fall, Congress passed an omnibus bill which provided for the construction of three roads to California. Two of the roads—one running from El Paso to Fort Yuma, and a second from Fort Kearny to the Carson Valley—would be built under the Interior Department's supervision. The third road—from Fort Defiance to the Colorado River—would be under the War Department's control. Beale was an ideal choice to head the military survey because of his previous explorations and travels in the Southwest. [2]

On April 22, 1857, Secretary of War John B. Floyd notified Beale of his appointment as superintendent of the wagon road from Fort Defiance to the mouth of the Mojave River. In his instructions, Floyd stated that it was "supposed" that the Mojave joined the Colorado. In reality, the Mojave was an intermittent desert stream which disappeared into the sands some eighty miles west of the Colorado. Beale would proceed to New Mexico as soon as possible and organize his work party, which would contain from thirty-five to fifty men. As superintendent, Beale would earn $3,000 per year, plus traveling expenses. His topographer would draw $2,500 annual pay, while the doctor and surveyor would be allotted three to five dollars per day.

The government instructed Beale to take ten wagons to convey his camp equipment, tools, and provisions and to "demonstrate practically that the road may be passed over with heavy wagons." To expedite passage, the work party would also "make all watering places and fords easily accessible to wagons." Beale would make estimates as to the cost of constructing bridges wherever necessary on the route, and if time permitted and funds remained, he should retrace his route and improve the road's difficult spots. At Fort Defiance, Beale's party would be given an escort of twenty-five men for the passage across northwestern New Mexico, inhabited by several tribes of hostile Indians, including the Navajos. On all occasions the survey party would attempt to conciliate Indians through presents and acts of kindness. To cover any eventuality, Beale's cousin, Gwin Heap, second in command of the survey forces, would take charge in the event of Beale's death. On the expedition

Beale also would take up to twenty-five camels to California, with the view to "test their usefulness, endurance and economy." He could hire as many of the Arabs and Turks who had accompanied the camels from the Middle East as he required. They would prove invaluable in handling the camels.[3]

The evening before Beale left Washington, Thomas Hart Benton arranged a sumptuous feast in his honor. A number of Washington dignitaries attended, including the secretary of war, who suffered an attack of severe indigestion as a result of the grand meal. Benton toasted Beale and expressed the hope that the wagon road would speed the building of a transcontinental railroad, which had been Benton's pet project for many years.

Secretary Floyd warned Beale to be careful about his finances. He would issue a duplicate voucher for money disbursements and transmit the originals promptly to the War Department. To help Beale keep a tight check on the expedition expenses, Floyd sent an itemized list of his funds and how they would be disbursed. Salaries consumed the majority of the appropriation—$20,360. Floyd allocated $6,125 for provisions and $12,000 for tools and road equipment. Camp and garrison equipment was set at $2,000, while wagons, mules, and transportation equipment constituted a sizeable $15,000. Miscellaneous items, including two India rubber boats, and presents for the Indians totalled $2,000.[4]

In early May of 1857, Beale headed west, accompanied by Gwin Heap, and Lieutenant C. F. Thorburn, a naval officer whom Beale had known during the Mexican War. En route they made purchases for the journey. By the twentieth the party reached Louisville and took lodgings at the Galt House, the city's best, while they investigated the local mule market. Boarding a steamboat they were in New Orleans by the twenty-sixth, and roughly two weeks later, on June 6, the Beale group reached Indianola, Texas. Here Beale organized a wagon train to carry supplies.[5]

Here he also purchased a black slave named Jourdan. Supposedly he learned that Jourdan was going to be sold to a "cruel taskmaster," so he bought the black for $1,500 (he later recalled) and set him free. But in 1857, Beale desperately needed money, and it appeared that Jourdan assumed an indentured status as an employee of Beale. The bill of sale described the Negro as twenty-five to thirty years in age, copper-colored, healthy, and sensible. In the years to come, Jourdan and Beale became close friends and the ex-slave worked for Beale for many years.[6]

Beale's train of ten wagons left Indianola in early June, bound for Camp Verde, where they would find the camels. Beale and his assistants traveled in an army ambulance, painted a bright red. On the thirteenth an argument between Beale and Heap occurred. Beale had placed Heap in charge of the wagon train, while he rode off to hunt stray mules. After getting eight wagons across a stream Heap assumed the remaining wagons would cross without trouble and left. Two of the wagons, however, negotiated the stream only with great difficulty and were late in reaching camp. That evening Beale spoke "in a very harsh and ungentlemanly manner" to Heap, "telling him that he had not performed his duty as wagon master." The argument grew heated, and Heap finally declared he was resigning his post as assistant superintendent. Although he had quarrelled with Beale, Heap's resignation in a large measure resulted from his tiring with the "vagabond life" he had been leading for several years.[7]

At San Antonio, the party rested. A few men, including Beale, went to Camp Verde to procure the expedition's camels. On June 21, Beale, Joe Bell, and Ham Porter returned with the camels. The strange beasts scared the mules and horses, which thrashed about excitedly in their corrals. Within a few days, the animals grew to tolerate the presence of the camels. In the meantime, Beale's men attempted to master the complicated art of packing the camels' loads—a task far different from packing a mule. On the twenty-fifth the expedition left San Antonio, heading across west Texas for New Mexico.

The party traveled slowly for the first few days, while the camels developed strength to carry their heavy loads. At first the animals lagged behind the wagons, but after several days, they grew stronger and kept up with the rest of the train. Beale spent a wretched Fourth of July on the trail, drenched from a steady rain. He tried to ease his discomfort with several bottles of brandy, presented to him by a Philadelphia friend.[8]

Beale ordered his men to watch closely for hostile Indians known to be active in west Texas. No incidents occurred, however, and by July 17, the caravan had reached Fort Davis. Ten days later, the caravan moved on toward El Paso. Beale observed the camels closely and marveled at their ability to eat mesquite bushes and other thorny plants in preference to grass. Camels did not have to be shod, and they were more surefooted than mules. A camel picked up its feet and planted them without any slippage, in contrast to mules which raised their hooves with a slipping motion. It had been feared that the unshod camels would soon become footsore, but the fear was quickly dispelled.[9]

From El Paso, the party moved up the Rio Grande, with the camels' fame preceding them. At adobe villages along the trail, people came out to marvel at the caravan. Some asked Beale whether he was ringmaster of a circus, perhaps because of Beale's bright red ambulance, which looked similar to a circus wagon. Beale enjoyed the ruse. In his diary, he recorded the following exchange between himself and a local crowd:

"Dis show wagon, no?"
I replied, "Yes."
"Ah, ha!" You be de showmans, no?"
"Yes, sir."
"What you gottee more on camelos? Gottee any dogs?"
"Yes, monkeys, too, and more."
"Whatee more?"
"Horse more."
"Whatee cando horse?"
"Stand on his head, and drink a glass of wine."
"Valgame Dios! What a people these are to have a horse stand on his head, and drink a glass of wine."[10]

By early August of 1857, Beale had reached Albuquerque and put his party in camp. He departed headquarters for Santa Fe and made arrangements for a military escort on the route west. Beale had some trouble with his camel drivers and recommended that to move a half-drunken Turkish driver required a "copious supply of oil of the boot" and "a good tough piece of wagon spoke, aimed tolerably *high.*" On August 15, the party left the "fandangos and other pleasures" of Albuquerque and started for Fort Defiance, some 160 miles to the west. Beale had now mastered the art of camel riding and was constantly aboard his favorite white dromedary, "Seid."[11]

The journey to Fort Defiance, across a parched, hot mesa country, took ten days. A few miles east of the post, Captain Josiah H. Carlisle, Second Artillery, greeted the caravan. In his diary, Beale penned that "it was most refreshing to see the captain's servant throw off the folds of a blanket from a tub in the bottom of the wagon, and expose several large and glistening blocks of ice, while at the same time the captain produced a delicate flask of 'red eye.' " Beale spent two days at Fort Defiance.[12]

On August 27 the expedition left the fort with an escort of twenty soldiers, picked men, who accompanied the party along with a large number of Mexican laborers and assistants, making a total of approximately seventy men. The work of the wagon road survey now began. "No one who has not commanded an expedition of this kind . . . can imagine the anxiety with which I start upon this journey," wrote Beale. He vowed his determination to make the wagon road survey a success; his reputation depended upon it. Beale intended to follow roughly the railroad route that Lieutenant Amiel Weeks Whipple had charted across the wilderness of northern Arizona along the thirty-fifth parallel in 1853. Beale frequently consulted Whipple's report, plus the meager report of Francois X. Aubry, explorer and guide, who also traveled through the same region.

On August 29, Beale, aboard Seid, lumbered into the Zuni villages, near the present-day Arizona line. [13]

After bartering for corn at Zuni, the party headed almost due west into unknown country. The days on the road were monotonous. The men would arise before sunup, and by seven o'clock were slowly plodding westward. The leaders felt a great sense of exploration and discovery. Beale acted as if he were the first man to see the region, although he confided to his journal that they frequently followed the faint tracks of Whipple's wagons. He was cognizant that later emigrants needed knowledge about the countryside, so he jotted notes on game, forage, and water. In the explorer's tradition, he bestowed names on prominent landmarks, many of which were officially adopted. On September 5, the party saw a distant peak on the horizon, the San Francisco Mountain, which served as a guiding landmark. The country through which they passed had abundant grass. "What a stock country!" was the frequent comment by members of the party. Beale predicted a large population for northwestern New Mexico (northern Arizona), once the threat of the Navajos had been removed or controlled by military posts. [14]

Farther west, the leaders of the expedition and even common road laborers expressed their astonishment at the meadows and pine forests of north-central Arizona. A true sportsman, Beale noted with enthusiasm the richness of the wild game—bears, deer, antelope, partridges, and squirrels. By mid-September, Beale had taken over the role of the expedition's guide as the "wretch" he had employed at Albuquerque was the "most ignorant and irresolute old ass extant." Beale continued to name landmarks after the members of the party and even chiseled the place names into nearby rocks to ensure their permanence.

In his diary (which later became his official report), Beale repeatedly praised the road. Frequently the party made twenty miles per day with mules that had pulled heavily loaded wagons for more than eighteen hundred miles. The camels were even less troubled by the countryside than the mules. Beale believed that with camels alone he could have averaged forty miles per day. The rocky ground posed no problem for them, nor did they require forage or more than an occasional drink of water. [15]

Indians constantly worried Beale. On September 26, he returned from a scouting expedition and found no guards around the campfire. He decided precautions against Indian attacks had grown much too lax and vowed to teach his men a lesson. As Beale approached his camp, he fired his pistol into the air and gave an Indian war hoop. "Indians, Indians! Here they are, the d——n rascals, give them hell boys," he shouted. Beale's men flew into action. Several men grabbed muskets and charged toward Beale's location. In the excitement, Beale's horse bolted and galloped wildly for several miles. May Humphries Stacey, an assistant, recorded in his diary that as a result of his mock attack "Mr. Beale was very sick all night, vomiting, and in much pain." Beale was thoroughly humiliated when he learned that he had "attacked" an abandoned campfire. While on his scouting expedition, his men had relocated their camp fifty yards away.[16]

On September 27, 1857, at a camp one hundred miles east of the Colorado River, Beale wrote a letter to Secretary Floyd. The party had found abundant grass, timber, and water all along the route. One could not praise the camels too highly. Beale exploded the old absurdity that their feet would break down on rocky ground. Recently the party had crossed the roughest volcanic rock, and the camels were unaffected. Beale predicted the road would become the "great emigrant route to California." The road was two hundred miles shorter than any other route and passed through fertile, well-watered country, abundant with grass, and in northern Arizona it ran through one of the "finest forests of pine timber possible to conceive."[17]

As he continued west, Beale felt an increasing confidence. On October 9, he named peaks after James Buchanan and Thomas Hart Benton. Shortly thereafter, he christened another mountain after Harry Edwards, his brother-in-law, and then named Engle's Pass, after his mother-in-law's prominent Pennsylvania family. On October 13, the expedition encountered several Mojave Indians, who fled in fear. Several days later, Beale met a large number of Indians near the Colorado River. One greeted him with fractured English: "God damn my soul eyes. How do do! How do do." The Mojaves grew watermelons, cantaloupes, and pumpkins, and they traded their produce for Beale's old shirts, handkerchiefs, and other items. The party also obtained corn and beans from the Indians.[18]

At the Colorado River, Beale floated his wagons across on the inflatable Indian rubber rafts. On October 20, to the delight and surprise of the entire party, the camels easily swam across the wide river. Ten mules and two horses drowned in the crossing, but the Indians profited from their loss. They fished out the carcasses and feasted on the remains. Beale tried to get an Indian guide to take him down river to Fort Yuma but could not secure one.

At the Colorado, Beale drew up another lengthy report to Secretary Floyd. He stressed the level terrain, the large stands of timber, water and grass, and fertile soil as far west as the Bill Williams Fork. At the ford on the Colorado, which he named Beale's Crossing, the river was two hundred yards wide, nineteen feet deep, and flowed at a constant three miles per hour. He predicted that the river was navigable for the largest steamer. It was a wonderful country; even the climate was healthful. Not a single man had required medical attention during the trip. The camels had more than proved their worth, and Beale looked forward to the "time when they will be in general use in all parts of the country."[19]

On November 9, Beale and an assistant lumbered into Los Angeles aboard two dromedaries, startling the local townspeople. They reined up at a hotel, and the camels kneeled down to permit the riders to dismount. A large, curious crowd, mostly Mexicans, gathered around the animals. After shaking countless hands and hearing numerous congratulations, Beale went inside and wrote a short note to his wife, which he commenced by stating: "I have this moment dismounted from my dromedary. . . ." He told Mary Beale that his trip had been a "perfect and brilliant success from beginning to end." Everyone arrived safely; he had not lost a man or camel on the expedition.[20]

With an escort of some fifty dragoons from Fort Tejon, led by Major George A. H. Blake, Beale organized a caravan, including camels, to retrace his route to New Mexico. The party left on January 10, 1858. At the Colorado River, Beale found the steamer *General Jesup*, commanded by George A. Johnson, who had just returned from forty miles up river. Beale congratulated Johnson on his successful trip, and on the twenty-third wrote Secretary Floyd about the voyage. Beale believed it to be the most important ever made on the western side of the Rocky Mountains, for it opened up a large territory for future development. Beale also commented on the Indians—estimated to number 1,500—who lived in the valley at Beale's Crossing. These Indians should be given presents of clothing and blankets in order to keep them friendly. Peaceful relations were especially important at this time because a dispute with the Mormons threatened to erupt into full-scale warfare.[21]

According to Beale the road along the thirty-fifth parallel was easily negotiable, even in midwinter. There was deep snow in the vicinity of San Francisco Peak, but elsewhere he saw only small patches. The winter weather was so mild that Beale and his men never bothered to pitch their tents, even when they camped in the deep pine forests along the route. The coldest temperature recorded was eighteen degrees, registered on February 5 at four in the morning. On February 24, Beale's party reached Albuquerque. One month later, he was in Kansas City.[22]

By mid-April of 1858, Beale had arrived in Washington and found that the War Department was impressed with his work. Secretary Floyd was enthusiastic about the military advantages of Beale's road. In time, he saw the road serving as a dividing line between the nomadic Indian tribes inhabiting Utah and northern Arizona, and the lands to the south. In conversation with bureaucrats, Beale stressed that in time the thirty-fifth parallel route could carry the major emigration to the Pacific, provided the government constructed military posts, bridges, and dams on certain seasonal streams to ensure a water supply. An additional $100,000 appropriation from Congress was needed to complete the improvements on the road. Secretary Floyd sent Beale's journal (slightly edited), along with a cover letter, to the House of Representatives, where it was ordered to be published.[23]

In early August, Beale was asked to lead a second road expedition. Congress had granted the War Department an additional $75,000 to construct bridges and improve the road running from Ft. Smith, Arkansas to Albuquerque, New Mexico and on to California. Once again, Beale would test the camels' practicality. Floyd concluded that the appropriation was insufficient to build a completed road across the route's entire length to California. Instead, Beale should concentrate his attention and money on improving the road's most difficult stretches.[24]

As he contemplated another western expedition, Beale stood on the threshold of realizing his dream of becoming a "man of rank." His salary had been increased to $4,000—a substantial income—but more important, his ranching operations in California, under the able management of his partner, S. A. Bishop, had prospered. In fact, only two men paid more property taxes in Los Angeles County. Abel Stearns, one of the largest landholders in the state was assessed at $186,586. Juan Temple was second on the tax rolls at $89,556. Beale and Bishop's wealth was estimated at $47,900.[25]

By late October of 1858, Beale reached Fort Smith, via Memphis, and prepared to organize the expedition. He learned that warfare had broken out across the plains between the Comanches and the U.S. Army, threatening his prospects for success. The wagon road passed through the heart of the Comanches' homeland. Beale requested that Lieutenant Alexander E. Steen, leader of the military escort, draw upon the military at Fort Smith for two artillery field pieces.[26]

Before leaving Fort Smith, Beale wrote a letter to his wife. His letter revealed that he occasionally gambled in business ventures. He informed her that he had sold his interest in a mail contract for $2,500, as the contract had not proved lucrative. He also inquired about the property that he and Mary recently had purchased near Chester, Pennsylvania. Beale forecasted that the land's value would increase dramatically as the community grew. He urged Mary to have this property recorded in the name of Mary Ann Edwards, Beale's mother-in-law, and then conveyed to Mary Beale as a gift. In that fashion, said Beale, the property "shall not become liable for my debts."

Beale instructed Mary to take care of certain vital chores in California.

Beale wanted his employee Jourdan, who had been on the camel expedition with him, to check on the camels, then in California. The camels must be kept constantly visible before the public so "people can see they *are in use.*" Beale had begun to realize that his reputation was closely attached to the camels. On the matter of the new road, Beale admitted that parts of it presented almost insurmountable problems to transportation, particularly the section near the Colorado River. She should ask Bishop, or preferably Fred Kerlin, to try to improve the road in that area. Tell Fred, Beale said to his wife, that *"my reputation* is in his hands, and that is dearer to me *than life itself."*[27]

On October 28, 1858, Beale's road party departed. George Beale had difficulty in obtaining guides. The men his brother wanted refused to serve because of the Comanche troubles. Jesse Chisholm, who agreed to serve as a guide, warned that the Comanches would "burn every blade of grass" and that in a few days they would not have a single animal left. Beale chose to ignore the warning. In addition to the Beales, the principal members of the second expedition were Harry B. Edwards, first assistant; J. M. Bell, secretary and assistant; William P. Floyd, surgeon and assistant; and J. R. Crump, engineer and astronomer.[28]

Beale charted his wagon road almost due west from Fort Smith, following the course of the Canadian River. He took considerable interest in the activities of Dick the Delaware and Little Axe, two Indians employed to provide fresh meat for the party. Game abounded—deer, turkey, prairie chicken, and quail. Beale even hunted for sport with his greyhounds, Buck and Fannie, when he could find the time. He kept a close eye on the vegetation and in his diary recorded the various types of grasses, trees, shrubs, and other plants he saw along the road.[29]

One hundred eight miles west of Fort Smith, Beale met several mail stages awaiting his arrival. R. Frank Green held a contract with the government to carry the mail from Neosho, Missouri to Santa Fe, but the recent fighting with the Comanches made it impossible to travel without an escort. Green hoped to travel with Beale and his military escort. The escort under Lieutenant Steen had dropped behind, however. In fact, the escort of soldiers found it difficult to keep up with the road-building party. On November 15, Beale and the stagecoaches halted to wait for Steen to catch up. He also sent Harry Edwards back over the road to supervise the construction of bridges over the streams Beale had designated.[30]

Beale now grew restless. By November 22, Lieutenant Steen was still not in sight, and Beale recorded in his journal that "we are getting disgustingly tired of waiting for our escort." Beale figured that Steen was averaging only five and one-half miles per day. The road party had sixty days of provisions, but they might run out of food before they reached New Mexico. Beale finally received a letter from Steen asking if the road party intended to wait for its escort or to cross Indian country without soldiers. This infuriated Beale. They had been on the road for twenty-six days and were only about two hundred miles from Fort Smith. Winter was fast approaching. Already, the Canadian was encrusted with ice on the edges. On November 26, Steen's escort finally rode up, Beale now felt that the combined force of 130 men was sufficient to take care of any Indians that might foolishly attack his expedition.[31]

The next day P. G. Breckenridge, a young member of the party, wandered away from the camp and was lost. Beale was greatly annoyed by having to halt again in order to look for the youth. Breckenridge apparently had friends in high government circles who demanded that the boy be taken on the expedition. Beale confided to his diary that such persons invariably became a burden on everybody. They soon became "disgusted and humiliated to see how badly they compare with men, infinitely beneath them in birth and fortune, in all that makes *a man* upon the plains." A search party found Breckenridge on the following day about two miles from camp. He had wandered over the prairie some forty miles. "So much for these Greenhorn annoyances," wrote Beale.[32]

Beale pushed the party to increase its speed in order to reach winter quarters in New Mexico. He maintained a busy schedule. Some two hundred twenty miles west of Fort Smith, he selected a promising site for a military post on the eastern edge of the Comanche homeland. Occasionally the party halted in order to improve the road. They worked mainly on riverbanks, cutting down the slopes so that wagons could pass.[33]

By early December the weather on the plains had grown exceedingly cold. On the evening of December 7 Beale wrote in his diary that the temperature was "as cold as I have ever known it." Mules died in the freezing weather, and the whole party felt the gloom. They had expected to find the climate much warmer along that latitude. Still, Beale maintained his unbridled optimism. The more he saw of the Canadian River Valley, the more he became convinced that it offered "decidedly the most level line for a railroad to be found for the same distance between the Pacific and Atlantic."[34]

The party entered New Mexico and spent Christmas Day at Laguna Colorado, a pond of muddy water. Twenty-five wild turkeys, preserved by the icy weather, had been saved for the occasion, and everyone enjoyed a feast of turkey, deer, antelope, raccoon, prairie dog, and grouse. Three days later the caravan crossed the divide between the Canadian and the Pecos rivers and reached Hatch's Ranch, where they would spend the most trying weeks of the winter.[35]

Beale wrote a letter to Mary. Some people might censure him for leaving his escort some 250 miles behind, but Harry Edwards, who had left the train near Fort Smith could explain the reason for the decision. Beale had not heard from Fred Kerlin, but he expected him to join the party before long. He described the journey as a simple routine trip. "As usual," Beale wrote, "I have brought all my men through without the loss of a single one, nor have I abandoned a wagon on the road." He told Mary to tell "our dear children . . . how I thought tenderly and affectionately of them on a bitter Christmas day in the year 1858, plodding along two hours before daylight until camping time, on a weary road." Beale also praised his brother George—"the best man of my party."[36]

In New Mexico, Beale learned of the Rose Massacre. During the previous summer a group of emigrants, which included the Rose family, were traveling on his wagon road to California and had been attacked by Mojave Indians at the Colorado River. In Albuquerque, Beale later talked with several of the survivors. Under the leadership of J. L. Rose, the wagon train had left Albuquerque in late June, and at the urging of local residents, they decided to follow Beale's newly surveyed road to California. The train had fared reasonably well until it came within sight of the Colorado River. Here the Mojaves struck. Eight persons were killed and thirteen seriously wounded. After the clash, the survivors joined another westbound group of emigrants, and they all turned back toward Albuquerque. In describing the incident to Secretary Floyd Beale said it was madness to attempt to travel over the wagon road until a military post was established on the Colorado River. Beale also urged that the army give a "dreadful retribution" to the Mojaves.[37]

Beale described the road he had just traveled over. Although his instructions said nothing about examining the countryside for a railroad, Beale told Floyd that every member of his party was impressed with the level, broad valley of the Canadian River, frequently five miles wide. Beale's civil engineer, Crump, estimated it would cost only $2,000 per mile to grade and prepare the roadbed for the laying of track. Enough trees grew along the banks of the stream or in the vicinity to furnish the necessary railroad ties. In many places, rails could be laid in a straight line for thirty miles without a single curve in the track. Although his mentor, Thomas Hart Benton, had recently died, Beale pushed the senator's dream of a great national road to the Pacific. Beale told Floyd that an emigrant road for wagons, a livestock road, and a railroad could all run side by side along the Canadian River.[38]

Beale's exploits had not gone unnoticed. The editors of the New Orleans *Picayune* declared: "Just think of a fine river bottom to travel on from Fort Smith almost to the centre of the continent—level all the way, abounding in the finest grass, wood and water, and so straight as not to deviate ten miles north and south of a given parallel." In Chester, Pennsylvania, Mary E. Beale was pleased with the success of her husband. Although only thirty-six, he was described by the local newspaper as the "beau ideal of perseverance and pluck, of endurance under fatigue, and of love of adventure."[39]

In January of 1859, Fred Kerlin arrived at Hatch's Ranch and reported the "most gratifying intelligence" from Beale's California rancho. Kerlin calculated that within one year, Beale would have a permanent income from the ranch of over $10,000 per year. Beale passed the happy news to Mary in Chester. "It seems hardly credible," he wrote, "that we have so nearly reached our haven, after so many struggles against misfortune." Bishop had approximately $25,000 on hand awaiting investment. When the money was placed into sheep or cattle, and combined with the yearly stock price increases it would result in a *"Fortune"*! Beale stated that he longed to enjoy a vacation. First, he would take a long rest. Then, he would take the entire family to Europe and spend a summer in Florence and the winter in Rome. How nice it would be, he told Mary, to be "in a beautiful country surrounded by everything refined and elegant." He encouraged Mary to cast aside her aversion to sea voyages and even proposed to take along her aunt and mother, provided they promised not to abuse his independent views concerning "religion."[40]

Beale was treated royally by the residents and government officials in Santa Fe and Albuquerque. All encouraged his plans for the wagon road and railroad. Beale sent Fred Kerlin back to the Liebre Rancho and was amazed that one could take a stage from Santa Fe south to El Paso, and then westward to Los Angeles. Beale paused in Santa Fe, resting his mules for the remainder of the trip, and wrote another letter to his wife. With a bold confidence, he stated "my name must be connected forever in the history and progress of this vast country."[41]

Beale left Santa Fe for Taos, riding in the army ambulance thoughtfully provided by Major James L. Donaldson. He spent several pleasant days with Kit Carson, who agreed to return over the icy road to Santa Fe in order to continue their reunion for a few more days. At Santa Fe, Beale learned that his camp at Hatch's Ranch had been visited by the "Bedouans of America," the Comanches, who desired to negotiate terms of peace with him. The Indians declared their confidence in Beale and said they would await his arrival. Carson and Beale hurried to Hatch's Ranch, but by the time they reached there, the Indians had departed.[42]

The Comanche leaders had assured George Beale, who had represented his brother, that their intentions were peaceful. They would allow stages to travel through their country from Neosho to Albuquerque, but they would never permit settlements or houses to be built on the Canadian River. They plainly warned that any white man who attempted to settle on that river would be killed. A second delegation of Indians, Kiowas, also visited George Beale and stated similar feelings. In relaying this conversation to Secretary Floyd, Ned Beale suggested that building several military posts in the Comanche country would soon settle the question. For example, a post could be established at the mouth of Utah Creek and the Canadian, and within a few months a hundred families would settle there.

While at Hatch's Ranch, Beale also gave attention to a wagon line that would straighten out the route running east from Anton Chico to the Canadian River. He discovered in his explorations that the Canadian River actually ran thirty-five miles farther west than indicated on his map. At that point, the river bent abruptly northward, but another stream, the Conchas, flowed into the Canadian from the west. Only a gentle divide separated the Conchas from the Gallinas; Hatch's Ranch was on the Gallinas. This was only one instance where Beale sought to straighten out the wagon road by personal exploration. In a letter dated February 15, 1859, Beale wrote Secretary Floyd that "for a *railroad* line, the Canadian River bottom, the valley of the Conchas and the intervening country, between the headwaters of the latter and Anton Chico, offer every facility."[43]

On February 26, Beale broke winter encampment at Hatch's Ranch and started west for the Rio Grande. Three days later, the party encountered one of the drilling crews connected with Captain John Pope's artesian well operations, yet another example of Jefferson Davis's desire to open the arid Southwest. If Pope accomplished his task, stated Beale, "he will have rendered better service to New Mexico than anyone alive." When the caravan reached Albuquerque, Beale invested ten dollars in a lottery, and won a beautiful, double-barreled English shotgun, valued at two hundred fifty dollars. But more important than the lucky lottery ticket was a resolution by the New Mexico Legislature on March 5, thanking Beale for his wagon road survey which showed the thirty-fifth parallel route to be the cheapest and shortest avenue to the Pacific.[44]

From Albuquerque, Beale penned a letter to his wife. He hoped to reach the Colorado River by May 1, he said, and return to the East by August. It seemed an "interminable time" until he would see Mary again, but "we must not complain." Beale included in his letter a story for his three-year-old son, Truxtun. On the way to Albuquerque the wind blew so hard during a freezing snowstorm that he could not keep the blankets on himself. But the following day, he walked twenty-five miles, without every crying. Trux should try to copy his father and always be a good boy, and "never worry his dear Mother by crying, or running out on the Rail Road track" which passed within a few hundred yards of their home in Chester. Beale told Mary that he was very lonesome and ended the letter by asking her to "kiss our little darlings for me a thousand times. . . ."[45]

Beale's westbound expedition was accompanied by a party of emigrants, including some members of the Rose party. On March 12, while in western New Mexico, the group was lightly blanketed by a brief snowfall, and Beale took the opportunity to write another letter home. Mary should tell Truxtun and daughter Mary (nicknamed Mame) about the children of the emigrant train who traveled with him. Earlier, when the Indians attacked the Rose party, many "poor little children were obliged to walk over the road with their feet bleeding at every step," he related. Beale promised to "raise the hair of many a devilish Indian this time for all the pain and suffering they have caused these harmless people." He warned his children that if they misbehaved he would have to trade them to the Indians on his next trip west. Truxtun, who was prone to antics, would almost surely have to be traded regardless, Beale jokingly wrote.[46]

Beale now headed for the Zuni villages. Near Inscription Rock he halted and set a detail to work improving the road where it crossed the continental divide. Beale's commissary—a large herd of sheep being driven as a food supply—attracted two Indians from a nearby community, who attempted to steal several of the animals. They were apprehended, and Beale ordered them flogged as a summary lesson in justice. By March 27, the caravan reached Zuni and was met by George Beale, who had gone ahead and purchased a large quantity of corn. Proceeding west, at Navajo Springs, on March 31, Beale carelessly stepped into a mud spring, similar to quicksand, and sank to his waist before being rescued. Beale jotted a warning to future travelers in his journal. Several days later the party reached the Little Colorado River.[47]

Beale was intrigued by the mystery of the ancient inhabitants of the Southwest. On a nearby hillside, he found the remains of an old pueblo. Investigating the site, Beale exhumed a much decayed skeleton and noted the small earthenware jars placed at the forehead and on each side of the corpse. He planned to take the jars back to the East, along with some agate arrowheads. Opportunities for such sidetrips were rare, for almost daily he supervised the road crew as they moved boulders, blazed trees, and dug down difficult sections. The party reached San Francisco Mountain on April 12, with a light snow falling.[48]

While his official journal spoke of the road in flattering terms, Beale's letters to his wife gave a more realistic view. Winter had struck with "most unrelenting severity," he wrote Mary. A ferocious wind had blown constantly since October. The wind carried sand which had cut his face until it bled, and everyone's hair, mouth, ears, nostrils, and clothes were filled with a fine sand. It was a harsh, difficult journey.

On April 18, while Beale and his party were digging out a basin for a spring some miles west of the San Francisco Mountain, two riders approached, mounted on dromedaries. Beale immediately recognized "Seid," his favorite Egyptian camel. The two men were Samuel Bishop and Hadji Ali, a camel driver, who had accompanied Beale on the first expedition. That evening in camp Bishop described recent developments concerning the Mojave Indians. Earlier, Fred Kerlin had applied to Brigadier General Newman S. Clarke, commanding the Department of California, for an escort to accompany his wagons loaded with provisions to supply Beale's party when it reached the Colorado River. Clarke was gathering an expeditionary force at Fort Yuma to strike the Mojaves and could not comply. Bishop gathered a civilian force of thirty-eight men, plus several employees of the Central Overland Mail Company, which had been unable to transport the mail for several months over Beale's Road, and left Los Angeles on March 1. The party took ten camels and six wagons pulled by mules.[49]

Bishop said his party reached the Colorado on the nineteenth and was greeted by some seven hundred armed, hostile Indians. Claiming to be Mojaves, Paiutes, and Yumas, they brandished their bows and arrows and war clubs. Bishop met briefly with a headman, explained the object of his visit, and then gave each chieftain a shirt, while at the same time dispersing one hundred pounds of tobacco. On the morning of March 20, he attempted to cross the river in an Indian rubber boat but was driven back. Attacked by an Indian band on the California side of the river, the Americans fought for some three hours and killed a number of Indians. Bishop gave orders to scalp every dead Indian and sent a messenger down river to seek military assistance from Major William Hoffman at Fort Yuma. Learning on April 5 that Hoffman would be delayed, Bishop decided to reduce his force and cross the Colorado at a point north of the Mojave villages. The supplies were buried or cached at Paiute Creek, and the wagons were sent to the California settlements. Crossing the river with several camels, Bishop headed for Beale's train.

Beale was pleased with Bishop's success but miffed by the army's response. He sarcastically wrote in his diary that he "hoped the gallant seven hundred under Major Hoffman will find no great trouble in subduing the tribe which has been so badly beaten by the forty men and boys under my command." Bishop also brought the mail with him aboard the camels. Thus it was that the first mail west (on the first expedition) and now east over the thirty-fifth parallel route had been carried by camels. Beale emphasized this in a letter to his wife. She must "tell Harry (Edwards) to let it be *distinctly* understood that the *first* mail over the *Beale* route was brought by the camels, by Beale, *partner* S. A. Bishop." If Harry was not at home, Mary should send the story to John W. Forney, editor of the Philadelphia *Press*, or to the *Observer*.[50]

Beale's party now continued west once again, improving the road and marking important springs. At several points, Beale completely realigned the road from his first expedition. Occasionally, the Indians hampered progress. At Truxtun's Spring, named the previous year after his son and grandfather, the Indians stole a mule. On April 28, the following day, the Indians again stole a mule and killed yet another. One member of the party came close to being speared by an arrow shot at him. Beale grew angry with this harassment and planned a trap. He knew that the Indians closely watched the road builders during the day and prowled at night. So one evening after sundown, he ordered the camp moved several miles away from the first site. A dead mule was left in plain view at the first site, and several men climbed into the rocks, hoping the Indians would venture in and claim the carcass. At daybreak, as the "red brothers" entered the camp site, the men opened fire, killing four. Scalps were brought back as "vouchers." Beale was highly elated with his tactical skill and noted in his diary that "it was a good practical joke—a merrie jeste of ye white man and ye Indian."[51]

On the following day, April 30, 1859, Beale saw the Colorado River and prepared his men to fight the Mojave Indians. He was soon greeted by American soldiers, however, and learned to his surprise that Major Hoffman had arrived at the Mojave villages ten days before with 600 men. On the twenty-third, Hoffman dictated a peace treaty to the Indians, and the tribes readily accepted. On May 4, Beale's party crossed the Colorado River. There he learned that the large cache, carefully buried by Bishop, had been dug up by Hoffman's soldiers and the contents stolen. Leaving his work party and emigrants at the river, Beale and several others headed for Los Angeles to obtain supplies.

Beale arrived in Los Angeles on May 12 and immediately purchased provisions for his men. Wasting no time, Beale dispatched forty pack mules loaded with supplies for the Colorado. Once the supplies arrived his work crew resumed their labors on the road.[52]

Angered by the theft of his provisions, Beale wrote a long letter to Major Hoffman. The theft had caused Beale's men to subsist on short rations and had delayed an important public project. The supplies cached were in large quantities, Beale said. According to Bishop, the cache contained 2,700 pounds of flour, 1,700 pounds of bacon, 600 pounds of beans, 400 pounds of sugar, 200 pounds of coffee, 100 pounds of rice, 100 pounds of dried beef, and lesser amounts of tobacco, soap, mustard, and pepper. Only eighty pounds of bacon were recovered. Hoffman replied to Beale on May 14 stating that such a large amount of stores "could not possibly have been taken from the cache by the troops." It would have been impossible to have kept such quantities a secret from their officers. Beale broached the subject of the theft in a letter to Secretary Floyd, who ordered an investigation and courts martial for soldiers involved in the thefts.[53]

Beale also related the theft to his wife. He was highly critical of Hoffman and his soldiers, stating that "the only distinction they have gained in the bloodless campaign" was the robbery. The emigrants should have been avenged before any peace treaty was concluded. "Within twenty steps of the place where Hoffman with his thousand men made this treaty," Beale continued in hot anger, "we saw sticking in the rough bark of the trees the golden hair of a child whose brains the bloody savages had knocked out. . . ." Beale surely regretted that he had not had a chance to surprise the Mojave camp.[54]

From Fort Tejon, Beale wrote Secretary Floyd and praised the camels. He apologized for failing to mention them in recent reports simply because they had ceased to be novelties. Every day, he employed the camels in the "severest toil," and his "admiration for them so far from diminishing increases every day." Many persons had feared the camels would not breed well in captivity, but this belief had proved unfounded. Several calves were born and were alive in full, vigorous health. Beale sincerely hoped that Congress would act favorably on the importation of "this useful animal." No one who had used them would trade camels for three times their number in horses or mules.[55]

While most California newspapers praised Beale's success with the road expedition, a reporter with Hoffman's expedition spoke differently. Rasey Biven, writing for the *Alta*, stated that Beale's Crossing on the Colorado River was "no crossing at all" for part of the year. When the Colorado rose in the late spring and early summer, the channel widened, creating sloughs and bayous on the banks which were almost impassable. Biven also said the Beale route was totally impractical due to the mountainous nature of the countryside between the Colorado River and the Rio Grande. Biven then addressed some remarks at Beale. Discoverers of new roads while in the government's employ, he said, "should be made to re-cross them with an immigrant train and take along their families." Such discoverers "would stand a good chance of being shot by the immigrants." The Mojave trail in California was no better, according to the reporter. It crossed the "worst desert to be found between the Pacific and the Rio Grande." Biven warned potential emigrants in the Mississippi Valley that the Beale Road was a "most worthless route."[56]

Los Angeles newspapers and the San Francisco *Herald* praised the new road. The *Herald* relied heavily upon the word of Samuel Bishop who described the route as "an excellent road throughout its whole length, with abundant supplies of wood, water, and grass. . . ." In Los Angeles, both the *Star* and the *Southern Vineyard* supported the new road. W. T. B. Sandford, prominent in Phineas Banning's transportation firm, checked the road for himself and found it good and hard, with water readily obtainable, even in summer.[57]

The *Alta California* continued to dissent, perhaps realizing that a southern road would take trade away from the northern part of the state. A correspondent from Fort Mojave, perhaps Biven, stated that Beale's party at San Francisco Mountain had difficulty with water and had to rely on a water tank wagon while working on a section of the road. From a Mr. Smith of the Overland Mail, the writer learned that "there is in fact, no road from here to Santa Fe." The writer urged the *Alta* to "show up the humbuggery of Mr. Beale." On June 11, the *Alta* advised all emigrants to avoid the Beale road. West of the Rio Grande, it was very rough. The Colorado River crossing was near impossible. In sum, the road was "almost impassable for a large emigrant train," and the route was also dangerous. Even the Tubac *Weekly Arizonian* urged travelers to avoid the hardships of the Beale Road and follow the southern overland route, where water and grass were supposedly abundant.[58]

Beale departed for the Colorado River in mid-June of 1859. At Fort Mojave, according to the *Alta's* correspondent, Beale "blew, of course, very much while here, about his road." Beale continued to work on the road: he changed its course to avoid difficult spots, marked new springs, and improved rough places. By July 29, Beale had arrived in Albuquerque and took time to write his wife and children. "I do not know what the people in the East think of what we have done but I know we have done good service," he stated. On August 24, Beale reached Kansas City, Missouri. Here the local *Journal of Commerce* praised his accomplishments. Beale had made the fastest crossing of the southwestern part of the continent on record for wagon travel and had proved "beyond question" that the thirty-fifth parallel route was the best line yet explored for either a railroad or a wagon road. When Beale's achievements were added to those of his other trips, one could not doubt that "he has done more of the practical character to develop and open up the overland travel of the continent, than any other man who had preceded him." Beale reached Chester in September and set to work on his report to Floyd.[59]

Shortly after he returned home, Beale learned of the death of his friend David C. Broderick, U.S. senator from California. Broderick died from a wound received in a duel with David S. Terry, a leader of California's Chivalry Democrats. Since early 1857, the California Democrats had been split between free-soil forces, led by Broderick and calling themselves Anti-Lecompton Democrats, and the pro-Southern Chivalry, led by Senator Gwin. Although a Southerner by birth, Beale had grown close to Broderick, who frequently visited Beale's homes in Chester and at the Tejon. John Hickman, an important Pennsylvania politician, later said that he had seen Beale and Broderick have many long interviews together and that "Broderick loved Beale." Sometime after the senator's death, Beale purchased a large oil portrait of his friend which hung in Beale's home for the rest of his life.[60]

Equally distressing to Beale was the rising criticism over his wagon road. In September the Los Angeles *Star* reversed its opinion on the Beale Road. The paper quoted the *Missouri Republican,* which stated that many wagon trains departing from Texas and Arkansas over Beale's Road had been forced to turn back with great losses—and then took the southern route through El Paso, Tucson, Yuma, to Los Angeles. According to many emigrants, "the 'Beale route' is worse than a humbug—it is a swindle."[61]

On December 15, 1859, Beale submitted his final report on his wagon road expedition to Secretary Floyd. In a cover letter, he expressed more concern over a railroad to California than with a wagon road. His frequent references to the steepness of the grades, thirty to fifty feet per mile, which would hardly be noticed by wagons, reflected his interest in the railroad. Beale and his civil engineer went so far as to estimate the cost of constructing a railroad with double track, running from Fort Smith to San Felipe, near Albuquerque. This estimate of $21,391,100 included grading the roadbed, masonry construction, track, engineering expenses, and equipment. Beale concluded: "It is the shortest, the best timbered, the best grassed, the best watered, and certainly, in point of grade, better than any other line between the two oceans. . . ." But a touch of pessimism permeated Beale's report, for he sensed that increasing sectional animosities had doomed the adoption of his route for the railroad.[62]

For two years, Edward Beale had been constantly at work in the Far Southwest, exploring new country and building a wagon road to California. At the same time, he had tested the practicality of employing camels in the arid reaches of the West and found the animals highly valuable. Despite his recommendations to the War Department, the camel experiment was abandoned. In time, it would be remembered as simply a strange idea, presided over by a quixotic man. But Beale's Road was a different story. Within a few years, the road became a major east-west commercial artery, and some twenty years later a great railroad was built along Beale's suggested route. In opening this highway Beale joined the small group of explorers who left an enduring mark on the American West during the nineteenth century.

Chapter 8

SURVEYOR GENERAL
OF CALIFORNIA

Some day the archives of our country will tell why Lincoln made
me Surveyor-General. It had nothing to do with rod or chain, but
much to do with the metes and bounds of the Union.
                                          —Edward F. Beale

Upon returning to the East, Beale pondered his achievements over the
past two and a half years. He knew that he had laid out what he regarded as the best transcontinental railroad route to the Pacific, but he
was equally aware that the nation's widening North-South political divi-
sions would block passage of a Pacific Railroad Bill. More pressing,
however, was Beale's present unemployment, so he turned his attention
to securing yet another government position.

The development of a Panamanian crossing momentarily attracted
his interest. The United States recently had secured a conditional contract from Colombia to survey a passage from Chiriqui Grande on the
Caribbean through Panama to Golfito on the Pacific. Commercial men
already were talking of the advantages of an interoceanic canal, and Beale
jumped at the opportunity to head the reconnaissance. He tendered his
services to the Navy Department, and on December 10, 1859, Navy
Secretary Isaac Toucey agreed to appoint Beale to head the expedition
provided he would demand no compensation for his work. These terms
were unsuitable.[1]

Although the isthmian reconnaissance was aborted, Beale could be
content with his California interests. The Tejon rancho prospered. Ac-

cording to the 1860 census, his partner, Samuel Bishop, listed a personal wealth of $119,950, and his real estate at $40,000. Moreover, Beale's title to La Liebre Rancho, owned previously by Jose Maria Flores, had been confirmed by a federal district court. Some years before, Beale had secured Flores's property rights for only $1,500. Additionally, Beale also sold a lot in San Francisco at this time, realizing a nice profit. He and Bishop also sold the mining, timber, and water rights to 1,280 acres on the Liebre property.[2]

In the past Beale had owed his business success in large measure to his political friendships and his official appointments. Friends had supported him for office, and he always had access to powerful associates. But now, the Democratic Party was on the verge of splitting into north and south wings. Beale's conscience and personal interests forced him to seek the counsel of certain friends, such as prominent Pennsylvanians John W. Forney and John Hickman, as to the political winds. The editor of the Philadelphia *Press*, Forney, like Beale, had been a longtime backer of James Buchanan but broke with him over the disastrous Kansas policy and joined Stephen Douglas, David C. Broderick, and others in attacking the president. By 1860, Forney was elected to the House of Representatives where he sat as clerk, a powerful post. Hickman, also a congressman, was a friend of Mary Beale's family. In April of 1860, Hickman forsook the Democratic Party and committed himself to the Republicans.

Grudgingly, Beale also decided to renounce the Democrats and became a reluctant Republican. In April he attended a Democratic caucus in Washington and was outspoken about his feelings. Forney reported to California Senator Milton S. Latham that "Ned Beale, a Southern man, was the most bitter Republican present at the meeting." Beale stated to his friends that he had not swung to the Republican Party from affection, but that force and ill treatment had driven him there. Many important Democrats shared Beale's views and felt forced to embrace the new party because of the incompetency of the Democracy's leadership. Beale felt personally slighted as well. In 1857 Buchanan had refused to reappoint him to the position of California Indian superintendent and more recently had not supported his name for the Panama survey.[3]

In the charged political atmosphere, politics even crept into the sanctuary of worship. Beale and his family regularly attended services at St. John's Episcopal Church in Washington, with its congregation noted for being aristocratic and Southern. One Sunday, the rector of St. John's who reflected the sympathies of a majority of his parishioners, urged the congregation to pray for the success of the Southern cause. Beale, newly converted to Republicanism, became furious at the minister's action, and rose from his pew. Marching out of the service at the head of his family, Beale publicly vowed that "he would never go to church again."[4]

In the early summer of 1860, Beale once again headed for California to look after his business interests. Traveling with Fred Kerlin, a frequent companion, he reached Westport, Missouri in mid-July and started down the Santa Fe Trail. In Santa Fe, Beale heard about recent Navajo hostilities, and later, at Fort Defiance, learned that the Navajos had attacked that post the previous April 30. Beale received a somewhat garbled version of the incident and understood that the Navajos had overrun the soldiers and controlled the post for six hours. In reality, the fierce warriors only came close to capturing the sutler's store and were rebuffed after a two-hour battle. Leaving Defiance, Beale hit the Beale Road, traveling with fourteen men, two wagons, and forty animals. Along much of the route, the party saw signs of hostile Indians. On September 15, Beale reached Fort Mojave on the Colorado River. He pronounced the wagon road to California in excellent condition but warned travelers that the Indian bands along the route still posed a grave menace. After crossing the Colorado River, where they lost three animals in the swift current, Beale's group continued across the hot sands of the Mojave Desert, then moved hurriedly toward the Tejon Ranch.[5]

From Samuel Bishop, Beale learned that the ranch was prospering. Their sheep and cattle operations were showing a profit, and they enjoyed the distinction of being listed as the fifth largest landowners in Los Angeles County, with an estimated wealth of $56,000. Already they had surpassed the old ranching enterprises of the Pico Brothers—Pio and Andres.[6]

During the fall of 1860, Beale became apprehensive about his future in California. Like the nation, California was a divided state with a strong Southern element in the southern counties. In the November election, Lincoln managed to win the state, but Democrat John C. Breckinridge swept Los Angeles County by a two-to-one margin. As a Republican, Beale became pessimistic about remaining in the state and contemplated the sale of his ranch. By December, he had received an offer of $70,000 for the Tejon, with $10,000 in cash and the remainder to be paid in five years.[7] Meanwhile, the political friends of Mary Beale's family promised to lobby for a federal position for Beale in California. While awaiting Lincoln's inauguration, Beale decided against the sale of the ranch, probably because he wanted full payment in cash.[8]

Other business matters also occupied Beale's attention during these months. He swapped several pieces of San Francisco real estate with his brother-in-law Harry Edwards and put in a bid to acquire the government sawmill at Fort Tejon. The War Department planned to close the post, believing that the fort served no useful purpose. Lieutenant

Colonel Thomas Swords, deputy quartermaster general, promised Beale that he would make every effort to obtain the Tejon sawmill for him. The government owed Beale a debt for his "gallantry and exertions at and after the battle of San Pasqual a thousand times more than it will ever be in the power of the Quartermaster Department to repay," Swords said.[9]

Although Beale coveted the sawmill, he did not wish to see the fort abandoned. In February, he joined Bishop, Kerlin, and eighty-five other petitioners in a protest to Brigadier General Albert S. Johnston, commanding the Pacific Department. The petitioners were against dismantling the fort and predicted that without its protection, settlers would be "left to the mercy of the ruthless savages, and a beautiful district about to be reclaimed by civilization again abandoned to its original condition." Beale and Bishop probably would lose more than anyone else as settlers and the fort directly benefited their ranching operation. Influenced by the public outcry, the army postponed for an indefinite time the abandonment of the fort.[10]

On January 28, 1861, the pony express brought ominous news to San Francisco. Under the heading, "The Beginnings of Civil War," the *Bulletin* stated that a South Carolinian battery had fired upon the *Star of the West*, a merchantman carrying reinforcements to Fort Sumter. Indeed, war was close at hand. On March 4, a weary James Buchanan turned over the presidency to Abraham Lincoln. Many western politicians worried about the new president's appointments. Edward Baker, an old friend of Lincoln's from Illinois days, had been elected senator from Oregon, and it was rumored that Baker would control federal patronage on the West Coast, including California.[11]

California's most lucrative political appointment was collector of the port of San Francisco. This position offered the greatest number of local patronage jobs, and the collector earned substantial fees, with the possibility of supplements from unofficial sources. Beale may have desired the collectorship or the post of superintendent of the mint, but the competition was too keen. R. J. Stevens, Baker's son-in-law, seemed certain to receive one of the top spots. Under these circumstances, Beale instructed his Pennsylvania backers, Forney and Hickman, to promote him for surveyor general. He called the slot the "handsomest in the state," perhaps recognizing the office's potential for a man interested in land.[12]

On March 13, Abraham Lincoln received a letter from John Hickman which strongly urged the candidacy of Beale as surveyor general of California. Hickman recited Beale's heroic contributions during the Mexican War, his daring "Ride Across Mexico," and his gallant service as government dispatch bearer. He also praised Beale's conduct as superintendent of wagon roads and added that his candidate had "never failed in any enterprise he has undertaken, where severe courage, energy and persevering exertion could accomplish his purpose." The president should weigh the fact heavily, counseled Hickman, that Beale was descended from a Southern family, but had become an early advocate of Republican principles. Beale could help keep the Anti-Lecompton Democrats (pro-Union) loyal. The late Senator Broderick, the martyred hero of antislavery groups in California, had been a close, trusted friend of Beale, and always stopped to visit with Beale and his family, whether in California, Pennsylvania, or Washington. "I have been at too many interviews between these long tried friends to be ignorant of their relations," he added, and declared that it was "a high eulogium to say that Broderick loved Beale." Hickman concluded by praising Beale's fine education and sound judgment. His appointment would prove the "sound discretion of the appointing power."[13]

Others wrote letters in Beale's behalf. Congressman Francis P. Blair, Jr. of Missouri, a state of critical importance to the Union, wrote Interior Secretary Caleb B. Smith, urging Beale's appointment. He recited a litany of Beale's achievements and dubbed him the "most successful pioneer in California." Blair also noted Beale's close friendship with David C. Broderick and said that the interest of both the party and the country would be served by his appointment. J. F. Potter of Wisconsin also backed Beale in a letter to Secretary Smith and labeled him a "devoted self-sacrificing friend." Despite these appeals, the appointment remained unfilled.[14]

John W. Forney, editor and congressman, also backed Beale. Forney wrote Lincoln that both Congressman Francis Blair and Secretary of War Simon Cameron also favored Beale. As Beale had never met Cameron, the secretary's support doubtless came through a tie with the Edwards family. Forney made an eloquent plea. He recounted Beale's years of government service and his opposition to Buchanan's policies, adding that he had told the president his faults to his face. Forney melodramatically dragged in David Broderick, whose Lecomptom Democrats held the key to power in California. If Beale had been with Broderick at the fatal encounter with Judge Terry, Broderick would still be alive and sitting in the United States Senate. If the martyred Broderick could now appear, the one request he would make of Lincoln, Forney stated, would be to appoint Edward F. Beale as surveyor general of California. Beale was a rare breed—a Southerner, who advocated the Republican Party's doctrines. Many Southerners liked and respected Beale. But men such as William Gwin, who hoped to take California out of the Union, were his persistent enemies. Beale had always opposed them.[15]

Lincoln was persuaded. Beale seemed the best political appointment that could be made. On April 29, the news of Beale's selection reached San Francisco, carried by pony express. In the *Bulletin*, Simonton stated that Beale's appointment would deepen the ill feeling among the California politicians. Lincoln had bestowed yet another office on a former Democrat.[16]

Beale was at the Tejon ranch when he learned of his appointment. Delighted, he quickly went to Los Angeles, where he found a letter from his wife stating that she would join him in California if he became federal surveyor general. Beale caught the steamer *Senator* at San Pedro and sailed up the coast to San Francisco, arriving in the city at noon on May 11. Discovering that Mary Beale had not reached the city, he wrote her a hasty letter, which told of his elation with the new appointment. On June 1, the local *Alta California* ran an article on the transfer of power to the incoming bureaucrats under the heading: "The faithful to Abraham receive their reward to-day." Beale was duly listed as surveyor general.[17]

Dramatic events had taken place in the eastern United States during the spring of 1861. The Confederate States of America had been formed and an attack made on Fort Sumter. On April 14 the fort fell, and Lincoln called for 75,000 militia volunteers. War threatened to engulf the nation. Departments such as the General Land Office, not essential to the war effort, soon found their budgets slashed by Congress as the nation prepared to finance the swollen operations of the War Department. One of the first letters that Surveyor General Beale received from James M. Edmunds, commissioner of the General Land Office, carried explicit orders to reduce expenses in his district. Public land surveys would have to be decisively curtailed, as Congress had granted the Land Office only a small appropriation for the next fiscal year.[18]

Beale possessed a knack for taking a routine job and making it important and visible. Upon becoming surveyor general, he heard rumors that Mexican Californians might lean toward the Confederacy and thus present a large block of dissidents in the Far West. In several places, the Bear Flag had been briefly raised after the fall of Fort Sumter. On June 3, Beale addressed a letter to Andres Pico, the Mexican hero of San Pasqual and a leading Breckinridge Democrat. He bluntly asked him whether he favored "maintaining the Federal Government of the United States at all hazards, or if you favor, under any circumstances a Pacific Republic, and the secession of this state." Beale declared that a strong movement for rebellion existed in the southern portion of the state, which could lead to the "utter ruin of every interest in that part of California, and to scenes of violence and bloodshed dreadful to contemplate."

Pico responded with a strong endorsement for the federal union. Before the attack on Fort Sumter, Pico admitted, he had favored Breckinridge's party, but now one must choose sides. Pico declared himself "unconditionally and at all hazards" for the Constitution of the Union. He cheerfully offered the federal government his services as a soldier and his financial support. His brother Pio Pico echoed the same sentiments. Several California newspapers published the Beale-Pico correspondence, which helped to influence the Californio attitude toward the war.[19]

As major battles loomed in the East between Union and Confederate armies, Beale requested a military command. On July 10, he wrote to Lincoln and requested a commission. Under normal circumstances, he stated, the federal office he enjoyed would leave nothing more to desire, but he felt that he owed "more in this hour of trial than mere performance of duty in a position of ease and quiet." Beale wanted "to offer [his] life for the flag." A number of newspapers, including Forney's Philadelphia *Press,* later reproduced Beale's patriotic letter to Lincoln. Hickman was alarmed and on August 24 wrote to Mrs. Beale, suggesting that her brother Harry Edwards should write to the president to refuse Beale's request. Beale's friends and family, however, had no need to fear. On July 15, the United States Senate had confirmed Beale's nomination, and two days later he was commissioned as surveyor general of California.[20]

Five days after writing to Lincoln, Beale greeted Mary and his four children, who arrived at San Francisco aboard the steamer *Golden Gate.* Mrs. Beale also brought her favorite carriage team—Ned and Barney. Beale doubtless told her of his recent letter to Lincoln offering his services as a soldier. The family reunion was not a happy occasion, as a tragedy struck the Beale family on August 11 with the death of Samuel Edwards Beale, the youngest son, two years old. The Beales deeply mourned their loss.[21]

Beale found his position as surveyor general to be quite challenging. Learning that Congress had slashed the budget for office expenses, Beale apprised Commissioner Edmunds on August 26 that even with reduced rent, there would be a deficit. His expenses—messenger salary, postage, stationery, coal, and sundries—would run at least $1,750 over the $3,000 appropriation.

On September 15, 1861, Beale mailed his first annual report as surveyor general to Washington. It went overland in a tin mailing case by stagecoach. As the report indicated, most of the work in his office was routine—instructions to deputy field surveyors, drawing maps of public surveys and private land claims, continual updating of surveying work connected with the land sale, examination of surveyors' field notes, and keeping the books and accounts of the office. Beale's staff consisted of ten men. Included were Fred E. Kerlin, his friend and companion for over a decade, and Francis Bret Harte, an aspiring author and poet whom Beale may have employed as a favor to Mrs. John C. Fremont. Edward Conway served as chief clerk.[22]

Beale stated in his report that within a year the federal courts would approve and order surveys for a number of Mexican land grants. These munificent gifts of land, an unsettled problem since 1848, played a key role in the progress of the public surveys, for they covered some of the state's best land. Public lands surrounding the grants could not be surveyed and sold by the government until the grants themselves had been confirmed and their boundaries fixed. Consequently, thousands of acres of excellent land, which could be readily sold by the General Land Office, had never been surveyed. Beale asked for an appropriation of $50,000 for surveying private land claims, and $150,000 for public land surveys. He noted that his predecessors had concentrated their surveys on desert lands, worthless for agricultural purposes, due to the ease of working on flat terrain. The government paid deputy surveyors by the mile, and desert areas took less work and required fewer sightings and measurements. Unfortunately, settlers could not be attracted to buy those wastelands.

Beale believed that the land between the Sacramento River Valley and the Pacific Ocean presented a rich region for homesteads. Also, the northeastern portion of the state appeared ready for survey and sale. Due to long-standing importance of mining to the state, Beale urged that the General Land Office consider extending township lines over mineral districts. Mining development required a large capital investment, and Beale felt that mine owners deserved permanent title to their properties. Beale knew a great deal about mining expenses, for he had invested in such ventures. Although a civil war had erupted, he nevertheless hoped that Congress would appropriate $200,000 for surveying in California.[23]

Always a man of diverse interests, Beale did not permit his official duties to absorb all his energy. Military affairs, for instance, also concerned him. In early September, Brigadier General Edwin V. Sumner, commanding the Pacific Department, asked his advice on the best route across Mexico for an attack against Confederate Texas. Beale replied that the best highway ran from San Blas eastward, via Tepic, Guadalajara, and Queretaro. The road out of Mazatlan was impassable for wagons. On a more northern route Guaymas to El Paso, water was almost nonexistent, and once an army reached El Paso, commanders would have to contend with a long supply train, which would be an easy prey for hostile Indians.

Beale believed that an invasion of Texas from a Mexican port on the Gulf of Mexico, such as Vera Cruz, might be better advised. Here, Union naval power, that is, steamers, could be used effectively. From his intimate knowledge of the Far Southwest, Beale asserted "that a large force—say 5,000 men—cannot march from here (California) by the Gila on Texas and keep up its supplies. . . ." Beale's advice impressed Sumner, who wrote the adjutant general in Washington and urged a serious reconsideration of a projected overland attack against Texas. An invasion by sea seemed more plausible.[24]

Beale presided over a large domain. A large well-lighted room housed Land Commission records. Attorneys constantly worked here preparing arguments for land cases. One clerk, who handed the legal packages to the lawyers, always was in attendance; no papers were permitted to leave the office, and only the surveyor general's staff was allowed access to records storage areas. Another room contained instruments and large tables for the draftsmen, with a small adjoining room for all maps. The next room housed the clerks, as well as field notes and miscellaneous papers connected with the government surveys. Persons making inquiries on official business continually used the room. The fifth room contained fireproof safes which held all original papers. Finally there was Beale's office, with a large desk surrounded by the law library and other books of the surveyor general.[25]

By early 1862, the General Land Office in Washington had learned that a number of Southern sympathizers had obtained government land. Commissioner Edmunds sent a general circular to western surveyor generals and land office agents on the subject and ordered that all purchasers of government land must take an oath of allegiance to the United States government. The resources of the nation "cannot be squandered on those individuals who aid and abet treason," stated Edmunds. Shortly after receiving this circular, Beale again heard from Washington. In a letter of February 10, Edmunds directed that deputy surveyors in their field notes report on (1) precious minerals and ores; (2) deposits of copper, lead, iron, and tin; (3) coal; (4) salt; (5) condition of soil; (6) timber; and (7) improvements on the land. Edmunds also urged Beale to try to unsort the conflicting land claims in California. He pointed out that in some instances military bounty land locations had been made on private land grants, and California state land selections also on occasion fell on private property. Exchanges would have to be effected. Confirmed Mexican land grants held priority by law.[26]

Despite the press of official duties, Beale managed to visit his ranch from time to time, and to keep informed of developments in southern California. His brother-in-law, Harry Edwards, for instance, attempted to gain the post of U.S. district attorney at Los Angeles, but Hickman's influence could not swing the appointment. Edwards earlier had served for several months as captain of the Union Blues of Chester, Pennsylvania, who had gallantly marched off to battle in May of 1861. He then returned to California, where he held several surveying contracts provided by his generous relative in San Francisco.[27]

Los Angeles and southern California continued to be disturbed by disunion sentiment, spearheaded by the Los Angeles *Star*. In the fall election of 1861, the Union Party had suffered a thorough defeat. The Los Angeles *Southern News*, a Union paper in spite of its title, brooded: "Secession and disunion have carried the day, and years of repentance cannot wash out the stain. . . ." At the Tejon, voting frauds had occurred, according to the *News*. In the important governor's race, Leland Stanford had supposedly received a large majority of the ballots cast at Tejon, but someone destroyed the ballots because the polls opened at the wrong hour. The leading politician there was a Samuel Bishop, Beale's partner, who William H. Brewer, a scientist, labeled a "rank Secessionist." Furthermore, the Los Angeles correspondent of the San Francisco *Alta California* stated that every resident of Los Angeles was suspected of treason, and "a lurking suspicion of a man's loyalty outweighs all his protestations or acts of fealty." Beale faced an uncomfortable course during these months. He was the Republican surveyor general but his property was located in a hostile section. Fortunately, Bishop was more in touch with the local sentiments.[28]

After holding the office of surveyor general for some seven months, Beale found that he could not reduce office expenses. In January of 1862, he wrote Commissioner Edmunds that a deficiency of $1,750 would definitely occur and reminded him that he had warned of the problem four months earlier. Beale boldly threatened to shut down the Surveyor General's Office, as he did not intend to assume personal liability for government expenses. Edmunds answered in kind and criticized Beale's expensive, needless purchases of office furniture and carpeting. In anger, Beale responded with an eleven-page letter, in which he defended his handling of funds, and declared that he had always practiced "rigid economy." Writing paper was always bought by the single ream or less, tracing cloth by the single bolt, and ink by the individual bottle. With indignation, he informed Commissioner Edmunds that he invited a thorough investigation of his accounts.[29]

For Fred Kerlin, who worked as chief clerk of the Indian Superintendency from 1852 to 1854, it must have occurred that Beale's career was following a familiar pattern. Once again, Beale appeared to be traveling toward a collision with his Washington superior.

Chapter 9

"MONARCH OF ALL HE HAS SURVEYED"

Lincoln: "Senator, what sort of fellow is this man Beale of California?"

Senator: " 'A pretty good fellow, Mr. President, was the ready response. 'Why?' "

Lincoln: "Well I appointed him Surveyor-General out there, and I understand he is monarch of all he has surveyed."
—Washington, January, 1864

In early April, Beale worried about Edmunds's criticisms and sought to justify his purchases to the commissioner. On April 3, he explained two recent purchases. He had bought two rolls of tracing paper, rather than one, because the rolls were the last supply in the San Francisco market, and no others were due to arrive from the East. He also had purchased a stove to heat the archives room. The stove was expensive, Beale admitted, but the archives required the safest model available. In his letters of explanation, he continued to complain about the Treasury Department's delay in paying bills, telling Edmunds that the local post office had threatened to discontinue service if the government did not pay in advance. [1]

In June, Beale received his annual instructions and budget from Washington. Congress had approved a fiscal appropriation for the California surveyor general, which allowed $10,000 for surveying, far below the amount Beale had requested. An additional $4,000 was tagged for office expenses—rent, fuel, books, and stationery. Salaries totaled $15,000, which included Beale's stipend of $4,500. Of the $10,000 designated for surveying, Beale was to focus first on confirmed private land claims (Beale's suggestion), and to subdivide only such townships as were required. Commissioner Edmunds deemed the appropriation "quite sufficient in view of the limited extent of fieldwork authorized for the next fiscal year." Exasperated by Beale's inability to cut expenses, he ordered him to reduce the number of clerks in his office.

About the same time that he got his annual instructions, Beale learned that the Surveyor General's Office in Nevada had been closed and that district added to California. For Nevada's surveys, Beale obtained an additional $5,000. All work there would be in districts where township lines had been run and therefore would simply be subdivision work. Furthermore, Beale would authorize surveys only on land valuable for timber, agricultural purposes, or actual settlement. Deputy surveyors engaged in fieldwork would be paid the following rate: $20 per mile for base, meridian and standard parallel line; $12 per mile for township and section lines. These rates recently had been lowered in Oregon and probably would drop in California and Nevada as well.[2]

Edmunds also commented on procedures for letting contracts. Beale had questioned a recent law that stipulated that contracts go to the lowest bidder, saying it would curtail his freedom to select the best people. His brother-in-law, Harry Edwards, for instance, occasionally was given lucrative surveying contracts. Attorney General Edward Bates ruled that a surveying contract fell outside the scope of the "lowest bidder law." Surveying demanded more than simple fidelity and integrity; it required a certain kind of skill and knowledge. In other words, Beale retained a wide latitude in passing out the highly desirable contracts.[3]

By reducing the General Land Office budget, the federal government did not intend to halt the sale of public land or prevent settlers on public land from securing titles. California Senator Milton S. Latham backed a bill that permitted settlers on unsurveyed public lands to obtain patents by paying for the expenses of a government survey. This presumably was for the benefit of the settler, but in actual practice, the small farmer might be forced to wait years if his farm was situated at a great distance from the nearest established lines. On June 2, 1862, when the bill became law, Commissioner Edmunds also said that the $10,000 originally in Beale's budget for surveying private land grant claims would be applied only to public lands. As in the case of settlers, holders of Mexican grants would be required to pay for the official surveys in order to obtain patent.[4]

Edmunds placed strict controls on Beale's ability to bind the government to a surveying contract. Before a contract was considered final, the document would be forwarded to Washington for review and approval. Only after the General Land Office had approved the survey would Beale be permitted to authorize the work. Accompanying the contract, the surveyor general must forward a statement which explained the necessity for the survey. Clearly unhappy with Beale's deficiency, Edmunds informed Beale on June 9 that he had asked Congress for a deficiency appropriation to cover Beale's excessive expenditures. Senator Latham of California played a key role in securing additional funds.[5]

During June, 1862, Beale found a new location for his office, as Adolph Sutro had grown tired of delayed payments. The Customs House remained unavailable; Collector Ira Rankin could find only one room. Finally, with luck, Beale found quarters in a building opposite the post office and Customs House, saving $600 per year in rent. Once again, the surveyor general's office temporarily closed its doors to move to another location. Beale made an arrangement with the new proprietor, Mr. Lent, who thought that his agreement called for payments in gold. Lent expressed displeasure when Beale later handed him legal tender notes.[6]

As surveyor general of California, Beale was required to deal with a problem that was shared by several other western states—swamp and overflowed lands. By a congressional act of September 28, 1850, the federal government donated to California all swamp or tule lands within its boundaries, hoping the land could be drained and reclaimed for agriculture. A survey of swamplands was made in the 1850s, but its result was disputed by the state. A wide difference of opinion existed between the state and national government over the amount of swamp and overflowed land in California. The land was located chiefly along the San Joaquin and Sacramento rivers, but marshlands also existed along the shores of San Francisco, San Pablo, and Suisun Bays. The federal government estimated some 700,000 acres were involved, while the state surveyor general generously believed the total was over four million acres.

Colonel Thomas Baker, a state senator with pro-Southern views, became especially interested in this question. Baker recently had invested in a canal project designed to reclaim a section in the Tulare Lake-Kern Lake region (near present-day Bakersfield) and felt the federal survey had grossly underestimated the amount of tule lands there. The federal government seemed to acknowledge that a mistake might have occurred by setting up a procedure for a claimant of undesignated swampland.

Baker indicated to Beale in mid-May of 1862 that the procedure for acquiring the swampland was almost impossible to fulfill. The federal government required him to secure an affidavit from the deputy surveyor who made the original survey, stating that the lands were indeed swampland. This was a peculiar requirement, for it demanded that the surveyor admit that he had made an error on the initial survey. Baker stood to lose or gain a vast amount of real estate, and he asked Beale for his assistance. An error could easily occur, Baker pointed out, because land which appeared solid in the autumn might be overflowed in the spring. Beale promised to present the question to Commissioner Edmunds, but with the tight budget, he felt that an early adjustment would be unlikely.[7]

Beale wrote to A. M. Winn, president of the state Swamp Land Commission, whose office was in Sacramento, to clarify and explain the federal government's position in the matter. Beale saw the General Land Office in Washington as the major stumbling block preventing the transfer of land to California, a transfer held in abeyance for twelve years. Commissioner Edmunds insisted "upon the Swamp character of the land being proved, as of the date of the Act of Congress, viz 28th September 1850." Beale sympathized with the state's problem of proving swampland claims in regions that were uninhabited at that time. In fact, he declared that on the basis of his long residence in the state it would be impossible for his state to meet the requirement and urged that "a more enlarged construction be placed upon the terms of this Act." Beale suggested that the secretary of the interior perhaps could view with favor those claims backed by documentary support.

Two weeks later, on May 26, Beale sent Winn a plan under which California could receive federal swamplands. First, the state should draw up a list of swamp claims. Where claims were made on tracts regarded as farmland, detailed plat maps should be provided. The plats should indicate the boundaries of the swampland for future checking by the United States Surveyor General's Office. Second, the state should obtain the affidavit of the deputy surveyor who made the township survey (the point to which Baker had objected). If that was impossible, the state's agent should explain in an affidavit the absence of the former. Third, affidavits from the assistant deputy surveyor, or no less than two respectable witnesses must be procured. Once the state complied with these stipulations, Beale would feel obliged to direct his office to examine the questionable property, and then report the matter to Washington.[8]

Legal difficulties over California swampland continued for many years. The state government sold land which the United States had claimed as swampland and therefore had not been donated to California. Altogether, titles covering roughly 50,000 acres were uncertain. Despite his promise to Thomas Baker, Beale personally held little interest in tule land, spending most of his time with mineral claims and Mexican grants. Baker's letter may have sparked a small interest, however, for shortly thereafter Beale purchased some eighty acres of tule land on Steamboat Slough in

Santa Clara County and also bought two acres of dry land from Abel Stearns, located near the Mission Dolores.[9]

Notwithstanding the tight Civil War budget, Beale hoped to expand his operations in the coming fiscal year. In early August, Beale paid Wells-Fargo seventy-five dollars for carrying the Nevada surveyor general's records over the Sierra Nevada to San Francisco, and the Carson City office was closed. On the ninth, he submitted his annual budget request to Washington. He asked for an extraordinary $150,000 for public surveying in California, and $100,000 for Nevada. He also suggested hefty increases in funds for office expenses. Beale forwarded with his report several contracts to Edmunds for approval of payment. Two were claims by Beale's brother-in-law Harry Edwards for surveying the Channel Islands of Santa Cruz and Santa Rosa, while a third was from George H. Thompson for surveying Beale's Rancho La Liebre.[10]

When Edmunds learned that Beale had charged the $1,028 survey of La Liebre to the government, he railed at Beale's audacity. Writing on October 8, he declared that all claims must be paid by the owners of the property surveyed. Beale had been informed of this fact in early June. The "foregoing illegality"—the Thompson survey of La Liebre—was compounded by the fact that the Land Office records indicated that the ranch had never been confirmed by the district court. Other surveys that Beale had authorized fell within the same category and included the surveys of Ranchos Castac and El Tejon. When the Edwards survey of the Channel Islands was added to the surveys of the three ranchos, the sum exhausted the entire surveying appropriation for the fiscal year—$10,000. Meanwhile, Beale fortuitously cancelled Edwards's $5,000 claim.[11]

On November 11, Beale responded to Commissioner Edmunds's angry letter about the La Liebre survey. He stated that prior to the letter of June 7, all of Edmunds's communications had directed that the surveying funds should be applied to private grants. "It appeared to be the express wish of the department to have the surveys of private land claims executed in preference to those of public lands," Beale wrote. With regard to the specific case of La Liebre, he enclosed the court's decision in *Jose Maria Flores* v. *the United States*, filed with the California Surveyor General's Office on March 10, 1862. Beale had issued instructions on April 17 to E. Hadly for the La Liebre survey, but Hadly had only completed part of the work, leaving abruptly for a gold strike on the Colorado River. On June 15, Beale issued surveying instructions to George H. Thompson, who proceeded to the ranch and began to run his lines. While Thompson was in the field, Beale received the June 7 letter. A clerk in his office placed the wrong date (July instead of June) on Thompson's instructions, Beale innocently stated. The same individual also placed the wrong months on the surveying contracts for Ranchos Castac and El Tejon. In all the correspondence, Beale never acknowledged his ownership of La Liebre.[12]

Edmunds received Beale's response and in early December ordered that Deputy Surveyor Thompson be paid. The patents to the ranchos would be withheld from the claimants, however, until they liquidated the expenses of the survey. About the same time, he reviewed Beale's requested appropriation for California and Nevada ($150,000 and $100,000, respectively) and reduced them to $25,000 ($15,000 for California and $10,000 for Nevada). The requested amount was small, but most of the surveying work had been curtailed. During the fiscal year ending June 30, 1862, some 390,000 acres of private land claims had been surveyed in California, in addition to 106,000 acres of public land. The total acreage surveyed in California since American acquisition totalled approximately nineteen million acres.[13]

Beale was becoming one of the largest property owners in California. In addition to his ownership of La Liebre Ranch, he acquired key springs and watercourses at strategic points adjoining the Liebre grant. In so doing, he prevented competition and doubled his ranch size without a big expense. In December of 1862, he acquired Willow Springs in the Antelope Valley some thirty miles east of Liebre headquarters, and the best spring in the area. East of Willow Springs stretched the desolate Mojave Desert which effectively secured the eastern boundary of his sprawling property. Samuel A. Bishop, Beale's partner, owned the nearby Rancho Castac, a Mexican land grant close to Fort Tejon, and Beale may have held an interest in Bishop's ranch as well as in the El Tejon grant, owned by Juan Temple. The Tejon grant (Beale called his ranch Tejon or Liebre during these years) was adjacent to Castac and several miles north of the Liebre. As surveyor general, Beale had ordered all of these properties surveyed at government expense, an indication of his interest in their value and potential.[14]

A correspondent for the San Francisco *Evening Bulletin* touring the country north of Los Angeles in 1862 commented on Beale's properties. He described the headquarters (presumably Liebre) as "a very extensive and handsome establishment, where everything has been planned and executed on a baronial scale. Here are enclosed and cultivated fields, with a spacious mansion, huge barns and every manner of outhouse that taste could suggest or convenience require." The visitor smelled an "odor of nationality" about the place, suggesting that in former times the property and its improvements had belonged to the federal government. Continuing north toward Visalia, the reporter occasionally asked about the ownership of the countryside. Invariably, the reply was the same—"owned by Lieut. Beale or his partners." An Irishman who had helped survey 49,000 acres for Beale told the reporter "he believed Beale had since bout out the United States *intirely* [sic]."[15]

Beale did not overlook any opportunity to improve the value of his property. He obtained a franchise to construct a turnpike over San Fernando Mountain, north of Los Angeles, to Fort Tejon, when the original holders found the project too expensive to complete after the heavy winter rains of 1861–62 washed out the road. San Fernando Hill posed the main problem: a very steep, impassable grade that required extensive cutting and grading. Beale hired a crew to make a road through the hill at Beale's Cut. Several months later, when he asked the Los Angeles Board of Supervisors for approval, the agency demanded that Beale further improve the road or forfeit his contract. On two previous occasions, first in 1854 and again in 1858, the steep grade had been lowered for stages, but it still proved all but impassable.[16]

In the fall of 1862, Beale became increasingly active in mining activities in southern California. In June, he had been one of the incorporators of the Soledad Gold, Silver, and Copper Mining Company, capitalized for $780,000; he and four others served as trustees. Located in the vicinity of Soledad Canyon, the mine was construed to have a rich potential but would require a substantial investment to develop the resources.

Then in the fall, Beale joined others investing in the silver mines which had been discovered in a mountain of white slate in the desert east of the Sierras. Tests of silver ore during the late summer yielded $1000 per ton and excited assayists declared the ore superior to the famed Washoe silver of the Comstock. Throughout the fall, miners had returned from the Slate Range with stories of its richness, marred by tales of ovenlike temperatures and paucity of water. In November, Beale and four others organized six separate mining companies to work the Slate Range District. They named the companies: the Albany Company, Cataraugus Company, Rochester Company, Philadelphia Company, New York Company, and the Slate Range Company, each capitalized at $315,000. Each partner controlled a total of 2,520 shares of stock, valued at $525,000 on paper, in the six companies. The Searles brothers, Dennis and John, well-known denizens of California's southeastern deserts, had discovered the Slate Range mines.[17]

Late in November of 1862, Beale expanded his interest in the Slate Range mines. In that parched wasteland, water was as important as high grade ore, so he had his associates organized the Slate Range Water Company, capitalized at $105,000. The company planned to draw water from Drum Centre, Jawbone, and Manhattan canyons and New Gulch, hoping to monopolize the local water supply. By early January of 1863, San Francisco newspapers including the respected *Mining and Scientific Press,* printed reports on the Slate Range District. The strike was called "fabulous" and "most astonishing." Mining companies in the Slate Range District even applied to the state legislature for a tram railroad charter to run from the mines to Kern River, where wood grew plentiful.[18]

Beale companies also began moving in heavy equipment. A crushing mill was hauled in from Los Angeles and placed in operation. Eight stamps, powered by a thirty horse engine, soon were crushing ore. The mill processed ore from Beale mines and contracted with other companies in the Slate Range. Meanwhile, John Searles, Beale's manager, started tunneling toward the discovery claim of the Morrow Mine, probably the richest mine of the Slate Range. Favorable reports were sent to the newspapers. Dennis Searles informed the San Francisco *Bulletin* that the Antrim Mine would probably yield $4,000 per ton. In late February, the *Bulletin* described new leads of "unsurpassed richness" which have been discovered in the Slate Range and "lay Washoe in the shade." Even coal had been found.[19]

Not all visitors to the Slate Range came away impressed. Levi Parsons called the mining district a virtual humbug. A Mr. Robinson returned from the mines and said that wood, water, and grass could not be found within a radius of forty-five miles. The available water was bad, and the recently vaunted coal refused to burn after several hours of testing. Shortly thereafter, an uprising of Owen's River Indians forced the temporary abandonment of the mines.[20]

Beale soon learned to his dismay that the Indian Department had decided to relocate the tribe at the old Tejon reserve, which was now his property. Without consulting him, the government removed eight hundred Indians to the reserve in July of 1863. Beale was furious when he learned of the action. In January, he had refused a request to place the Owen's River tribe at Tejon. With reports from the ranch manager W. W. Hudson that Indian cattle had destroyed his orchard and vineyard, Beale contacted J. P. Wentworth, California superintendent of Indian affairs, and demanded to know on what grounds Wentworth had placed the Indians on private property "protected by the sanctity" of a grant patent. Three days later, on July 27, Beale received an urgent telegram from the ranch. The local commander at Fort Tejon had threatened to put Hudson in irons if he did not leave the Beale ranch immediately. Beale quickly contacted General George Wright, an old friend who was commanding the Department of the Pacific, and asked for an explanation of this "most unwarrantable and unjustifiable act of oppression and military violence."

Indian Superintendent Wentworth attempted to calm Beale by asking if he would permit the Indian Department to rent the Tejon reserve so that the Owen's River Indians might remain there. Beale replied on July 29 that he was in the business of raising stock and that in a few years, he would require all of his property for that purpose. Because the Indian Department would be greatly inconvenienced by an immediate removal of the tribe, however, Beale offered to rent the property to the government at the rate of one dollar per acre per year.

Wentworth interpreted Beale's earlier protests as a ploy to obtain rental of the property. "If I rent at all it will only be as a great favor, and one only reluctantly granted," Beale retorted on August 11 and clarified his offer. Under no circumstances would he permit the Owen's River Indians to stay at Tejon. The previous summer the tribe had twice defeated troops sent against them and committed "atrocious murders and outrages." One hour's violence could destroy all of Beale's livestock. He demanded an immediate removal of the Owen's River tribe. His offer to rent applied only to the Indians who had resided at the Tejon for twelve years. He would prefer to have them removed as well, but he would consent to rent a portion of the ranch for them. Eventually, an agreement was reached. When the Owen's River tribe departed, Beale rented the 1,200-acre reserve at a fee of $1000 per year.[21]

During 1863, Beale devoted little time to his post as surveyor general. In March, he again complained to Commissioner Edmunds about the method of paying the departments' employees. Once again the employees had been forced to go for six months without pay, and their credit was nearly exhausted. As legal tender notes fluctuated from 50 to 70 percent of face value, Beale urged that payment be made in gold for the employee's sake. Beale's landlord also felt the pinch from depreciated greenbacks and demanded that the rent be paid in gold.

Edmunds felt little sympathy for Beale's problems. He wrote on April 22, 1863 that any government employee who felt that it was a hardship to take the government's paper "ought in justice both to themselves and the government to be relieved from such hardship by removal from office." Burdens resulting from the war were inevitable, Edmunds said. A month later, on May 18, Edmunds forwarded annual instructions to Beale for the coming fiscal year. Congress had appropriated $25,000 ($10,000 for Nevada and $15,000 for California). During the coming year Beale would survey land along the proposed transcontinental rail route in preparation for sale and settlement. No surveys should be made in the vicinity of the California-Nevada boundary, however, for the dividing line was still uncertain. Edmunds wanted to prevent overlapping surveys.[22]

On May 25, 1863, Beale sent Commissioner Edmunds a final certificate from the United States District Court of Southern California, which showed that the owners of Rancho El Tejon were entitled to a patent. Although the recorded owners were Ignacio del Valle and Juan Temple, several persons, including the Indian Office, referred to Beale as the owner. This probably resulted from an unrecorded lease of the property to Beale by Temple and del Valle. All of the improvements which Beale had made earlier as Indian superintendent, as well as the military improvements around Fort Tejon, were located on this sprawling land grant. Beale may even have been a partial owner of El Tejon. William Brewer, a scientist employed by the California geological survey, visited the Tejon in 1862 and mentioned that Beale had purchased the property that year as a Spanish claim, and that it had recently been confirmed as a valid grant. Brewer also described the Liebre Rancho, which Beale owned, as being an immense domain of eleven leagues, eighty square miles, controlling nearly all the water and forage for an area three times that size. In fact, Beale controlled all valuable land east of the Liebre and west of the Mojave Desert.[23]

In Washington, the General Land Office grew increasingly unhappy with Beale's deficit. He had sent in contracts which pushed the California budget to $13,444, which was $3,444 over the limit for the year. Acting Commissioner Joseph S. Wilson exceedingly regretted that Beale could not show a "more scrupulous regard" for public money. By incurring such a liability, Beale had directly violated a fixed policy, and the government would not assume any responsibility for unpaid accounts. The only way the government could pay the deputy surveyors would be with monies the ranch owners paid into the U.S. Treasury. Contracts for surveying included La Liebre (owned by Beale)—$1,028.18, El Tejon (owned by Ignacio del Valle and Juan Temple, and leased/rented to Beale)—$1,279.27, and the Castac (owned by Samuel A. Bishop, Beale's partner)—$389.63. Wilson asked whether Beale had consulted with the owners of the various ranches on the question of payment.

Beale replied on July 9, denying that he had exceeded his appropriation. According to his computation, his expenses stood well within the budget. The General Land Office had applied for a deficiency incurred by J. W. Manderville Beale's predecessor, against his accounts. A new bookkeeping operation began when the position changed hands. Beale felt that he should be charged only with those liabilities he had incurred and declared that he had shown the "most scrupulous regard in keeping within the limits authorized by my department." Beale failed to mention any correspondence between his office and the ranch owners, but in an earlier letter he noted that he had duly forwarded the patent of Rancho El Tejon to the parties entitled to receive it. That action seemed to puncture Edmunds's plan to require the rancho owners to pay for surveys before receiving their patents.[24]

As surveyor general of California, Beale occupied the perfect position for advancing his own interests in land matters. Even after a federal court made a final decision in favor of a grantee, a survey was required before the patent was issued. Until the patent's receipt, the grantee lacked title. With a limited staff and a paltry budget, the surveyor general found that he had far more work than he could ever perform. Therefore, some owners of Mexican grants waited ten to twenty years before obtaining patents. During Beale's tenure, however, grants held by Beale or his friends received a quick survey at government expense.

Beale's interest in land extended far beyond the Liebre Ranch. On July 25, he sent the General Land Office an innocuous note which stated that H. W. Carpentier was entitled to a draft of forty dollars for platting the Arroyo Seco grant. Located in Amador County in the Sierra foothills near Jackson, Arroyo Seco was yet another property which Beale held as a partial owner. This Mexican grant contained 48,857.52 acres, according to Beale's office, and covered potential mineral property as well as Jackson and Ione valleys claimed by farmers and a small community, Ione. Throughout the 1850s the ownership of the property was disputed in the courts, as Andres Pico, the grantee, battled a settlers' league determined to keep their holdings.

Eventually, Pico tired of the struggle. On December 10, 1861, he sold the Arroyo Seco to J. Mora Moss, H. W. Carpentier, Herman Wohler, and Edward F. Beale. Amid charges of bribery and perjury, Judge Ogden Hoffman, federal district judge for northern California, reversed an earlier decision and confirmed the grant's authenticity in the fall of 1862. The settlers' hopes faded abruptly. An appeal to the Supreme Court of the United States failed when the court refused to hear the case. In a last effort the Arroyo Seco settlers petitioned President Lincoln and Attorney General Bates. Several hundred citizens stated that they stood to lose their "little farms and poor homes, which have cost us long years of toil and privation." Almost all of the settlers' holdings were small farms and varied from fifty to one hundred and sixty acres. Their petition implied that the "men of great wealth"—Beale, Moss, Wohler, and Carpentier—had used their money and influence to overturn the decision of the Board of Land Commissioners and Judge Hall McAllister, Hoffman's predecessor. Lincoln refused to listen to the petition. Beale and his associates readied themselves to make handsome profits by selling the settlers their former homes and farms.[25]

While most of Beale's investments prospered, he suffered a minor setback in March and April of 1863. Once again the city fathers of Los

Angeles refused to accept his roadwork on the San Fernando Hill and ordered the turnpike further improved or the contract forfeited. The Board of Supervisors tantalized Beale with the offer of a twenty-year contract for tolls when the road met certain standards.[26]

Shortly thereafter, in late April, another personal tragedy struck. On April 27, Beale was shocked to hear the sad news of Fred Kerlin's death. Kerlin had been a passenger aboard the steamer *Milton Willis* which was destroyed in a fiery explosion at San Pedro. Beale felt Kerlin's loss deeply. Fred Kerlin had accompanied him to California as his chief clerk for the Indian superintendency, traveled with him on the "Central Route to the Pacific", aided on the wagon-road survey and camel experiment, and most recently worked in the surveyor general's office. The Los Angeles *Star* eulogized Kerlin as a fit representative of the "noble aspiration of ambitious youth."[27]

In mid-July, Beale joined other residents of San Francisco in applauding recent Union victories in the East. On July 8, San Francisco heard that Lee's invasion of Pennsylvania had been turned back at the crossroads hamlet of Gettysburg, and Vicksburg, Mississippi had fallen to the army of U. S. Grant. A strong Unionist, Beale was ecstatic, but he probably regretted the resulting drop in the price of gold. With effort, Beale remembered that in the 1850s in San Francisco there was an army officer named Sam Grant. He was one of the few men who did not join the faddish handball craze, and in fact, Grant could not play the game. But times change.[28]

In the summer of 1863, Beale turned his attention south to Mexico, a country which had long interested him. By late May, Benito Juarez's Mexican army had been driven north by the French forces which held possession of Puebla and Mexico City. The American Civil War consumed all the energies of the United States, and little attention could be paid to the potential threat of a European monarchy on the southern border of the nation. Beale corresponded with Thomas Brown, U.S. Treasury agent for the Pacific Coast, and urged that the time was perfect for American acquisition of lower California. From Brown, perhaps Beale learned that Salmon P. Chase, treasury secretary, held similar views.

On August 5, Beale wrote to Secretary Chase and described the importance of Baja California to the United States. He pointed out the excellent harbors to be found on both the Pacific and Gulf of California and added that the Baja peninsula was filled "with mineral wealth of every description." If Baja, plus a small portion of the opposite coast could be obtained the United States would *"possess the mouth of the Colorado destined to be as important to us on the Pacific as is the Mississippi to the Eastern States,"* Beale explained. The Colorado River in time would become of supreme importance for the welfare of the Pacific region. Cotton, sugar, tobacco, and other crops could be grown on the rich bottomlands. The nearby mountains of the Colorado River area "abound in vast resources and in mineral wealth." The French knew the region's importance, Beale warned, and if the United States did not act quickly, it would soon be too late.

Beale proposed to Chase that the United States purchase the desired land from the Juarez government. The Mexicans obviously needed the money in order to secure arms to continue the fight against the French. Beale even knew where to find the men to occupy the territory once purchased. Five thousand men could be drawn from the Military Department of New Mexico, where they were "entirely useless," and promptly placed in La Paz and Guaymas. He concluded his letter to Chase by warning that future residents of California would "not hold the memory of that administration in high respect which will have allowed a foreign power to collect a toll at the mouth of the Mississippi of the Pacific, after having lost the opportunity of its acquisition for our own people."[29]

A month later, on September 5, 1863, Chase responded. He agreed about the desirability of acquiring Baja California and regretted that General Winfield Scott had not established a protectorate in Mexico during the war of 1846–48. Chase blamed the timidity of the Whig leaders and the "slave-holding oligarchy" for blocking such a policy which would have "prevented all our present troubles so far as French domination in Mexico is concerned." Chase now feared that the Juarez government was too broken to negotiate, but he promised to confer with the president and the secretary of state on the topic.[30]

In early September, Beale forwarded his annual report to Commissioner Edmunds. He began by stating that the "meagre appropriations of the past three years have much reduced the work in the field." He had concentrated his surveying work on the main lines of travel eastward to Nevada and the Atlantic states and thereby obeyed the instructions to survey the property intended for the Central Pacific Railroad. In Nevada, Beale concentrated on surveying in the Truckee River valley, once again land intended to assist the railroad. He asked for permission to survey the land in the vicinity of Pyramid Lake and Walker River Indian reservation, for it contained some of the best agricultural land in the region. If Nevada continued to fill up with miners, Beale feared a shortage of surveyed agricultural lands.

Beale focused his report on mineral lands. Many California businessmen feared that the federal government intended to tax heavily or even seize important mining properties. In early May, President Lincoln had ordered the seizure of the New Almaden quicksilver mine, probably the most valuable mining property in the nation. A vociferous public out-cry forced the revocation of the "surreptitious order," as Beale termed the action. Beale subtly warned Commissioner Edmunds and Lincoln that "indiscreet or ignorant interference and meddling" with this impor-tant subject—mining—might mean the loss of California for the Union.

Beale then suggested answers to the vexing problems posed by min-eral lands. First, the United States should adopt, if feasible, the Spanish mining laws for the Pacific Coast. Second, Beale proposed a general con-gress of the mining states to meet at San Francisco and advise the United States Congress in the adoption of a general mining code. "A whole-some code," he wrote, "would satisfy the requirements of the people, and weld forever the patriotism of the Pacific to the federal government." Third, Beale recommended that the federal government deed to the states and territories all mineral lands, stipulating that money derived from their sale be used for charitable institutions, schools, fortifications, and similar purposes. This would allow the states to enact mining laws to fit regional and local differences. Beale termed the revision of mining laws a "work worthy of the best intellects of the nation."[31]

Throughout the late summer and fall of 1863, the feud between Ed-munds and Beale deepened. On August 29, Edmunds responded with vehemence to Beale's letter of July 9, denying the charge of excessive expenditures. Edmunds said that when Beale's predecessor told him that his accounts were "settled up," he was either mistaken or lying for sev-eral thousand dollars remained outstanding at that time. Edmunds had advised Beale on July 18, 1862 that the shortage existed. He questioned how, in only eighteen days into the fiscal year, Beale could have spent an entire year's appropriation of $10,000. Edmunds seemed to suspect Beale of attempting to hide something in the matter of the surveying contracts. Even if Edmunds's letter had arrived after the contracts to survey the ranchos had been signed, Beale could have ordered its can-cellation. The simmering dispute was reminiscent of the Beale-Manypenny difficulties of 1854.[32]

As the months wore on, Edmunds continued to charge Beale with irresponsibility—and Beale continued to insist upon his scrupulous re-gard for economy. Nevertheless, Edmunds once again had to ask Con-gress for a deficiency appropriation to cover the overrun of the fourth quarter of the preceding fiscal year. He ordered Beale to cut down on expenditures by reducing the office staff. Beale promised to do this in the fourth quarter (April–June of 1864) because he did not want to turn out any clerks, most of whom had families, during the winter when em-ployment was harder to find.[33]

Meanwhile, at the Tejon ranch, Beale's operation continued to prosper. On October 7, he signed a five-year partnership agreement with Alex Godey which placed Godey in charge of all ranch business related to sheep production, such as buying and selling, but stipulated that Godey could not sell any portion of the ranch itself. An old friend of Beale's Godey had recently been appointed Indian agent at the Tejon reservation, which provided a convenient market for Beale's livestock. Having resolved his troubles with the Indian Department, he now held a contract to supply the Indians at Tejon with two hundred head of cattle. The military authorities at Fort Tejon had been ordered to stop harassing ranch employees. Beale made occasional visits to the ranch, but most of the time he stayed in San Francisco, living with his family at 821 Bush Street, between Mason and Taylor streets, several blocks west of the commercial district.[34]

Beale's interest in Mexican affairs continued to deepen. On October 29, Charles James, San Francisco collector of customs, wrote a letter to Secretary Salmon P. Chase, which postulated an ingenious plan to acquire control of the month of the Colorado River. James suggested that Beale could purchase several floating land grants in Mexican territory on the Colorado River. Once he had established his personal ownership, the question of sovereignty over the land could be taken up with Mexico. The land could either be purchased by Beale as a private individual and a later arrangement made to transfer it to the United States, or possibly the government could authorize Beale to purchase the land for the public domain at a price not in excess of $100,000. Washington officials, probably amazed at the suggestion, declined the bizarre proposal.

In October, Beale read a newspaper account of a speech that Secretary Chase made in Cincinnati on October 12 in which he vowed not to allow France to have her own way in Mexico. Encouraged, he again wrote Chase and urged the acquisition of lower California. If Mexico retained that property forever, Beale wrote, it would always be to America's disadvantage, but should France control the land, it would be "ruinous to our commercial prospects on that part of the Coast." Beale then suggested the floating grants scheme, a proposition he had discussed with Treasury Agent Brown and Collector James. He wanted Chase to understand that he did not underrate the hazards of a war with France but felt the risk should be taken. A secret purchase treaty could be made with the Juarez government and kept hidden until the Confederates had been defeated. Beale's plan may have tempted Chase, but Lincoln opposed it. Beale's dabbling in foreign affairs did not enhance his stature in Washington.[35]

By December of 1863, Commissioner Edmunds had grown tired of Beale's conduct in operating the California office. The General Land Office had checked closely on Beale's personal activities and found several irregularities. Edmunds wrote to the Los Angeles Register and informed him that the Washington office had discovered two illegal entries in Beale's name. The violations, however, were not too serious for they were located on the Liebre Rancho, owned by Beale. Then, on December 3, Edmunds found an error in a contract which Beale had recently made with Eben H. Dyer. He suspended the questionable agreement and requested Beale to cancel the $7,500 contract for the survey of some sixteen townships and fractional townships at twelve dollars per mile. Edmunds declared that the survey site was located in the Humboldt River area of eastern Nevada, an inhospitable place, sixty miles from the nearest standard line. He failed to see how the survey could be accomplished without first surveying the exterior lines and perhaps an additional standard line. The contract was either a serious mistake or an attempt at fraud.[36]

On January 7, 1864, Mr. Lent, who rented offices to the surveyor general, complained to Edmunds. The proprietor had been forced to raise the rent to take into account the depreciated treasury notes with which the government paid its obligations. Lent's building faced the Customs House, at the corner of Washington and Battery, and was close to the business district. He rented the bottom floor for $350 per month in gold. He chaffed at the delayed payment and said that once again the rent was six months overdue. Lent felt that Beale had deceived him when the offices were first rented, as the surveyor general led him to understand that the payments would be in gold.[37]

In mid-January, Edmunds learned of still another illegal land entry made by Beale. More than four months earlier, on August 20, Beale had filed on the N 1/2 of the NW 1/4 of Section 2, and the NE 1/4 of the SW 1/4 of Section 3, both entries in Township 7N, Range 16W, San Bernardino Meridian Base. "The tracts called for have never been surveyed and offered at public sale according to law, and hence, are not subject to private entry," fumed Edmunds. The entries "should not, therefore have been allowed, and they will be cancelled by this office," he continued. Edmunds then directed Register Ramirez to notify Beale of the cancellation and suggested that Beale apply for a return of his purchase money. The illegal entries, Edmunds realized, could not have been a simple mistake on Beale's part. Beale knew the status of public surveys in California better than anyone else and had attempted illegally to claim choice property, probably water courses, near his ranch.[38]

In California, Beale continued to spend time with his own interests.

On January 11, his partnership with Alex Godey was terminated. Beale was dissatisfied with Godey's management and his failure to account for money expended, as well as for using an excessive amount of provisions. The 11,092 sheep were divided: 3,356 to Godey and 6,706 to Beale. All debts incurred by the partnership would be paid by Beale. Five days later, he and six men located the Bride of Abydos Mine in the San Fernando Mining District, four miles east of Beale's Cut. Thomas Bisset, John Bisset, John Moore, Oscar Moore, Oliver Robbins, and R. H. Robbins were associated with Beale in the venture. The entry described the Bride of Abydos as a gold, silver, and copper mining enterprise, whose claim ran for some 1,600 feet. Beale conducted still other business in January. On the thirtieth, he formed a partnership for sheep raising with Robert S. Baker, a Los Angeles businessman.[39]

In Washington, a decision to remove Beale was near. Lincoln, several members of the California delegation and Commissioner Edmunds held meetings concerning Beale's activities. Cornelius Cole, Republican senator from California, urged Lincoln to refrain from making any removals in California for which Cole might be held responsible. On the other hand, John Conness, Republican senator from Sacramento and the main California political power in Washington, took a strong stand. Conness inquired about the deficiency appropriation for Beale, and Edmunds responded: "This excess of the appropriation of $11,000 (office expenses) was created in violation of the explicit instructions of this office." Conness then pushed Beale's removal and refused to support him for any other position on the Pacific Coast.

By early February, unofficial word of Beale's removal had reached California. Lauren Upson, editor of the Sacramento *Union* and a strong Conness supporter, would be his successor. The Los Angeles *Star* gloated over Beale's dismissal and indicated that "renegade Southerners seem to have the luck of getting *into* office under the present Administration, but somehow or other they can't *stay* in." The *Star's* editor conveniently summarized Beale's career. Miraculously, Beale had held public office in California under five consecutive administrations and had "boxed the political compass as often as any other living man—big or little—from radical pro-slaveryism to radical abolitionism—from Dr. Gwin to Starr King—from Jeff. Davis to Abe Lincoln." Beale's political and moral gymnastics would not suffice to keep himself in power. "His present master, whose shoes he has so faithfully brushed," continued the *Star*, "do not trust him. They go upon the very sensible ground that a man who will desert one cause is not likely to be faithful to another."[40]

On February 16, Lincoln nominated Lauren Upson as surveyor general of California. The United States Senate on February 23 confirmed his appointment, and on February 25, 1864, Upson received his commission. Edmunds informed Beale of his removal and leveled a final complaint against him. The surveyor general's office had failed to forward to Washington the reports from the various local land offices—Los Angeles, San Francisco, Humboldt, Stockton, and Visalia. Records covering cash selections, warrants and homestead entries, sales, and locations, had not been received for many months. Edmunds stated that the local offices all informed him that these reports had been regularly forwarded to Beale's San Francisco office. It was yet another example of Beale's incompetence and neglect of duty.

The loss of the surveyor general's post angered Beale but did not surprise him. Almost by instinct, he eyed another appointment. Rumors circulated in San Francisco that General George Wright would soon relinquish command of the Department of the Pacific. For a long time, Beale had desired a military command. This time, however, his political sensitivity failed when he asked John Conness to back his candidacy. Conness told Lincoln that he had "no recommendation to make" in Beale's behalf and killed Beale's slim chance for a military command. The San Francisco *Bulletin* heard of the bid for a military appointment and called it "a good joke." Beale's public career in California had reached an end.[41]

During his two and one-half years as surveyor general, Beale personified the problems of the General Land Office in the mid-nineteenth century. Like many office holders, he devoted his efforts to advancing his own fortunes and used his official position to obtain land both for himself and his friends. At the same time, Beale ignored the Homestead Law, supposedly designed to help small farmers, and concentrated on aiding railroads and large mining companies. Admittedly, little public surveying could be performed with a diminutive budget, but instead of ordering surveys on farming land, Beale squandered a year's budget on personal surveys. He also followed accepted practice and handed out surveying contracts to friends and relatives. Always a kind employer, Beale fought for his office staff, while continuing to neglect his public duties.

But Beale did not regard his tenure as surveyor general as a failure. He could view with smug satisfaction his accomplishments. He carved out an immense estate in California and thereby achieved his boyhood dream of becoming a "man of rank." Almost twenty-five years before, young midshipman Beale had penned a cryptic phrase in his diary: "He who has never committed a crime cannot appreciate virtue." By 1864, Beale had achieved an appreciation of virtue. Fortunately, the government never took legal action against him; his transgressions violated ethics rather than laws. Nineteenth-century standards for public morality permitted a wide attitude when it came to profiting from a public job.

Beale was forty-two years old when he left office. Thus far, his contradictory career showed earnest ideals frequently compromised by pecuniary desires. Twelve years before, Beale had become entangled in Indian Department contracts and partisan politics, which destroyed a sincere effort to help California's Indian population. With few exceptions, as surveyor general Beale permitted nothing to block his grand opportunity to grasp the "main chance."

Bayard Taylor

Emily Beale McLean, the youngest daughter, about 1880. (*Courtesy National Trust for Historic Preservation.*)

Decatur House in the 1880s. (*Courtesy National Trust for Historic Preservation.*)

Washington DC
January 10th 1883

I hereby leave all my
property personal real
and mixed to my wife
Mary Edwards Beale
E. F. Beale,

Witness
U. S. Grant
W. T. Sherman

Will of Edward F. Beale, January 10, 1883, which was witnessed by U.S. Grant and
W. T. Sherman. (*Courtesy Library of Congress.*)

In 1888–89, Beale wanted to sell El Tejon Ranch. He commissioned Carleton E. Watkins, one of San Francisco's most prestigious photographers, to come to the ranch and produce an album that could be used as an aid to the sale. Most of these photographs have not been previously reproduced, and a small selection of eight are presented here. *(Courtesy Tejon Ranch Company.)*

View of the patio at El Tejon Ranch headquarters, looking east.

Formerly the hospital at Fort Tejon, this building was used to house the *vaqueros* of El Tejon Ranch.

Kitchen at
El Tejon
Ranch.

Indians in Tejon
Canyon

Catholic
Church
at the
Indian
rancheria.

Beale experimented with citrus trees at El Tejon Ranch. Shown here are orange trees.

Wild grape fence shows the agricultural abundance of the land.

Ranch stables.

Access to El Tejon Ranch was improved
with Beale's Cut in the San Gabriel
Mountains. *(Courtesy Dennis Alward.)*

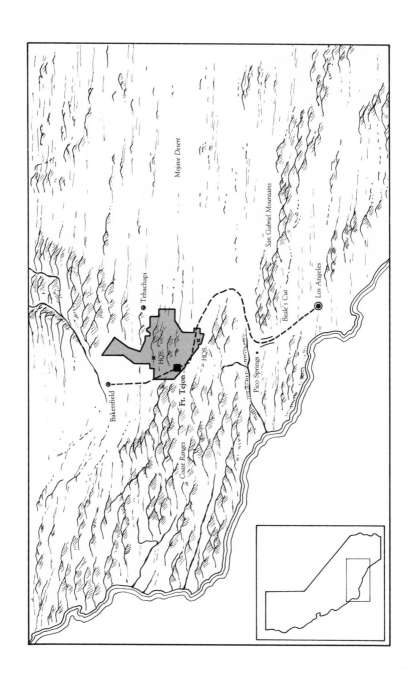

164

Chapter 10

A VOCAL REPUBLICAN

"Carthage must be destroyed!" was once the cry of the Romans—
"Death to Slavery!" should be ours. I know the accursed thing,
and have seen it, and lived among its foul abominations. I have
bought great, stalwart men, nearly white, from the slave block,
and freed them, and felt their warm tears of gratitude for it; and I
trust, when all my heavy sins are weighed, and the awful balance
trembles to the left hand, those crystal drops will incline the beam
to the side of mercy for my soul. Thank God! I never stained it
with the sale of humanity.

—Beale, speech, November 7, 1864

After his dismissal as the surveyor general of California, Beale concentrated on his business interests. In March of 1864, in San Francisco, he heard the welcome news that the Board of Supervisors in Los Angeles had finally approved his work on San Fernando Hill. The road was now safe and passable, although in some places the steep grade averaged a one-foot climb to every five linear feet. At the base of the south grade stood the small adobe toll house of Beale's collector—O. P. Robbins, who was always ready to lift the wooden pole, which spanned the road. The Los Angeles *Star* praised the new road's "great importance to the country" and noted that the builder undoubtedly had spent a sizeable sum of money in cutting down the hill. With his twenty-year contract, Beale would average several hundred dollars per month in toll receipts. Years later, when the contract expired, the road had paid for itself several times.[1]

Chapter 10

In mid-March, someone showed Beale a letter which implied that his removal from the Surveyor General's Office had resulted from Beale's disloyal statements. Months before, on September 29, 1863, Commissioner Edmunds had been shocked when he read Beale's annual report with its intemperate criticism of the federal mining policy. Edmunds wrote to John Usher, secretary of the interior, and warned that Beale had hinted at seditious or revolutionary consequences in California if mining policy did not change. He also pointed out Beale's indelicate reference to Lincoln's "surreptitious order" to seize the New Almaden Mine. On the basis of this annual report, Edmunds had suspected Beale's loyalty. When he learned of the letter's contents, Beale raged with anger that his loyalty and patriotism had been questioned.

On May 12, 1864, in the San Francisco *Bulletin,* Beale addressed an open letter "To the People of California" and defended his 1863 report. Quoting extensively from the document, he reviewed his suggestions about a mining congress and the need for a new mining code. His thinking was unchanged. Regarding his "surreptitious order" statement, everyone in San Francisco in July of 1863 knew that businessmen on Montgomery Street had responded like angry bees when the news of the New Almaden seizure reached the city. Fortunately, the order was retracted when the government learned of California's response. Was the order surreptitious? Beale quoted Major General Henry W. Halleck's telegram to prominent attorney and mineowner Frederick Billings: "The order for a military occupation of New Almaden was surreptitiously obtained." Possibly, Edmunds reacted with such vehemence because he and Usher had been responsible for the order, Beale suggested.

If the government taxed the mines, California's mountains would be depopulated, Beale predicted. Miners would rush to Mexico where governmental policy was more understanding. The government would have to force the miners to pay taxes, and such coercion would lead to a collision between the government and the people. Adopting the style of a stump speaker, Beale harangued: "Tax the miner! Why, you had as well tax the blessed atmosphere we breathe!"

Turning to the loyalty issue, Beale reiterated that the federal government risked the loss of California if it pursued such a short-sighted policy. *"We are loyal,"* explained Beale, "but not beyond the point of self-respect." As for Edmunds's accusations against himself, Beale called the charges "beneath contempt." He had more wounds on his body, suffered during years of loyal public service, than Edmunds could count years in office. Beale had heard that when the California delegation was interrogated about his removal, one member replied: "Let him slide; he is only a habitual officeholder." The characterization was true, Beale brashly admitted,

166

but only half true. He was also a "hereditary officeholder." One of his ancestors had died in the act of speaking to George Washington at the site of Braddock's defeat; another had fallen at the side of John Paul Jones. His father had served heroically during the war of 1812, and Beale modestly reminded his readers of his own valorous deeds at San Pasqual. A bitter man, Beale stated that he never again would seek a place in public affairs.

The *Bulletin's* editor felt compelled to comment on Beale's letter. He chided Beale for not displaying the good temper of a man who had " 'received his appointment without gratification,' and 'lost it without regret.' " The *Bulletin* reluctantly acknowledged that Beale was right on the question of taxing the mines. But, he was wrong on secession. Even if the federal government enacted the hated tax, the state should remain loyal.[2]

Throughout these months, Beale's own mining properties continued to produce. According to the Los Angeles *Star,* the Slate Range Mill was turning out "bullion in quantities." The mining syndicate had recently received excellent news from the district. Silver had taken the place of lead as the alloy of gold, making a rich combination. It was almost too good to be true.[3]

Feeling that he had properly defended himself, Beale turned his attention to other matters. In the spring of 1864, he plunged deeply into Mexican affairs, when a Juarista agent named Placido Vega arrived in San Francisco and tried to secure American backers for his government's struggle against the French. Vega found two men ready to aid the Mexican cause—Thomas Brown, special agent of the U.S. Treasury Department, and Edward F. Beale. Vega enticed Beale and his friends with mineral-lease concessions, one of which was the lucrative Carmen Island salt deposits, located in the Gulf of California. With the exception of a poor grade of salt gathered in the Alameda salt marshes, all salt used in California was imported. Carmen Island contributed the greatest percentage, some 4,000 tons in 1862. Due to heavy use in mining, salt prices had soared to forty dollars per ton, and Vega's concession looked most attractive.

Beale and several associates quickly organized the Carmen Island Salt Company, with offices in San Francisco and New York, to operate the salt mines. The company was capitalized at $250,000, and the listed incorporators were Beale, Albert H. Osborn, Jose Maria Aguirre, and Placido Vega. Mexico offered the company a twenty-year lease at an annual fee of $20,000 per year. The Juarez government, in desperate need of funds, insisted on an initial cash payment of $200,000 to cover the first ten years of the lease. Osborn handled the sale of the stock and showed prospective purchasers elaborate charts indicating that within ten years a $1,000 investment would return $6,700 in dividends. For Juarez and Mexico, at any rate, the scheme proved successful. Vega secured enough money from the Carmen Island lease to purchase the equipment necessary for Mexico to manufacture her own rifles, in addition to a significant quantity of armaments. Beale always felt that his investment helped to make a difference in the struggle against the French forces.[4]

Difficulties did occur, however. In early April of 1864, Charles James, collector of customs at San Francisco, seized 3,000 arms aboard the *John L. Stephens* bound for Juarez's forces. The shipment violated American neutrality laws, which forbade the shipping of weapons to either of the belligerents, France or Mexico. Collector James kept in close touch with French officials in San Francisco, and rumors circulated that in return for bribes, James permitted arms destined for the French forces to pass through the Golden Gate unmolested. In July, James learned from French spies that Vega planned another shipment. He confiscated some 20,000 rifles, eighteen cannons, and considerable ammunition. The weapons had been purchased in Hamburg, Germany, and Vega swore under oath that he would return the arms to the manufacturer and thus comply with American law.[5]

Worried about his salt concession, Beale decided to assist the Mexican cause publicly, and he entered the arms dispute. Vega argued with some plausibility that since American officials (Beale and Brown) had aided him, he believed the shipment legal. Beale could not plead ignorance of American neutrality law, however, like Vega. Instead, he sent a strongly worded letter to Collector James and hinted that "French gold" had overcome the official's integrity. Beale knew that James held orders from the United States government to prohibit the export of arms to Mexico. But the collector should realize that with the Southern states in rebellion, the government was forced to say one thing, while secretly desiring another.

If James could not evade his orders, Beale suggested that he disobey them and "go out of office with the consciousness of having done at least one good thing." The arms must go through, or history would regard James's name as the "synonym of everything that is humanly base," Beale predicted. While obeying a neutrality law enacted to fit the peculiar conditions of the Civil War, James was violating a cardinal article of American diplomatic faith—the Monroe doctrine. "On the continent of America, and in the nineteenth century," Beale asked, "are you willing to checkmate the advance of liberty with a King?"[6]

James refused to budge and wrote Beale that "it was a mistake to suppose that the language of menace, contumely, and insult" would prevent him from carrying out the president's expressed orders. Earlier, Treasury Agent Thomas Brown had told James the arms would be returned to Hamburg; now, Beale indicated that they were destined for Mexico. James vowed to enforce the law, and his confiscation order stood.[7]

Beale prepared to move from San Francisco to the East. His wife preferred to live near her family home in Chester, Pennsylvania, and Beale had lost his fondness for San Francisco. The Tejon Ranch prospered and did not require his attention. The Beales sailed in late summer of 1864. He was armed with a flattering letter of introduction to Treasury Secretary Chase, provided by Treasury Agent Thomas Brown. Edward Beale, Brown said, regarded himself as a disciple of the secretary and in fact had labeled Chase the "foremost statesman of the age."[8]

A heated presidential campaign was underway when Beale reached Chester. Although he had opposed Lincoln's renomination in early 1864, possibly hoping for Chase, Beale now worked with vigor for the Republican incumbent. To quiet lingering doubts about his loyalty, he felt that he should contribute personally to a Republican victory. Beale was well known in Chester and his offer to deliver a major political speech on Monday, November 7, election eve, was welcomed.

On the appointed day, Beale arose before a crowded audience at National Hall in Chester and stated his reason for seeking a public forum. In the future, he wanted no person to ever point to his son and daughters and declare: "Those are the children of a Traitor." Beale's speech, replete with classical allusions and overblown rhetoric, proved effective. He pummeled the Democrats and linked them to various secret societies operating throughout the North. These organizations would stop at nothing to achieve their ends, Beale warned, and they would even use assassination and terror. As a former Democrat, Beale now hoped to convince Democrats to vote for Lincoln. Only the previous day, he said, an old acquaintance had ridiculed him for defecting from Andrew Jackson's party. Beale had responded that he had left the Democratic Party when it "became the synonym of treason." In the coming election, the speaker declared, the voters had only two possible choices. They could choose either the party which proposed to sell out the country for a disgraceful peace or the party which promised to preserve the nation free for the future.[9]

Beale commented on the candidates for the presidency. He admitted with candor that Lincoln had not been his first choice, but he now pledged to support the president "with all my heart and soul as long as he is true to the country." Lincoln might not be the best Republican, but the election of McClellan would be tragedy. McClellan was responsible for a "series of disasters such as are without a parallel in the history of war," stated Beale. If McClellan "had been Caesar, the smallest boy in Rome would have grown to be a gray-haired Senator, while Julius McClellan doubted and hesitated on the banks of the Rubicon." Should McClellan win the presidency, the result would be "national suicide."

By this stage of his career, Beale had embraced the radical wing of the Republican Party. He urged his listeners not to fear being called Abolitionists. "It is a prouder title than any Americans have ever sought before," he explained. In discussing slavery, Beale reflected his own attitude about blacks. Grievous wrongs had been committed in the past and must now be righted. Perhaps in the early ages of the earth, God had placed a curse on Negroes, but Beale urged his listeners to beseech God "to accept this awful war as an expiation of their crime. Surely, Christ died upon the blessed cross as well for their sake as for ours." Beale spoke with personal knowledge of slavery: he was a Southerner from a slaveholding family. "Death to Slavery!" should be an American battle cry, Beale exhorted his audience. During his life, he had stained his soul with many heavy sins, but he could proudly declare: "Thank God! I never stained it with the sale of humanity." Beale's speech ended with rousing applause from the audience.[10]

A week after his address, Beale mailed Simon Cameron, boss of Pennsylvania politics, a printed copy. In a cover letter, he indicated that Harry Edwards, a "warm friend" of Cameron, had suggested that the remarks might please the senator. The pamphlet reached Cameron but was misplaced and was discovered only on Christmas Day, shortly before dinner. Cameron read the tract and thoroughly enjoyed it. The following day, he wrote Beale that his speech had added greatly to the festive holiday. It proved the judgment "of our departed friend Broderick in electing you as one of his most trusted friends." Cameron invited Beale to visit his home in Harrisburg whenever possible. Beale had courted and won an important ally.[11]

Disturbing news now came from one of Beale's California properties. A Settler's League on the Arroyo Seco grant, owned by Beale and three others, had resisted the efforts of a United States marshal to evict local residents. Some fifty men armed with rifles and pistols met the marshal and suggested that he return to San Francisco. The marshal complied. Then, Captain Augustus W. Starr, Second California Cavalry, received a federal order to dispossess the settlers from the Beale property. On February 11, 1865, Starr took a troop of seventy-five soldiers to Ione. Herman Wohler, one of the owners of the grant, directed the troops in removing settlers, who either had refused to pay for their property or were unable to do so. On the seventeenth, the troops expelled some fifty persons from their homes in Jackson Valley. Celebrating his success two nights later at Ione, Wohler was struck by a bullet in the chest, fired through a window. [12]

The wound was serious. Captain Starr and his cavalrymen searched the Arroyo Seco vicinity for the assassin; in San Francisco a $1,500 reward was posted. The San Francisco *Alta California* acknowledged that perhaps the Settlers' League held a valid complaint against Wohler, Beale, Moss, and Carpentier but declared that "wrongs cannot be righted by a resort to lawless violence." Despite the intensive search and substantial reward, the gunman was never captured. The incident at Ione, however, encouraged the grant owners to rent to the settlers their former lands on lenient terms. [13]

The spring of 1865 found Beale once again in California. He enjoyed being on the ranch at the time of livestock sales and equally enjoyed helping with the cattle roundup. On the morning of May 1, from six until noon, Beale rode some forty miles, helping to collect the cattle. For the rest of the day, until after dark, he and his Mexican vaqueros labored on the rodeo grounds sorting out five hundred head, destined for the San Francisco market. As the herd was being driven into a corral for the night, something frightened the cattle, and they stampeded. Beale spent the following day once again rounding up cattle, assisted by some fifty neighbors, Indians, and employees. The vaqueros were superbly mounted, but the work was so strenuous they changed horses every two hours. Beale's romantic nature delighted in the sight of colorfully garbed "Mexicans careening at full speed over the plains." Finally, on May 3, the roundup was completed, and Hudson, the ranch manager, started a herd up the central valley toward San Francisco.

This was Beale's first separation from his family in several years, and he missed his wife and children. In writing a long letter to his children, Beale revealed insights into his personality. As his youngest daughter Emily shared her mother's dislike for dogs, he sent her a true story about one dog's heroism, which illustrated the worth and nobility of the canine species.

Recently, the shepherd on the Tejon, accompanied only by his sheep dog, had driven a flock of sheep to market in San Francisco and returned via the San Joaquin Valley. One night the man and dog camped in a dense tule growth on the shores of Tulare Lake. About midnight the shepherd was awakened by the dog "jumping vehemently on his breast, and barking violently, and tearing at the blanket which covered him." All around him the dry tule was afire. They fled to safety, saved by the dog. "Let this adventure teach you, my little Em, more charity for dogs . . . ," Beale wrote. "God has given to them many noble traits and endowments which should frequently make his more favored creations envious, or rather emulous, of their goodness." Emily should also find out how the Romans once rewarded a dog who saved the life of a citizen of Rome. In imitation, Beale planned to fashion a suitable reward for Tejon's hero.

Beale also penned instructions about studies for his oldest daughter Mary. He promised her a European holiday when she turned eighteen, provided that she had become an accomplished woman by that time. To be accomplished required a knowledge of Latin and at least two modern foreign languages. He suggested that Mary read poetry extensively and proceeded to give her a lengthy, albeit superficial, analysis of the nature of the muse. From his memory, he quoted lines of verse that merited attention. Keats's "St. Agnes Eve," for instance, was described by Beale as expressing "the most refined and delicate shade of thought." As a young man, Beale had imitated the romantic style in his own verses to Mary's mother.

Music should also be seriously studied, and Beale described how the "sister of Poetry" aided mankind. "Some sentiments or feelings," he wrote, existed "utterly beyond the power of expression by words,—as insubstantial and impalpable to the touch of words as any midsummer cloud." Music touched these misty regions. The combined beauties of Poetry and Music, Beale continued, "like the wild flowers of our plains here, are as various as they are innumerable."

Growing tired, Beale only addressed a few words to his wife. He told her that he planned on accompanying the largest of his three herds of cattle to San Francisco, probably sometime in June. "I am determined not to leave here until out of debt to every living creature, and my income greatly increased for us at home," he vowed. Possibly the failure of several of his mining ventures had placed him in debt. Most likely, however, Beale worried about how to pay a $21,000 promissory note due Juan Temple on June 9, 1865.[14]

Almost three months earlier, on February 9, 1865, Beale had purchased from Temple yet another Mexican land grant—El Tejon (the Badger)—which included his old 1852 Indian reservation. Roughly shaped like an hourglass, the 97,000-acre ranch covered the Tehachapi Mountains and foothills north of his La Liebre ranch. Thirty-five miles in length, with the width varying from six to fifteen miles, the Tejon grant more than doubled the size of Beale's original Tejon ranch. The grant included highly desirable grazing lands. Beale's worries about paying Temple proved unfounded. His cattle sales in San Francisco proved successful, and on June 12, Beale paid Temple $21,000 dollars in gold coins.

But Beale was not finished with land grant purchases. Between La Liebre and El Tejon lay a diamond-shaped grant—Los Alamos y Agua Caliente (Cottonwoods and Warm Water). Beale acquired this grant of approximately 26,500 acres for the small sum of $1,500; the price was low because title was clouded with debts and liens.[15]

Beale's speculative instincts soon turned to a new topic in California—oil development. The recent boom in Pennsylvania had been sparked by Benjamin Silliman, Jr., head of Yale's chemistry department. In April of 1864, Silliman arrived in California to examine mining properties on the West Coast, including petroleum deposits. After surveying a number of sites, he announced that the best site in California for petroleum production was the Ojai Rancho, near Santa Barbara. Silliman advised Thomas Scott, vice-president of the Pennsylvania Railroad, that ten wells bored on the Ojai would produce a net profit of $1,365,000. Scott and his associates were impressed. They purchased the rancho and incorporated three companies to bring in the oil fields. Actually, Edward Conway, Beale's chief clerk, probably was the first to recognize oil possibilities in California. Conway organized and headed E. Conway & Company, a $60,000 incorporation which held scattered oil properties in the vicinity of Ojai Ranch. Beale may have held an interest in Conway's company because he paid for Silliman's investigation of the Conway interests and advanced $7,000 for the company's use.[16]

Soon after his return to California in the spring of 1865, Beale learned of oil at Pico Springs, ten miles northwest of Beale's Cut. Earlier, Andres Pico said he held title to Pico Springs, but Beale had informed his old friend that unsurveyed public land could not be held simply by recording one's claim. The land law gave precedence to residence and occupancy of the property. Ironically, the occupants of Pico Springs were Jesus Hernandez and Ramon Perea, vaqueros of Don Andres who, according to one account, had stumbled across the oil seepages while hunting. In January of 1865, Pico's son, Romulo, filed for the site.[17]

In May, Beale and his new ranching partner, Robert S. Baker, stopped at Pico Springs and visited with Hernandez and Perea. The two vaqueros were incensed with Andres Pico, they learned. Don Andres seemed certain to make a fortune on the oil springs, but the two discoverers had received nothing. The two men had already talked to a lawyer who recommended that they file a claim to the springs by right of occupancy. Hernandez said he would sell his title to anyone except Pico, and Beale learned that an offer had already been made. Always quick to recognize a profitable opportunity, Beale and Baker acted immediately and purchased the claim from Hernandez and Perea for three hundred dollars. On May 22, out of friendship Beale explained to Andres Pico how the title had been purchased and promised that should the title prove valid, they would deed one-half interest to him. From his knowledge of the land office, Beale assured Pico that the Hernandez and Perea title would stand.[18]

By June, Beale and several associates had organized the San Fernando Petroleum Mining District. Meetings were held at O. P. Robbins's tollhouse on Beale's Cut. In July, Beale and Baker, together with B. Van Stephenson, Charles Leaming, Sanford Lyon, A. B. Chapman, and Romulo Pico, bought out eighty-nine claimants and organized the Mammoth Company. The holdings ran for several thousand feet in Petroleum Canyon above Pico Springs. Beale and his associates dominated the San Fernando District. Leaming occupied the post of district recorder and carefully watched the claim entries and locations. Robbins acted as the poll inspector for any voting in the district. Sanford Lyons, who ran a sheep ranch eight or nine miles away, provided the actual labor for the oil production.[19]

By the fall of 1865, the Beale firm was producing small quantities of oil from surface seepages. They shipped some of it to San Francisco where Hayward, Coleman and Company refined the crude into lamp and lubricating oil. The refiner reported that the Pico oil contained 45 percent illuminating oil, 40 percent lubricating oil, and 15 percent residuum. The quality was very superior, but once the Pennsylvania oil fields began to produce in quantity, following the Civil War, it became cheaper to buy Pennsylvania products in California. Nevertheless, the small California oil companies continued to struggle along.[20]

By September of 1865 Beale once again had sailed for the East. Fortunately, some friends in California watched out for his interests. On September 30, the Los Angeles *Tri-Weekly News* carried an official notice from the county sheriff, Tomas W. Sanchez, announcing the sale of Beale's Rancho Los Alamos y Agua Caliente. Beale had purchased the property, in part, from Agustin and Refugio Olvera, perhaps without knowing that the Third District Court had ordered Olvera's property sold at public auction in order to meet financial obligations in Santa Clara County. On October 10, in front of the Los Angeles district courthouse, Sheriff Sanchez auctioned off the property. When the gavel fell, the highest bidders were Beale's friends, Adolph Pfisher and Sherman O. Houghton, who paid $39.80 for Olvera's interest, and a potentially troublesome fight over the ownership of Los Alamos y Agua Caliente was neatly avoided.[21]

When Beale arrived back in Chester, the *Delaware County Republican* hailed him as a prophet. The newspaper's editor, Y. S. Walter, reminded readers that in Beale's election speech in November of 1864, he had warned about traitors who would use assassination and murder to further their ends. Lincoln's assassination in April had sadly fulfilled Beale's "prophetic warning." Once again, Beale planned to speak at National Hall in Chester on election eve. The title of his November 6 address was "The Enfranchisement of the Colored Race."[22]

In his address Beale presented a convincing case for allowing blacks to vote, basing his argument upon observation, common sense, Christianity, and political expediency. He tried to show that prejudice toward Negroes was not a natural feeling, but a learned or acquired one. Common sense showed that Negro labor was productive—the South had financed the recent war on that basis. He stated that no difference existed between "an uneducated, uninstructed white man, and an uneducated, uninstructed colored man." In Chester, one daily could observe black and white common laborers working together in perfect harmony. With education and the passage of time, the black man would be the equal of the white.

Beale emphasized that he did not refer to social equality. In a free society, social equality—every person financially equal to each other—was an impossibility. Talented and dilligent individuals would always rise, and the same principle applied to Negroes. In time, if given equal opportunity, their race would stratify into upper, middle, and lower classes. At a distant day, upper-class Negroes would mingle with their white peers, for distinctions of rank were natural, in contrast to the artificial distinction of race.

It was strange, Beale stated, that many persons who romanticized the Indian looked with contempt on the Negro. Beale knew both Negroes and Indians from years of close contact, and he pronounced Negroes far more intelligent and industrious. The noble savage was simply a creation of literature. Those fine-sounding speeches of Indians, he said, "belong to the poetic fancy of an Indian agent or accomplished interpreter, who could not understand a word of the language he pretended to translate." While he fully recognized the grievous wrongs inflicted over the years against Indians, he nonetheless reiterated that the "colored race is infinitely superior to the foremost tribes of Indians on this broad continent." Blacks worked with industry; most Indians disliked hard labor. Yet, blacks were denied the right to vote, while Indians voted in several places including Kansas. White men never felt degraded voting next to Shawnees or Delawares.[23]

Slavery had fostered an "unjust prejudice" against Negroes. In Europe, no such prejudice existed. Beale admitted that Africa had not produced high civilizations, but he blamed climatic conditions rather than race. The tropics fostered a languid state in individuals. Too much was provided by the environment without the need for hard work. Chance had happened to place Negroes in such an environment. Portuguese and Spaniards who ventured to the tropics showed a similar degeneracy. That same rule of climate would even apply to industrious white Americans, if they lived in such a region.

Beale next discussed a practical reason for allowing Negroes to vote. The Southern states soon would be back in the Union. "Does anyone doubt the continued disloyalty of the South?" he asked his audience. If Southern Negroes could vote, they would divide the old unity of the South and help hold that section in check for years to come. On the other hand, if white Southerners were allowed to go their own way, they would replace slavery with serfdom. Beale warned that the nation was "reconstructing too rapidly," and before the former rebel states gained readmission, "we should demand and secure some substantial guarantee for the colored race." Once restored to their full rights, the Southern people would "fight you as obstinately and arrogantly as ever," he warned.

As he neared the end of his speech, Beale turned to general themes. He appealed to Pennsylvanians to disregard the actions of other Northern states, reminding them the citizens of their state were the descendants of liberal-minded William Penn and Benjamin Franklin. Beale urged the granting of the franchise to Negroes, not because it would keep the South in subjugation, nor from charity, but "because *it is right and just.*" The only laws that could legitimately be applied to blacks were those applied to white Americans as well. Negroes had served in the military during the Civil War, and many had paid taxes. For those two reasons, in addition to all others, they should be allowed to vote.[24]

The response to Beale's speech was largely favorable. Congressman William D. Kelley of Philadelphia wrote of his intense gratification on hearing the speech and declared his pride that such a noble utterance had been made by a Pennsylvanian. Kelley told Beale that if cheap pamphlet copies of the speech could be printed, he would gladly purchase "a couple of thousand" for his constituents. Additional praise came from distant parts of the nation. The Wayne County Equal Rights Association (Detroit) adopted a resolution which declared that Beale's sentiments "should meet with the hearty concurrence of every Colored man and woman in the State of Michigan."[25]

Despite the success of his Chester speech, Beale quickly faced west. His California properties required attention. On his ranchos, he concentrated more efforts on the production of sheep, probably because sheep could withstand a severe drought better than cattle. He still hoped to achieve a success with his oil ventures, even though his other mining ventures collapsed. The Slate Range companies, which appeared so promising in the early 1860s, had folded. In January of 1866, the Los Angeles *Semi-Weekly News* announced that the Los Angeles District Court has ordered B. F. Mathews, sheriff of San Bernardino County, to sell the properties of the Beale syndicate at auction.[26]

Beale's oil interests fared somewhat better. Sanford Lyons continued to stay near Pico Springs and produced eight to twelve barrels of crude oil per week in a primitive fashion. In June of 1866, Stephen F. Peckham, another eastern oil expert, visited the San Fernando District. Peckham seemed dubious of Silliman's report on the oil at Pico Springs. The sample had yielded 40 to 50 percent kerosene upon distillation. Peckham secured a portion of the oil which Silliman had used in his experiment. The analysis convinced the young scientist that Silliman had been duped by a concoction taken from Canada Larga near the Ojai and mixed with an equal part of Devoe's kerosene, a common eastern brand sold in California. Peckham's own sample from Pico yielded 13.5 percent kerosene.[27]

On July 3, 1866, Christopher Leaming, an associate of Beale and recorder for the San Fernando Mining District, reported on recent developments at Pico Springs. Several companies in the vicinity were in production, with one company at Wiley Springs turning out a steady six barrels per day. The San Fernando Petroleum Company, under the superintendence of P. J. Hughes, bored a well and struck oil at 168 feet. Leaming indicated that stock in the San Fernando Company was selling for $4.50 per foot, which gave a value to the entire claim of $450,000. He urged Beale to sell the Mammoth Claim and estimated the Mammoth's worth at $222,750, or one-half the value of San Fernando property. If Beale could sell the claim for only one dollar per foot, it was still an attractive sum—$99,000.

Leaming also told Beale of Peckham's visit to Pico Springs. The refining specialist said that he had completed a tour of all oil properties in California and pronounced that "he would not give the Pico Spring for all of the celebrated Ojai Ranch." The statement seemed strange coming from a man employed by the Philadelphia and California Petroleum Company, which had been organized to exploit the Ojai riches. Peckham also stated that although the Pico Springs were "the most valuable . . . natural outflow yet discovered," the total production in the entire San Fernando District amounted to little more than prospective operations.

The Los Angeles *Semi-Weekly News* recognized the problem of the high cost of transporting crude oil and urged the building of a refinery in southern California. Interest at San Fernando, however, began to taper off. Then, in May of 1867, Peckham published an article entitled "On the Supposed Falsification of Samples of California Petroleum," which appeared in the prestigious *American Journal of Science and Arts.* The apparent Silliman fraud was exposed regarding the Pico Springs oil. Silliman never told who gave him the oil sample from Pico, but the professor did say that he was a respectable gentleman (undoubtedly an owner of Pico Springs).[28]

In the fall of 1866, Beale acquired still another Mexican land grant. On October 13, he purchased Rancho Castac from his business partner Robert S. Baker, paying a munificent sum of $65,000 and assuming Baker's mortgage to Samuel A. Bishop for $45,000. The price was high because it included all the cattle, horses, sheep, and mules, including some 6,000 head of Durham and American cattle. Beale also acquired Bishop's S B brand. In the future, Beale would brand all his animals with the distinctive El Tejon brand, the Cross and Crescent, which he himself devised. The Tejon brand carried more symbolic elements than most, for it represented a spiritual and physical meeting of East and West, an idea which had intrigued Beale ever since the days of his midshipman's service. In acquiring Rancho Castac, Beale also bought the abandoned buildings of Fort Tejon. The Havilah *Weekly Courier* called the property the "most substantial and best furnished" outside of San Francisco.[29]

In the late 1860s, Edward Beale began to spend more time in the East. In 1867 he remained almost entirely in Chester with his family, interrupting the summer to take a lengthy European trip. He was firmly entrenched in Chester's society where his wife's relatives played a leading part. Beale's home, situated only a half block from the Philadelphia, Wilmington, and Baltimore Railroad, was a convenient stopping point for friends traveling from New York to Washington.[30]

The Beale Mansion was a well-known landmark. The house was situated on the middle of several spacious acres, bordering Edgmont Road, north of Sixth Street. It was bounded on the north by the Friends Burial Ground and on the west by Chester Creek, which flowed into the Delaware River. Chester's business section was located south of Beale's property, between the railroad and the Delaware River. Chester was a growing community and eventually the Beale property, encompassing eight or nine city blocks, would be quite valuable. In 1867, the only building there was the Beale home, which was modern in every way, with running water, even to the upper floors. Water from Chester Creek was pumped to a tank located on the top floor, and the water then circulated through the home.

Chester abounded with relatives of Mary Edwards Beale. Her brother, Harry Edwards, owned several pieces of property. He lived about one-half mile from the Beale Mansion and near the Pennsylvania Military Academy, where Truxtun Beale attended school. The Stacey, Engle,

Kerlin, and Porter families, all connected by familial ties to the Beales, also lived in Chester.[31]

Visitors to the Beale Mansion always remembered the library, which seemed to mirror the owner's personality. The magnificent head of a giant elk, which he had killed on a western expedition, dominated the room. Hanging from each tip of the spreading antlers were mementos of Beale's past—Indian beadwork pouches, a pair of ancient Spanish spurs with enormous rowels, pistols, and knives. In the corners of the library were relics associated with Kit Carson, Commodore Stockton, and other famous persons from the early days of California's history. Each item had a story connected with it, and Beale liked to embellish his tales about daring deeds in the Far West.[32]

All Beale property in Chester was recorded in Mary Edwards Beale's name. She had inherited the land and apparently continued her owner-ship after marriage. One important legal advantage resulted from this practice. If a court ordered Beale to sell property in order to pay off the debts from a business failure, property owned by Mary Edwards Beale would be free from liability. Aware of this advantage, Beale placed all of his California properties in Mary's name in order to avoid possible losses from speculations grown awry.

Dun and Bradstreet's investigators examined Beale at this time and reported that he was "very keen, shrewd & far sighted." Both Beale and partner Baker appeared steady and industrious. They owned 60,000 to 70,000 sheep, according to Dun and Bradstreet, but they only reported half that number to tax assessors. The combined net worth of the part-nership was estimated at $500,000. This figure did not include Beale's interest in Arroyo Seco, various California mines, or stock and bond holdings. Recently, Beale had surpassed Phineas Banning, the transpor-tation king, as Los Angeles County's number one taxpayer. Beale paid $13,242 in taxes, while Banning paid $11,900.[33]

Reports from California told of recent damages from winter storms. During the winter of 1867–68, the long drought began to kill Beale's livestock. Then, immense sandstorms swept across the plains. The sheep-shearing house of Beale and Baker was destroyed by high winds. Over $20,000 worth of livestock was lost to drought and other causes. Finally, the rains came. By February of 1868, a Tejon resident could once again describe the ranch grass as excellent.[34]

By the summer of 1868, Beale had gained a prominent position in the Republican Party in Delaware County. In the fall elections, he spoke eloquently about Grant's presidential aspirations and delivered several speeches in Chester, Media, and other Pennsylvania communities. On Friday, October 23, he delivered a major address at Lincoln Hall in

Chester. Without resorting to name calling, Beale pushed his belief that only men who had supported the Union during the Civil War should ever be permitted to hold public office. His talk emphasized the proper reconstruction of the South, the virtues of candidate Grant, and the problem of debt and taxation.

Beale opened his address with a spirited attack upon the South and Democrats. President Andrew Johnson had been delinquent in his duties, Beale charged, particularly for permitting former rebels to organize assassination bands such as the Ku Klux Klan. The time had arrived, for the Southern people "to give up murder as a fine art and go to work." The United States government must make it clear to the South that "treason, neither armed or under the cloak of politics, can ever succeed on American soil." Beale fully supported Congress's program of reconstruction. The Democrats, however, planned to undo the achievements of congressional reconstruction and once again plunge the South into chaos, confusion, and crime. Beale acknowledged that some good Democrats existed. Every Democrat was not a rebel, but every rebel had been a Democrat, a fact which should make every man suspicious of that party.

Beale then attempted to compare the qualifications of the two candidates for the presidency—Horatio Seymour and U. S. Grant. During the Civil War, Seymour had served as New York's governor, but he was always "cold to the cause of the Union." Beale charged Seymour with encouraging the draft rioters in New York City in 1863. He could not think of a single instance during the recent hostilities where Seymour had given evidence of "self-sacrificing support" for the Union.[35]

Certainly everyone knew General Grant by his works—"the imperishable labors of a patriot." Democrats charged that Grant knew nothing about statesmanship and lacked Seymour's experience to govern the nation. Beale argued that a man who could preside over the complex movements of a dozen armies certainly possessed the ability to govern a nation. Grant's character was the important item to consider. He was a man with *"common sense,* wedded to integrity, and an inflexible determination to do justice, and enforce it." Should a war break out with Great Britain over the Alabama claims, which man would make a better wartime president, Grant or Seymour?

The Democrats seemed to be attracting voters by pounding one issue— high taxes and the nation's war debt. Beale acknowledged that taxes seemed high, but he disagreed with the Democrats' proposal to write off the debt. The international economic position of the United States would be ruined. Immigrants still flooded to the United States, a sure sign that Americans were not oppressed. Beale then quoted from a Democratic resolution which urged the "equalization of every species of property according to its real value, including Government bonds and securities." The next innovation from the Democrats would be taxes on bread, milk, and churches. Taxes fell far more heavily on the rich, who could afford to pay them, than on the middle and lower classes. The equalization proposal would actually increase the taxes of those less able to pay.

With supreme confidence, Beale predicted a Republican victory. He forecast that President Grant would faithfully and with a sense of justice administer the Reconstruction laws. With a clear vision, Beale foresaw the United States becoming the leading commercial nation in the world because of energetic men like Grant. Someday, Beale predicted, "a grateful people will raise a mighty pyramid, tall and solid as that of the Egyptian Cheops, and dedicate it, with blessings, to GRANT, the Peacemaker, eighteenth President of the United States." The audience applauded heartily. A Pennsylvania newspaper called Beale's speech "one of the very best addresses" of the current campaign. The Philadelphia *Press* predicted that the talk would have an impact upon the election. Grant won the presidency by an overwhelming vote.[36]

During the four years following his dismissal as surveyor general in California, Edward Beale had experienced remarkable successes. His California enterprises had generally prospered, and his landholdings had swelled with several new additions. In the East, Beale's persuasive speeches on behalf of Negro rights and Republican candidates earned him the recognition and friendship of influential politicians. Forty-six years old in 1868, he possessed wealth, education, and experience; his opinions counted. Nevertheless, Beale stood on the periphery of the American political scene. Little reason existed to believe that Grant's election would cause a dramatic change in Beale's life in future years. As yet, he had never met the new president.

Chapter 11

RANCHO EL TEJON
& DECATUR HOUSE

The rancho from which I write this—the Tejon it is called—seems
to me . . . the finest property in the United States in a single
hand. It contains nearly 200,000 acres, and lies at the junction of
the Sierra Nevada with the Coast Range. . . . You may ride for
eight miles on the county road upon this great estate. It supports
this year over 100,000 sheep; and it has a peasantry of its own. . . .
—Charles Nordhoff

Mrs. Grant and I will take pleasure in dining with you any day
this week after Tuesday that may suit you, unless Mrs. Grant should
be detained by company which she is now expecting. I can accept
for myself without conditions.
—President U. S. Grant to Beale
November 30, 1873

Beale left for California in December of 1869. For the first time in his
life, he rode the entire distance to the coast by railroad. Upon arriving
in San Francisco, he discovered that the Central Pacific planned additional railroad construction in the state, including a railroad down the
San Joaquin Valley, then possibly east to the Colorado River. The Big
Four had introduced a bill into the California legislature to provide for
the railroad's construction. The bill proposed that each county through
which the railroad would pass be permitted to vote a local subsidy of
$6,000 per mile for construction. The counties affected were San Joaquin,
Merced, Fresno, Tulare, and Kern. The last-named county, carved from
Los Angeles and Tulare counties in 1866, included more than three-

quarters of Beale's holdings. Some local businessmen hoped to profit from an influx of settlers upon agricultural lands, but Beale saw the tax as a threat which could undermine his ranching operations at the Tejon.[1]

In the San Francisco *Examiner* of February 26, 1870, Beale addressed an "Open Letter to the Senators of the State of California." He railed against the bill, which was urged by a "powerful and interested company." In Kern County, he roughly computed that the railroad would run one hundred twenty miles and require a subsidy of $720,000, based on $6,000 per mile. This great tax burden would fall on some 1,500 persons (an underestimation of the number of taxpayers). Beale analyzed Kern County. Most residents were Southerners—poor men, who found the existing county tax difficult to pay. Agriculture did not flourish in Kern without irrigation, and conditions which permitted irrigation existed in only a few places. The railroad company trumpeted Kern County's potentialities after irrigation became widespread, but Beale stated that such a method of farming went against the "genius of our people." Irrigation required engineering skills, constant labor on ditches and furrows, and expensive canals, dams, gates, and aqueducts. Small-scale orchards and vineyards might be possible, but large-scale irrigation was not practicable. Beale scoffed at the idea that irrigation would attract settlers who could pay for the railroad. Kern County, for the foreseeable future, would remain a grazing region. Poor soil and skimpy rainfall made intensive agriculture impossible.

Beale said that the Central Pacific, which owned the projected Southern Pacific, had contacted him and argued that his vast estate of over 200,000 acres would be greatly enhanced in value by the railroad. With twenty years of experience, Beale had reaffirmed that the land was only fit for grazing—"unless nature changes our seasons, climate and soil." The Central Pacific, Beale said, had asked him if he trusted the honesty of the county's residents and their ability to understand the issue. He answered "no" to both propositions. Most of the residents in Kern County were vaqueros who could be easily influenced by a promise of "temporary excitement." In any referendum on the question, the voters would be "tampered with" by the railroad. In the long run, Beale saw the ruin of his ranching interests if the bill became law. The tax would fall on the county's few wealthy men, and Beale was the wealthiest. Carried away by his words, Beale attacked the proposed bill, calling it a measure that would bring "ruin and disaster to myself, my friends, and my county."[2]

In the Bakersfield *Courier* of March 22, 1870, Andrew R. Jackson, a local leader, spoke in behalf of the county's farmers. He took exception to Beale's statement that Kern County could never be anything but a grazing land. As long as Beale held thousands of acres at a "marginal assessment," he had no desire for railroads, for they meant "population, small farms, cash valuations, neighbors, taxes, thoroughfares, fences, and all those etceteras that make large domains in a free country anything but desirable or profitable property." Moreover, Beale was not a fit representative to speak for the people of Kern County; he had never lived there since the county was organized and only made occasional "flying visits" to his ranch. Jackson said he had no great sympathy for the railroad men, but if they managed to drive out the large landholders, like Beale, they would "deserve the thanks of man and woman." Jackson added that stockmen still upheld the open-range principle in Kern County and backed their arguments with wild bands of "broad horned beeves that would trample a poor man's crops in the dust and in a moments time lay waste the fruits of a season's labors."[3]

Despite the efforts of the Central Pacific Railroad and men like Jackson, Beale won the fight. On the copy of his "Open Letter to the Senators" which he later placed in his library files, he gleefully penciled: "Bill defeated by one vote! The Railroad got nothing. EFB." In time, the Southern Pacific would build through the valley, and farmers and socialists would dub it the "Octopus." But by that time, Beale had reached an understanding with Collis P. Huntington, and he no longer worried about the railroad.[4]

Beale returned to Chester, well satisfied with the results of his California trip. In April of 1870, he heard from poet Bayard Taylor for the first time in years, and plans were laid for Beale and his oldest daughter Mary to visit with the Taylors. Beale complimented Taylor on his magnificent job of translating Faust in the original meters, acclaimed the best English translation ever produced of Goethe's classic. Taylor had recently spent several years in the diplomatic service, and the old friends of the 1850s had many amusing stories to exchange.

At the end of April, the Beales held a small party at the Beale Mansion in Chester. Senators Simon Cameron and Charles Sumner, the latter from Massachusetts, attended. Beale had met Sumner many years before at Thomas Hart Benton's Washington residence. In his invitation to the famous Radical Republican leader, Beale had noted that he had missed Sumner's lecture on the caste system and earnestly desired a copy. Although the conversations of the Sunday gathering never came to light, Sumner had already opposed the Grant administration on several issues, and a split within the party was in the wind. Although firmly in the camp of the Grant Republicans, Beale possessed credentials on black rights that were similar to Sumner's, albeit on a lesser scale. If Beale's Sunday social was intended to serve as a bridge to the Massachusetts senator, it failed terribly, for Beale apparently never saw Sumner again. Perhaps Bayard Taylor knew that politics would arise at the party, for he suddenly found his work schedule too hectic and declined Beale's invitation to attend.[5]

Beale remained in the public eye. In July he received a letter from the National Labor Union at Detroit which not only surprised him but forced public commentary. The letter attributed America's problems to the accumulation of capital by an aristocratic upper class. At the same time, the National Labor Union blamed the Chinese immigration for keeping down workers' wages. Either the labor union mistakenly thought that Beale would support their socialist cause, or they hoped to provoke a response to bolster their contention that rich capitalists wanted cheap foreign labor for exploitation. Although the letter originated in Michigan, the sentiments expressed had been growing for several years in California, particularly after an 1868 treaty further eased the entrance of Chinese laborers into the United States.

On August 6, Beale answered the National Labor Union with a lengthy letter, which was reproduced in several newspapers in Pennsylvania and California. First, Beale replied to the Marxian analysis of American society. In a common-sense approach, he argued that the wealthy men, the upper class had almost always been laborers or workers in their younger days, but by ability and genius had climbed the ladder. An hereditary aristocracy of wealth did not exist in America. The wealthy families of early days who had lived in the Chester area, Beale said, had seen their old estates divided among children. Some of those descendants now found themselves as laborers. The system was open and fluid.

The socialists charged that the workers produced the wealth of American society but did not receive the full benefit of their labor. Beale responded that in all fields—politics, business, literature, or whatever— former workers held prominent positions. He granted that as a philosophy the utopian society envisioned by the National Labor Union had certain merits, but it should not be mistaken for the real world. Always there would be rich and poor. America gave all men equal opportunity to succeed or fail, and each year Beale saw the country growing more democratic. The National Labor Union should consider the status of workers in foreign countries before criticizing the American laborer's position. "I think our working people as a whole, the happiest, freest and best paid and cared for and educated, on earth," Beale stated.[6]

Then he replied to the attack on Chinese immigrants. Beale knew the Chinese from long years of association in California and found them admirable and industrious, whether as independent businessmen, tenants, or common laborers. He believed that Americans could learn and profit from knowledge brought by the Chinese. Already, tea cultivation had begun in California. In time, Beale predicted, the United States would produce a finer silk than China and learn the art of making chinaware. As for character traits, the Chinese were "intelligent, painstaking, frugal and temperate." It was not American working men who objected to Chinese laborers, but other foreign immigrants, Beale indicated.

The National Labor Union severely criticized the "coolie system" of labor under which Chinese were hired in their homeland and brought to the United States under contracts which called for a specific term of labor in exchange for passage. Beale saw nothing wrong with the system. Many Americans went to the California gold fields in 1849 under similar contracts. As to the charge that the Chinese would paganize American institutions, Beale felt the possibility was slim. "I believe the Rock of Ages, on which Christ built his church, is stronger than the bubble of Mahomet, or the fallacies of Buddah," he proclaimed.[7]

Sometime in 1870–71, Beale met with President Grant in Washington to discuss the possibility of obtaining the appointment of minister to Constantinople. Wayne MacVeagh, Cameron's son-in-law and the present minister, was planning to resign the position in Turkey and return home within the next few months. Beale told Grant that his candidacy had the backing of Simon Cameron, John Forney, and John Hickman. Grant possessed an uncommon talent for neatly turning aside a request with an apparently favorable response. He told Beale that he could not commit himself with a positive promise concerning the opening, but Beale "would be in every way most agreeable" as MacVeagh's successor.

While in San Francisco in April of 1871, Beale noticed a newspaper item which rumored another's name for the diplomatic post. He immediately wrote Cameron from the Grand Hotel and asked the senator to "be candid" in the matter. If Beale was to have the appointment, he would conclude his business in California and return to the East. If not, he would spend more time in the West. This had been the most profitable year of his life, and if President Grant chose to send him abroad he would be in "splendid financial condition." Only wealthy men could afford a minister's post, he believed, due to the expenses associated with representing the United States.[8]

Later in West Chester, Beale saw MacVeagh, and the minister to Turkey said Cameron had not suggested Beale's name to Grant. Piqued by this statement, he wrote the senator on September 9 and said he felt "great disappointment" about the matter. "It will look to the President as though I had misrepresented the fact, when I said to him that you were my friend in this matter and would present me, as your choice for the position," Beale explained. He hoped Cameron would tell Grant that the sentiment which he had conveyed to the president had indeed been the truth. Beale did not want his standing with Grant affected by the apparent misrepresentation.

Beale told Cameron that he did not want the post for a long time, six months would be enough. He would willingly compare his record of service to the country with George H. Boker, the leading candidate, on any occasion. The Union League of Philadelphia backed Boker, but Beale said the group only represented the "social feeling" of a select few and did not represent Philadelphia. He urged Cameron to see the president and "state your feelings and wishes, and expectation in this matter as my friend, *decidedly.*" Beale did not want the post for the "paltry salary," which was insignificant to a man with his fortune. He wanted the post because it would be personally gratifying. Although he failed to receive the Turkish appointment, the Beales by mid-September were socializing with the Camerons at Chester. The incident illustrated a lifelong feature of Beale's personality. Quick to anger, he forgave readily, even when it involved a minister's appointment that he coveted.[9]

In mid-August, Beale had been shocked and angered by reading a recent issue of *Harper's Weekly.* A poem by Joaquin Miller entitled "Kit Carson's Ride" covered the entire front page. Beale considered the poem a crude slander on the memory of his old friend, who had died four years earlier in May of 1868. Miller described a fictional ride in which Carson stole a beautiful Comanche bride from her people, then fled over the plains. Unfortunately, the dry prairie grass somehow caught fire. In order to travel as lightly as possible before the pursuing flames, both Carson and the Indian maiden stripped off their garments until "bare as when born." At this dramatic juncture, a herd of stampeding buffalo joined the mad flight before the conflagration. For readers who lacked imagination, a thoughtful illustrator provided a half-page etching of the frenzied scene. The Brazos River became the goal of the two desperate, naked riders and thousands of shaggy beasts. Kit was mounted on the faster horse, stolen from his bride's father, and gradually his lover fell further behind. Carson's instinct for self-preservation overcame his sense of duty and love, and he abandoned his girl friend to the fire and the buffalo.[10]

Wretched by any standard, Miller's poem offended Beale by portraying Carson in an unfavorable and uncharacteristic role. He felt duty bound to defend publicly the memory of the man who twenty-five years before had saved his life. He wrote a lengthy letter to the editor of the Chester *Republican,* attacking Miller and eulogizing Carson. He signed the anonymous article with the pseudonym "El Mariposo."

As a general rule in poetry, began El Mariposo, when a poet departed from known facts, he used his poetic license to exaggerate the virtues of a departed hero rather than to slander a man by making him ridiculous and indecent. Beale urged Carson's relatives to file a lawsuit against Miller for defamation. It was too bad that Carson had not counted among his coups the "scalp of Joaquin." He concluded that "Kit Carson's Ride" was moral poison and ought to be put on a high shelf, away from children, and forgotten.

Miller's poem on Carson served one valuable purpose: it forced Beale to pen a memorable character sketch of the famous frontiersman:

> Dear old Kit! Not such as this poet painted you, do I recall the man I loved. . . . No man this to take his woman's horse, because it was faster than his own, and leave her to a prairie fire while he galloped to twaddle, in tumid bosh, over "her marvellous eyes." Oh, Kit, my heart beats quicker, even now old fellow, when I think of the time twenty-five years ago, when I lay on the burning sands of the great desert, under a mesquite bush, . . . and then under that sun of flame and on those burning sands, without a thought of ever seeing water again, you poured upon my fevered lips, the last drop in camp from your canteen. Oh, Kit! I think again of afterwards on the bloody Gila, where we fought all night and travelled all day, with each man his bit of mule meat, and no other food, and when I so worn from a hurt could go no further, begged you to leave me there and save yourself, I see you leaning on that old, long Hawkins gun of yours (mine now) and looking out of those clear blue eyes at me with a surprised reproach, as one who takes an insult from a friend.
>
> Oh, wise of counsel, strong of arm, brave of heart and gentle of nature, how bitterly have you been maligned.[11]

But Beale was not yet finished with Miller. Shortly thereafter, he penned a long poem in which Carson's spirit returned to Earth to thank Beale for his efforts to preserve his memory. Given the poetic standards of the day, Beale surpassed Miller at creating verses.

Beale's quarrel with Miller reached national proportions, extending from San Francisco to New York. Miller answered Beale with a card published in the New York *Tribune* on September 22, 1871. He chided Carson's friends for ignoring the scout's death and argued that his poem had attempted "to preserve the memory of this truly brave and good man." Miller felt his portrait was true. Attempting to shift attention away from Carson, Miller spent words on a discussion of his reason for allowing the Indian girl to die: "She represents a race that is passing away. It would have been contrary to the order of things to have allowed her to escape." Miller analyzed the outcry which his poem had aroused by stating that if it had created sympathy for the Indian's fate the poem was "more perfect than I had thought." The quarrel did not swirl around the Indian's plight, however, but around the attack on Carson.[12]

Charles Nordhoff, a correspondent for the New York *Herald* and *Harper's,* visited Beale at the Tejon in the fall of 1872. Nordhoff planned to write about California and describe the advantages of the state. Beale gave the reporter the full freedom of his vast rancho and treated him like a visiting dignitary. The reporter, in turn, wrote a fine description of the Tejon Ranch.

"The rancho from which I write this—the Tejon it is called—seems to me," Nordhoff stated, "about the finest property in the United States in a single hand." It contained some 200,000 acres and was located at the junction of the Sierra Nevada with the Coast Range. Over 100,000 sheep lived on the Tejon, and it took eight to nine weeks to shear the entire flock. The sheep were divided into "bands" which contained from 1,300 to 2,000 sheep under the care of shepherd. Each band had a range limited by the available water in the area. Each night the shepherd drove the animals into a corral and retired to sleep on a nearby *tepestra* close to the corral's entrance. The *tepestra,* a high platform, was raised some twelve feet off the ground with solid, implanted poles and afforded protection from grizzly bears, still plentiful in the region. Other creatures—mountain lions, wildcats, fox and coyotes—constantly menaced the sheep.[13]

Various nationalities of men served as shepherds at the Tejon. Beale employed Spaniards, Chinese, and Scotsmen. Approximately once a week, a ration master from a regional station came by the various flocks with a supply mule and gave the shepherd his rations for the upcoming week. The ration master also counted the sheep each week. Any missing animals had to be accounted for by the shepherd, who was occasionally allowed to butcher a sheep for food. Ration masters were subordinate to the majordomo, who examined the pasturage and made sure that new pastures were available when needed. He kept the corrals in order and handled the hiring of extra laborers at lambing time. The majordomo also checked the sheep regularly to prevent scab, virtually the only disease which bothered California sheep. Almost an isolated world, the Tejon required many other types of workers. There was a general superintendent, bookkeeper, storekeeper, blacksmiths, teamsters, ploughmen, gardeners, and servants.

Nordhoff was surprised to find that some three hundred Indians still resided on the ranch composing a "happy, tolerably thrifty and very comfortable" peasantry. They had been allowed to enclose small tracts of land, and Beale's manager purchased their surplus produce. These were the same Indians who were living in such primitive conditions when Beale established the Tejon reservation in the 1850s. These once savage men were "as civilized as a good many who come in emigrant ships from Europe to New York," Nordhoff ventured. They were a contrast to the Indians on the Tule River Reservation, who were idlers, gamblers, and simply "good for nothing."[14]

Perhaps in return for Beale's hospitality, Nordhoff took on an assignment for Beale. He had learned that Thomas R. Bard wished to dispose of the Simi Ranch, a sizeable piece of real estate, one-third the size of the Tejon. As Nordhoff was also writing about Santa Barbara and Ojai Ranch, based on information from Bard, Beale asked him sound out Bard on the price of the Simi property. The reporter told Bard that some of his friends might be interested in buying investment property, and Bard offered the Simi Rancho, located west of San Fernando, for $130,000 in gold. Nordhoff reported the sum to Beale, who thought the price was too steep.[15]

Nordhoff was one of California's most important promoters. In his articles, he described a land blessed by a mild climate, with unlimited opportunity, almost a newfound Eden. The Bakersfield *Weekly Courier* was very grateful for Nordhoff's praise of southern California and reiterated to skeptics that everything Nordhoff said was absolutely true. Quoting the correspondent, the *Courier* declared: "The poor in this state are a very small class, and there is no poverty in the European sense. The means of subsistence are easy beyond the belief of an eastern man." Several years later, Nordhoff took advantage of the California boom and wrote *California: For Health, Pleasure, and Residence.* Fittingly, he dedicated the book to Edward F. Beale, a man who had promoted California for most of his life.[16]

Bakersfield, the county seat, had become the dominant community in Kern County. Based on agriculture, it had an excellent location in the southern San Joaquin Valley. On July 6, the *Bakersfield Kern County Weekly Courier* announced that an expensive, modern building was going up—the Beale Hotel, still another project of Edward F. Beale. As Bakersfield was known for sizzling summer heat, the architect planned to situate the building in such a manner as to admit breezes to every part of the structure. There would be water pipes throughout, and the three-story building would have suites for families, in short, all the comforts of a first-class hotel.[17]

Late in the spring of 1872, Beale returned to the East and spent several weeks at the summer resort community of Long Branch, on the New

Jersey coast. President Grant also liked to retreat in summer to this seaside town, known for cool breezes and excellent carriage roads. It was perhaps natural that two men who shared a common passion for the American trotter horse should develop a friendship. Beale, who worshipped prominent men, treasured every line of correspondence from the president. On September 9, a messenger appeared at Beale's door at Long Branch with a note from Grant, which stated: "Mrs. Grant and I will be pleased to have you dine with us, socially, this afternoon at two o'clock."[18]

The two men found they had much in common. From his days in California, Grant knew something of Beale's early career. Possibly the fact that Beale had not held a military rank during the Civil War somehow appealed to Grant, who found little entertainment in reminiscing about the war. Beale's well-known storytelling ability complemented Grant's usual reticence. The two families also had common characteristics. The children were roughly the same age, and both Julia Dent Grant and Mary Edwards Beale suffered from eye trouble. Mrs. Grant's brothers had also known Beale before the war. Grant seemed irresistibly attracted to men of wealth, and Beale appeared to be one of the wealthiest. On political and social matters, Grant and Beale's views coincided. Grant may have wanted Beale to speak for him during the upcoming election, but unlike past years, Beale did not make speeches during the campaign. In the years that followed they shared an ongoing friendship.

The lengthy illness of Mary Ann Edwards, Beale's mother-in-law, helped to curtail Beale's political activity. Her death came after months of patient suffering, apparently from cancer, and once again Beale took up his pen and wrote an obituary. "She filled the brightest ideal of home excellence," he said. Mrs. Edwards had "neither time nor inclination for the prattle and gossip of society." In her seventy-three years, she had displayed firmness of character and a loving, quiet, religious strength. Even during her painful dying months, she was "consoled by the most profound Christian faith," perhaps inherited from her Quaker ancestors. Beale was named the executor of Mrs. Edwards's estate, but he signed the task over to Harry Edwards. The estate was valued at $19,218 and was divided between Harry Edwards, Mary Edwards Beale, and Abby L. Kerlin, a sister of the deceased. The property included eight mortgages and a sizeable amount of stock. Leaving Harry Edwards to handle the administration of the estate, Beale, his wife, and two daughters left Chester in the fall of 1872 to spend the winter months in San Francisco. The family was accompanied by Abby Kerlin, the widow of John Kerlin, president of the Bank of Delaware County and a prominent Chester attorney.[19]

In the presidential election of 1872, Grant won an easy victory. Beale's cousin, Admiral David Dixon Porter, attended the victory party and apparently sounded out various possibilities for Beale. The next day, Porter wrote Senator Cameron and described briefly his evening with President Grant, who had reacted to the landslide victory "in his usual quiet way." Then Porter bluntly queried: "Has it ever struck you what a splendid Secretary of the Navy Cousin Edward Beale would make." Grant liked Beale very much, and the president had told Porter that he owed a great deal to Pennsylvania and Cameron. "Excuse me for giving this hint," apologized Porter, "but I am very fond of Beale and want to see him occupy a position I know he would do honor to."[20]

Before long, a number of newspapers reported that Beale's name was being mentioned for the position of secretary of the navy. A Chester paper said that Beale possessed "all the qualifications necessary to fill so distinguished a position." His selection would not only please the entire body of naval officers, but the general public as well. Even distant Bakersfield heard the story and gave more precise information. George Robeson, current navy secretary, would replace George Bancroft as minister to Berlin, and Beale would then step into Robeson's vacant post. The Bakersfield *Weekly Courier* added that Beale had reached the age in life when the "intellect is most clear and vigorous." Complementing Beale's fine mind was a certain special fitness for office—his great administrative ability acquired from holding a variety of public offices in earlier years. When Robeson remained at his post, the rumors about Beale ceased.[21]

Meanwhile, Beale's sheep business had suffered a serious setback. The 1870s ushered in a boom period for southern California, with extensive speculation. Ordinarily, Beale and Baker would sell their wool locally, but in 1872 they gambled and shipped 175,000 pounds to Boston in hopes of getting a better price. The cargo was insured against loss, but on November 9, an immense fire swept the business district of Boston and destroyed the harbor warehouses. The entire shipment of Beale and Baker wool was lost. Then, the insurance companies failed, and the partners were faced with a loss of $50,000. Shrugging off the loss, Beale and his family spent the winter in San Francisco, lodging at the Grand Hotel and enjoying the city's social life.[22]

Before returning East in March of 1873, Beale learned about the government's difficulties with the Modoc Indians in northern California. Originally inhabitants of the Tule Lake region, the Modocs had been forced to give up their ancestral lands and move to an Oregon reservation which they shared with traditional enemies, the Klamaths. In 1872, after conflicts with the Klamaths and the government failure to supply them with food, the Modocs fled the reservation and returned to their old home. The cavalry was sent in pursuit. The Indians eluded the soldiers and hid in the extensive lava beds south of Tule Lake. Beale took special interest in these developments for he regarded the Indian Department as responsible for the problem. He fully sympathized with the Indians' desire to live in their homeland. In mid-April at Chester, he heard that at a council meeting with the Indians, General E. R. S. Canby had been killed by the Modoc leader Captain Jack. With the speed of a brush fire, hatred against the Indians swept over the nation. Many persons called for total extermination of the Modocs.[23]

Beale took it upon himself to defend the tribe in three substantial articles in the Chester *Republican.* Although Beale deplored the murder of Canby, he pointed out that the nation was "reaping what we have sown" with regard to the Native American. "The Modoc Indians are fighting for a right to live where God created them," he stated. The origin of the Modoc War went back some twenty years. Immediately prior to his appointment as California Indian superintendent in 1852, an Indian fighter named Ben Wright engineered a massacre of the Modocs. According to Beale, the dead included the father of Captain Jack. At the urging of a few stockmen, the government had removed the tribe to Oregon, but the Indians "concluded to return to their own country rather than be starved by the Government and shot by the Klamaths."[24]

Beale asked the question: "Having taken from them their land, must we now wipe out their tribe from the face of the earth?" No good reason existed for the tribe's removal in the first place, and the "doctrine of extermination is unworthy of the civilization of the age in which we live." He called upon President Grant to save the Modoc tribe from annihilation and thereby spare the nation the disgrace of an official massacre.

The affair ended when soldiers eventually forced the Modocs to surrender. The feared massacre did not take place. A trial was held, and Captain Jack and three colleagues were convicted and executed. The judgment was harsher than Beale would have dealt the Indians. Doubtless he felt disgusted when he learned that Captain Jack's body had been disinterred, embalmed, and sent East for public exhibition.[25]

For some time, Beale had contemplated moving to Washington to be closer to the nation's political life. In February of 1871, he had purchased for $60,000 the red brick, three-story Decatur House, occupied since 1862 by government offices. After the purchase, which was recorded in Mary Edwards Beale's name, Beale asked William Belknap, secretary of war, and Brigadier General Amos Eaton, commissary general of subsistence, to vacate the building as soon as possible. On January 2, 1872, Beale informed General Eaton that he anticipated moving into the house in September. When the government turned the property over to Beale, the army's heavy use required extensive repairs. Throughout 1873, workmen labored on the home under Beale's close supervision.[26]

A reporter for the Washington *Capital* toured the Decatur House after Beale's renovation and predicted that "without doubt the old Decatur mansion will again rank first among the fashionable residences of our city." Rumors already were circulating that during the coming winter season the house would contain some of Washington's "most distinguished gentlemen and ladies." The *Capital* reporter was impressed with Beale's taste and selection in decorating the dining room, the library, the billiard room, and the conservatory, all located on the main floor. Upon ascending the stairs, one entered the north drawingroom, "without exception, the finest room in any private residence in the city." The second floor also contained the south drawing room, boasting French gray side walls with Japanese paneling and borders.[27]

With the sole exception of the White House, the Decatur House was the most historic private residence in the capital. Designed by Benjamin H. Latrobe, the home was constructed by Commodore Stephen Decatur, who moved into the building in 1819. Although a model of architectural simplicity, the house reflected Latrobe's genius, particularly in the elegant, domed vestibule. In the years following Decatur's death in 1822, a succession of the nation's most important men occupied the house. Henry Clay, Martin Van Buren, Edward Livingston, and George M. Dallas resided in Decatur House at various times. Beale was determined to make the house the center of Washington society.

Located on the corner of Jackson Place and H Street, the Decatur House faced Lafayette Park, which was dominated by a bronze statue of Andrew Jackson superbly mounted on a rearing charger. Across the open square and on the south side of the park was the White House. Beale was certain to see the president frequently. In other homes around Lafayette Park lived many of the political leaders of the nation, and Beale fully realized a dramatic change in his life would be forthcoming. Finally, in the fall of 1873, the house was ready for occupancy. On October 3, the Chester *Republican* noted with "deep regret" that Beale and his family had left the previous day for the house in Washington.[28]

According to local tradition, the Washington social season officially opened on January 1, but most hosts commenced entertaining in November. The Beales held their first parties about this time and made a highly favorable impression. In early December, they gave an elaborate dinner party, attended by President and Mrs. Grant, General and Mrs. William T. Sherman, Secretary and Mrs. Hamilton Fish, and Admiral and Mrs. David D. Porter. Throughout the winter season the local newspapers frequently mentioned the Beales or activities at the Decatur House. Beale was thanked by the Washington *Star*'s society reporter for reviving the "hospitality for which the Decatur House was celebrated in the olden times." Almost every week, the second floor ball room was "crowded with fashionable guests."[29]

While Beale entertained in Washington, his business interests in California took an unpleasant turn. In late 1873, he joined with Senator John P. Jones of Nevada in a scheme to develop a new port facility at Truxtun (near Santa Monica) which would divert shipping from Wilmington. Named for Beale's son and grandfather, Truxtun was half the distance from Los Angeles—much closer than was Wilmington on San Pedro Bay. The project included a proposed short-line railroad, called the Truxtun and Los Angeles. On January 2, 1874, Beale purchased an option on Rancho San Vicente y Santa Monica from Robert S. Baker, his Tejon partner. Under the agreement, Beale and Thomas Sheppard agreed to forfeit a $20,000 down payment should they decide against the purchase. The Wilmington *Enterprise* and Los Angeles businessmen, heavily invested in shipping and transportation in Wilmington, opposed the Beale and Jones scheme. Soon afterwards, Baker withdrew from the sheep-raising partnership to pursue his own interests in Los Angeles.[30]

But the grandiose plans for Truxtun faltered. On May 26, Baker wrote to Beale in Washington that he should comply with the agreement to purchase the rancho and warned Beale not to expect preferential treatment. Then in July, Baker filed suit against Beale and Sheppard in California's Seventeenth District Court at Los Angeles. Baker brought the action to declare the legal forfeiture of the $20,000 deposit and to assure his absolute ownership of Rancho San Vicente y Santa Monica against any possible future claim by Beale. The court heard the case and the judgment went in favor of Baker. He was entitled to the $20,000 and kept full possession of the property.[31]

In the middle of the haggling, Beale in mid-June went to Chester to attend his son Truxtun's graduation from the Pennsylvania Military Academy. A top student, Truxtun delivered a speech about the connection between modern civilization and Christianity. All advances of commerce and industry stemmed from the true faith, he declared, and added that God used commercial agents to spread Christianity. Someday, Truxtun predicted, a world would exist in which paganism would belong entirely to the past, and free Christian commerce would be found everywhere. The local newspaper complimented Truxtun on the speech and predicted a bright future for him. His father was proud and wired a telegram to his wife: "Trux got through splendidly." The Beales now prepared for a summer at Long Branch, while Truxtun left to attend Columbia University.[32]

After the summer ended, Beale turned his attention to California matters. Although the Truxtun and Los Angeles Railroad was not revived, he continued work on the commercial facilities at Truxtun. Beale also rented the Tejon Ranch to H. W. Woodward, a man thoroughly acquainted with sheep production. The total wool clip for 1874 totalled 242,000 pounds (spring wool—112,000 pounds; fall wool—130,000 pounds), and was valued at $70,000. The Bakersfield *Weekly Courier* called the production the biggest known on any one ranch in either California or Nevada. The new overseer, J. C. Cutting, planned to develop the Tejon's potential even further.[33]

In order to satisfy his love for trotters, Beale looked for property near Washington that could be used as a horse farm. Near Hyattsville, Maryland, only ten miles from Decatur House, Beale discovered Ash Hill, a beautiful country estate of some one thousand acres. On a wooded ridge, above a grassy valley, rested a twelve-room house built in the 1840s. The house commanded a fine view of rolling hills and valleys, and at night the sparkling lights of Washington could be seen through the clear air. Beale fell in love with the property, and in 1875 he purchased Ash Hill for $50,000. Beale now planned his entrance into the ranks of successful breeders.[34]

President Grant also took an interest in Beale's farm and tried to coax Beale into purchasing some of his own stock. Grant owned a horse farm near St. Louis, and circumstances had forced him to liquidate his entire stock. With the depressed economy, he told Beale that the stock would bring 25 percent of its value. Grant urged Beale to purchase a second generation Hambletonian stallion which had won the first prize at the St. Louis Fair in 1875. Beale may have purchased several Grant horses, for Grant became a frequent visitor to Ash Hill during his last year and one-half in the White House.[35]

On September 13, 1875, Beale went to New York City to address the New York branch of the California Pioneers Society. He hoped to quiet stories about the recent death of his friend William C. Ralston and the collapse of the Bank of California. Many newspapers felt the bank had failed due to Ralston's speculations, and his death, presumably by suicide, was a permanent effort to avoid accountability. Although Ralston had committed illegal acts in a vain effort to stave off the bank's failure, Beale did not believe that the banker was a scoundrel. On many previous occasions, Ralston had helped either Beale or his friends. Consequently, Beale delivered a lengthy eulogy which emphasized the departed man's contributions.[36]

In the passing years, Beale seemed to have lost enthusiasm for his Pico Springs Oil development. His partner, Robert Baker, however, was optimistic about the property. In 1873, Beale and Baker had been part of an eighteen-man syndicate that organized the Los Angeles Petroleum Refining Company and erected a primitive refinery at Lyons Station. Two years later, the company was deep in debt, and the refinery had closed. Star Oil Works of San Francisco then contacted Baker, who gave the company verbal permission to collect Pico Springs oil and drill on the claim in return to a one-eighth interest in all oil for Baker and Beale. In mid-August of 1875, Star Oil Works drilled a 120-foot well, which produced ten to twelve barrels a day. This well—Pico No. One—became the West's first commercial oil well. [37]

Other companies now expressed interest in the San Fernando District. With a ten-million-dollar capitalization, the San Francisco Petroleum Company began drilling one-half mile east of Pico, using the finest equipment available. In February of 1876, Sanford Lyon, working for Beale, Baker, and others, drilled a 170-foot well, near Pico No. One. Star Oil now decided something more substantial than Baker's word should be obtained, and negotiations produced a 1,000-foot lease around Pico Springs for three years. Baker signed the lease in Beale's behalf. After the lease's expiration, all oil wells would pass to Beale, Baker, Leaming, and Lyon. [38]

But Beale's attention was largely on other things. His income from the Tejon Ranch was secure, and in the years from 1868 he devoted much of his life to pastimes. Through his friendship with Grant and his devotion to Stalwart Republican principles, Beale finally earned a reward. One day in early 1876, while riding in a carriage, Grant turned to Beale and said: "Beale, I sent your name to the Senate to-day as minister to Austria." Genuinely surprised, Beale remonstrated about leaving the country, perhaps hoping to take an active role in the presidential campaign which promised to be close and hotly contested. "I took that all into consideration," said Grant, "but I knew it would please Mrs. Beale and your daughters, so don't let us talk about it, old fellow." Despite his feeble protests, Beale was delighted. [39]

Chapter 12

MINISTER TO THE COURT AT VIENNA

To me this seems the least homogeneous nation in the world. It is a most complicated government. There is an Austrian as well as a Hungarian Parliament. There are laws prohibiting certain things in Austria, which are encouraged and permitted in Hungary. The language of the two countries is totally distinct, and what is worse, the sentiments of the two people very much opposed. At present they are held together by the mutual necessity of one for the other, but when divided by such a powerful feeling, as will be evoked by the Russo-Turkish war, its condition cannot but be regarded as critical and precarious.

—Beale on Austria-Hungary
March 31, 1877

On March 22, 1876, following a business trip to California, Beale learned from Senator Cameron that President Grant would soon send his name to the Senate to be confirmed as the new minister to Austria-Hungary. The appointment gave Grant a chance to pay a political debt to Pennsylvania and Simon Cameron before he left office. He also wanted to give his friend Edward Beale a present. Cameron promised his full support in steering the nomination through the Senate, adding that little opposition was expected there. Hamilton Fish, who knew Beale from Decatur House receptions, felt that the choice was an excellent one.[1]

In late May, Beale's nomination to the Court of Vienna was made public. Most newspapers reacted favorably and printed biographical sketches, many highly inaccurate, describing Beale's unusual career.

Charles Nordhoff supplied the New York *World* with one of the best sketches. The celebrated writer recited Beale's heroism in the Mexican War, his contribution to the Gold Rush, the development of the California Indian reservation system, the camel experiment and wagon road surveys, and the surveyor generalship. Nordhoff noted Beale's ability with foreign languages and his understanding of public issues. Beale was among the first in Pennsylvania "to urge in public speeches that a vote should be given to the colored people." The *New York Times* stated that Beale was a man of culture, whose name had been "mentioned by rumor in connection with several other federal appointments." The *Times* knew about the friendship between Grant and Beale, but inaccurately traced its origins back to the pre-Civil War days in California.[2]

But during his long years in California, Beale had made numerous political enemies. Thomas Sim King, editor of the San Francisco *Bulletin* and brother of long-dead James King of William, had hated Beale ever since the violent days of 1856.[3]

On May 25 and 27, 1876, the *Bulletin* published long sketches of Beale's career and charged the new minister with repeated acts of corruption and malfeasance during his tenure in various public offices in California. As Indian superintendent, Beale supposedly had spent $750,000 on improvements at Fort Tejon, which he later acquired by a fraudulent land grant. By controlling precious water, Beale had expanded his ranch to the size of the state of Massachusetts. On numerous occasions, the *Bulletin* continued, Beale hired front men to file for property which he bought in order to keep down the prices. The key to Beale's acquisition of land was his appointment as surveyor general. "It is little to say that he administered the affairs of that office in a scandalous manner," stated the editor. The attack on Beale even reached back to the old charge that Beale connived with Fremont to obtain government cattle contracts, twenty-five years before. On June 5, the *New York Times* echoed these charges, saying that Beale did not possess a single quality necessary for a statesman. He was "hot-headed, vain and weak" and not a fit representative to send abroad. Because his candidacy had strong support, Beale declined to answer the charges publicly.[4]

Beale wrote his son Truxtun about the attacks. He could easily refute such slanderous statements, but "mendacious miscreants" hoped to provoke a public dialogue by the articles. Beale reminded Truxtun that Thomas King, the *Bulletin's* editor, was a "fugitive from Missouri Justice," a charge that frequently circulated during the days of the 1856 Committee of Vigilance. Beale then commented on the specific accusations. First, the construction of Fort Tejon occurred after Beale left the Indian superintendent's office. Regarding the Fremont cattle transaction, he either forgot the arrangements or lied to his son, saying that when he was appointed Indian superintendent, he had not seen Fremont for a long time. "I never bought a single head of cattle from him of any kind whatever in my life," said Beale. The accusations about his landholdings were also spurious. Beale had purchased legitimate Mexican grants, which anyone with the inclination and the money could do. "What advantage could I possibly gain for this purpose by being Surveyor General?" he asked.[5]

Despite the newspaper accusations, Beale's nomination was easily confirmed. Personal congratulations came from several persons, including Bayard Taylor and Cousin Ambrose W. Thompson. Taylor, who had some experience in the foreign service, said "if you like the position, I rejoice for your sake, but I rejoice for the country's sake, anyhow." For the first time in many years, Beale was again in the national news. *Harper's Weekly* noticed the appointment and published a distorted personal sketch. On June 6, he took his oath and accepted the position.[6]

On the following day, Beale received a letter of instructions from Secretary of State Hamilton Fish. As minister, he would earn a salary of $12,000 per year. Fish included a letter from Grant to Emperor Franz Joseph, the ruler of Austria-Hungary, a list of diplomatic agents abroad, and a letter of credit for London, where Beale would draw his salary. Fish concluded by saying that the State Department was confident that Beale's "intelligent and zealous attention to the interests of the United States" would further improve the already cordial relations between the two nations. By July, Beale and his family had sailed for Europe.[7]

On July 31, Beale reached Vienna and was greeted by J. F. Delaplaine, the charge d'affaires. As a student of European history, Beale knew that the once all-powerful House of Hapsburg had been severely weakened by the events of the nineteenth century. Austria-Hungary was governed by a limited monarchy. Two parliaments and a constitution somewhat checked the autocratic rule of Emperor Franz Joseph. Nevertheless, Franz Joseph dominated the dual monarchy as important offices, such as finance, foreign affairs, and the army, came under his direct control. Although the Hapsburgs boasted of their ancient heritage, the oldest royal family in Europe, the empire trembled with instability. Austria and Hungary appeared to most visitors to be two distinct nations with different laws and governments, over which the monarchy had reared a superstructure. In 1876 the most pressing question in Austria and throughout Europe concerned the ultimate fate of Turkey's Christian provinces. This sticky problem, known as the Eastern Question, posed a source for endless confrontations between various powers—particularly for Great Britain, Russia, and Austria-Hungary.[8]

Chapter 12

On August 7, at the Foreign Ministry, Beale in the company of Delaplaine and Count Gyula (Julius) Andrassy, was ushered into the emperor's presence. The usually icy and aloof personality of Franz Joseph was replaced with a demeanor of "graceful affability and courtesy," the new minister wrote. Official letters were exchanged. Somehow Joseph had learned of Beale's career in the American West and with obvious delight inquired about his experiences with the American Indians. Probably Andrassy had provided the emperor with the information that Beale enjoyed hunting, for the emperor told Beale he would find him a "most acceptable comrade" for the chase.

Two days later, Beale was granted a formal audience with Franz Joseph. The American minister presented the personal letter from President Grant and expressed the president's regard for both the emperor and the peoples of the empire. Beale pledged to work for the continued good relations between the two countries. The emperor asked Beale to convey to Grant his warmest feelings and mentioned the hospitality shown the Austrian exhibits at the Philadelphia Centennial Exposition, as well as the cordial treatment which the Imperial Navy's ships always received in American ports. Joseph also wanted to express his friendship for the many thousands of naturalized American citizens who had been born in the empire. As on the occasion of their first meeting, the audience concluded with a discussion of hunting. Surely, the emperor must have felt pangs of jealousy when Beale recounted stories of his hunting antelope, buffalo, and grizzly bears.[9]

Beale seemed off to a splendid start. He entertained hopes that he would become an intimate associate of the monarch. But as time passed, the promises about hunting did not materialize, and Beale worried about an apparent coolness he felt at court. Count Andrassy hinted that the problem lay in Mexico, and he asked Beale to tell him about the country, particularly about the French intervention and Maximilian, Joseph's favorite younger brother. Someone had told Franz Joseph that Beale had aided the Juaristas, who had eventually executed Maximilian. With candor, Beale gave an American's interpretation of the French intervention. He admitted his own involvement in the liberal cause, but, of course, he had nothing to do directly with Maximilian's death. Andrassy was impressed, and on the following day he advised the emperor that Beale was the "only man who has ever made the Mexican tragedy clear to me. You should speak with him." Beale was summoned to a private breakfast at Schoenbrunn, the emperor's summer residence in Vienna. The American elaborated on his defense of Juarez. Joseph was pleased and a friendly relationship ensued.[10]

After surmounting this major hurdle, Beale turned his attention to

202

the war between Serbia and Turkey. On August 14, he sent Secretary Fish a lengthy analysis of the conflict, based upon conversations with a number of Europeans. The conflict, he insisted, was primarily religious in nature. Almost every Christian he spoke to had urged support for the Christian population of Turkey. In order to elicit opinions, Beale had adopted the tactic of defending Turkey's action. Invariably, his listener rebuffed him. The war could conceivably engulf the entire continent of Europe. Beale doubted that the Turkish massacres of Christians had been official policy but believed it a natural outcome of strong religious animosities. Only the problem of dividing the spoils kept the major powers out of the conflict. "With all this we (United States) have, happily, as a nation, no immediate concern," Beale concluded.[11]

Four days later, Beale sent a dispatch to the State Department indicating his strong support for the unfortunate Christians in Turkey's Christian lands. Confirmed reports of massacres of Christians by Turks had reached Vienna. Beale bitterly reported that the Turkish irregulars "especially commend themselves to the execration of humanity in general." He shuddered at hearing of outrages and the "grossest licentiousness added to an insatiable thirst for plunder." As a Christian, civilized nation, the United States must oppose the Turks. "Our Indians are gentle doves compared with these people," Beale stated, concluding his dispatch with eloquence: "To create a desert and call it peace is not a new art, but to revive it as a lost one belongs to the warfare of the modern Turks. . . ."[12]

Three weeks later the mismatched war between Serbia and Turkey ended, with the Turks victorious at the battle of Alexinatz. Beale's views on the Eastern Question were always clouded by his own Christian faith and by the Austrian Foreign Ministry, which supplied much of his information. On September 8, he proposed to Secretary Fish what he called an obvious solution to the problem. Serbia, Bosnia, and Romania should unite themselves into a confederation modeled upon the United States. Such a combination would make a powerful country and could command the respect of all its neighbors: Austria-Hungary, Russia, and Turkey.

Ultimately, Beale forecast, the Christians would win out. But the European powers would have to take action. Turkey was like an old boiler ready to explode at any minute. On August 31, a new sultan, Abdul Hamid, had come to power, but he was characterized by Beale as a man with a "sullen and gloomy temper." Christians under Turkish rule would continue to suffer until their progressive, docile, humane, and industrious characteristics overcame the backwardness of the Turks. Beale quoted Sir Gardiner Wilkinson to indicate his own opinion of Turkey. " 'It is the only instance of a nation having reached its zenith of power without having been civilized,' " said Wilkinson, who added: " 'It came to Europe as a horde, it became powerful as a horde and it remains a horde.' "[13]

As American minister, Beale frequently found himself involved in work far removed from an analysis of European politics. Shortly after arriving in Vienna, he undertook a thorough inventory of the American legation, including archives, furniture, photographs, and even an itemized list of the books in the library. Beale also had regular duties which involved signing passport renewals, overseeing the bookkeeping of the legation, and handling the problems of Americans living in Austria.[14]

Throughout his stay in Vienna, Beale sent dispatches to the State Department concerning the difficulties with Turkey. If the peace negotiations between Turkey and Serbia should prove a success, he wrote, at best they would produce a future full of anxiety and "liable at any moment to set Europe in a blaze of war." There was only one solution to the conflict. The "Gordian knot" must be cut by the termination of Turkish rule over the Christian provinces in Europe. Due to the strong religious bent of the Russian empire and an ancient desire for an outlet to the Mediterranean, Russia took a special interest in defending the Christians. A war between Russia and Turkey would be a foregone conclusion, but should Russia gain control of the Christian provinces, Austria would feel threatened.

Beale tried to analyze the complicated international scene. Germany did not wish to see Russia in a powerful position, while Great Britain seemed to support the Turks, who provided a commercial advantage by blocking the Bosphorus Straits. Any shift could cause problems. Beale believed that Russia was pursuing the proper course. The czar, at least, had chosen the morally correct side of the argument. "All things considered," wrote Beale, "I am glad our country is not on this continent for the outlook is not encouraging. There is festering to a head a most irrepressible conflict between Muhammedanism and Christianity."[15]

Beale and his family also spent a great deal of time attending the countless social functions in the capital and hosting dinners and balls at the American legation. He also watched for interesting publications that might prove useful to the government. From time to time, he would forward a shipment to Washington. Despite the press of his duties, Beale found time to engage fully in the social life of the Viennese court. His adventures in the American West made him a much sought after guest for parties. His wife and two daughters thoroughly enjoyed themselves, while Truxtun spent the winter in Paris and studied French. The San

Francisco *Alta California* of October 19 wrote that the official receptions given by Beale were the most conspicuous in Vienna. The social life was romantic, sparkling with the splendor of European nobility. Soon, Beale's oldest daughter, Mary, fell for the charms of an attractive Russian diplomat, George Bahkmeteff, and despite her father's strong objections, the courtship became serious.[16]

Beale also found time to enjoy hunting at Ischl, the emperor's country estate, and to discuss horses with Empress Elizabeth, wife of Franz Joseph, one of the best riders he had ever met. Elizabeth spent much of her life traveling about Europe, engaging in equestrian contests, and attending horseshows. The lovely empress was such an accomplished horsewoman that she could perform stunts on horseback generally seen only at a circus. Almost every man at the Viennese court, including Beale, was captivated by Elizabeth's beauty, which she maintained by a series of faddish diets. For the rest of his life, Beale treasured a photograph of the empress which she presented to him.[17]

On December 14 Beale thought of a way to involve the United States in the quagmire of the Eastern Question. He suggested to Secretary Fish that conditions might be right "to discuss our rights of free use of the Straits of the Bosphorus, and the assertion of such rights, as natural to all American ships." Under the existing situation, Turkey denied the United States free passage. All ships had to anchor and wait upon the permission of the sultan. England liked the regulation for it tied up the Russian fleet. Yet, the straits constituted a "natural high way of the sea," and if the United States allowed Turkey to control the Bosphorus, England might someday attempt to shut off the Mediterranean Sea at Gibraltar. The United States had never signed the protocol which gave Turkey this privilege and therefore should not be held to it. American commerce was growing in the area, Beale indicated, and free access would speed its development.

Although Beale's idea was intriguing, Fish did not believe the time ripe for such a negotiation. A basic principle of American foreign policy was non-involvement in European affairs. American entanglement in the morass of the Eastern Question might even weaken the Monroe Doctrine in the western hemisphere.[18]

After spending a week with Franz Joseph at Ischl, Beale in late January of 1877 filed a report on the Constantinople peace conference. The results seemed discouraging. Turkey declined to accept any propositions, and Russia vowed independent action to aid the Turkish Christians. The czar said he would compel Turkey to recognize the rights of the Christians. Beale had heard that when Russia mobilized her army, it was found incapable of waging war. The armistice between Turkey and Serbia would expire on March 1, and Beale could not predict how many countries would be involved in the anticipated hostilities. If war resulted, the blame lay with Britain, for the previous spring that nation had encouraged the Turks by failing to join the other powers in protesting against the mistreatment of the Turkish Christians. "It is quite certain also to my mind," said Beale, "that all Europe must, within a very few years, undergo a fearful political fermentation, from which it will emerge purified."[19]

In late January, Beale received an invitation from Austrian Baron Orezy to visit the government farms at Kisber, Hungary. Early one morning, he caught a train and reached his destination that evening. A government carriage took him from the depot to the castle where he met Baron von Soest, who provided the "guest of the Empire" with room and servant. For three days, Beale toured and inspected the 45,000-acre farm devoted to agriculture and horse breeding.

At Kisber, Beale learned much about European agriculture. He compared Kisber's farmers with their American counterparts and wrote Secretary Fish that the American farmer was much better off. Wages, for instance, hovered around 25¢ per day for men, and less for women. Laborers seldom ate meat, and the principal diet staple was a brown or rye bread, supplemented by potatoes and onions. Beale was surprised by the women fieldworkers. The husky Hungarian females "took an equal amount of the hardest labor with the men." The women could be seen constantly in the fields reaping with cradles, cutting with scythes, pruning grapevines in the vineyards. On the nearby roads, Beale saw burly women carrying heavy baskets and wooden tubs on their backs, while others pulled small wagons, loaded with commodities. As an American Victorian, Beale was both impressed and shocked.

On the whole, Austrian farming was not as scientific as in the United States. Beale saw some mechanized farming and reported all the skilled laborers regarded the American made "Johnston Mower and Reaper and Self-Binder" as the best piece of farming equipment in the world. Unfortunately, peasant farmers were not as quick-witted as Americans. If a machine contained even slightly complicated parts, the item would be unsalable.

Beale was impressed by certain farming techniques. The fields, for instance, did not require fencing. On forested land, the government enforced the strictest economy. Wherever timber was cut, saplings were always planted. Laws forbade the use of trees as firewood. Only twigs and scraps were burned, and Austrian conservation required that woody trimmings from the grapevines be saved. "This contrasts very strongly with our wasteful destruction of forest trees, all over our country, and the loss of which will doubtless come to be severely felt by our successors in the land," Beale predicted. Finally, Austrian farmers used large quantities of fertilizers and manures to replenish soil nutrients.

But if the farming methods impressed Beale, the animal breeding astounded him. During his three-day stay at Kisber, he never saw a lean cow or horse. Lower Austria's long-horned cattle caught his attention. One giant animal carried four-foot horns and was sixteen hands high, the size of a horse. But as a horse fancier, Beale spent most of his stay in the large stables. Never in his life had he seen such a vast arena devoted to breeding. Franz Joseph had concentrated his attention on developing and improving every variety of horse and had achieved impressive results. Beale attributed the change to the novel breeding techniques. During the cold winter months the horses remained permanently indoors in spacious, heated stables, with knee-deep straw. The stables were so large that seventy-five horses had an ample area to exercise. In summer, the horses were taken outside to pastures. Beale also noticed that colts received a rich oat diet from birth and could eat as much food as they wanted.

In only a few years, Beale felt, all of Austria would be dominated by a superior breed of horse. The government operated a breeding program throughout the provinces which sent over one hundred of the finest stallions to various breeding stations. For a nominal fee, roughly two dollars, a peasant could have his mare serviced by the finest blooded horses in the world. The breeding program did not solely emphasize race horses. They had also developed a superior breed of draft horses. During the nineteenth century one did not have to state the obvious military application of Joseph's concentrated breeding efforts. Cavalry still dominated European warfare.[20]

After his pleasant stay at Kisber, Beale returned to Vienna to prepare for the marriage of his daughter Mary to George Bahkmeteff, the Russian diplomat. Beale had opposed the wedding, but when his daughter insisted he gave his consent and approval. Mary was ecstatic and wrote Senator Cameron about her pending wedding. Mary told Cameron, whom the Beale children regarded as a member of the family, that she was "going to break the promise I made you when I left home, and I'm going to marry a foreigner." She then described a recent ball her family had attended at the emperor's court. The display of brilliant uniforms of the men and the glittering diamonds of the ladies made an unforgettable impression on her. But she loyally insisted that none looked finer than her mother who had dined in the company of Empress Elizabeth and assorted royalty. In an aside, Mary chided the old senator about the results of the 1876 presidential election and urged him not to "let Tilden get into the White House."[21]

On February 11, 1877, Mary (Mamie) Beale and George Bahkmeteff were married. All of Europe attended the wedding, according to Beale, including a number of ambassadors. After the wedding, the party adjourned for a lively breakfast. Four days later Beale admitted to Cameron that Mamie married with "my consent," but he still believed that "American girls should marry in their own country." He asked Cameron to use his influence with Hamilton Fish to see if he could obtain a leave of absence to visit the United States.

Two months earlier, Beale had requested a leave, but Grant did not feel authorized to grant leaves which would extend beyond his term of office. By mid-February Beale's business affairs absolutely demanded his return for a short time. He also had grown tired of the post. He wrote Cameron that many persons would want his post, and "they will be very welcome to it." Beale did not want to be recalled, for such an act had a certain stigma to it. He wanted to have the satisfaction of resigning from an official position for a change. Presumably, if Tilden won the election, there would be no problem about obtaining a leave. Beale admitted to Cameron that he had not been impressed by European royal splendor. The court balls, for instance, were "pleasant enough, but no nicer than the President's."[22]

By telegraph Beale learned that the disputed presidential election had been resolved and Rutherford B. Hayes inaugurated president. In an exuberant letter to Fish, Beale commented on the election. "The whole country and I may say the whole world is to be congratulated on the result . . . ," he said. In any other country, the disputed election would have caused a violent struggle, but the peaceful resolution illustrated the "good sense of our people and their capacity for self-government." Throughout Europe, the supporters of democratic government applauded the result, while the monarchists were depressed. The aristocratic classes had believed that the Hayes-Tilden contest would terminate in the failure of the American form of government. Now monarchs and aristocrats had cause to worry. It was a nice time to be minister to Austria.[23]

Shortly after the inauguration of President Hayes, Beale took time to congratulate General Grant on his retirement. "No man of whom History makes mention is more to be envied than you," he wrote. Beale wished a long, happy life for Grant. He indirectly hinted at the strife that had plagued the recent election but said that when party sentiment faded Grant would be remembered "as the greatest central figure of the age." Beale then praised Grant for preserving "freedom" intact and passing the precious commodity to his successor. He did not intend to flatter Grant with his letter; he simply wanted to express his sincere gratitude and friendship. Beale hoped that in the future he would continue to enjoy Grant's warm friendship.[24]

On April 6, Beale learned from the new secretary of state, William S. Evarts, by telegraph that he could take a sixty-day leave of absence from his post in Vienna. He was very grateful for this respite and replied that he hoped to take his leave on about May 1. His tenure as minister was drawing to a close.

In mid-April, Beale attended a large dinner at the English embassy in Vienna and found to his surprise a general belief that America would align with Russia in event of a general European war. The Turkish ambassador, Alesha Pasha, took Beale aside and said: "So I see your country will go with Russia—against us!" Beale quickly responded: "Not at all. It would be in opposition to one of our cardinal political doctrines to interfere in European affairs. We wish commerce and peace with all, but alliance with none as against another." Someone then referred to a newspaper article in which the American minister to St. Petersburg had supposedly stated that the United States stood ready to defend Russia. Beale stated with force that "no such speech had ever been made anywhere in Europe by an American minister." When another foreign minister suggested that secret instructions had been given, Beale replied there were no secret instructions. If there were, he would know about them. Beale told Secretary Evarts that the Turkish minister was visibly relieved, but that twice during the same evening he had to repeat his assertions of American neutrality.[25]

On April 21, Beale sent his last dispatch to the State Department on the subject of the approaching European war. Russia would declare war on Turkey at any hour, he believed, and England would enter the war as Turkey's ally. Austria was uncertain; the Hapsburg Empire could go either way. If Franz Joseph allied with Russia, Hungary would be offended. An alliance with Turkey, though less likely, would strengthen Austria commercially and militarily through England's support. Neutrality seemed both impossible and unsafe to Beale. The Russian-Turkish war might engage nearly every important European state. As a perfect neutral, the United States "cannot fail to reap a rich harvest of commercial advantages." A major war would require arms, corn, wheat, wool, iron, and all types of manufactured articles. The war might give the United States the opportunity to seize the commanding commercial position it had held prior to the Civil War.[26]

On the same day that he penned his last dispatch, Beale and his family departed from Vienna. Prior to leaving, he called upon Count Andrassy, who had displayed good sense and genuine friendship, and thanked him for his hospitality and courtesy. He told Andrassy that Delaplaine would take charge of the American legation. By mid-May, Beale had visited the White House and tendered his resignation to President Hayes. It would take effect after July 1.[27]

As American minister to Austria-Hungary in 1876–77, Edward Beale had displayed an exceptional talent for international diplomacy, although his abilities had not been tested by a crisis. His command of foreign languages complemented his education and warm personality to make him an admirable representative of the United States. By his honesty in explaining the Mexican troubles and his love for horses and hunting, Beale had won the trust and friendship of both Emperor Franz Joseph and Empress Elizabeth. If he had remained minister for a longer period, Beale might have contributed significantly to American influence in Europe. But most diplomatic appointments in the nineteenth century rewarded party loyalty, and his selection was no exception. He had wanted the minister's position for personal gratification, and now he was satisfied.

Chapter 13

FRIEND OF
GENERAL GRANT

Necessarily at my age, and living where I do, I have known many
great men, but they were all like some fine fruit specked with
imperfection. He only was without blemish. They were great men—
great soldiers—great judges—great statesmen, but when you looked
them all over they were not like the kind friend I have lost and
who is buried today. They were simply great men. He alone was
both great and good!

—Beale's Eulogy for Grant
August 8, 1885

Late in life, Edward F. Beale told California historian H. H. Bancroft
that, following his return from Vienna in 1877, he became an idler, a
person without purpose. If true, Beale displayed a most peculiar form of
idleness, for he seemed constantly busy during these years. He plunged
into several important business ventures, principally the development
of California petroleum and the construction of a Nicaraguan canal. But
the overriding feature of this period was his close friendship with ex-
President Grant. From this friendship, Beale acquired an important place
in the ranks of the Stalwart Republicans, loyal followers of the former
president, and the Decatur House became the social center of the capital city.

Upon reaching the United States in the late spring of 1877, Beale
left immediately for California to check on his diverse business interests
there. With his partner Robert S. Baker, he went to the San Francisco
offices of California Star Oil Works and requested payment of their one-

eighth royalty on Pico oil. Pico No. One had begun to show significant production, and the two men demanded that California Star affirm that it had leased the Pico premises solely from Beale and Baker. California Star refused to acknowledge their claim, having learned that in August of 1865 the Pico claim had been relocated. Possibly other men were legally entitled to share in the ownership and perhaps Beale and Baker's claim was illegal. The company attempted to compromise with Beale and Baker, but they insisted upon their rights. No agreement was reached. Shortly thereafter, Beale visited his Tejon Ranch and then returned East.[1] Baker seemed more worried about losing the Pico than Beale because he had recently invested heavily in the Baker Block, a substantial multistory structure in Los Angeles. Beale chided Baker and reminded him that he had built the Baker Block against Beale's recommendations. He hoped the building would not ruin him.[2]

On March 22, 1878, Beale and Baker filed suit against California Star Oil Works. They asked the company to pay the overdue royalty, plus $150,000 in damages. Almost simultaneously, the California Star filed suit in San Francisco for the purpose of determining the ownership of the Pico claim. Beale and Baker reportedly declined a $50,000 settlement from Star Oil. The cases dragged through the rest of the year as legal battles occurred in San Francisco and Los Angeles district courts, the Los Angeles Land Office, and in the General Land Office in Washington.[3]

Beale and his wife sailed on April 11 for Europe to visit Mamie and George Bahkmeteff. In May, the Beales were joined by General and Mrs. Grant. They visited the Paris Exposition together, and according to Julia Grant's memoirs, they had "many happy excursions together." Beale remembered that he and Grant walked the city's streets until two o'clock in the morning. For the two horse fanciers, a highlight of their stay was a visit to what Grant dubbed the "Horse Oppera." Sometime in late May or early June, the Beales returned to the United States.[4]

The fall of 1878 found Beale ill at the Decatur House. He worried about the Pico Springs cases, which had been inconclusive, and wondered why Robert Baker had not written him. Rumors circulated that John D. Rockefeller's Standard Oil Company had bought out Beale and Baker's interests for $75,000, but the stories proved false. Meanwhile, he seemed to worry about his own fortunes, as some investments apparently had failed. On January 1, 1879, he wrote Baker that "I never was so poor in my life before." He told Baker that if he would send some encouraging news from California, he would "come out again and buck at some chance thing."[5]

While Beale fretted over his financial position, he continued to receive letters from Grant. Grant found the recent elections encouraging, particularly the senatorial elections of Roscoe Conkling and Donald Cameron, both Decatur House intimates. He also reiterated his admiration for the United States. "We are the most progressive freest and richest people on earth, but don't know it or appreciate it," he told Beale. Grant had also heard about a recent society wedding to which Emily Beale and U. S. Grant, Jr. had driven with a magnificent team of horses. The Grant family were encouraging a match between "Buck" Grant, and Beale's youngest daughter, but Beale opposed the idea. The Grants lacked substantial wealth.[6]

Edward Beale worried about the reform movement in California. When he attempted to sell the Rancho Laguna for Robert Baker, he found that the proposed new state constitution for California would make the sale impossible. The constitution would curtail the large landed estates through heavy taxation. Beale believed that California stood "on the verge of the worst sort of Communism." Writer Charles Nordhoff had always wanted to invest in a western rancho, but with the movement to revise the state constitution, he would not buy an inch of California property. An important influence on the movement was Henry George's famous work, *Progress and Poverty*, which appeared at this time. George had lived for a long period in California and saw the unequal distribution of land there as the major reason for poverty. Beale read the book, complimented George on his philosophic frankness, and added that the people whom George desired to reach with *Progress and Poverty* would never hear of it. But Beale was mistaken. George's sentiments were close to being enacted into law through the new constitution. Led by Denis Kearney, the proponents were as rabidly anti-Chinese as they were anti-estate owners. Kearney's followers should allow all Chinese into the state who desired to come, said Beale, for under the new constitution it would be impossible to "get any white men to live in such a state." Beale's fears proved unfounded. When the California Constitution of 1879 was ratified, it contained almost nothing to curtail the state's private landholdings.[7]

With the fear of "communism" removed, Beale and Baker continued to wrestle with the Pico Oil Springs matter. Beale worked in Washington to obtain a patent to the springs through college scrip, while Baker sought to perfect a title through the deed of Hernandez and Perea, the two vaqueros who filed on the site. But evidence seemed to indicate that the two vaqueros had never filed a homestead entry on the 160 acres, as Baker alleged. As soon as he submitted his application to the Los Angeles Land Office, based on a "lost" record, it was rejected. On April 12, 1879, the lease Baker and Beale had given Star Oil Works expired. Instead of ownership reverting to the partners, a San Francisco court appointed a receiver until the dispute over ownership was settled. Beale also learned that Lloyd Tevis, president of Wells, Fargo, and Company, had taken over the battle on behalf of Star Oil.

The opposition had grown too powerful. As Beale and Baker both needed money they agreed to a compromise with Star Oil. In return for signing over their rights to the Pico, they received a three-sevenths interest in California Star, or 4,286 shares of stock. The way had been cleared at last for the development of Pico oil. Over the next ten years, both Baker and Beale received substantial dividends from their holdings in California Star Oil Works. In time, after additional mergers, California Star evolved into Standard Oil of California.[8]

One of the reasons that Beale had surrendered on the oil claim derived from unsettled conditions on the Tejon Ranch. Robert M. Pogson, his manager at the Tejon, had reported that the extended drought had vitally affected the pastures. At this time the ranch contained 10,000 head of cattle and 68,000 head of sheep, but Beale was in the process of converting strictly to cattle. The livestock brokerage firm of Shoobert & Beale (Truxtun had joined the business) had advised that no demand existed for sheep in California. After trying to rent grassland in Los Angeles and San Diego counties, Beale ordered his majordomo, J. J. Lopez, to drive 16,000 head to sheep to the two mountain counties of Mono and Inyo near the Nevada border. On May 15, 1879, the drive got under way, headed for Willow Springs. Herbert Beecher, the son of Beale's friend, the Reverend Henry Ward Beecher, accompanied the drive in an effort to learn the business.[9]

At Big Pine, in Owen's Valley, Lopez received instructions from Beale to move the sheep across the scorching, desolate Nevada desert to Pioche, a booming mining camp, near the Utah border, two hundred fifty miles away. W. W. Hudson arrived to guide the party to Pioche. Before the drive started, Beale was offered one dollar per head at Independence, California for the sheep, but he declined to sell. The drive for Pioche began. When only thirty miles into Nevada, Hudson and Lopez received word from Beale that the band had been sold to Morton E. Post and to head the sheep to Green River, Wyoming.

In mid-July, the thirsty sheep became scattered on the Nevada desert, and Beale decided to meet Lopez and Hudson at Eureka in central Nevada. When he finally located the drive, Beale blamed Lopez and Hudson for the losses because they had failed to explore the desert in advance. On August 3, Beale wrote Baker from Eureka about the loss. "My feelings after two days hard riding through dust to find this little remnant of what might have been a fortune has not put me in a frame of mind to enjoy very much this filthy mining town," he said. The market was glutted and Post would only pay thirty-three cents per head. After all the hardships and risks, Beale would receive only $5,000 for the sheep. Recalling the $16,000 he had declined at Independence, Beale wrote: "Dull is no word to express my feelings."[10]

In early November, Beale got a letter from Grant, whose party had reached San Francisco. He agreed to join the Beales at the Decatur House shortly after Christmas but wanted no involvements in lavish dinner parties or other entertainments. Grant desired a restful visit, with an opportunity to visit Beale's farm and see the horses, particularly the Turkish Arabians. Later in the month, he reached the East and wrote Beale again. The receptions he endured following his return from the world tour had nearly pulled him to pieces. Grant enjoyed the hero's return, however, and called the welcome "most hearty and gratifying." He told Beale that he especially wanted to talk about a project they had been mutually interested in for quite some time—the construction of a canal across Nicaragua.[11]

Beale had been fascinated with the idea of an interoceanic canal since the mid-1840s when he first visited Central America as a lowly passed midshipman in the navy. During Grant's administration, he and Grant's boyhood friend Admiral Daniel Ammen had strongly advocated a Nicaraguan canal.[12]

Ammen and Beale organized an "initatory society" to promote the idea of a Nicaraguan canal and to take steps toward gaining the cooperation of Nicaragua. Among the members of the newly formed Provisional Interoceanic Canal Society were Beale, Ammen, George W. Riggs, George B. McClellan, Seth Phelps, and Levi P. Morton. Beale and Ammen believed that they needed General Grant to head their organization to attract investors. The question was apparently resolved when Grant wrote Ammen that if the American people would embrace the Nicaragua route in earnest, the only practical route as he saw it, he would give the project all conceivable aid. Several weeks later, he proposed a formula for the canal's construction. First, there must be a treaty between the United States and Nicaragua. Then, by act of Congress the canal should be incorporated. Grant suggested a figure of $100 million as the subscription amount and urged that the entire issue of stock be subscribed before work commenced.[13]

Quickly, Ammen, Beale, and others began to work on the incorporation. On November 27, Grant expressed to Beale a concern about European backers of the project. Undoubtedly, their money would be crucial for the canal construction, but Congress might reject a bill that hinted of European control. Perhaps the act of incorporation could list only the American incorporators, Grant suggested, with the European backers to be filled in at a later date. Beale should also take steps to contact the Nicaraguan government to work out the terms of the concession.[14]

On December 27, Grant and his family arrived in Washington for a brief visit with the Beales. Earlier, he had declined an invitation from President Hayes to stay at the White House. A large crowd gathered at the Baltimore and Potomac Station to greet the ex-president. Distinguished politicians were on hand to join the Beale family in welcoming Grant. When General Grant came to the carriage with lovely Emily Beale on his arm, the crowd cheered. With a lift of his hat, Grant acknowledged the reception, and the party boarded carriages for a quick dash to the Decatur House.

Beale tried to make Grant's visit a quiet and restful one. The dinner at the Decatur House on December 27 was attended only by the Beale and Grant families, Senator and Mrs. Donald Cameron, and Admiral Ammen. On Sunday morning, Grant and Beale attended services at the Metropolitan Methodist Episcopal Church, where they sat in the "Grant Pew." The visit to church was hightly unusual for Beale. Grant had managed to make him break his vow never to attend church, a vow he had kept since 1860. Throughout the day, prominent callers dropped by the Decatur House to pay their respects. Grant and Beale strolled over to the various governmental departments and then drove out to Bloomingdale to pay a call on Emily Beale (Beale's mother). They also visited Beale's Ash Hill farm and admired the horses. The two men then paid a brief call at the White House, chatting with Mrs. Hayes, as the president was out of town. While lodged with Beale, Grant saw Sherman, Sheridan, Levi P. Morton, Secretary William Evarts, Congressman James A. Garfield, Senator William B. Allison, and other prominent Republicans. On December 31, the Grant party departed Washington, bound for a winter in the South and Cuba.[15]

Midwinter of 1880 found Beale once again in California. At the Tejon, he checked on the efforts to convert the ranch to cattle producton. The change was proceeding on schedule. The ranch currently ran 15,000 head of cattle, and Beale planned to expand the number to 25,000 head. A seasonal ranching pattern had now been established which would remain unchanged for the rest of Beale's life. Every June herders would drive the cattle to summer pastures, high up in the mountains, where they would stay until mid-October. The herds then would be rounded up for shipment to market or for trailing to lower winter pastures. At Bealville, where the Southern Pacific Railroad crossed the northern edge of the ranch, cattle were loaded for shipment to markets east and west.[16]

While visiting California, Beale granted interviews to several newspapers. Not surprisingly, he strongly championed the election of Grant to a third term as president. "The cry of rotation in office is the curse of our affairs," he said. A man like Grant, who had shown for eight years his ability to handle national affairs skillfully, should not be declared ineligible for office by a slogan. On the contrary, Grant's experience should constitute a major reason for his reelection. The United States needed more continuity in office and less "political excitement," Beale said. Grant had displayed administrative abilities far greater than any of his predecessors in office and in fact was the "greatest and most remarkable man of the century." Beale knew that his friend would not seek the nomination, but should the Republican convention insist upon his candidacy for the nation's good he would be forced to accept. Beale reminded the reporter that Grant was in excellent health. [17]

In his interviews, Beale also commented on railroad developments. The Atlantic and Pacific Railroad was building along the thirty-fifth parallel across Arizona, heading toward California, he said, and soon would reach the state, breaking the Southern Pacific's monopoly. Beale held several thousand shares of stock in the company and even had granted the railroad a right-of-way across the Tejon Ranch. This would provide a better line than the Southern Pacific's convoluted tracks which climbed steeply through the Tehachapi Loop. The A & P, Beale believed, would also build a competing line into San Francisco via the peninsula, but he warned oceanside communities not to expect a coast railroad. The rugged California coastline made construction costs exorbitant and impractical. San Francisco faced a bright future. In thirty-five years, he had seen the community transformed from an isolated village of five houses to a metropolis of 300,000 residents, the greatest city on the Pacific coast. Beale believed that San Francisco's prosperity would continue unabated, and eventually, the Golden Gate city would become the "Queen City of the World."

Beale then turned his attention to the Nicaraguan canal. He firmly believed that the development should be an American controlled and protected enterprise, ignoring the fact that many Europeans would invest in the project. If Europe should interfere with American interests in the western hemisphere, the United States could simply cut off their supply of grains. If that occurred European nations would change the Lord's Prayer to read: " 'Oh America! Give us this day our daily bread.' "[18]

When Beale returned East, he found the Nicaraguan project in trouble. Despite his earlier promises of support, Grant had failed to take an active interest in the matter. Without Grant's support, which to Ammen and Beale meant Grant's presidency of the Provisional Society, the likelihood of Congress incorporating an agency to construct such a project diminished. Frederick Billings, the railroad magnate, added his name to the society, but Grant's lack of interest was costly and embittered his old friend Ammen. Other investments had claimed his attention and funds. Jesse Grant, the general's son, became an associate of James B. Eads, the famous bridge builder, in an enterprise to build a ship-railway across the Tehuantepec Isthumus in Mexico. The far-fetched scheme called for port facilities that would bodily lift cargo ships onto enormous railway flatcars. A slow-moving train would then tow the cars and ships across the isthmus. Both Beale and Ammen felt that Grant had been duped by Eads. If Eads's plan proved possible, there would be no reason for a canal, and the engineer promised it would be far less costly to construct.

The supporters of both the canal project and the ship-railway scheme became active. Nicaragua and Mexico respectively granted the desired concessions. In Congress fairly strong support developed for the Nicaraguan canal. The bill for canal incorporation was reported out of committee without a dissenting vote, but the ship-railway bill caused a storm of protest in the House of Representatives and was tabled. As the session ended, the Eads supporters combined forces with the American Panama Canal Syndicate, recipient of a 2.5-million-franc annuity, to block the Nicaraguan Canal Company's bill. Beale's group seemed stymied. [19]

Unlike Daniel Ammen, Beale ignored Grant's fickle support and remained a close friend of the former president. He advised Grant against lending his backing to the San Pedro Mining Company of New Mexico, which had offered Grant the company's presidency, a good salary, plus a sizeable quantity of stock. At first, Grant hesitated to follow Beale's advice, but he later learned that promoters were using him to push the mine's stock and declined the positon. Both Beale and Grant played limited roles in Garfield's election campaign in the fall of 1880, probably because they were not enthusiastic about Garfield's nomination. [20]

By November of 1880, Beale probably was the most influential resident of the District of Columbia. Yet, without a real political base, Beale would never wield more than influence. Consequently, on November 19, he publicly called for a constitutional amendment granting home rule to the District of Columbia. Residents should have all the rights of other American citizens, he said, including the right to vote and elect representatives. The amendment anticipated a form of statehood for the district. In his endorsement, Beale did not mention the importance that home rule would have on his own political fortunes, but if the district elected senators and representatives, Beale might gain one of those offices. Unfortunately, the amendment was greeted with little support outside of Washington, and the issue soon faded from the scene. [21]

During the winter of 1880–81, Beale was involved in numerous activities. As a social leader of Washington, he was selected to serve on President-elect Garfield's inaugural committee. But such a festive assignment consumed very little time, and he spent considerably more attention on developments relating to the Nicaraguan canal. Progress stalled on the incorporation bill, and passage grew less and less likely. Railroad promoters actively opposed the canal, stating that goods could be transported far cheaper by railroad. Grant had invested heavily in Mexican railroads and threw his support in that direction. During the winter, the Beale family visited the Grants in New York City, which rapidly was becoming Grant's adopted hometown.[22]

Throughout the 1880s, Edward Beale was Washington's most famous host. The Decatur House served as the unofficial headquarters for Republican Stalwarts, men who believed in General Grant and old-fashioned Republicanism. It also was the meeting place of all important men, regardless of party affiliation. Beale and his family even gained the friendship of a new neighbor, Henry Adams, noted scholar and descendant of the famous family. Although Adams abhorred Stalwart Republicans, Beale frequently entertained Henry and his wife Marian as dinner guests at Decatur House. Beale's daughter Emily, noted for her slashing sarcastic wit, charmed Adams and frequently visited the Adams's home. In 1880, Adams produced an anonymous book entitled *Democracy* which skillfully ridiculed the Washington community. A leading female character in the *roman à clef* was Virginia Dare, a thinly disguised Emily Beale. Adams recorded that Mr. Dare, Virginia's father, achieved his wealth as a "claim agent, or some such thing, and is said to have made his money by cheating his clients out of their claims." Emily Beale was embarrassed by her scandalous portrayal in *Democracy*, which said she violated "every rule of propriety" and could always be found absorbed in a flirtation with a foreign legation secretary.

Adams freely sought the entertainment and spectacle which Beale's circle afforded. Sometimes, however, he felt guilty about compromising his principles and asked: "What could be of a world that divided a man against himself and compelled morality to be selective?" The presence of powerful men, plus Emily's wit, made Beale's parties irresistible. On one occasion, a recently displaced politician, George Robeson, asked Emily if she knew of a permanent position for him. Emily replied without hesitation: "Why you know the penitentiary has been yawning for you for years!"[23]

Beale's dinners always featured the famous and powerful. At a typical dinner in January of 1881, Henry Adams sat next to General Sherman. Beyond Sherman loomed the "great" Roscoe Conkling of New York, who looked "more asinine and offensive than ever," observed Adams.

For Marian Adams, a high point was the after-dinner game "Fun in a Fog," or blindman's bluff, which had become an international fad. Even the dour figure of General Sherman could be seen with tears of laughter in his eyes watching the antics of the stumbling blindfolded victims. Not surprisingly, dinner with the Beales became an almost weekly affair for the Adamses. Certainly, Beale's parties surpassed the White House entertainments, where both Henry and his wife had recently become ill from drinking Potomac River water.[24]

Stalwart Republicans, like Beale, did not expect favors from James A. Garfield's new administration, and they got none. When Garfield succumbed to an assassin's bullet on September 2, 1881, after a valiant three-month struggle to live, the outlook for Stalwarts improved remarkably. Chester Arthur, the new president, had been known in the past as a leading Stalwart Republican. Grant and Beale expected to be rewarded for their loyalty. The ex-president fully believed he would be given a strong voice in naming important political appointments. Some of Grant's suggestions sounded unusual, almost ludicrous. On October 8, for instance, he recommended that Arthur appoint John Jacob Astor as secretary of the treasury. But the appointment which Grant most strongly pushed was Edward F. Beale for secretary of the navy.[25]

By early November of 1881, newspapers in the East and in California were supporting Beale for an appointment. Marian Adams reported to her Massachusetts relatives that Beale would be better than any other Stalwart, for he had promised not to allow stealing. The Washington *Republic* said that Beale's fitness for the office could not be questioned, and if he gained a position, it would be a "bad time for jobbers and cheating contractors."[26]

In early 1882, Beale wrote a long leaflet for distribution, which he called "Common Sense About the Navy—A Talk with Gen. Edward F. Beale." He designed the piece to answer charges that he lacked knowledge about the modern navy. Beale indicated that he would propose radical changes if he became navy secretary. The United States Navy must be prepared to fight a war with Great Britain, a lifelong fear of Beale's. Should such a war eventuate, the navy needed a fleet of swift, armored gunships to cripple British commerce. He suggested that light vessels be equipped with only one long gun. Speed would be the only criterion for a ship's size.

Beale proposed other radical changes. As navy secretary, he would eliminate the highest grades of officers, and make captain the top attainable rank. Such a suggestion was anathema to high-ranking American officers, who had fought for many years to gain the rank of admiral. In addition, Beale disliked the Naval Academy and sarcastically called it a university. A simple naval school, supplemented by the old-fashioned type of education which he himself had received, would produce the best officers. In sum, Beale suggested a dramatic and complete reorganization of the navy.[27]

President Arthur faced a thorny problem in filling the Navy Department. James G. Blaine, Garfield's secretary of state, had pushed New Hampshire's William E. Chandler for the appointment and had the New England states behind him. Arthur had already yielded two major appointments to Grant's friends: Frederic Frelinghuysen as secretary of state, and Timothy Howe as postmaster general. Of course, Beale was Grant's favorite, but the man's strange statements about naval reforms gave Arthur a valid reason for selecting Chandler over Beale. Chandler's appointment angered Grant, who told Beale he would ask no more favors of Arthur's administration.[28]

On February 4, 1882, Edward Beale celebrated his sixtieth birthday. With the Tejon Ranch under able supervision, he devoted himself almost entirely to Washington's political and social scene. In the late 1870s, and 1880s, he also began to break up the extensive family holdings in Chester, Pennsylvania. Selling a large number of lots from the land his wife had inherited, he arranged mortgages which provided a substantial additional income. In 1881, Beale had erected a multistory building called the "Beale Block" in downtown Chester, renting spaces for offices and stores and also invested in the stock of various companies, particularly railroads. His financial condition appeared stable. Although several times a millionaire, he was far from being one of America's wealthiest men.[29]

Beale and his family enjoyed a quiet year in 1882. In late May, Beale penned an elegiac obituary for Y. S. Walter, longtime editor and publisher of the Chester *Delaware County Republican*. For many years, Walter had given Beale almost unlimited access to his newspaper columns, printing his thoughts on international affairs and even his poetry. In early July, the Beale family left the heat of Washington and traveled to Long Branch, New Jersey, where they visited with the Grants. Some months later, Emily and Truxtun stayed with the Grants at their home in New York City. In early December, Grant gave Beale his Arabian horse, Leopard, with no strings attached. The year ended on a happy note.[30]

On New Year's Day, 1883, the Beale's gave the Grants an elaborate reception at the Decatur House. Shortly before their arrival, a reporter called and found Beale "immersed in a volume of ancient history and puffing on a fragrant cigarette." Beale generously gave the man a detailed account of the preparations for the reception. The visit seemed almost the kickoff for a political campaign. The Republican nomination for the 1884 presidential election was wide open with Arthur choosing not to be a candidate. Henry Adams observed the tumultous greeting accorded Grant from a distance, having declined an invitation to attend the "big crush at Beales." Adams regarded the Republican Party as a "burst bladder" and jokingly wrote his friend John Hay that Emily Beale had forced him to declare in favor of Senator John A. Logan of Illinois—which hinted that the Stalwart Beales no longer were promoting Grant for another term in the White House.[31]

Once Grant settled in at Decatur House, he began a series of dinners and visits. One evening at the Beales's, a crowd of laboring men gathered in front of the house and commenced to sing and cheer, hoping to attract Grant's attention. Finally, Grant opened the front door and walked out onto a small porch. He told the men that he had heard their cheering and had "tried to convince General Beale, with whom I am dining, that this demonstration was intended in his honor, but his modesty prevented him from accepting my statement." The occasion of Grant's visit may have provided Beale with an unusual opportunity. On January 10, he hastily drafted a will. "I hereby leave all my property personal real and mixed to my wife Mary Edwards Beale," he wrote. He then asked two of the nation's most famous men to affix their signatures as witnesses—U. S. Grant and William T. Sherman.[32]

On April 13, 1883, at Delmonico's restaurant in New York City, Beale delivered a speech at a banquet honoring Porfirio Diaz, ex-president of Mexico. The gathering included some of America's wealthiest financiers, including Jay Gould, Cyrus Field, Jr., Perry Belmont, and J. B. Houston. General Grant also attended. In his speech, Beale described a visit he had once made to El Cid's tomb at Burgos and declared that Benito Juarez, whom Diaz had aided, was the Mexican Cid. Beale then compared Diaz to Alexander Hamilton and said: "He struck the rock of national credit and abundant streams flowed forth." Diaz had reorganized the Mexican civil service, the Mexican army, and the judicial system. But Diaz's most important achievement, Beale declared, was throwing "open to the enterprise of the world the vast resources of his country."[33]

In October of 1883 and again in January of 1884, the Beale family visited the Grants in New York City. There seemed to be considerable support for the third term for Grant, and Beale invited him to Washington to discuss the matter. In championing Grant, Beale quickly became aware that James G. Blaine was far in the lead for the nomination. On March 18, Beale attempted to bring Grant and Blaine together, but Grant refused, saying: "I do not want to meet him." At Beale's insistence, Grant soon moderated his position. "If General Beale invites me to dinner, and also invites Mr. Blaine, of course I should not refuse to go," Grant told a reporter. The newspaper story described Beale as "anxious to be the President-maker for the next term." Possessing a great talent for bringing men of every shade of opinion together, he hoped to reconcile Grant and Blaine "through the amenities of the stomach."[34]

Beale's manipulations were rudely interrupted by word that the banking house of Ward and Grant had failed. Grant had invested his entire savings plus borrowed money in the banking business of Ferdinand Ward, a New York sharpster, and Grant's son, Ulysses, Jr. The failure pauperized Grant, who found himself deeply in debt. The bank's collapse also had other repercussions. Grant and Ward had recently thrown their support to the Maritime Canal Company of Nicaragua, which Beale and Ammen had organized from the Provisional Society. The bank's failure doomed the latest effort to build a canal, and the hard-gained Nicaragua concession lapsed on September 30, 1884.[35]

Beale sought support in Congress for a retirement bill for Grant to help ease his financial burden. On June 26, Grant thanked him for his efforts. He had followed the bill through Congress and predicted that it would not pass during the current session. He did not mention to Beale that his desperate financial straits had caused him to seek money by composing magazine articles dealing with his Civil War career.[36]

In early October of 1884, Emily Beale married John R. McLean, who owned and edited the Cincinnati *Enquirer*. Emily had failed to interest William Sturgis Bigelow, a relative of Marian Adams, who said that the earlier romance failed when "the sawdust came out of the California doll." Emily and John McLean had met at Deer Park, Maryland, where the Beales had recently begun to spend some of the summer months. The marriage took place on October 4, in the Decatur House before a small circle of close family friends. Somewhat surprised that Washington's most famous eligible lady would have such a quiet wedding, a reporter stopped Beale, on his way to visit the Grants and questioned him about the wedding. "I think that is the way to be married," Beale replied, adding: "I was married that way, and I have been very fortunate in my marriage."[37]

Republican prospects for the upcoming November election looked gloomy. The difficulty seemed to lie in the Stalwart Republicans' refusal to embrace candidate Blaine. Beale, however, found no difficulty in supporting Blaine. As a regular Republican, he traditionally supported the party nominee. Republican difficulties seemed to date from that fateful day in March, when Grant refused Beale's request to meet with Blaine. In October, with the election of Grover Cleveland threatening, the three men—Grant, Blaine, and Beale—sat down before an open fireplace in the Decatur House, and Grant pledged to urge his friends to support Blaine. In the few days remaining before the election, the Stalwarts manifested a new and remarkable enthusiasm for Blaine, but the Republican resurgence was too late. Democrat Cleveland won the election.[38]

In the fall of 1884, Beale visited Grant in New York City and found him hard at work on his military memoirs. The two men took time to tour Charles Backman's stables, and Beale may have purchased some horses for his Maryland farm. Grant had not attended Emily's recent wedding, but he knew the McLean family intimately and told his friend that he would be well pleased with his son-in-law. On this trip Beale doubtless learned that Grant had been having trouble with his throat, which in time would be diagnosed as terminal cancer.[39]

By mid-December Beale grew apprehensive over his friend's illness. When invited to spend New Year's 1885 at Decatur House, Grant replied that his throat condition would not permit him to travel. Swallowing had become very painful, and even talking presented difficulties. He added that his doctor did not hold out much hope that he would improve. Beale passed the information of Grant's illness to a newspaper reporter but said that he did not know the nature of his ill health. Beale speculated that the failure of Grant and Ward, combined with Grant's debt of $150,000 to William H. Vanderbilt, had brought on depression. In partial payment to Vanderbilt, Grant had turned over to the millionaire his sword, military awards, and medals. "It is just like him not to let me know that his straits are so desperate," Beale said. "I had no idea they were anything like this, and it is my belief that his illness which I could not account for is caused by his anxiety," Beale concluded.[40]

The parties at the Decatur House continued as usual. One Christmas entertainment stood out from all the rest. This was a children's masquerade party, with the children and parents of prominent Washingtonians being invited. The list of adults who attended read like a presidential reception: Blaine, Sheridan, Logan, Donald Cameron, General William B. Hazen, George Bancroft, W. W. Corcoran, Senator Shelby Cullom, Jay Cooke, Charles Nordhoff, Jerome Bonaparte, Admiral C. R. P. Rodgers, and many other notables. The evening's high point arrived when General Beale, disguised as Father Christmas, entered the room wearing an enormous white bearskin. The children ran and clustered about Beale, who was garbed with snowy white beard and mustache and crackling icicles.[41]

Parties, however, did not prevent Beale from thinking about Grant's misfortunes. He asked the support of Cyrus W. Field and William T. Sherman in raising a fund in Grant's behalf. In early January of 1885, Grant heard of their fund and ordered his friends to stop their efforts. His pride would not allow him to accept charity, and he hoped his memoirs would ease his financial burden. Beale and other friends then channeled their efforts into securing a military pension for Grant. In late January, in response to an invitation to visit the Decatur House, the sick man replied that he would gladly come, but he required a doctor's daily attention.[42]

On May 21, 1885, Emily Beale, eighty-seven-year-old mother of E. F. Beale, died at her home of Bloomingdale. She had lived a long life, and had seen her son become one of the nation's famous personages. Her husband George Beale had died fifty years earlier, and Emily never remarried.[43]

Beale had hardly recovered from his mother's death, when word circulated that U. S. Grant was dying from cancer. In the early summer, Grant was taken from New York City to Mount McGregor, a cool, healthful spot in upstate New York. Like many other Americans, Beale journeyed to Mount McGregor and visited the dying Civil War hero. Grant struggled valiantly in a grim race to complete his memoirs before the disease totally incapacitated him. When Grant completed his writing task, his publisher, Mark Twain, assured him that his book would pull the family out of debt with considerable money left over.[44]

In late July, Grant's death was awaited hourly. Reporters began to visit Beale for revelations about the dying man's personal life. As readers were well acquainted with Grant's military genius, Beale dwelled on his personal characteristics. As seen by his closest friend, Grant's dominant traits consisted of "guilelessness of character, even temperment and great magnanimity." As to the old charge that Grant drank excessively, Beale responded by stating that he had never seen him affected by alcohol, even when he and Grant had walked the streets of Paris until two o'clock in the morning. Actually, the two men frequently drank together.

Beale remembered other traits of his friend. Whenever Grant stayed at the Decatur House, school children would leave their autograph books for the famous signature. Late at night, Beale and Grant would return from a long reception tired and sleepy, but Grant always insisted on signing the autograph books before he went to bed. He knew that the children would stop for the books on their way to school in the morning, and he refused to disappoint them.[45]

On the morning of July 23, 1885, Beale received the long-expected telegram from Fred Grant: "Father died at eight o'clock this morning." As Washington's church bells began to toll, a dispute broke out over the final resting place of Grant's body. Beale urged in public and private that Grant, as a national figure, should be interred somewhere in the nation's capital. At the suggestion of Washington friends, Beale and General Sheridan toured the District of Columbia to find a suitable burial site. The two men decided on three possible locations: (1) the Soldier's

Home, near Winfield Scott's monument; (2) Arlington Cemetery; and (3) the new circle between the Washington Monument and the White House.

Beale headed a delegation which presented to the Grant family a set of resolutions from prominent Washingtonians on the subject; of course, the final decision rested with the family. But Beale moved too slow. New York City, also desirous of securing Grant's remains, moved with surprising celerity and offered the family a location in Riverside Park on the Hudson River. The family promptly accepted.[46]

On August 6, Fred Grant again contacted Beale and asked him "as my father's dear friend," to join the family in funeral services. Grant's funeral procession through New York City produced one of the greatest spectacles of the nineteenth century. Beale rode in a carriage that contained the immediate family. Prior to starting in the procession for Riverside Park, Fred Grant, who had seen mountains of worthless newspaper articles about his father, mused "if only some one who knew my father well, would write of him as a man and a friend, how much it would gratify us all." Beale volunteered to draft a eulogy on the spur of the moment. He probably read the tribute at graveside or in private to the family on the day of the funeral.[47]

Beale's eulogy was simple, but moving. He portrayed Grant as the *"good man,"* not as history's great man. He stressed Grant's nature: truthful, serene, candid, and simple. Grant disliked hunting and regarded such sport as cruelty. He possessed a pleasant wit, liked stories, but would not tolerate a tale which concealed an impure thought. In speech, he was absolutely clean-tongued. During their years together, Beale had never heard Grant use an expletive. In habit and expression, Grant was the most modest man Beale had ever met. Grant influenced everyone who came near him by a "sort of inexpressible moral force." Beale concluded by comparing Grant to other great men he had known:

> Necessarily at my age, and living where I do, I have known many great men, but they were all like some fine fruit specked with imperfection. He only was without blemish. They were great men— great soldiers—great judges—great statesmen, but when you looked them all over they were not like the kind friend I have lost and who is buried today. They were simply great men. He alone was both great and good!

What the poet Horace had said of himself with arrogance, Grant could have repeated in perfect truth: "I have built a monument more lasting than bronze."[48]

Grant's death closed an important era of Beale's life. The years from 1877 to 1885 witnessed a dramatic change and growth in Edward F. Beale's social and political influence. As Grant's closest friend, he found himself an influential member of the Stalwart faction of the Republican Party, and he opened the Decatur House to Republicans of all varieties. The Beales were the unchallenged leaders of Washington society. A politician who had never received an invitation to a Decatur House party must have felt like an American pariah.

Even with his total involvement in Washington affairs, Beale still made a yearly visit to the Tejon Ranch. He retained the robust health of his youth, despite his age. When an occasion demanded physical endurance, he could perform feats that would have severely taxed a far younger man. Such an incident had occurred during the summer sheep drive of 1879. Nevertheless, Grant's death made a forceful impact on Beale's life. He would no longer live in the glow of publicity which had radiated about the famous man. Both Grant and Beale had been born in 1822. In the summer of 1885, Beale could feel the weight of the years.

Chapter 14

"NO MORE ROCKY MOUNTAINS"

I would be willing to hear many an "arrer" sing in the air and the
sharp crack of many an old "Hawkins rifle" again, to be as young
as in those happy days. But the times change and we change with
them, and there are no more buffalo, and no more Indians, and
no more Rocky Mountains. Were there ever any, or was it all a
last night's dream?

> —E. F. Beale
> April 30, 1887

Early in 1886, Beale and his associates in the Maritime Canal Company
of Nicaragua found Cleveland's administration highly favorable to their
canal plans. Thomas F. Bayard, secretary of state, wrote to Beale on
January 13, and said that the president regarded the proposals with great
favor. Bayard promised to obtain the services of A. G. Menocal, the
engineer who had played an important role in the earlier Nicaraguan
dealings. Once again, hopes soared for the transoceanic canal.[1]

About this time, Beale experienced a grandfather's joy for the first
time. Emily Beale McLean gave birth to a son, and the parents christened the child Edward Beale McLean. At the baby's baptism on January 27, members of the Grant family were in attendance, in addition to
the Beales and McLeans. Emily McLean had recently embarked on a
career as a Washington hostess, following in the footsteps of her parents.
Her mother's health, meanwhile, had failed significantly. By the fall of
1886, Mrs. Beale was almost totally blind from the eye affliction which
had plagued her entire life.

Recently, the Beales had renewed their old friendship with the Fremonts. General John C. Fremont, who had served for several years as governor of Arizona Territory, was far from prosperous. Perhaps in imitation of Grant, Fremont struggled diligently to write his memoirs. Beale contributed a humorous anecdotal piece on the Mexican War in California to the manuscript. One day, the two men appeared before a surprised government clerk, and Beale duly applied for a pension from the Mexican War. Fremont witnessed and verified his friend's statement of service.[2]

In early October, Beale left on the train for California. Always solicitous of his wife's health, he wrote from Chicago, saying: "I would gladly give my life to have you restored to sight." In mid-October, Beale arrived at the Tejon Ranch. As soon as he washed off the dust from the trip, he hurried to a small house nearby, where his longtime majordomo, Chico Acuna, lay near death. Just before he arrived, Chico has asked: "Has not the Patron come yet?" The old man wanted desperately to see Beale before he died. Chico had worked at the Tejon since the mid-1850s, and much of the ranch's success had been due to his honesty and good sense. When Beale appeared at Chico's bedside, the old vaquero used his last remaining strength to embrace the Patron. Then he began to sink rapidly. Beale held the old man's hands until they stiffened in death. "This has been the saddest day I ever passed on the Rancho," Beale wrote to Mary. "How we shall do without his wise counsel and knowledge I do not know. I feel inexpressibly sad. He has been so true and faithful these many long years. The Tejon without him will never be the same to me."[3]

On October 19, the funeral for Chico was held at the Tejon Ranch. Beale suspended all work for the day. A funeral procession formed at Chico's house about a mile from the Tejon headquarters. Beale had purchased a handsome coffin in Bakersfield, and the Tejon vaqueros carried the casket, frequently relieving each other. The procession chanted the burial service in Spanish, the men and women alternating verses. "I have never heard anything so solemn and sweet as this chant" Beale wrote. For a short time, the body rested in the parlor, where mourners filled the coffin with beautiful roses and other flowers. Then the time came for the burial. Beale, R. M. Pogson, Alex Godey, Jimmie Rosemyre, J. J. Lopez, and Chico Lopez acted as pall bearers. The men carried Chico's remains to the upper end of the rose garden. Beale said it was the most impressive funeral he had ever witnessed in his life.[4]

Time indeed was passing. On December 26, Beale sat by the bedside of another friend who lay dying in Washington. He had been a strong supporter of Senator John A. Logan and was with the Stalwart Republican when he died. In late April of 1887, Beale himself began experiencing ill health. Invited to attend a reunion of the California pioneers, he wrote Gordon C. Gorham, the secretary, that he was now paying the penalty for "the excesses of my youth and riotous living in the Rocky Mountains and on the great plains." Beale said that a severe attack of gout had immobilized him. He attributed his condition to a longtime diet in his early days of "mule meat stuffed with truffles and the rich fat of rusty bacon washed down with rare Johannisberger, drunk from a buffalo wallow full of polywogs and tadpoles." He found it hard to believe he had once been so young and happy. Now there were "no more buffalo, and no more Indians, and no more Rocky Mountains." In conclusion, he sadly asked: "Were there ever any, or was it all last night's dream?"[5]

In the spring of 1888, Beale left again for California. At Bakersfield, the community's leading citizens honored him with a testimonial banquet which lasted from eight o'clock until four o'clock the following morning. Several speakers recalled Beale's early contribution to the state and region, while others addressed more recent subjects. His attempt to get a railroad into Bakersfield, after the Southern Pacific had bypassed the town, drew repeated praise. Everyone listened attentively when Beale arose and spoke about the area's history and then about U. S. Grant. Afterward, he wrote his wife that the floral tribute which covered the long table especially impressed him. It was a train with the engine and tender full of "exquisite roses." Unknown to almost everyone present, Beale had laid plans for the sale of the Tejon Ranch. Upon his return to the East, Beale declined a nomination for a congressional seat, stating that his many business engagements would probably call him away during the upcoming campaign.[6]

Beale continued to give close attention to Ash Hill, his horse farm in Maryland. Grant's Arabians, Leopard and Linden Tree, were quartered there, and they sired a number of offspring. Ash Hill presented a modern training layout, complete with two race courses. Beale, however, was spending less and less time at the farm. In the fall of 1888, William F. Cody (Buffalo Bill) arranged to winter the buffalo and animals connected with his Wild West show at Ash Hill until the following spring.[7]

Beale took an active role in the election campaign of 1888. In the fall of 1887, Beale had helped to organize the National Republican League, headquartered in Washington and designed to give direction to Republican efforts. The Republican League elected Beale as its first president. Other prominent members were Frederick Douglass, John P. Newman, William B. Allison, Cornelius Cole, Stephen B. Elkins, John Hay, John Sherman, William M. Evarts, J. C. Cannon, Shelby Cullom, J. N. Dolph, and George F. Edmunds. In time, many more Republicans joined, and during the 1888 campaign, the league encouraged every important Republican politician to visit the Washington office.

Beale's selection as league president prompted several newspapers to mention his name as a possible presidential candidate. Once local paper said: "If we could have our way, Washington should furnish a President of the United States, and his name would be—Edward Fitzgerald Beale." But the Beale movement was not really serious, and Beale worked hard for Benjamin Harrison.[8]

Shortly after Harrison's victory, Beale was asked to chair the inaugural reception committee, a position of honor. Beale accepted and immediately began contacting prominent Republicans to serve with him. The Grant family also agreed to stay with the Beales during the inauguration. Unexpected events in California, however, called Beale away, and he had to resign from the inaugural committee and rush west.[9]

Beale came close to selling the Tejon Ranch. Senator Stephen Dorsey believed he could sell the ranch for him, but it would be expensive and require a bond, and a reasonable length of time. U. S. Grant, Jr. relayed Dorsey's offer to Beale, but he declined to place the property in Dorsey's hands. In California, Beale drew up a lengthy memorandum on the property. He began by itemizing the Tejon's acreage:

El Tejon Rancho	97,612 acres
Los Alamos	26,626 acres
Castac Rancho	22,178 acres
La Liebre	48,799 acres
Railroad lands	54,000 acres
Purchased from settlers	20,000 acres
	269,215 acres

Beale emphasized in the memorandum that the Tejon Ranch (all the properties) was used at present almost entirely for ranching purposes. He stressed, however, the way in which property values would soar if the owner of the property would subdivide the land and sell parcels to settlers. Already, the Atlantic and Pacific Railroad was building a line across the Tejon and promised to complete the line by 1891.[10]

What would draw settlers to the Tejon Ranch? According to Beale, the ranch contained some of the best farming land in California. His farm at the ranch headquarters produced all types of vegetables, grains, forage, and fruits, and he insisted the same crops could be grown almost anywhere on the ranch's 130,000 acres of arable land. An additional 150,000 acres offered fine grazing land—forested and well watered. Beale suggested that a prospective buyer might want to continue the ranching business, as he sold off lots to potential farmers. The prospectus indicated that the entire property was fenced and had never been mined. Placer and gold mines were known to exist in the area. Castac Lake, a one-hundred-and-fifty-acre blue jewel in the mountains, would be close to the new railroad line and could make a fine resort. Charles Nordhoff had called the Tejon the most valuable property in America owned by a single individual, and Beale estimated its worth at $3.5 million.[11]

By the spring of 1889, Beale considered three offers, but none seemed good. Charles Nordhoff, acting as Beale's agent, received a request for an option from an English promoter who felt certain he could sell the ranch. The unnamed Englishman planned to raise the asking price to $4. million. If he was lucky and sold the ranch, he would gain a tidy commission. Beale feared that he might be drifting into the "London Promoter trick." If the Englishman could not sell the ranch, the Tejon would be committed to a six-month option. Should a buyer appear elsewhere during that period, permission to sell the ranch would have to come from the London promoter. The commission for the sale would have to be split. Beale advised Nordhoff to pursue the matter further and determine whether a real person was actually interested in buying the ranch, or if, as he suspected, it was simply a scheme to tie up the property.[12]

As Beale attempted to sell the Tejon Ranch, another venture of long-standing, the Maritime Canal Company of Nicaragua, was incorporated by the US Congress. There had been prolonged debate on the act. A member of the House from New York rankled tempers when he charged that the Maritime Company was a mere "stock jobbing concern, . . . played by certain sharpers to filch honest people out of their money." On February 20, 1889, the act was passed; listed among the incorporators were Beale, Daniel Ammen, Hiram Hitchcock, Frederic Billings, A. G. Menocal, James Roosevelt, and others. Capitalized for $100 million (one million shares @ $100 each), the Maritime Canal Company retained the prerogative of doubling the capitalization to $200 million, an enormous sum. The company was owned by the Nicaragua Canal Construction Company, which was owned by an almost identical group of men—Beale, Ammen, and their associates. The construction company had obtained a concession from the Nicaraguan government and sold it to the Maritime Canal Company for 120,000 shares of stock, or $12 million on paper. It was agreed that the construction company would stay in business and undertake the building of the canal. Payment would be in the form of addition stock in the Maritime Company. With the incorporation act, it suddenly appeared that Beale might become one of America's wealthiest men.[13]

Admiral Ammen exuded confidence about the canal's construction. On March 12, 1889, he wrote Beale a letter and reminisced about the beginning of the Nicaragua canal venture. "Had it not been for the meeting in your house of Menocal and myself with you, at this moment a French canal would now be established," he said. Ammen was certain the canal would be constructed by their American company.[14]

Beale still continued fairly active. He never found a buyer for the Tejon Ranch, but he may not have been too serious about selling the property. His children—Truxtun, Emily and Mary—frequently visited at the Decatur House in Washington. Due to his father's political connections, Truxtun Beale was appointed by President Harrison to the post of American consul in Greece, after having wearied of managing the Tejon Ranch. Mary Beale Bahkmeteff's husband George had risen quickly in the czar's diplomatic service, and the Bahkmeteffs had already resided in several European capitals. Emily Beale McLean's husband John seemed destined to become a powerful man. He now owned the Washington *Post* and presided over the Washington Gas Light Company.[15]

When Beale visited California, he made arrangements for the Hunter family, who had recently moved to the Tejon Ranch from Illinois, to take charge of Rose Station, a traveler's inn on the road between Bakersfield and Los Angeles. Beale soon discovered that Mary Hunter possessed an aptitude for writing both prose and poetry. The young woman was fascinated by Beale's stories about the region, and she accompanied him on several occasions when he rode over the Tejon. Impressed with her poetry, Beale sent several selections to Mrs. John A. Logan, who enjoyed them immensely. Unlike the Hunter family which seemed skeptical of Mary's writing ambitions, Beale encouraged her. In later years, after Beale's death, five of Mary Hunter Austin's works bore the stamp of Beale and El Tejon: *The Flock, Land of Little Rain, Isidro,* the *Arrowmaker,* and *The Ford.* A chaper of *The Flock* described J. J. Lopez, the Tejon majordomo. Beale provided the main plot for *Isidro,* and *The Arrowmaker* may also have used Beale's ideas. Throughout his life, Beale maintained an interest in literature and writers. The stories he provided the youg woman were reminiscent of the days he had spent with poet Bayard Taylor, forty years before.[16]

Occasionally, the Beales would cross Lafayette Square and visit President Harrison or attend an official state function. President Harrison kindly remembered the Beale family in February of 1892 and sent them a beautiful pair of canvasback ducks, which he had bagged on a recent hunting expedition. Beale thanked the president and said that as an old sportsman, he could well appreciate the gift. "I hope the country will always afford such good ducks, and that it may be forever blessed with such a good 'dux,' " Beale punned.[17]

The year 1892 was not a happy one. In April Beale made a solemn journey to Chester to take care of the estate of his brother-in-law Harry Edwards. Harry had recently died at the age of sixty-six. Beale spend a few days in Chester before returning to Washington. On the twenty-first he wrote Mary a letter about Harry's business matters, a gloomy letter in which Beale mentioned his poor health. In recent years, his once robust health had deteriorated greatly. Some weeks later, Beale had learned that his grandiose plan for a Nicaraguan canal had again failed. Only a miracle would prevent the Maritime Company from declaring bankruptcy.[18]

The days moved quickly. The winter of 1892 found Beale seriously ill. His disease was diagnosed as jaundice, produced by a liver disease, probably cirrhosis. By late March, Beale was confined to his bed in the Decatur House; his complexion yellowed with the disease's onslaught.[19]

Beale felt certain he was dying. He dictated a memorandum to C. W. Kerlin, his wife's cousin and Fred Kerlin's brother. In the event of his death, he directed that Robert M. Pogson take full control of the Tejon Ranch. There should be no authority over him, including Truxtun. Pogson was an honest and faithful man, with great experience. Beale said he did not want Truxtun to live at the Tejon for "he never liked it and would soon weary of that sort of life." He intended no slight to his son, however. Truxtun had proved a most "creditable member of the family and deserves all praise for the manner in which he had conducted himself." Beale contemplated the ranch's sale setting the asking price at $3 million. If the sale occurred, Pogson would receive $420,000, and if the manager located the purchaser, he would also earn a full 5 percent commission. On April 18, Beale added a codicil, stating his arrangements for Pogson required that he remain in Mary E. Beale's employ until the Tejon was sold.[20]

In mid-April Beale slowly weakened, but the presence of friends and family comforted him. Only Truxtun was absent, but the faithful son was hurrying home from Europe. Feeling the end was near, the dying man dictated a last loving letter to his son:

> Dear Trux: I wish you to live with your Mother and take care of her and cherish her—remember the devotion she has always shown you. You have done all that I have asked of you and have acquired a well earned high reputation. Enjoy the rest of your life, I do not wish you to go to the ranch. It is a wearing life and Pogson is quite competent to conduct it, and moreover, I want you near your Mother, who will need all your assistance. Go to California

occasionally and look into our affairs. That is all that is necessary.
Goodby my dear boy. I have always loved you and been very proud of you.

Your affectionate Father,
E. F. Beale

On the night of April 21, Beale rallied from his illness, and on the following morning he appeared considerably stronger. But his strength proved fictitious. As the day wore on, he grew steadily weaker. At 3:30 P.M., Edward Beale died peacefully. He was seventy-one years old.[21]

Newspapers throughout the nation marked Beale's passing. Laudatory obituaries described his fabulous career in frequently inaccurate stories. On April 27, Truxtun arrived in Washington, and the funeral was held on the following day. An Episcopal service was held at ten o'clock in the morning in the reception room on the second floor of the Decatur House, the scene of so many parties in the past. A plain black coffin, covered with fragrant roses, was located in the center of the room. An absolute silence filled the old house, broken only by the clergyman's voice. Many prominent men were in attendance, including California Senators Leland Stanford and Stephen White. With the last solemn word of the service, pallbearers carried the flower-covered coffin out of the room. From the lower hallway, the quiet sobbing of the old family servants was heard. Beale's pallbearers made a distinguished procession: Vice-President Levi P. Morton, Supreme Court Justice Stephen J. Field, Senator Henry Cabot Lodge, Judge Bancroft Davis, Admiral Daniel Ammen, and several others. A hearse carried Beale's remains to the train depot, where C. W. Kerlin took charge.[22]

Before his death, Beale expressed a strong desire to have his body cremated. Truxtun, Kerlin, and several close friends accompanied the remains to the crematorium at Loudon Park Cemetery at Baltimore. Here, Truxtun asked that the coffin be opened, and he took a last farewell look at his father. Then he abruptly left the building and returned to Washington.[23]

The ashes were taken to the Chester Rural Cemetery and interred in the Edwards family plot. Nearby rested Samuel Edwards Beale, the infant who had died in California in 1861. A short distance away lay the graves of the Edwards and Kerlin families, close friends in life, now together in death. Beyond the grassy green hillside sat William Penn's old community, and in the distance, the Delaware River flowed quietly past the pier at the foot of Edgmont Avenue.

A F T E R W O R D

In his long life (1822–93), Edward F. Beale had witnessed many of the historic events of the nineteenth century. At times, he played a leading role on center stage, but on other occasions he was either a minor actor or simply an engrossed spectator. But Beale's vantage point always offered a unique view and provides historians with an additional tool to illuminate the institutions, people, and events that affected his life. Naval officer, rancher, explorer, politician, humanitarian, and diplomat— Beale left an enduring legacy in several different areas.

In the Mexican War of 1846–48, Beale had served with distinction, revealing by his acts, qualities of leadership and heroism. After the Battle of San Pasqual, where he fought gallantly, Beale sought additional avenues to gain success and fame. In the summer of 1848, while still a passed midshipman, Beale volunteered to carry to the East the exciting news of the California gold discovery. When he arrived in New York City, his enthusiasm, along with his golden samples, helped spark the great rush west. Beale's name filled the columns of every eastern newspaper, and he quickly learned the value of publicity. Continuing his career as a military dispatch carrier, he made certain that the public read about his exploits. Fame and public recognition played a key role in achieving success in America.

Despite his efforts at self-promotion, Beale's career did not fit the classic pattern of the self-made man. Political friends and influential relatives played the decisive role in his career. His military service brought him into close proximity with Robert F. Stockton, Samuel F. Du Pont, and John C. Fremont, and he assiduously cultivated friendships with these men. In early 1847, when a dispute broke out in California between Fremont and General Stephen W. Kearny, Beale wisely decided to side with Fremont and stood ready to testify about Kearny's incompetence at the Battle at San Pasqual. Through the Fremonts, Beale befriended Senator Thomas Hart Benton, who provided influence and took an interest in his career. About this time Beale also met Bayard Taylor, a well-known New York reporter, en route west to write a book about the Gold Rush. He volunteered to serve as Taylor's guide, and not surprisingly Taylor's *Eldorado*, probably the best firsthand account of the epic rush, was dedicated to Edward F. Beale.

Beale not only had a talent for making the right friends, but also possessed the good fortune of marrying into influential family. His marriage to Mary Edwards brought an entree into the important political circles in Pennsylvania. Mary's father, Samuel Edwards, had been a leading Pennsylvlania Democrat during Andrew Jackson's presidency, and James Buchanan regarded Edwards as one of his closest political associates. Other Edwards ties extended to Simon Cameron and John Clayton. Such powerful allies, combined with Beale's own political acquaintances, engineered his appointment as California's first superintendent of Indian affairs in 1852.

In California, Beale made a lasting contribution to Indian-white relations in the United States. When he arrived in California, white settlers, swarming over the state in search of mineral wealth and farmland, were driving the Indians from their homes or exterminating them. The United States Senate had recently rejected a plan to place the California Indians on reservations because the subsistence costs appeared astronomical. Beale discovered a workable solution. He urged the government to place the Indians on reservations, where Indian Office employees would instruct them in the arts of husbandry. In short, Beale proposed a return to the old Spanish Mission System, which had operated so effectively at an earlier time in California. When Beale was removed from office in 1854, the experiment seemed on the road to success. After the Civil War, Beale's concept of the self-sufficient reservation, designed to alter Indian culture through education, dominated the federal government's Indian policy.

Beginning in 1857, Beale supervised the construction of a wagon road across the Southwest. For two and a half years, he worked on the highway which passed through desolate, isolated country, peopled only by nomadic Indians. In locating the shortest route to California, Beale frequently explored unknown country. At this time, Beale also empha-

238

sized the route's suitability for a transcontinental railroad. Without the sectional animosity of the period, the transcontinental railroad might have been built over Beale's road. Finally, in conjunction with the wagon road project Beale tested the army's camels for possible use in the Far West.

Although he was born into a slaveholding family, Beale always felt a sense of *noblesse oblige* for Indians, Negroes, and Chinese. In 1860, he switched party allegiance and became a Republican out of principle. After Lincoln's election, Beale's friends lobbied diligently to secure his appointment as California's surveyor general. Beale's tenure in that office was less than distinguished. He devoted much of his time to his personal business affairs and neglected government work. He also used his powers to confirm title to several Mexican land grants—a practice which was unethical, though apparently legal. Speculating heavily in California mines, Beale fought a contemplated change in the federal mining law which would tax mining properties. His hot-headed response, plus his irregular dealings in land, led to his dismissal.

After the war, Beale settled in Chester, Pennsylvania and divided his time between his California interests and eastern politics. During these years, the Tejon Ranch grew into a lucrative spread of 250,000 acres and provided a substantial income. He also made his first investments in petroleum properties, which would one day become Standard Oil of California. Beale's political forays remained limited to making an occasional speech and developing friendships among important politicans. In 1865, he embraced the radical wing of the Republican Party and was one of the first men in Pennsylvania to urge that black Americans be given the right to vote. Articles by Beale frequently appeared in Pennsylvania newspapers. Two important articles defended the Modoc Indians and protested mistreatment of Chinese.

The purchase of the Decatur House in 1871 in Washington D.C. marked a dramatic change in Edward Beale's life. He began to entertain on a lavish scale and made contacts with many important politicans. President Grant discovered that he and Beale shared many interests, particularly a fondness for fine horses. In time, they became fast friends. Beale made the Decatur House a social center of the nation's capital and gradually acquired a position of influence in the Republican Party. If Grant had made a bid for a third term and won, Beale might have emerged as one of the country's most powerful men. During the last years of his life, Beale kept active in politics and business.

Beale counted among his friends some of the nation's most distinguished men. Figures as diverse as Kit Carson, Bayard Taylor, Charles Nordhoff, U. S. Grant, John C. Fremont, Thomas Hart Benton, Rob-

ert F. Stockton, Simon Cameron, and David C. Broderick were all captivated by Beale's personality. What kind of man was Edward F. Beale?

His character and personality seemed as complicated and contradictory as the American nation itself. Slightly below medium stature, Beale
was driven by a nervous energy which animated his body with almost
involuntary, jerky movements. His entire life seemed a blur of constant
motion. Beale enjoyed telling stories about his western adventures, but
he was far from being a latter-day version of Davy Crockett. He constantly worked at his education and prided himself on being well-read in
philosophy, fiction, poetry, and history. He also acquired an expert ability to judge paintings and learned several foreign languages. In fact, his
linguistic abilities spawned a tale that he had taught himself Syrian in
order to speak to his camels in their native tongue. A sophisticated
easterner, Beale had endured all the hardships of life in the Far West.
His skill at woodcraft and desert survival rivaled any mountain man's.
As a young man, Beale enjoyed the sport of hunting; when he grew older,
he loved horse racing. To many men of different walks of life, Beale
was a jovial entertaining companion.

But there existed another side to Beale's character. He sought pecuniary success with a single-minded intensity. He endeavored to profit from
every government position he held and was successful in the effort. He
was a ruthless businessman who could take away a settler's home through
a legal manipulation of the land law. Although he was a man who laughed
easily, he also was quick to anger. Beale was considered "dangerous"
when aroused and could become violent. In 1855, he challenged the
commissioner of Indian affairs to a duel. On several occasions, public
drunkness created problems for him. Chameleon-like, Beale could take
on the coloring of whatever background upon which he was placed. It
made him congenial to many people, but others wondered at his sincerity.

It was unfortunate that Beale never wrote an autobiography. His letters,
poetry, diaries, and official reports showed a remarkable ability to write
descriptively with honest feelings. His failure to produce a volume about
his life probably explains his absence from many accounts of American
history. Beale admitted that writing posed an unpleasant chore, and in
later years, he wrote only when absolutely necessary. In 1912, Stephen
Bonsal, who knew Truxtun Beale, produced a biography of Beale that
did little more than string together quotations from Beale's published
reports. In failing to treat his subject seriously, Bonsal consigned Beale
to the dustbins of history. As a result he has almost been forgotten.

Yet Edward F. Beale was a man whose historic contributions were truly
multifold—explorer, rancher, naval officer, humanitarian, politician,
businessman, and diplomat. As a lifelong student of history, Beale per-

ceived that he would leave a mark in the great sweep of nineteenth-century development in America. On a cold January day in 1859, while he labored to build a wagon road across the Far Southwest, Beale wrote his wife: "My name must be connected forever in the history and progress of this vast country." It was an accurate assessment of an extraordinary career.

Shortly after Beale's death in 1893, an unnamed friend tried to sum up his life. Edward Fitzgerald Beale was "one of the most variously gifted of Americans," he said, and "to have enjoyed the privilege of a personal acquaintance with him may fairly be said to have been equal to a liberal education."[24]

N O T E S

Chapter 1

1. San Francisco *News Letter*, April 29, 1893. Stephen Bonsal, *Edward Fitz-gerald Beale: A Pioneer in the Path of Empire, 1822–1903* (New York: G. P. Putnam's Sons, 1912).

2. "The Statement from Gen. E. F. Beale for Mr. Hubert Howe Bancroft," undated [ca. 1888], Bancroft Library, University of California [B-UC], 1. San Francisco *Bulletin*, May 12, 1864. Frances B. S. Hodges, *The Beale Family of Virginia* (Ann Arbor: Edwards Brothers, Inc., 1956), 10–11, 138. According to Frances B. S. Hodges, a genealogist, the name Beale is Celtic in origin and derived from the ancient Druidic god "Beal."

3. "Beale Statement," 1, B-UC. "Death of Mrs. Emily Beale," undated newspaper clipping [May 1885], Decatur House Papers [DHP], Library of Congress [LC]. Eugene S. Ferguson, *Truxtun of the Constellation: the Life of Commodore Thomas Truxtun, U.S. Navy, 1755–1822* (Baltimore: Johns Hopkins Press, 1956), passim; Hodges, *Beale Family of Virginia*, 137–38. George Beale (widow-Emily), Pension and Bounty Land Warrant File, April 12, 1836, Records Relating to Pension and Bounty Land Claims, 1773–1942, Records of the Veteran's Administration [RVA], Record Group [RG] 15, National Archives [NA].

4. George Beale to Paul Hamilton, January 10, 1812, Acceptances File—1812; "Memo Showing the Amount of Duty Performed by Each of the Pursers . . .," Inactive Files, Box 1 (1830), Naval Records Collecton [NRC], Records of the Office of Naval Records and Library [RONRL], RG 45, NA. Hodges, *Beale Family of Virginia*, 138. G. Beale, Pension and Bounty Land Warrant Files, RVA.

5. "Beale Statement," 2, B-UC. *Plan of the City of Washington . . .* [map, 1792] (Ithaca: Historic Urban Plans, 1964); Hodges, *Beale Family of Virginia*, 65–68, 72.

6. Marie Beale [Oge], *Decatur House and Its Inhabitants* (Washington, D.C.: National Trust for Historic Preservation, 1954), 68; Hodges, *Beale Family of*

Virginia, 138. "Beale Statement," 2, B-UC. "Memo Showing Duty Performed by Pursers," Inactive Files, Box 1 (1830), NRC, RONRL.

7. "Beale Statement," 2-3, B-UC. Hodges, *Beale Family of Virginia,* 138.

8. W. C. Repitti to Laurence R. Cook, November 24, 1951, Correspondence File, Rolle-Cook Collection, Occidental College, Los Angeles. John M. Daley, *Georgetown University: Origin and Early Years* (Washington, D.C.: Georgetown University Press, 1957), 223–29, 239–41, 266.

9. "Beale Statement," 1-2, B-UC. Hodges, *Beale Family of Virginia,* 142. Entries for George Beale, Georgetown Assessment Book, 1835–39, and City of Washington Tax Books, 1834, Wards 1–4, Records of the Government of the District of Columbia, RG 351, NA.

10. "Beale Statement," 3, B-UC. Beale, *Decatur House and Its Inhabitants,* 69–70.

11. Beale to Secretary of the Navy, December 15, 1836, Acceptances—Vol. A–B, 1809–38, RONL. Henry L. Burr, *Education in the Early Navy* (Philadelphia: privately printed, 1939), 38–41.

12. "Edward F. Beale," Records of Officers, Entry 2183, M-330, Roll 5, Records of the Bureau of Naval Personnel [RBNP], RG 24, NA. "Annual Report of the Secretary of the Navy, 1837," *Senate Executive Document [SED] 1,* 25 Congress, 2 Session (Serial 314), 715–16. Bonsal, *Edward Fitzgerald Beale,* 5. "Statement of the Names, Age, Tonnage, and Number of Guns of Each Vessel . . .," *House Executive Document [HED] 132,* 27 Cong., 3 Sess. (Serial 421), 173.

13. Burr, *Early Navy,* 69. Journal of E. F. Beale [ca. 1842–45], DHP, LC.

14. Susan Dallas (ed.), *Diary of George Mifflin Dallas* (Philadelphia: J. B. Lippincott Company, 1892), 7–10. "Beale," Records of Officers, Entries 1711, 2183, M-330, Rolls 5–6. "Annual Report of the Secretary of the Navy, 1837," *SED 1,* 25 Cong., 2 Sess., 715–16. Beale to J. K. Paulding, July 25, 1839, Acceptances—1839, RONRL.

15. Beale Journal [1842–45], DHP, LC. The physical description is based on Beale's earliest portrait, a miniature, located in the Decatur House, Washington, D.C.

16. "Beale," Records of Officers, Entry 1711, M-330, Roll 6. "Annual Report of the Secretary of the Navy, 1841," *HED 2,* 27 Cong., 2 Sess. (Serial 401), 348. Beale to Paulding, November 12 and 24, 1840, Letters Received by the Secretary of the Navy from Officers Below the Rank of Commander [LR-SNBC], RONRL. "Annual Report of the Secretary of the Navy, 1840," *HED 2,* 26 Cong., 2 Sess. (Serial 382), 403, 445.

17. "Beale," Records of Officers, Entry 1711, M-330, Roll 6. Beale to George Badger, August 31, 1841, LR-SNBC.

18. Burr, *Early Navy,* 149–58; Daniel Ammen, *The Old Navy and the New* (Philadelphia: J. B. Lippincott Company, 1891), 94–97. Beale to Truxtun Beale, Sunday, September 12 [1841], quoted in Maria Scott Beale Chance, *A Chronical of the Family of Edward F. Beale of Philadelphia* (Haverford, Penn.: privately printed, 1943), 34–35.

19. Burr, *Early Navy,* 156; Chance, *Edward F. Beale of Philadelphia,* 33–34; Bonsal, *Edward Fitzgerald Beale,* 4–5.

20. Ammen, *Old Navy*, 94–97; Burr, *Early Navy*, 158–63.

21. Proceedings of Board of Examinaton of Midshipmen, June 13–29, 1842, Records of the United States Naval Academy [RNA], RG 405, NA. Ammen, *Old Navy*, 95–98. "Beale Statement," 3, B-UC.

22. Beale to Abel Upshur, August 1, 1842, Acceptances—1842, RONRL. "Beale," Records of Officers, Entry 1711, M-330, Roll 6. Beale to John Mason, October 7, 1844, and Mason to Beale, October 9 and 24, 1844, LR-SNBC. Burr, Early Navy, 184–86.

23. Beale Journal [ca. 1842–45], DHP, L.C. This notebook, hardly a diary as the entries are skimpy and largely undated, covers several years of Beale's life, following his graduation from the naval school. While of little value in determining what Beale was doing on a particular day, or year, the journal provides a penetrating look at Beale's philosophy of life during his early naval career. The journal pages are not numbered and are frequently blank.

24. Beale Journal [ca. 1842–45], DHP, LC.

25. Ibid.

26. "Beale," Records of Officers, Entry 1711, M-330, Roll 6. Allen Johnson and Dumas Malone (eds.), *The Dictionary of American Biography [DAB]* (20 vols.; New York: Charles Scribner's Sons, 1935), XVIII, 48–49; Walter Colton, *Deck and Port: Or, Incidents of a Cruise in the United States Frigate Congress to California* (New York: A. S. Barnes and Burr, 1860), 323–24, 358–59, describes Stockton's sermons.

27. Glenn Price, *Origins of the War with Mexico: The Polk-Stockton Intrigue* (Austin: University of Texas Press, 1967), 76–77. Beale to George Bancroft, March 13 and 25, 1845, LR-SNBC. "Beale Statement," 3, B-UC.

28. Price, *Origins of the War with Mexico*, 108; Justin Smith, *Annexation of Texas* (New York: Baker and Taylor Co., 1911), 447–48.

29. "Beale," Records of Officers, Entry 1711, M-330, Roll 6. Price, *Origins of the War With Mexico*, 150–151. James Buchanan to George Bancroft, July 17, 1845, DHP, LC. Beale to Bancroft, September 2, 1845, LR-SNBC.

30. "Beale Statement," 3, B-UC. Milo M. Quaife (ed.), *The Diary of James K. Polk, During His Presidency, 1845 to 1849* (4 vols., Chicago: A. C. McClurg, 1910), I, passim.

31. "Beale," Records of Officers, Entry 1711, M-330, Roll 6. Burr, *Early Navy*, 86; Colton, *Deck and Port*, 295–96.

32. Colton, *Deck and Port*, 13–15; Washington *National Intelligencer*, October 30, November 4, 1845, Beale to Mrs. Samuel F. Du Pont, October 28, 1845, S. F. Du Pont Papers, Eleutherian Mills Historical Library, Greenville, Wilmington, Delaware.

33. Washington *National Intelligencer*, November 4, 1845.

34. Colton, *Deck and Port*, 22–23, 38, 45–46; K. Jack Bauer, *Surfboats and Horse Marines: U.S. Naval Operations in the Mexican War, 1846–48* (Annapolis: United States Naval Institute, 1969), 254.

35. Colton, *Deck and Port*, 45–46. "Beale Statement," 3–4, B-UC.

36. "Beale Statement," 4; B-UC. Beale to Bancroft, February 23, 1846, LR-SNBC. Quaife, *Diary of James K. Polk*, I, 242–43.

37. Bancroft to Beale, March 7, 1846, LR-SNBC. Stockton to Beale, April

13, 1846, Robert F. Stockton Papers, Princeton University. Colton, *Deck and Port*, 295–96, 299–326, passim.

38. Ibid., 326–89, passim. "Beale Statement," 4, B-UC.

Chapter 2

1. Andrew Rolle, *California: A History* New York: Thomas Y. Crowell Company, 1969), 193–96; K. Jack Bauer, *The Mexican War, 1846–48* (New York): Macmillan Company, 1974), 11–29; Bauer, *Surfboats and Horse Marines*, 158–62.

2. Bauer, *Surfboats and Horse Marines*, 135–63, passim. See also John A. Hussey, "The United States and the Bear Flag Revolt" (Ph.D. Dissertation, University of California, 1941).

3. "Beale Statement," 7, B-UC; Stockton to Beale, July 29, 1846, Stockton Papers, Princeton; Stockton to Bancroft, August 22, 1846, Pacific Squadron Letters, 1841–86, M-89, Roll 33. Bauer, *Surfboats and Horse Marines*, 165–70.

4. Bauer, *Surfboats and Horse Marines*, 177. "Beale Statement," 6, B-UC; Stockton to Beale, October 3, 1846, Stockton Letterbook, 369, Stockton Papers, Princeton.

5. John C. Fremont, *Memoirs of My Life* (2 vols., Chicago: Belford, Clarke, 1887), I, 574–75. Louis McLane to Jacob Rink Snyder, ca. October, 1846, Jacob R. Snyder Papers, Society of California Pioneers, San Francisco.

6. Fremont, *Memoirs of My Life*, I, 574–75; Mary Lee Spence and Donald Jackson (eds.), *The Expeditions of John C. Fremont* (5 vols., Urbana: University of Illinois Press, 1970), II, 208n.

7. Spence and Jackson, *Expeditions of Fremont*, II, 209–10; Bauer, *Surfboats and Horse Marines*, 180–82.

8. "Beale Statement, 7–8, B-UC. Washington *National Intelligencer*, March 20, 1847, reproduces a letter from San Diego of November 25, 1846.

9. "Beale Statement," 7–8, B-UC. Kearny to Stockton, December 2, 1846, and Stockton to Kearny, December 3, 1846, in Samuel J. Bayard, *Sketch of the Life of Com. Robert F. Stockton* (New York: Derby & Jackson, 1856), 131–32, 133. Arthur Woodward, *Lances at San Pasqual* (San Francisco: California Historical Society, 1948), 19.

10. Woodward, *San Pasqual*, 19. Sally C. Johns, "The Battle of San Pasqual" (M.A. thesis, University of San Diego, 1972), 73.

11. Woodward, *San Pasqual*, 23–25, "Beale Statement," 8, B-UC. William H. Davis, *Sixty Years in California* (San Francisco: A. J. Leary, 1889), 420; Dwight L. Clark (ed.), *The Original Journals of Henry Smith Turner—With Stephen Watts Kearny to New Mexico and California, 1846–1847* (Norman: University of Oklahoma Press, 1966), 106.

12. Jones, "Battle of San Pasqual," 77–79; George W. Ames, Jr., "Gillespie and the Conquest of California: Part III," *California Historical Society Quarterly* [CHSQ], XVII (December 1938), 341: Woodward, *Lances at San Pasqual*, 29.

13. Ames, "Gillespie and the Conquest of California," 341–42; Woodward, *Lances at San Pasqual*, 29; Samuel F. Du Pont, *Extracts from the Private Journal Letters of Captain S. F. Du Pont* (Wilmington: privately printed, 1885), 101.

William Emory, "Notes of a Military Reconnaissance from Fort Leavenworth, in Missouri, to San Diego, in California," *HED 41*, 30 Cong.; 1 Sess. (Serial 517), 108.

14. George W. Ames, Jr. (ed.), "A Doctor Comes to California: Part II," XXI (December 1942), 335; Ames, "Gillespie and the Conquest of California,: 342–43; Johns, "Battle of San Pasqual," 82–91; Du Pont, *Private Journal Letters*, 102.

15. Turner to Stockton, December 6, 1846, Pacific Squadron Letters, M-89, Roll 33. Johns, "Battle of San Pasqual," 95. Thomas Hart Benton, "Speech on the Nomination of General Kearny," *Congressional Globe*, 30 Cong., 1 Sess., XIX, Appendix, 982. Bayard, *Stockton*, 133–34.

16. Johns, "Battle of San Pasqual," 98–101. Benton, "Speech on Kearny," 981–82.

17. Benton, "Speech on Kearny," 982. "Notes on San Pasqual," June 19, 1976, author's files.

18. Benton, "Speech on Kearny," 982–83.

19. Ibid.; Fred B. Rogers, *Filings from an Old Saw* (San Francisco: John Howell, 1956), 87.

20. Benton, "Speech on Kearny," 983.

21. Ibid., 978; Johns, "Battle of San Pasqual," 117–18. James Mills (comp.), "Historical Landmarks of San Diego County," *Journal of San Diego History*, V (January 1959), 13.

22. Beale, "Remarks of General Beale at the Banquet in Honor of General Diaz," April 13, 1883, printed sheet, DHP, LC.

23. Bauer, *Surfboats and Horse Marines*, 191–201. "Beale Statement," 8–9, B-UC.

24. Bauer, *Surfboats and Horse Marines*, 202–204.

25. Stockton to Beale, January 27, 1847, Letterbook, 496, Stockton Papers, Princeton.

26. J. W. Revere, et al., to Beale, December 21, 1846, and Beale to Messrs. R. L. Tilghman et al., January 26, 1847, in Washington *National Intelligencer*, May 26, 1847.

27. Stockton to Beale, February 12, 15, 1847, Letterbook, 517–18, Stockton Papers, Princeton.

28. Spence and Jackson, *Expeditions of John C. Fremont*, II, 361–62; El Mariposo [Beale] to editor, Chester (Penn.) *Delaware County Republican* [August–September], 1871, clipping, DHP, LC.

29. Washington *Union*, May 25, 1847. David Lavender, *Bent's Fort* (New York: Doubleday, 1954), 271–97, passim.

30. Louise Barry, *The Beginning of the West: Annals of the Kansas Gateway to the American West, 1540–1854* (Topeka: Kansas State Historical Society, 1972), 670, 682–83.

31. E. F. Beale to John Y. Mason, May 31, 1847, LR-SNBC. Stockton's dispatches, which Beale carried to Washington, appear in Pacific Squadron Letters, M-89, Roll 33. Quaife, *Diary of Polk*, II, 492–93, III, 52–55. Beale to S. F. Du Pont [undated—1848], S. F. Du Pont Papers.

32. Beale to Mason, August (?), 1847; Mason to Benton, August 27, 1847, DHP, LC. Beale to S. F. Du Pont, undated [March–April, 1848], S. F. Du Pont Papers.

33. Jessie Benton Fremont to Beale, September 20, 1847, in Spence and Jackson, *Expeditions of Fremont*, II, 387–88.

34. "Court Martial of John C. Fremont," *SED 33*, 30 Cong., 1 Sess. (Serial 507), 269.

35. Ibid., 269–72.

36. John Appleton, Acting Secretary of the Navy, to Beale, December 30, 1847, LR-SNBC. Beale to Mrs. S. F. Du Pont, December 23, 29, 1847, and January 5, 1848, and undated [January 7, 1848], S. F. Du Pont Papers.

37. Beale to Mason, February 18 (1848), LR-SNBC.

38. Jones to Mason, March 6, 1848, Pacific Squadron Letters, M-89, Roll 34. Beale to Du Pont, undated [March–April, 1848], S. F. Du Pont Papers.

39. Bauer, *Mexican War*, 350, and Chapter 19, passim. James McCrane to Lieutenant Fabius Stanley, March 9, 1852; and Stanley to Beale, March 11, 1852, in "File of Edward F. Beale," No. 159, Special Files of the Office of Indian Affairs [OIA], 1807–1904, M-574, Roll 33, Records of the Bureau of Indian Affairs, RG 75, NA. Bonsal, *Edward Fitzgerald Beale*, 39–40.

Chapter 3

1. Rodman W. Paul, *California Gold: The Beginning of Mining in the Far West* (Lincoln: University of Nebraska Press, 1965), 16–19; Rolle, *California*, 215.

2. Jones to Mason, July 29, 1848, Pacific Squadron Letters, M-89, Roll 34. Bonsal, *Edward Fitzgerald Beale*, 40. "A Ride Across Mexico," Washington *National Intelligencer*, September 28, 1848.

3. "A Ride Across Mexico," Washington *National Intelligencer*, September 28, 1848. Nathan Clifford to James Buchanan, August 21, 1848, Dispatches from United States Ministers to Mexico, Records of the Department of State, RG 59, M-97, Roll 14.

4. "A Ride Across Mexico," Washington *National Intelligencer*, September 28, 1848.

5. Ibid. Beale to Polk, September 19, 1848, James K. Polk Papers, LC microfilm, Roll 53. Quaife, *Diary of Polk*, III, 124–35. *History of San Luis Obispo County, California, With Illustrations and Biographical Sketches of its Prominent Men and Pioneers* (Oakland, Cal.: Thompson and West, 1883), 112. In an 1881 interview, Beale stated that he entered the president's office and found Polk in the middle of a chess game. After listening to Beale, the president brushed aside the story of the gold discovery by suggesting that Beale and his fellow officers were probably speculating in city lots in San Francisco and hoped to induce an immigration.

6. Washington *National Intelligencer*, September 21, 1848. San Francisco *Alta California*, January 18, 1849, reproduced articles from the Baltimore *Sun*, September 20, 1848, and Washington *Union*, September 19, 1848. Ralph P. Bieber, "California Gold Mania," *Mississippi Valley Historical Review [MVHR]*, XXXV (June 1948), 9–17; John W. Caughey, *Gold Is the Cornerstone* (Berkeley and Los Angeles: University of California Press, 1948), 39–45; Harvey Lewis Carter, *"Dear Old Kit," the Historical Kit Carson* (Norman: University of Okla-

homa Press, 1968), 120–21. Santa Fe Weekly *Republican*, June 27, 1848. Walter Colton, *Three Years in California* (New York: A. S. Barnes and Co., 1851), 242–44. Beale's news had been preceded by an article in the New York *Herald* on August 18 from a member of the New York Volunteers in California, but it attracted little attention. On September 12, the New Orleans *Picayune* published an article on the California gold discovery based upon a Mexico City interview with Beale. The author described California as "destined to become probably the richest and most important country on the continent." Lieutenant Lucien Loeser, the U.S. Army's counterpart to Beale, did not reach Washington until December 5, long after Beale's arrival, but by this time even President Polk was impressed. Harvey Carter in *Dear Old Kit* speculates that Kit Carson, who left California via the Gila route on May 9, probably carried letters and messages concerning the gold strike. Carson reached Santa Fe on June 19. The Santa Fe *Republican* reported the arrival of his party but stated "they bring no news of importance, more than that every thing was perfectly quiet when they left." The month of May was apparently critical in the spread of the news on the West Coast. Reverent Walter Colton, alcalde at Monterey, did not record that the announcement of the gold discovery had reached Monterey until May 29, and even then, many residents reacted to the news with disbelief and incredulity. The Mississippi Valley likely received the exciting news from eastern newspapers.

7. Washington *National Intelligencer*, September 28, 1848. [William C. Jones], "A Ride Across Mexico," *Littell's Living Age*, XIX (October 21, 1848), 130–32. Beale disclosed the authorship of the article in a letter to Bayard Taylor. Beale to Taylor, March 28, 1850, Bayard Taylor Papers, Cornell University, Ithaca, New York.

8. "Message from the President of the United States with Copies of the Correspondence in Relation to the Boundaries of Texas . . .," *SED 24*, 31 Cong., 1 Sess. (Serial 554), 4–7. Leroy R. Hafen and Ann W. Hafen (eds.), *Fremont's Fourth Expedition* (Glendale, Cal.: Arthur H. Clark Company, 1960), 19–22. Beale to S. F. Du Pont, October 27, 1848, S. F. Du Pont Papers.

9. Beale to Du Pont, October 27, 1848, S. F. Du Pont Papers, James Hamilton, *Life in Earnest* (New York: Robert Carter, 1848), 21, 94, 104. Henry Graham Ashmead, *History of Delaware County, Pennsylvania* (Philadelphia: L. A. Everts & Company, 1884), 248.

10. Barry, *The Beginning of the West*, 786–87. Beale to Harry Edwards, December 3, 1848, DHP, LC.

11. Hafen and Hafen, *Fremont's Fourth Expedition*, 88. Beale to Edwards, December 3, 1848, DHP, LC.

12. San Francisco *Alta California*, Supplement, March 29, 1849. Washington *National Intelligencer*, May 31, 1849. "Correspondence in Relation to Boundaries," *SED 24*, 31 Cong., 1 Sess. (Serial 554), 7.

13. San Francisco *Alta California*, March 29, 1848. Allan Nevins, *Fremont: Pathmarker of the West* (New York: Appleton-Century Co., 1939), 368–69.

14. Washington *National Intelligencer*, May 31, April 7, 1849.

15. Ibid., May 31, 1849. Philadelphia *North American*, June 12, 1849. New York *Herald*, June 14, 1849.

16. New York *Herald*, June 1, 1849. *Panama Star*, May 13, 1849, clippng in DHP, LC. Washington *National Intelligencer*, June 1, 1849.

17. Washington *National Intelligencer,* May 31, 1849. Jessie Benton Fremont, *A Year of American Travel: A Narrative of Personal Experience* (San Francisco: Book Club of California, 1960), 58–59.

18. New York *Herald,* May 30, 1849.

19. P. T. Barnum to Beale, May 27 (29?), 1849, DHP, LC. New York *Herald,* May 30, 1849.

20. New York *Herald,* May 30, 1849.

21. Ibid., May 30, June 6, 1849. Washington *National Intelligencer,* June 2, 1849.

22. New York *Herald,* June 6, 1849.

23. Ibid., June 8, 1849.

24. A copy of the marriage certificate of Edward F. Beale and Mary Engle Edwards, signed by M. R. Talbot, is in Edward F. Beale (Widow—Mary), Mexican War Pension File, RVA, RG 15, NA. New York *Herald,* June 29, 30, July 3, 1849. New York *Herald,* July 1, 1849.

25. Bayard Taylor, *Eldorado, or, Adventures in the Path of Empire* (2 vols.; New York: G.P. Putnam, 1850), I, vii–viii, 29–30. John W. Connor, "Connor's Early California; Statement of a Few Recollectons . . . ," [1878], 1–2, unpublished manuscript, B-UC.

26. Taylor, *Eldorado,* I, 31–42.

27. Ibid., I, 45–46. Thomas Scharf, "Amiel Weeks Whipple: Boundary and Railroad Surveys in the Southwest, 1849–1854" (M.A. thesis, University of San Diego, 1973), 72–73; Lewis B. Lesley, "The International Boundary Survey, 1848–50," *CHSQ,* IX (March 1930), 7.

28. Taylor, *Eldorado,* I, 55–61, San Francisco *Alta California,* Supplement August 23, 1849.

29. Taylor, *Eldorado,* I, 62–68.

30. Lesley, "International Boundary Survey," 7; Taylor, *Eldorado,* I, 70.

31. Taylor, *Eldorado,* I, 74–87.

32. Ibid., I, 121–33, 151–58, 192. Beale to Abel Stearns, October 4, 1849. Abel Stearns Papers, Huntington Library, San Marino, California. Beale apparently had been contemplating "life in earnest" in California. On October 4, he gave a power of attorney to Abel Stearns, a longtime American rancher in southern California. Beale authorized Stearns to obtain the San Bernardino Rancho for a sum not in excess of $25,000. He planned to make a down payment and then pay out the remainder on time. He also wished to purchase all of the ranch's livestock. Moreover, ever since his convalescence after the battle of San Pasqual, he had felt himself drawn to the life-style of the *Californios.* Unfortunately, he was unable to purchase the San Bernardino Rancho.

33. Beale to Taylor, October 15, 1849, Taylor Papers. Taylor to Thomas Buchanan Read, October 30, 1849; to R. H. Stoddard, October 31, 1849; to N. P. Willis, October 31, 1949, DHP, LC.

34. Jones to Beale, October 31, 1849; to William B. Preston, Secretary of the Navy, October 31, 1849, Pacific Squadron Letters, M-89, Roll 34. New York *Herald,* December 8, 1849.

35. Preston to Beale, August 6, 1849; Taylor to Beale, March 26, 1850, DHP, LC. Beale to Taylor, March 28, 1850, Taylor Papers.

36. Taylor to Beale, March 26, 1850; Fremont to Beale, April 17, 1850, DHP, LC. Beale to Taylor, March 28, 1850, Taylor Papers.

37. Fremont to Beale, April 17, 1850, DHP, LC. Beale to Taylor, March 28, 1850, Taylor Papers.

38. Beale to Taylor, May 7, 1850, Taylor Papers. San Francisco *Alta California,* June 20, 1850. Stockton and William H. Aspinwall to Beale, January 9, 1851, DHP, LC. San Francisco *Herald,* June 22, 1850. New York *Herald,* August 8, 1850, copied from the San Francisco *Herald* of July 1, 1850. This issue of the San Francisco *Herald* is apparently nonexistent today.

39. C. Gregory Crampton, "The Opening of the Mariposa Mining Region, 1849–1959, with particular reference to the Mexican Land Grant of John Charles Fremont" (Ph.D. dissertation, University of California, 1941), 170–71. Sacramento *Transcript,* September 13, 1850.

40. Fremont to Clayton, June 10, 1850; to Z. Taylor, June 10, 1850, Letters of Application and Recommendation during the Administrations of James K. Polk, Zachary Taylor, and Millard Fillmore, M-873, Roll 30.

41. Sacramento *Transcript,* September 13, 1850; Edmund Booth, *Edmund Booth— Forty-Niner* (Stockton: San Joaquin Pioneer and Historial Society, 1953), 27.

42. Fremont and Benton to Daniel Webster, September 3, 1850, Letters of Application, Fillmore, M-873, Roll 30. Fremont to Mary Ann Edwards, September 12, 1850, DHP, LC. Holman Hamilton, *Prologue to Conflict: The Crisis and Compromise of 1850* (New York: W. W. Norton & Company, 1966), 159–60. "Beale," Records of Officers, Entry 738, M-330, Roll 7.

43. Beale to Buchanan, November 2, 1850, James Buchanan Papers, Historical Society of Pennsylvania, Philadelphia. Buchanan to Beale, November 22, 1850, DHP, LC.

44. Stockton and Aspinwall to Beale, January 9, 1851, DHP, LC.

45. San Francisco *Alta California,* February 25, 1851.

46. George R. Stewart, *Committee of Vigilance: Revolution in San Francisco, 1851* (Boston: Houghton Mifflin Company, 1964), 3–39; Bonsal, *Edward Fitzgerald Beale,* 60–62.

47. San Francisco *Herald,* May 22, and May 31, 1851.

Chapter 4

1. Richard E. Crouter and Andrew F. Rolle, "Edward Fitzgerald Beale and the Indian Peace Commissioners in California, 1851–1854," Historical Society of Southern California [HSSC] *Quarterly,* XLII, (June 1960), 107–9; Sheburne F. Cook, *The Conflict Between the California Indians and White Civilizations* (Berkeley and Los Angeles: University of California Press, 1943), 1–115.

2. Crouter and Rolle, "Beale and the Peace Commissioners," 111–15. Charles Leonard, "Federal Indian Policy in th San Joaquin Valley, Its Application and Results" (Ph.D. dissertation, University of California, 1928), 183.

3. San Francisco *Alta California,* July 24, August 11, 1851; October 2, 1855. Leonard, "Indian Policy in the San Joaquin Valley," 183; Crouter and Rolle, "Beale and the Peace Commissoners," 114.

4. Crouter and Rolle, "Beale and the Peace Commissioners," 114–17. Thomas Hart Benton to Alexander Stuart, November 12, 1851, DHP, LC.

5. Fremont to George W. Wright, December 26, 1851, Wright Papers, Huntington Library, San Marino, Cal. William M. Gwin, Joseph W. McCorkle, and Edward Marshall [ca. December 1851] to Fillmore, Interior Department Appointment Papers: State of California, Records of the Office of the Secretary of the Interior, RG 48, NA. William H. Ellison (ed.), "Memoirs of the Hon. William M. Gwin: Part II," *CHSQ*, XIX (June 1940), 157–84.

6. Beale to Clayton, January 30, 1852, John M. Clayton Papers, LC; undated newspaper clippng (ca. 1842), DHP, LC. Lee Ann Clancey, Historical Society of Delaware, to author, December 15, 1976, author's files.

7. Affidavits of Henry B. Edwards and Beale, January 24, 1852, in "Message on Accounts of J. C. Fremont," *SED 109*, 34 Cong., 1 Sess. (Serial 825), 32–33.

8. Beale to Taylor, February 3, 1852, Taylor Papers; Bayard Taylor, "The Summer Camp," in *The Poems of Bayard Taylor* (Boston: Ticknor and Fields, 1866), 331.

9. *Congressional Globe*, 32 Cong., 1 Sess., XXIV, Part 1, 663–64; Washington *National Intelligencer*, March 4, 1852. Fillmore to U.S. Senate, March 4, 1852, Executive Nominations, Appointment Division, Volume 1-A, Records of the Department of Interior [RDI]; Fremont to Beale, March 8, 1852, LRCS, M-234, Roll 32. San Francisco *Alta Californian*, October 2, 1855.

10. James McCrane to Lt. Fabius Stanley, March 9, 1852; and Stanley to Beale, March 11, 1852; Alexander H. H. Stuart to CIA, March 11, 1852, all in LRCS, M-234, Roll 32.

11. Beale to Lea, March 18, 1852, "Report of the Secretary of the Interior, Communicating . . . the correspondence between the Department of the Interior and the Indian Agents and Commissioners in California," *SED 4*, 33 Cong., Special Sess. (Serial 688), 297. *United States Statutes at Large*, X, Chapter 103, 55–56.

12. San Francisco *Herald*, February 22, 1852. Redick McKee to John Bigler, April 5, 1852; Bigler to McKee, April 9, 1852, in "Interior Report," *SED 4*, 33 Cong., Special Sess., 310–18.

13. San Francisco *Herald*, April 13, 1852. Oliver Wozencraft to Lea. April 29, 1852, "Interior Report," *SED 4*, 33 Cong., Special Sess., 324. San Francisco *Evening Picayune* (April 1852), clipping in LRCS, M-234, Roll 32.

14. McKee to Lea, May 1, 1852, M-234, Roll 32. McKee to Fillmore, April 3, 1852, "Interior Report," *SED 4*, 33 Cong., Special Sess., 308.

15. Lea to Beale, May 8, 1852 (telegram); to Beale, May 10, 1852; and Beale to Lea, May 11, 1852, "Interior Report," *SED 4*, 33 Cong., Special Sess., 26, 326–30. Beale to Lea May 11, 1852, LRCS, M-234, Roll 32.

16. Crouter and Rolle, "Beale and the Indian Peace Commissioners," 119. Beale to Lea, April 7, 1852, LRCS, M-234, Roll 32.

17. Beale to Lea, July 14, 1852, "Interior Report," *SED 4*, 33 Cong., Special Sess., 344–45.

18. Stuart to Lea, July 26, 1852, LRCS, M-234, Roll 32. Lea to Beale, July 31, 1852, Letters Sent by the Office of Indian Affairs, 1824–81 [LS-OIA], M-21, Roll 46, Records of the BIA, RG 75, NA.

19. Beale to Lea, August 3, 1852, "Interior Report," *SED 4*, 33 Cong., Spe-

cial Sess., 358. San Francisco *Alta California,* September 6, 1852. *Congressional Globe,* 32 Cong., 1 Sess., XXIV, Part 3, 2172–79. William H. Ellison, "Federal Indian Policy in California, 1846–1860: (Ph.D. dissertation, University of California, 1919), 357–59. The long debate over California Indian affairs eventually resulted in a $100,000 appropriation, enacted into law on August 30, 1852.

20. Beale to Lea, September 16, 1852, "Interior Report," *SED 4,* 33 Cong., Special Sess., 361; "Memorandum of a conversation with agent Wozencraft," September 14, 1852, ibid., 368–69. On the same day that he talked with Wozencraft, Beale resigned from the U.S. Navy. Beale to Secretary of the Navy, September 14, 1852, Resignations of Officers, RG 45, NA.

21. Joel Brooks to Beale, September 21, 1852, "Interior Report," *SED 4,* 33 Cong., Special Sess., 369–70. H. C. Logan to Beale, September 21, 1852, ibid., 370. Ethan A. Hitchcock to Beale, September 21, 1852; Captain John H. Lindrum to Wozencraft, February 14, 1853, LRCS, M-234, Roll 33. Francis B. Heitman (comp.), *Historical Register and Dictionary of the United States Army* (2 vols., Washington, D.C.: Government Printing Office, 1903), 627–28.

22. Beale to Lea, September 30, 1852, "Interior Report," *SED 4,* 33 Cong., Special Sess., 366–67.

23. H. B. Edwards, Vouchers No. 1 and 8, October 7, 20, 1852, File of Edward F. Beale, No. 159, Special Files of the Office of Indian Affairs, M-574, Roll 33, RBIA, RG 75, NA. Beale to Lea, October 29, 1852, "Interior Report," *SED 4,* 33 Cong., Special Sess., 373. Peter Campbell, October 28, 1852, LRCS, M-234, Roll 32. *San Francisco Directory for the year 1852–3* (San Francisco: James M. Parker, 1852), 35.

24. Beale to Lea, October 29, 1852, "Interior Report," *SED 4,* 33 Cong., Special Sess., 373–74; Hitchcock Statement, October 31, 1852, ibid., 374–75.

25. Lea to Pearson B. Reading, September 15, 17, 1852, LS-OIA, M-21, Roll 46. Reading to Lea, September 10, October 5, 1852, LRCS, M-234, Roll 32. Beale to Lea, November 15, 1852, "Interior Report," *SED 4,* 33 Cong., Special Sess., 375; Wilson to Beale, November 11, 1852, ibid., 376–77.

26. Beale to Lea, November 11, 1852, "Interior Report," *SED 4,* 33 Cong., Special Sess., 377–80.

27. Hitchcock to Adjutant General, November 29, 1852, LRCS, M-234, Roll 33.

28. Beale to Wilson, November 5, 1852, LRCS, M-234, Roll 33; Beale to Wilson, November 22, 1852, B. D. Wilson Papers, Huntington Library. San Francisco *Herald,* December 1, 1852.

29. Beale to Lea, December 14, 23, 1852, "Interior Report," *SED 4,* Special Sess., 390–93.

30. Beale to Lea, December 14, 1852, "Interior Report," *SED 4,* Special Sess., 390–92. San Francisco *Herald,* January 11, 1853.

31. San Francisco *Herald,* January 11 and 15, 1853. Lea to Beale, December 2, 1852, LSOIA, M-21, Roll 46.

32. San Francisco *Herald,* January 11, 15, 1853. "Letter from the Secretary of the Interior, Communicating the Report of Edward F. Beale, . . . respecting the condition of Indian Affairs," *SED 57,* 32 Cong., 2 Sess. (Serial 665), 1–18, passim.

33. Stuart to William K. Sebastian, March 3, 1853 "Report of Beale," *SED 57*, 32 Cong., 2 Sess., 1; Ellison, "Federal Indian Policy in California," 374–76; *Congressional Globe*, 32 Cong., 2 Sess., 1085–86, 1162.

34. Beale to Lea, March 18, 1853; Pierce to McClelland, March 25, 1853, Special File 159, OIA, M-574, Roll 33. Beale to Lea, March 21, 1853, LRCS, M-234, Roll 33. McClelland [?] to Beale, March 26, 1853. DHP, LC. Mix to Beale, March 26, 1853, LS-OIA, M-21, Roll 47.

35. Beale to Lea, March 24, 1853; to McKee, March 31, 1853, Special File 159, OIA, M-574, Roll 33; Manypenny to Beale, March 31, 1853, LS-OIA, M-21, Roll 47.

36. Du Pont to Beale, April 13, 1853, DHP, LC. *New York Times,* April 14, 1853. See San Francisco *Herald,* April 22, 25, 30, 1853.

37. William H. Goetzmann, *Army Explorations in the American West, 1803–1863* (New Haven: Yale University Press, 1959), 262. Benton and Beale to Jefferson Davis, March 16, 1853; and Davis to Benton, March 19, 1853, in Gwin Harris Heap, *Central Route to the Pacific* (Glendale, Cal.: Arthur H. Clark Company, 1957), 283–85.

38. Davis to Benton, March 19, 1853, in Heap, *Central Route to the Pacific,* 285. William E. Parrish, *David Rice Atchison of Missouri, Border Politician* (Columbia: University of Missouri Press, 1961), 126–30. The San Francisco *Herald* on September 1, 1853.

39. McClelland to Beale, April 13, 1853, Special File 159, OIA, M-574, Roll 33. Jefferson City *Jefferson Inquirer* (Missouri), May 28, 1853, reprinted in Heap, *Central Route to the Pacific,* 57–71.

40. Beale to McClelland, April 30, 1853; and contract between Beale and Henry E. Young, May 6, 1853; Beale to Young, Voucher No. 14, October 10, 1853, Special File 159, OIA, M-574, Roll 33. Manypenny to Beale, May 9, 1853, LS-OIA, M-21, Roll 47.

41. Heap, *Central Route to the Pacific,* 85–120, passim; Santa Fe *Weekly Gazette,* June 11, 1853; San Francisco *Herald,* June 17, 1853.

42. Heap, *Central Route to the Pacific,* 121–63; Santa Fe *Weekly Gazette,* June 23, 1853. "Colorado Place Names (C)," *Colorado Magazine,* XVII (July 1940), 135.

43. Heap, *Central Route to the Pacific,* 183–91.

44. Los Angeles *Star,* July 16, 1853; San Francisco *Herald,* August 6, 16, 1853.

45. Los Angeles *Star,* September 3, 1853; Heap, *Central Route to the Pacific,* 21, 250–51; San Francisco *Alta California,* September 5, 1853; San Francisco *Herald,* September 5, 1853. Benton to Mary E. Beale, September 5, 1853; Benton to Beale, August 3, 1853, DHP, LC.

Chapter 5

1. Beale to Manypenny, August 22, 1853, "Annual Report of the Commissioner of Indian Affairs [CIA], 1853," *SED 1*, 31 Cong., 1 Sess. (Serial 690), 467–69.

2. San Francisco *Alta California,* September 22, 1853. George Stoneman,

Robert Williamson, John G. Parke to Beale, September 4, 1853, "Report of the CIA, 1853" *SED 1*, 33 Cong., 1 Sess., 478–79.

3. Stoneman, Williamson, and Parke to Beale, September 4, 1853, *SED 1*, 33 Cong., 1 Sess., 478–79. Beale to Lea, November 11, 1852, "Interior Report," *SED 4*, 33 Cong., Special Sess., 377–80.

4. San Francisco *Alta California*, September 22, 1853. Beale to Manypenny, August 22, 1853, "Report of the CIA, 1853," *SED 1*, 33 Cong., 1 Sess., 476–69.

5. San Francisco *Alta California*, September 22, 1853.

6. Beale to Manypenny, September 30, 1853, "Report of the CIA, 1853," *SED 1*, 33 Cong., 1 Sess., 469–72.

7. Edwards to Beale, September 20, 1853, "Report of the CIA, 1853," *SED 1*, 33 Cong., 1 Sess., 472–74.

8. Beale to Gwin and Latham, September 27, 1853; Gwin to Beale (October 1853); John B. Weller to Beale, October 2, 1853; J. A. McDougall to Beale, October 14, 1853, all in "Report of the CIA, 1853," *SED 1*, 33 Cong., 1 Sess., 475–78.

9. Beale to Manypenny, September 23, 1853, Special File 159, OIA, M-574, Roll 33. San Francisco *Herald*, October 9, 1853. Beale to Wilson, October 17, 1853, Benjamin D. Wilson Papers, Huntington Library, San Marino, Cal., San Francisco *Alta California*, October 17, 1853.

10. Beale to Manypenny, October 10, 1853, "Report of the CIA, 1853," *SED 1*, 33 Cong., 1 Sess., 474–75. Beale to Wilson, October 10, 15, 17, 1853, B. D. Wilson Papers.

11. San Francisco *Alta California*, November 1, 23, 1853.

12. San Francisco *Herald*, December 27, 1853.

13. Ignacio del Valle to Beale, November[?], 1853, LRCS, M-234, Roll 36. Beale to del Valle, December 28, 1853, LRCS, M-234, Roll 36.

14. Beale to Manypenny, December 28, 1853, Special File 159, OIA, M-574, Roll 33.

15. Manypenny to Beale, November 18, 1853, "Report of the CIA, 1853," *SED 1*, 33 Cong., 1 Sess., 480–81.

16. Beale to Manypenny, February 8, 1854, "Annual Report of the CIA, 1854," *HED 1*, 33 Cong., 2 Sess. (Serial 777), 506–8. See also Leonard, "Federal Indian Policy in the San Joaquin Valley," Chapter 7, 252–99.

17. Benton to Mary Edwards Beale, March 27, 1854; to Beale, April 2, 1854, DHP, LC. Washington *Evening Star*, June 13, 1854.

18. McClelland to Manypenny, January 5, 1854, Special File 159, OIA, M-574, Roll 33.

19. Manypenny to Beale, April 3 and 4, 1854; to Benton, April 8, 1854; to Senators Gwin and Weller, and Representatives McDougall and Latham, April 13, 1854, all in LS-OIA, M-21, Roll 49.

20. Manypenny to Senators Gwin and Weller, and Representatives McDougall and Latham, April 13, 1854, LS-OIA, M-21, Roll 49. Benton to Beale, April 2, 1854, DHP, LC.

21. San Francisco *Herald*, May 5, 1854. Beale to Manypenny, May 5, 1854, LRCS, M-234, Roll 33.

22. John E. Wool to Samuel Cooper, March 14, 1854; to Winfield Scott,

May 15, 1854; to Beale, May 15, 1854; Beale to Manypenny, May 16, 1854, all in LRCS, M-234, Roll 33. Davis to McClelland, June 22, 1854, LRCS, M-234, Roll 33. Wool urged an appropriation of $500,000 for Beale's "humane schemes." He said if Beale's plans proved as successful as the Tejon project, the military would be able to close several expensive posts. Jefferson Davis forwarded the suggestion to Secretary McClelland.

23. Beale to Manypenny, May 15, 1854, LRCS, M-234, Roll 34. Los Angeles *Star*, June 17, 24, 1854.

24. Washington *Evening Star*, June 2, July 17, 1854; Richard H. Weightman to Beale, April 20, 1855, LRCS, M-234, Roll 34. Washington *National Intelligencer*, July 17, 1854.

25. Beale to Thomas J. Henley, June 20, 1854, LRCS, M-234, Roll 33.

26. San Francisco *Alta California*, July 21, 1854; San Francisco *Herald*, July 4, 11, 1854. Beale to Henley, July 15, 1854, LRCS, M-234, Roll 33.

27. J. Ross Browne to James Guthrie, July 27, 1854, Special File 159, OIA, M-574, Roll 33. Browne to Lucy (Browne), July 15, October 16, 1854, in Lina F. Browne (ed.), *J. Ross Browne: His Letters, Journals and Writings* (Albuquerque: University of New Mexico Press, 1969), 174, 176–77.

28. Browne to Guthrie, July 27, 1854, Special File 159, OIA, M-574, Roll 33. San Francisco *Herald*, August 5, 8, 1854. Invoice of Public Property, Sebastian Military Reserve, August 7, 1854, LRCS, M-234, Roll 34. "Report of J. Ross Browne . . . concerning accounts, & c. of Supt. Beale," 19–20, Messages Suggesting Legislation or Submitting Specific Information or Documents, 35 Cong., Records of the U.S. Senate, RG 46, NA.

29. Henley to Manypenny, August 29, 1854, and enclosure, LRCS, M-234, Roll 33.

30. Browne to Guthrie, July 27, 1854; Henley to Manypenny, September 15, 1854; Charles E. Mix to Browne, September 2, 1854; all in Special File 159, OIA, M-574, Roll 33. "Browne Report," Messages Submitting Information, 35 Cong., Records of the U.S. Senate, RG 46, 40–42. Beale to Wilson, undated and October 14, 1854, Wilson Papers.

31. Beale to Wilson, undated (October, 1854), Wilson Papers.

32. Henley and Browne to Manypenny, October 15, 1854, Special File 159, OIA, M-574, Roll 33. San Francisco *Herald*, October 18, 1854. Browne to Lucy (Browne), October 18, 1854, in Browne, *Browne: Letters, Journals and Writings*, 177.

33. New York *Herald*, November 10, 1854; Washington *Evening Star*, November 15, 1854. Manypenny to Beale, November 24, 1854, LS-OIA, M-21, Roll 50. Beale to Manypenny, November 27, 1854, Special File 159, OIA, M-574, Roll 33. Most of the voluminous correspondence generated by Beale's accounts are in his Special File 159.

34. Manypenny to Beale, December 6, 21, 1854; Beale to Manypenny, December 14, 23, 1854; Special File 159, OIA, M-574, Roll 33.

35. Beale to Taylor, November 18, December 4, 1854, Taylor Papers.

36. Manypenny to Beale, December 27, 1854, LS-OIA, M-21, Roll 50. San Francisco *Herald*, December 31, 1854. David M. Goodman, *A Western Panorama, 1849–75: The Travels, Writings and Influence of J. Ross Browne* (Glendale, Cal.: Arthur H. Clark Company, 1966), 77.

37. "Browne Report," Messages Submitting Information, 35 Cong., Records of the U.S. Senate, RG 46, passim. Beale to Wilson, January 18, 1855, Wilson Papers, Huntington Library. Henley and Browne to Manypenny, October 15, 1854, Special File 159, OIA, M-574, Roll 33.

38. William H. Russell to Beale, February 18, 1855; John Guest to Beale, February 19, 1855, LRCS, M-234, Roll 34. Fremont to Beale, April 3, 1855, Special File 159, OIA, M-574, Roll 33.

39. James M. Brodhead to James Guthrie, April 9, 1855, "Message from the President . . . relating to the case of Edward F. Beale," SED 69, 34 Cong., 3 Sess. (Serial 881), 1–7. Washington Evening Star, April 18, 1855.

40. Richard H. Weightman to Beale, April 20, 1855; Luther Smoot to Beale, April 21, 1855, LRCS, M-234, Roll 34. Donald Chaput, Francois X. Aubry: Trader, Trailmaker, and Voyageur in the Southwest, 1846–1854 (Glendale, Cal.: Arthur H. Clark Company, 1975), 154–66.

41. Washington Evening Star, April 21, 1855; Washington Union, May 1, 1855; Washington National Intelligencer, May 15, 1855.

42. Beale to Pierce, April 20, 1855; Caleb Cushing to Manypenny, May 11, 1855, LRCS, M-234, Roll 34.

43. New York Tribune, April 21, 1855, stated that Beale "inflicted a severe castigation with his fists upon Col. Manypenny." E. Wallach to Manypenny, April 24, 27, 1855; and Manypenny to Wallach, April 24, 1855, LRCS, M-234, Roll 34, contains a dispute over Manypenny's statements to Wallach the previous summer. The feud between Commissioner Manypenny and Benton reached new heights in Washington National Intelligencer, April 28, May 15, 23, 1855; and Washington Union, May 1, 1855.

44. San Francisco Alta California, June 5, 1855; San Francisco Herald, May 17, 1855.

45. San Francisco Herald, May 31, 1855.

Chapter 6

1. W. C. Walker to Mary Edwards Beale, August 8, 1855, Deed Book 3, p. 141, Los Angeles County Records. The legal description of La Liebre is recorded in Ranchos Book, 535–42, Records of the County Recorder's Office, Los Angeles Archives and Records [LA-CAR], Los Angeles.

2. San Francisco Alta California, October 2, 1855.

3. Beale to B. D. Wilson, August 29, 1855, Wilson Papers.

4. James O'Meara, The Vigilance Committee of 1856 (San Francisco: James H. Barry, Publisher, 1887), 24–26; San Francisco Alta California, August 22, 1855. The San Francisco newspapers reproduced the minutes of the county board of supervisors which revealed Casey to be a strong supporter of common laborers. Hubert Howe Bancroft, Popular Tribunals (2 vols., San Francisco: History Company, 1887), II, 1–21, 42–43.

5. San Francisco Alta California, August 22 and 25, 1855; O'Meara, Vigilance Committee, 24–26.

6. O'Meara, Vigilance Committee, 26; San Francisco Alta California, August 26, 1855. John M. Myers, San Francisco's Reign of Terror (New York: Doubleday,

1966), 97. The American Party newspaper which strongly supported Beale was the *Southern Californian,* such as June 13 and 20, 1855.

7. Bancroft, *Popular Tribunals,* II, 29–33; San Francisco *Herald,* November 20, December 14, 15, 1855; San Francisco *Town Talk,* November 20, December 7, 8, 1855.

8. San Francisco *Herald,* January 13, 1855; Bancroft, *Popular Tribunals* II, 29–34; Richard H. Dillon (ed.), " 'Rejoice Ye Thieves and Harlots': The Vigilance Editorials of the San Francisco Journalist James King of William," *CHSQ,* XXXVII (June 1958), 137–69.

9. San Francisco *Alta California,* February 2, April 6, 1856.

10. Ibid., February 2, 1856. *National Cyclopaedia of American Biography* (56 vols., New York: James T. White and Company, 1898), XXVII, 407.

11. San Francisco *Herald,* June 5, 1856. William T. Sherman to Henry S. Turner, May 18, 1856, in Doyce B. Nunis (ed.), *The San Francisco Vigilance Committee of 1856: Three Views* (Los Angeles: Los Angeles Westerners, 1971) 150–55. Bancroft, *Popular Tribunals,* II, 28–29, 35–40, 72.

12. San Francisco *Herald,* May 17, 1856. Sherman to Turner, May 18, 1856, in Nunis, *Three Views,* 150–55. Bancroft, *Popular Tribunals,* II, 81–83.

13. Bancroft, *Popular Tribunals,* II, 183–93, 235–39.

14. San Francisco *Herald,* May 24, July 8, 1856. San Francisco *Alta California,* May 24, 1855.

15. San Francisco *Herald,* May 8, 14, 16, 26, 1856. Wool to Beale, September 21, 1858, DHP, LC.

16. William C. Kibbe to Beale, May 14, 1856, DHP, LC. J. Neely Johnson to Beale, May 26, 1856, Indian Wars File [IWF], California State Archives, Sacramento.

17. Beale to J. Neely Johnson, July 12, 1856, in San Francisco *Herald,* July 13, 1856. Heitman, *Historical Register,* I, 160, 636.

18. Beale to Johnson, July 12, 1856, IWF, California State Archives.

19. Ibid.

20. San Francisco *Herald,* June 13, September 10, 1856.

21. Bancroft, *Popular Tribunals,* II, 32; San Francisco *Herald,* July 11, 13, 15, 1856; San Francisco *Alta California,* July 13, 1856.

22. San Francisco *Alta California,* July 13, 1856; San Francisco *Herald,* July 15, 1856; David Scannell to Ira P. Rankin, July 15, 1856, in San Francisco *Alta California,* July 15, 1856.

23. San Francisco *Alta California,* July 17, 18, 1856; San Francisco *Herald,* July 19, 1856.

24. San Francisco *Alta California,* July 23, August 5, 8, 1856. George Whelan, president of the Board of Supervisors to Beale, August 7, 1856, DHP, LC. William C. Kibbe to Johnson, August 7, and 8, 1856, in Herbert G. Florcken (ed.), "The Law and Order View of the San Francisco Vigilance Committee of 1856,: Part IV" *CHSQ,* XV (September 1936), 247–48.

25. San Francisco *Alta California,* August 9–14, 16, 1856.

26. Richard Maxwell Brown, "Pivot of American Vigilantism: The San Francisco Vigilance Committee of 1856," in John A. Carroll (ed.), *Reflections of Western Historians* (Tucson: University of Arizona Press, 1969), 113–19; William H. Ellison, *A Self-governing Dominion: California, 1849–1860* (Berkeley

and Los Angeles: University of California Press, 1950), 244–65; Bancroft, *Popular Tribunals*, II, 132. San Francisco *Herald*, May 5, 1857. Doane ran unopposed for the sheriff's office, but Scannell remained in office. A court case resulted, as expected. The California Supreme Court declared on May 4, 1857, in *Charles Doane v. David Scannell*, that the Board of Supervisors which disallowed Scannell's bonds had not given the sheriff sufficient time to make the bonded amount before declaring the office vacant. Scannell was correct in assuming that he had never been removed from office, and the court reversed the decision of Judge Freelon.

27. San Francisco *Herald*, July 16, August 3, 1856.

28. Ibid., July 16, August 3, 5, 1856.

29. Ibid., August 5, 9, 1856; David A. Williams, *David C. Broderick—A Political Portrait* (San Marino: Huntington Library, 1969), 134.

30. Beale to Buchanan, September 5, 1856, Buchanan Papers. Buchanan to B. F. Washington, September 17, 1856, in San Francisco *Herald*, October 18, 1856.

31. Benton to Beale, September 1, 1856, DHP, LC; San Francisco *Herald*, September 24, 1856. The poem is from the *Camden Democrat* (New Jersey) August 30, 1856, DHP, LC.

32. September [?], 1856, undated newspaper clipping, Mary Edwards Scrapbook, DHP, LC.

33. Ibid.; Buchanan to Beale, October 3, 1856, DHP, LC.

34. San Francisco *Herald*, October 25, 1856. See Gerald Stanley, "The Republican Party in California, 1856–1868" (Ph.D. dissertation, University of Arizona, 1973).

35. San Francisco *Herald*, November 4, 1856.

36. San Francisco *Alta California*, November [7–10], 1856; Beale to Charles Fernald, December 5, 1856, in Cameron Rogers (ed.) *A County Judge in Arcady: Selected Private Papers of Charles Fernald, Pioneer California Jurist* (Glendale, Cal.: Arthur H. Clark Company, 1954), 95–96; San Francisco *Herald*, December 2, 1856.

37. Wool to Buchanan, January 15, 1857, State of California, 1849–1907, Interior Department Appointment Papers, Records of the Secretary of the Interior, RG 48.

38. New York *Herald*, February 14, 1857. San Francisco *Town Talk*, January 20, 1857.

Chapter 7

1. San Francisco *Herald*, April 21, 30, 1857. For the Broderick and Gwin dispute, see Williams, *Broderick*, 159–63.

2. San Francisco *Herald*, April 21, 1856, May 4, 1857. W. Turrentine Jackson, *Wagon Roads West: A Study of Federal Road Surveys and Construction in the Trans-Mississippi West, 1846–1869* (Berkeley and Los Angeles: University of California Press, 1952), 241–45.

3. John B. Floyd to Beale, April 22, 1857, Letters Sent by the Secretary of War, Relating to Military Affairs, 1800–89 [LSSW], Records of the Office of the Secretary of War (ROSW), RG 107, NA, M-6, Roll 39.

4. Floyd [aide of] to Beale, May 1, 1857, DHP, LC. Floyd to Beale, April 23, 1857, LSSW, ROSW, M-6, Roll 39. Beale to Buchanan, April 25, 1857, California Appointment Papers, Records of the Office of the Secretary of the Interior, RG 48, NA. Before departing for New Mexico, Beale visited the White House and requested that President Buchanan appoint Judge Thomas Sutherland as postmaster of San Francisco. He stated that Sutherland's appointment would be "highly satisfactory" to Senator Broderick.

5. Lesley B. Lewis (ed.), "Journal of May Humphreys Stacey," *Uncle Sam's Camels* (Glorieta, N.M.: Rio Grande Press, 1970), 21–34.

6. Baldridge, Sparks & Co. to Edward F. Beale, Bill of Sale, June 4, 1857, DHP, LC. Bonsal, *Edward Fitzgerald Beale*, 294–95.

7. Lewis, *Uncle Sam's Camels*, 37–38. Heap to Mrs. Heap, November 21, 1857, Camels Collection, AHS.

8. Lewis, *Uncle Sam's Camels*, 42–44. Edward F. Beale, "Wagon Road from Fort Defiance to the Colorado River," *HED 124*, 35 Cong., 1 Sess. (Serial 959), 15–19.

9. Beale to Floyd, July 24, 1857, Letters Received by the Secretary of War (LRSW), Registered Series, ROSW, M-221, Roll 181. Beale, "Fort Defiance Wagon Road," 20–29.

10. Beale, "Fort Defiance Wagon Road," 32. Stacey confirmed that the party frequently attracted curious crowds. Lewis, *Uncle Sam's Camels*, 74.

10. Beale, "Fort Defiance Wagon Road," 32–34.

12. Ibid., 36. Heitman, *Historical Register*, I, 282.

13. Beale, "Fort Defiance Wagon Road," 36–38. Fort Defiance Post Returns August, 1857, Returns from U.S. Military Posts, M-617, Roll 301, Records of United States Army Commands, RG 98, NA. Chaput, *Francois X. Aubry*, 123–49.

14. Beale, "Fort Defiance Wagon Road," 39–45.

15. Ibid., 45–53.

16. Ibid., 61; Lewis, *Uncle Sam's Camels*, 103–4.

17. Beale to Floyd, September 27, 1857, Camel File, Records of the Quartermaster General, RG 92, microfilm, Bakersfield Public Library, Bakersfield, Cal.

18. Beale, "Fort Defiance Wagon Road," 69–70, 72–75.

19. Ibid., 76. Beale to Floyd, October 18, 1857, in Bonsal, *Edward Fitzgerald Beale*, 211–17.

20. San Francisco *Herald*, November 26, 1857. Beale to Mary E. Beale, November 8, 1857, DHP, LC. San Francisco *Alta California*, November 26, 1857.

21. Beale to Floyd, January 23, 1858, LRSW, ROSW, M-221, Roll 183. Beale, "Fort Defiance Wagon Road," 76–77. George A. Johnson to editor, February 22, 1858, San Francisco *Herald*, March 14, 1858.

22. Goetzmann, *Army Exploration in the American West*, Ch. 7, 262–304. Beale to Floyd, March 23, 1858, LRSW, ROSW, M-221, Roll 183.

23. Beale to James L. Orr, April 28, 1858, in Beale, "Fort Defiance Wagon Road," 1–2. Floyd to Miguel A. Otero, May 22, 1858; to Robert J. Atkinson, Third Auditor, May 8, 1858, LSSW, ROSW, M-6, Roll 40.

24. Floyd to Beale, August 5, 1858, LSSW, ROSW, M-6, Roll 40.
25. Floyd to Beale, August 16, LSSW, ROSW, M-6, Roll 40. Los Angeles *Southern Vineyard,* September 18, 1858.
26. New Orleans *Picayune,* October 5, 1858. Beale to Alexander E. Steen, October 26, 1858; to Floyd, October 27, 1858, LRSW, ROSW, M-221, Roll 185. Ed Bearss and Arrell M. Gibson, *Fort Smith: Little Gibraltar on the Arkansas* (Norman: University of Oklahoma Press, 1969), 235–36.
27. Beale to Mary E. Beale, October 27, 1858, DHP, LC. San Francisco *Herald,* October 20, 1858. San Francisco *Herald,* November 12, 1858. The camel experiment had come under attack at this time from a number of army officers. The *New York Times,* on October 27, 1858, stated that Secretary of War Floyd was thoroughly convinced of their usefulness and had characterized the critics as simply prejudiced against a new idea. Meanwhile, in California, a number of camels strayed away from Fort Tejon which necessitated a camel roundup, under the direction of Samuel Bishop. After crossing the continent the camels now possessed an uncontrollable desire to "ramble about," according to Bishop.
28. San Francisco *Alta California,* November 20, 1858, quotes *Fort Smith Times,* October 27, 1858. Edward F. Beale, "Wagon Road—Fort Smith to Colorado River," *HED 42,* 36 Cong., 1 Sess (Serial 1048), 8.
29. Beale, "Fort Smith to Colorado River," 12–13, 28.
30. Beale, "Fort Smith to Colorado River," 13–15. Beale, "Fort Smith to Colorado River," manuscript diary, entry for November 21, 1858, DHP, LC.
31. Beale, "Fort Smith to Colorado River," 13–16. Beale, "Fort Smith to Colorado River," manuscript diary, entries for November 21, 22, 1858, DHP, LC.
32. Beale, "Fort Smith to Colorado River," 16–17. Beale, "Fort Smith to Colorado River," manuscript diary, entries for November 27, 28, 1858, DHP, LC.
33. Beale, "Fort Smith to Colorado River," 17–20.
34. Ibid., 20–22, 26–29. Beale, "Fort Smith to Colorado River," manuscript diary, entry for December 7, 1858, DHP, LC.
35. Beale, "Fort Smith to Colorado River," 29–30.
36. Beale to Mary E. Beale, December 29 [?], 1858, DHP, LC.
37. Beale to Floyd, January 3, 1859, LRSW, ROSW, M-221, Roll 185. John Udell, *Journal of John Udell . . .,* 1858 (New Haven: Yale University Library, 1952), 4–45.
38. Beale to Floyd, January 3, 1859, LRSW, ROSW, M-221, Roll 185.
39. New Orleans *Picayune,* May 20, 1859. Undated newspaper clipping (1859), DHP, LC. Beale to Mary E. Beale, January 25, 1859, DHP, LC. Beale described his own appearance in different terms to his wife: "As for me I change for the worse, and every one out here is laughing at my grey hair and battered weather-beaten appearance."
40. Beale to Mary E. Beale, January 21, 1859, DHP, LC.
41. Beale to Mary E. Beale, January 25, 1859, DHP, LC.
42. Ibid.; Beale to Mary E. Beale, February 7, 1859, DHP, LC.
43. Beale to Floyd, February 14, 15, 1859, LRSW, ROSW, RG 107, NA.
44. Beale, "Fort Smith to Colorado River," 33–34. Beale to Mary E. Beale,

March 14, 1859; and Resolution, New Mexico Territorial Legislature, March 5, 1859, DHP, LC.

45. Beale to Mary E. Beale, March 8, 1859, DHP, LC.

46. Beale to Mary E. Beale, March 14, 1859, DHP, LC. Beale, "Fort Smith to Colorado River,: 35.

47. Beale, "Fort Smith to Colorado River," 36–42.

48. Ibid., 42–44.

49. Ibid., 44–45. Beale to Mary E. Beale, April 18 [?], 1859, DHP, LC. Dennis G. Casebier, *The Mojave Road* (Norco, Cal.: Tales of the Mojave Road Publishing Co., 1975), 81–90; Los Angeles *Star*, March 26, 1859.

50. Casebier, *Mojave Road*, 90–92. Beale, "Fort Smith to Colorado River," 44–45. Beale, "Fort Smith to Colorado River," manuscript diary, entry for April 18, 1859, DHP, LC. Bishop to William Hoffman, March 24, 1859, in Los Angeles *Star*, April 16, 1859. Beale to Mary E. Beale, undated [April 18–19, 1859], DHP, LC.

51. Beale, "Fort Smith to Colorado River," 46–49.

52. Ibid., 48–49. San Francisco *Alta California*, May 17, 21, 22, 1859. Beale to Hoffman, May 13, 1859, Letters Received, Office of the Adjutant General [LROAG], Main Series, 1822–60, Records of the Office of the Adjutant General, RG 94, NA, M-567, Roll 597. Los Angeles *Star*, May 14, 21, 1859.

53. Beale to Hoffman, May 13, 1859; to Floyd, May 16, 1859; Bishop to Beale, May 13, 1859; Hoffman to Beale, May 14, 1859, all in LROAG, M-567, Roll 597. Beale to Mary E. Beale, May 17, 1859, DHP, LC. Los Angeles *Star*, February 4, 1860. Floyd to Beale, March 29, 1860, DHP, LC. Dennis G. Casebier, *Fort Pah-Ute, California* (Norco, Cal.: Tales of the Mojave Road Publishing Co., 1974), passim. A court martial was held a Fort Yuma, and the soldiers were found innocent of opening the caches. Secretary Floyd dissented from the findings of the court and stated in a letter to Beale and in General Orders that the enlisted men's actions were criminal and the officers who permitted the opening of the supply caches were "reprehensible" in their conduct. Floyd ordered that the troops involved pay for the stolen property out of their company funds or from their own rations.

54. Beale to Mary E. Beale, May 17, 1859, DHP, LC.

55. Beale to Floyd, May 23, 1859, LRSW, ROSW, M-221, Roll 187.

56. San Francisco *Alta California*, May 28, June 11, 1859. San Francisco *Alta California*, May 28, 1859. After meeting Beale in person, and being subjected to his exuberance and flattery, Biven published a statement that Beale should be commended for his "zeal and energy in exploring." The Beale Road would, however, never be adopted in place of the northern or southern overland route.

57. San Francisco *Herald*, June 1, 1859; Los Angeles *Star*, June 4, 1859; Los Angeles *Southern Vineyard*, July 15, 1859.

58. San Francisco *Alta California*, June 11, July 19, 1859; Tubac *Weekly Arizonian*, July 14, 1859.

59. Beale, "Fort Smith to Colorado River," 49-53. San Francisco *Alta California*, July 19, 1859. Beale to Mary E. Beale, July 30, 1859, DHP, LC. Los Angeles *Star*, October 1, 1859. Los Angeles *Southern Vineyard*, November 11, 1859, quotes from Kansas City *Journal of Commerce*, August 25, 1859.

60. Williams, *Broderick*, 239–47. John W. Forney to Abraham Lincoln, March 25, 1861; John Hickman to Lincoln, March 13, 1861, Lincoln Papers, LC microfilm, Roll 67. Undated newspaper clipping, DHP, LC. Forney to Lincoln, March 25, 1861, Lincoln Papers, LC microfilm, Roll 67. Beale to Mary E. Beale, February 3, 1859, DHP, LC. Beale found himself unable to avoid the arguments over slavery's extension. Although he had grown up in a slave-holding family, he detested the institution. Beale went so far as to tell Buchanan in person that he opposed the actions of the administration on this most sensitive subject. The split with Beale's Southern relatives also widened at this time.

61. Los Angeles *Star*, October 1, 1859.

62. Beale to Floyd, December 15, 1859, in Beale, "Fort Smith to Colorado River," 1–8.

Chapter 8

1. Isaac Toucey to Beale, December 10, 1859, DHP, LC.

2. Tejon Township, Los Angles County, page 38, Eighth Census of the United States: 1860, Records Bureau of the Census, RG 29, M-653, Roll 14. *Jose Maria Flores* v. *the United States*, August 26, 1862, Minute Book 3, page 335, Minutes of the U.S. District Court of Southern California, Records of the District Courts of the United States, RG 21, Roll 1. La Liebre was designated case number 170. Beale to Fabius Stanley, deed, April 29, 1859, DHP, LC. Bishop and Beale to John G. Downey, Henrique Miller, and Manuel Requena, April 30, 1860, Miscellaneous Records Book 1, 13–14, Records of the County Recorder's Office, LA-CAR, Los Angeles.

3. Edgar E. Robinson (ed.), "The Day Journal of Milton S. Latham," *CHSQ*, XI (March 1932), 15; John W. Forney," *DAB*, VI, 526–27. For information on John Hickman, see New York *Herald*, March 24, 1875.

4. Undated newspaper clipping [December 29?], 1979, DHP, LC.

5. Los Angeles *Star*, September 29, 1860; Frank McNitt, *Navajo Wars—Military Campaigns, Slave Raids, and Reprisals* (Albuquerque: University of New Mexico Press, 1972), 382–84.

6. Los Angeles *Star*, August 18, September 8, 22, October 21, November 10, 1860. Frances P. Farquhar (ed.), *Up and Down California in 1860–1864: The Journal of William H. Brewer* (Berkeley and Los Angeles: University of California Press, 1874), 384.

7. Los Angeles *Star*, October 21, November 10, 1860. Henry Toomy to Beale, December 2, 1860, DHP, LC.

8. Examination Board Report, La Liebre, January 28, 1861; Louis McLane to Beale, March 13, 1861; Toomy to Beale, April 17, 1861; and Toomy to Beale, telegram, undated, 1861, DHP, LC.

9. Los Angeles *Star*, January 26, 1861. Thomas Swords to Beale, January 19, 1861, DHP, LC.

10. Bishop, Beale, and Kerlin et al. to Albert S. Johnston, Petition, February, 1861, in *The War of the Rebellion: The Official Records of the Union and Confederate Armies* (139 vols., Washington, D.C.: Government Printing Office, 1891–96), Series I, Volume L, Part 1, 437. Clarence Cullimore, *Old Adobes of Forgotten Fort Tejon* (Bakersfield: Kern County Historical Society, 1949), 43–44.

11. San Francisco *Bulletin*, January 28, March 25, 1861.

12. San Francisco *Bulletin*, April 11, 1861. Beale to Mary E. Beale, May 11, 1861, DHP, LC.

13. John D. Hickman to Lincoln, March 13, 1861, Abraham Lincoln Papers, Roll 67, LC.

14. Francis P. Blair, Jr., to Caleb B. Smith, March 14, 1861; J. F. Potter to Smith, March 14, 1861, Lincoln Papers, Roll 67, LC.

15. John W. Forney to Lincoln, March 25, 1861, Abraham Lincoln Papers, Roll 67, LC. Beale to Simon Cameron, November 15, 1864, Simon Cameron Papers, LC.

16. San Francisco *Bulletin*, April 29, May 1861; San Francisco *Alta California*, April 30, 1861. "Beale Statement," 10, B-UC. In the late 1880s, Beale had trouble remembering the circumstances which surrounded his appointment as surveyor general. When interviewed by Hubert Howe Bancroft, Beale stated: "At the breaking out of the civil war of the rebellion, President Lincoln sent me without solicitation on my part, the commission of Surveyor General of California. I wrote him [that] instant that I did not want it, but would be very much obliged if he would give it to some-one else, and send me an appointment of any rank whatever in the union army."

17. Beale to Mary E. Beale, May 11, 1861, DHP, LC. San Francisco *Bulletin*, May 11, June 1, 1861.

18. James M. Edmunds to Beale, April 24, 1861, Letters Sent, Records of the Surveyor General of California [LS-SGC], Records of the Bureau of Land Management, RG 49, microfilm copy, author's files.

19. San Francisco *Alta California*, June 8, 1861; Los Angeles *Star*, June 15, 1861.

20. Beale to Lincoln, July 10, 1861, Abraham Lincoln Papers, Roll 67, LC, Hickman to Mary E. Beale, August 24, 1861, DHP, LC. Appointment of E. F. Beale, July 15, 1861, Interior Department Appointment Papers: State of California, 1849–1907, RG 48. Philadelphia *Press*, October 9, 1861.

21. San Francisco *Bulletin*, July 15, 1861.

22. Beale to Edmunds, September 15, 1861, in "Annual Report of the Commissioner of the General Land Office [GLO], 1861," *SED 1*, 37 Cong., 2 Sess. (Serial 1117), 537–65. Beale to Edmunds, August 29, 1861. Letters Received, General Land Office [LR-GLO], a microfilm copy, author's files.

23. Beale to Edmunds, September 15, 1861, in "Annual Report of the Commissioner of the GLO, 1861," 537–65.

24. Beale to Edwin V. Sumner, September 5, 1861, *Official Records*, Series I, Volume L, Part 1, 605; Sumner to E. D. Townsend, September 7, 1861, ibid., 610.

25. Beale to Edmunds, June 27, 1862, LRGLO.

26. Edmunds, General Circular, January 6, 1862; Edmunds to Beale, January 26, February 10, 1862, LSGLO.

27. Los Angeles *Semi-Weekly Southern News*, December 25, 1861; Farquhar, *Up and Down California*, 384. San Francisco *Alta California*, October 2, 1861.

28. Los Angeles *Semi-Weekly Southern News*, September 6, 11, 1861; Farquhar, *Up and Down California*, San Francisco *Alta California*, October 2, 1861.

29. Beale to Edmunds, January 3, March 19, 1862, LRGLO.

Notes

Chapter 9

1. Beale to Edmunds, March 4, April 3, 18, 1862, LRGLO.
2. Edmunds to Beale, May 20, 21, 1862, LSGLO.
3. Edmunds to Beale, May 30, 1862, LSGLO. Contracts with Harry Edwards mentioned in Edmunds to Beale, July 18, 1862, ibid.
4. San Francisco *Bulletin*, March 29, 1862; Edmunds to Beale, June 7, 1862, LSGLO.
5. Edmunds to Beale, June 5, 1862; Edmunds to Latham, June 9, 1862, LSGLO. Washington *National Intelligencer*, May 31, 1862.
6. Beale to Edmunds, June 27, July 10, August 7, 1862, LRGLO.
7. San Francisco *Alta California*, June 26, 28, 1861. Baker to Beale, May 21, 1862, Milton S. Latham Papers, California Historical Society [CHS], San Francisco. Naomi E. Bain, *The Story of Colonel Thomas Baker and the Founding of Bakersfield*, (Bakersfield: Kern County Historical Society, 1944), 16–18.
8. Beale to A. M. Winn, May 16, 26, 1862, Swamp and Overflow Lands File, Records of the Board of Swamp Land Commissioners, California State Archives, Sacramento.
9. San Francisco *Bulletin*, April 2, 1862. Beale, purchaser, June 6, 1862, Survey 65, Santa Clara County Swamp and Overflow Lands, Book Seven, p. 616, California State Land Commission Records, California State Archives, Sacramento. Beale to Abel Stearns, May 13, 1862, Stearns Papers.
10. Beale to Edmunds, August 7, 9, 1863, LRGLO. Beale to Edmunds, October 1, 1862, "Annual Report of the Commissioner of the GLO, 1862," *HED 1*, 37 Cong., 3 Sess. (Serial 1157), 133–44.
11. Edmunds to Beale, October 8, 1862, LSGLO. Beale to Edmunds, September 13, November 11, 1862, LRGLO.
12. Beale to Edmunds, November 11, 1862, LRGLO.
13. Edmunds to Beale, December 10, 1862, LSGLO. "Annual Report of the Commissioner of the GLO, 1862," 44–45, 143–44.
14. Property purchases made by Beale at this time are recorded in Patent Book One, p. 3; Patent Book Eleven, 304–5; Patent Book Twelve, 207–8, 209–11, Records of the County Recorder LA-CAR, Los Angeles.
15. San Francisco *Bulletin*, August 15, 1862.
16. Veinette S. Ripley, "The San Fernando Pass and the Pioneer Traffic That Went Over It: Part IV," HSSC *Quarterly*, XXX (June 1948), 114–17.
17. Los Angeles *Semi-Weekly Southern News*, June 20, July 23, 1862; San Francisco *Bulletin*, November 8, 9, 1863; San Franciso *Mining and Scientific Press*, October 7, 1862.
18. San Francisco *Bulletin*, November 26, 1862; January 6, 1863. San Francisco *Mining and Scientific Press*, January 6, 28, 1863.
19. San Francisco *Bulletin*, January 14, 28, February 3, 26, 1863.
20. San Francisco *Bulletin*, March 9, April 28, 1863.
21. J. P. Wentworth to William P. Dole, September 1, 1863; Beale to Wentworth, July 24, 29, August 11, 1863; Wentworth to Beale, July 29, August 10, 1863; all in "Annual Report of the CIA, 1863," *HED 1*, 38 Cong., 1 sess. (Serial 1182), 217–21. Beale to George Wright, July 27, 1863, DHP, LC.

Notes

22. Edmunds to Beale, May 18, 1863, LSGLO.

23. Beale to Edmunds, May 25, 1863, LRGLO. Farquhar, *Up and Down California*, 384–87.

24. Joseph G. Wilson to Beale, May 26, 1863, LSGLO. Beale to Edmunds, June 13, July 9, 1863, LRGLO.

25. Beale to Edmunds, July 25, 1863, LRGLO. "Plat of the Rancho Arroyo Seco," California Private Land Claims, Plats, Volume 4, Number 277, RG 49. *History of Amador County, California* (Oakland: Thompson and West, 1881), 243–47.

26. Los Angeles *Star*, April 4, 1863.

27. Ibid., May 2, 1863.

28. San Francisco *Bulletin*, July 7, 1863; Farquhar, *Up and Down California*, Edward F. Beale, *Address Delivered Before the Grant and Colfax Club of Chester* (Chester, Penn.: Y. S. Walter, Printer, 1868), 10.

29. Beale to Chase, August 5, 1863, reproduced in Bonsal, *Edward Fitzgerald Beale*, 261–63.

30. Chase to Beale, September 5, 1863, in Bonsal, *Edward Fitzgerald Beale*, 263–64.

31. Beale to Edmunds, September 1, 1863, "Annual Report of the Commissioner of the GLO, 1863," *HED 1*, 38 Cong., 1 sess. (Serial 1182), 117–28. Milton H. Shutes, "Abraham Lincoln and the New Almaden Mine," *CHSQ*, XV (March 1936, 3–20. "Annual Report of the Commissioner of the GLO, 1863," 118. In a footnote to Beale's published report of October 1, Edmunds stated that Beale made a gross error when he described Lincoln's order as "surreptitious."

32. Edmunds to Beale, August 29, 1863, LSGLO.

33. Beale to Edmunds, September 5, October 31, 1863, LRGLO. Edmunds to Beale, November 28, 1863, LSGLO.

34. Beale to Godey, October 7, 1863; Beale to Hudson, August 19, 1863; McLaughlin to R. C. Drum, September 23, 1863, DHP, LC. Henry G. Langley (comp.), *San Francisco Directory for the Year Commencing October 1863* (San Francisco: Excelsior Steam Presses, 1863), 62.

35. Charles James to Chase, October 29, 1863, DHP, LC. Beale to Chase, November 5, 1863, in Bonsal, *Edward Fitzgerald Beale*, 264–66.

36. Ramirez to Edmunds, November 25, 1863; Joseph Wilson to Ramirez, October 26, 1863, Los Angeles District Land Office, Federal Records Center (FRC) Laguna Niguel. Edmunds to Beale, December 3, 1863, LSGLO.

37. Lent to Edmunds, January 7, 1864, LRGLO.

38. Edmunds to Ramirez, January 19, 1864, Los Angeles District Land Office Records, FRC, Laguna Niguel.

39. Statement of Beale and Godey, January 11, 1864, DHP, LC. Bride of Abydos Claim, January 16, 1864, Miscellaneous Record Book One, 104, Records of the County Recorder's Office, LA-CAR, Los Angeles. Los Angeles *Star*, January 30, 1864.

40. Cornelius Cole to Lincoln, February [?], 1864, Abraham Lincoln Papers, Roll 69, LC. Edmunds to John Conness, February 2, 1864, LSGLO. Los Angeles *Star*, February 6, 1864.

41. Lauren Upson File, Records of the Appointments Division—California,

266

Office of the Secretary of the Interior, RG 48. Edmunds to Beale, March 10, 1864, LSGLO. Conness to Lincoln, February 6, 1864, Abraham Lincoln Papers, Roll 67, LC. San Francisco *Bulletin*, February 23, 1864.

Chapter 10

1. Los Angeles *Star*, March 5, 1864. Ripley, "San Fernando Pass," HSSC *Quarterly*, XXX, 118–21. Beale V. Jones, Case No. 4019, Old Files, Records of the Superior Court, LA-CAR, Los Angeles.

2. E. F. Beale, "Open Letter to the People of California"; Edmunds to John P. Usher, September 23, 1863, San Francisco *Bulletin*, May 12, 1864. John Conness to Salmon P. Chase, April 25, 1864, in San Francisco *Bulletin*, May 28, 1864.

3. Los Angeles *Star*, June 4, 1864.

4. Robert Ryal Miller, *Arms Across the Border: United States Aid to Juarez During the French Intervention in Mexico* (Philadelphia: American Philosophical Society, 1973), 16–18. *Proposals for the Organization of the Carmen Island Salt Company* (privately printed, 1864), copy in Placido Vegas Papers, B-UC. San Francisco *Bulletin*, February 16, 1963.

5. Miller, *Arms Across the Border*, 19.

6. Beale to James, July 16, 1864, in "Letter from the Secretary of War . . . in relation to a recent attempt to send arms . . . to Mexico," *SED 15*, 38 Cong., 2 Sess. (Serial 1209), 11–12.

7. James to Beale, July 20, 1864; Beale to James, July 22, 1864, in ibid., 12–13, 22.

8. Thomas Brown to Salmon P. Chase, July 19, 1864, DHP, LC.

9. E. F. Beale, *The Presidency, Speech of Lieut. E. F. Beale* (Chester, Penn.: privately printed, 1864), 1–6.

10. Ibid., 6–9.

11. Beale to Cameron, November 15, 1864, Simon Cameron Papers, Historical Society of Dauphin County, Harrisburg, Pennsylvania. Cameron to Beale, December 26, 1864, DHP, LC.

12. *History of Amador County*, 247,330. San Francisco *Alta California*, February 21, 1865; Heitman, *Historical Register*, I, 917.

13. San Francisco *Alta California*, February 22, 27, 1865; *History of Amador County*, 248, 333.

14. Beale to family, May 3, 1865, DHP, LC. Beale to Juan Temple, February 9, 1864, Mortgage Book Four, 422–24, Records of the County Recorder's Office, LA-CAR, Los Angeles.

15. Temple to Beale, February 9, 1865, Deed Book Seven, p. 94; Temple to Beale, June 12, 1865, Mortgage Book Four, 422–24, Records of the County Recorder's Office, LA-CAR, Los Angeles. For a full description of the Tejon as surveyed by Beale's office in 1862, see Ranchos Book, 5–13. James J. Gibbens and R. F. Gibbens to Beale, March 10, 1865, Deed Book Seven, p. 96; Cristobal Aguilar and Dolores Yorba de Aguilar to Beale, May 1, 1865, Deed Book Seven, 863; Agustin Olvera and Refugio O. de Olvera to Beale, May 1, 1865, Deed Book Seven, 183, all in Records of the County Recorder's Office, LA-CAR, Los Angeles.

16. Frank J. Taylor and Earl M. Welty, *Black Bonanza: How an Oil Hunt Grew into the Union Oil Company of California* (New York: McGraw-Hill, 1950), 29–34; Gerald T. White, *Formative Years in the Far West: A History of Standard Oil Company of California and Predecessors Through 1919* (New York: Appleton-Century-Crofts, 1962), 4–8, 27. Paul W. Gates, "Carpetbaggers Join the Rush for California Land," *CHSQ*, LVI (Summer 1977), 125–26. Shareholders in the Buenaventura Mission grant were Beale, 300 shares; B. G. Whitney, 53 shares; T. G. Phelps, 195 shares; L. Upson, 208 shares; S. J. Field, 521 shares; Jeremiah S. Black, 130 shares; and Edward Conway, 1,761 shares.

17. White, *Standard Oil*, 7–8, 28.

18. Beale and Robert S. Baker to Romulo Pico, May 22, 1864, Miscellaneous Record Book Three, 172–73, Records of the County Recorder's Office, LA-CAR, Los Angeles.

19. Los Angeles *Tri-Weekly News*, August 12, 1865. Beale et al., Mammoth Claim, July 22, 1865, Deed Book Seven, 292–95, Records of the County Recorder's Office, LA-CAR, Los Angeles. White, *Standard Oil*, 30.

20. Los Angeles *Tri-Weekly News*, November 4, 11, 1865; White, *Standard Oil*, 15–16.

21. Los Angeles *Tri-Weekly News*, September 30, 1865. Tomas W. Sanchez to Beale, May 9, 1866, Deed Book Eight, 33, Records of the County Recorder's Office, LA-CAR, Los Angeles.

22. Chester *Delaware County Republican* (Pennsylvania), June 23, 1865.

23. Edward F. Beale, *The Enfranchisement of the Colored Race* (Chester Penna. privately printed, 1865), 1–3.

24. Ibid., 2–11.

25. William D. Kelley to Beale, November 23, 1865; M. A. S. Cary to Beale, January 20, 1866, DHP, LC.

26. Ibid., January 9, February 2, 16, 1866.

27. Ibid., June 1, 1866; White, *Standard Oil*, 12; Stephen F. Peckham, "On the Supposed Falsification of samples of California Petroleum," *American Journal of Science and Arts*, Second Series, XLIII (May 1867), 345–51.

28. Christopher Leaming to Beale, July 3, 1866, Robert S. Baker Papers, Huntington Library, San Marino, Cal. Los Angeles *Semi-Weekly Southern News*, July 6, 1866; White, *Standard Oil*, 31,72; Peckham, "On the Falsification of California Petroleum," 345–51.

29. Baker to Beale, October 13, 1866, Deed Book Eight, p. 231, Records of the County Recorder's Office, Los Angeles County Archives and Records, Los Angeles. Earl Crowe, *Men of El Tejon: Empire in the Tehachapis* (Los Angeles: Ward Richie Press, 1957), 82–86; Havilah *Weekly Courier* (California), September 8, 1866.

30. Beale to [Charles] Beebe, November 15, 1867, Special Collections, UCLA Library, Los Angeles. "Map of the City of Chester," Henry W. Hopkins (comp.), *Atlas of Delaware County, Pennsylvania* Philadelphia: G. M. Hopkins, Publisher, 1870).

31. Samuel A. Newsome, "From Chester to Asia Minor to Texas to California Before the Civil War," Delaware County Historical Society *Bulletin*, XXII (January–February 1970), 1–2.

32. Chester *Times*, undated newspaper clipping (ca. 1933), Beale Miscellaneous File, Delaware County Historical Society, Chester, Penn.

33. "Map of the City of Chester," in Hopkins, *Delaware County*. Report of Beale and Baker, Kern County, Cal., Volume I, 292, Dun and Bradstreet Collection. Sacramento *Union*, September 27, 1866.

34. Havilah *Weekly Courier* (Cal.), February 8, 1868. Report on Beale and Baker, Kern County, Cal., volume I, 292, Dun and Bradstreet Collection.

35. Beale, *Grant and Colfax Address*, 1–13. Undated newspaper clippings [October, 1868], DHP, LC.

36. Beale, *Grant and Colfax Address*, 1–13.

Chapter 11

1. Mrs. Douglas Allen (comp.), "San Emidgio Ranch," manuscript, Vertical File, Bakersfield Public Library, Bakersfiled, Cal. Beale to Cameron, Simon Cameron Papers. Beale, "Open Letter to the Senators of the State of California," February, 1870, DHP, LC. William Harland Boyd, *California Middle Border: The Kern River Country, 1772–1880* (Richardson, Tex.: Havilah Press, 1972, 118–20. In February of 1869, Beale acquired a one-half interest in the San Emidgio Rancho from Cornelia Fremont Porter, daughter of John C. Fremont. Located fifteen miles west of Fort Tejon, the San Emidgio grant contained approximately 20,000 acres. Beale probably felt that in future years the grant might be necessary for grazing. In the summer of 1869, Joseph Palmer and Robert Page, two San Francisco businessmen, who held the remaining one-half interest, deeded their rights to Beale. Two years later, Beale disposed of the property.

2. San Francisco *Examiner*, February 26, 1870.

3. Bakersfield *Kern County Weekly Courier* (Cal.), March 22, 1870.

4. Beale, "Open Letter to the Senators," DHP, LC. H. Craig Miner, *The St. Louis-San Francisco Transcotinental Railroad: The Thirty-Fifth Parallel Project, 1853–1890* (Lawrence: University Press of Kansas, 1972), 47–51, 64–65; *Atlantic and Pacific Railroad, Route to the Ocean on the 35th Parallel. Extracts from Reports of E. F. Beale, Esq., and Lieut. Whipple* . . . (New York: Stockholders Job Printing Office, 1867). Joseph W. Snell to Gerald Thompson, May 13, 1975, author's files. Beale may have hoped that the Atlantic and Pacific Railroad, chartered by the United States Congress in 1866 would reach Kern County before the Southern Pacific. Beale was listed as an A & P director, along with John C. Fremont, A. P. K. Safford, William Gilpin, Phineas Banning, Frederick Billings, Levi Parsons, James B. Eads, and many other important men. In 1867, the A & P reprinted a section of Beale's report on the thirty-fifth parallel, which the railroad intended to follow. Beale apparently gave nothing to the railroad, other than the use of his name.

5. Beale to Taylor, April 3, 1870, Taylor Papers. Beale to Charles Sumner, April 18, 1870, Charles Sumner Papers, Harvard University, Cambridge, Mass. Taylor to Beale, April 21, DHP, LC.

6. Beale to the National Labor Union [Detroit, Mich.], August 6, 1870, in undated newspaper clippings, DHP, LC.

7. Ibid. At the turn of the century, Truxtun Beale, prominent in California politics, became an outspoken leader of the anti-Chinese movement, in sharp contrast to his father. San Francisco *Bulletin* [ca. 1900], clipping, DHP, LC.

8. Beale to Cameron, April 27, 1871. Container 13, Simon Cameron Papers, LC.

9. Beale to Cameron, August 4, September 9, 15, 1871, Container 13, Cameron Papers, LC.

10. Joaquin Miller, "Kit Carson's Ride," *Harper's Weekly*, XV (August 5, 1871), 713–14.

11. El Mariposo [Beale] to editor, Chester *Delaware County Republican* [August–September], 1871, clipping, DHP, LC.

12. [Beale], "Kit Carson's Shade," September 17, 1871, in Chester *Delaware County Republican* (September), 1871, clipping, DHP, LC. Joaquin Miller to editor, New York *Tribune*, September 22, 1871.

13. Bakersfield *Kern County Weekly Courier* (Cal.), November 2, December 14, 1872; Charles Nordhoff, *California: For Health, Pleasure and Residence* (New York: Harper and Brothers, 1872), 234–35.

14. Nordhoff, *California*, 235–37.

15. W. H. Hutchinson, *Oil, Land, and Politics: The California Career of Thomas Robert Bard* (2 vols., Norman: University of Oklahoma Press, 1965), I, 245.

16. Bakersfield *Kern County Weekly Courier* (Cal.), November 2, December 14, 1872. Nordhoff, *California*.

17. Bakersfield *Kern County Weekly Courier* (Cal.), July 6, 1872.

18. U. S. Grant to Beale, September 9, 1872, DHP, LC.

19. Mary Ann Edwards, Last Will and Testament and Codicils, Estate Inventory in Probate File [April 16, 1874], Records of Probate Court, Delaware County, Records, Media, Pennsylvania. Beale, "Obituary of Mary Ann Edwards," undated clipping, 1872, DHP, LC. Beale Miscellaneous File, DCHS. Ashmead, *History of Delaware County*, 264–66.

20. David D. Porter to Cameron, November 6, 1872, Container 13, Cameron Papers, LC.

21. Chester *Delaware County Republican* (Penn.), November 22, 1872. Beale Misc. File, DCHA, Chester. Bakersfield *Kern County Weekly Courier* (Cal.), March 22, 1873.

22. Crowe, *Men of El Tejon*, 77, 109; Harris Newmark, *Sixty Years in Southern California, 1853–1913* (Los Angeles: Teitlin & Van Brugge, 1970), 437.

23. Keith A. Murray, *The Modocs and Their War* (Norman: University of Oklahoma Press, 1959), is the standard account. Chester *Delaware County Republican* (Penn.), April [26?], 1873, newspaper clipping, DHP, LC.

24. Chester *Delaware County Republican* (Penn.), March 27, 1873. Beale Misc. File, DCHS, Chester. Chester *Delaware County Republican* (Penn.), April, 1873, clippings, DHP, LC.

25. Chester *Delaware County Republican* (Penn.), April, 1873, clippings, DHP, LC. Murray, *Modocs and Their War*, 300–17; Dee Brown, *Bury My Heart at Wounded Knee* (New York: Holt, Rinehart and Winston, 1971), 233.

26. Helen D. Bullock and Mrs. Terry B. Morton (eds.), *Decatur House* (Washington, D.C.: National Trust for Historic Preservation, 1967), 69–70;

Chester *Delaware County Republican* (Penn.), October 3, 1873. Beale Misc. File, DHCS, Chester. Heitman, *Historical Register*, I, 345.

27. Washington *Capital*, 1873, undated clipping, DHP, LC.

28. Bullock and Morton, *Decatur House*, passim; and Beale, *Decatur House and Its Inhabitants* are both good histories.

29. Chester *Delaware County Republican* (Washington, D.C.), December 12, 1873. Beale Misc. File, DCHS, Chester. Washington *Evening Star*, January 21, 24, 27, 28, and February 18, 1874.

30. Bakersfield *Kern County Weekly Courier* (Cal.), July 4, 1874; Newmark, *Sixty Years*, 459. *Baker v. Beale*, Case No. 2516, Old Files, Records of the Superior Court, LA-CAR, Los Angeles.

31. *Baker v. Beale*, Superior Court Records, LA-CAR, Los Angeles. The judgment was rendered on October 12, 1874.

32. Chester *Delaware County Republican* (Penn.), July [20?], 1874; Y. S. Walter to Beale, June 26, 1874; Beale to Mary E. Beale, telegram, June 19, 1874, all in DHP, LC.

33. Bakersfield *Kern County Weekly Courier* (Cal.), October 17, 1874; February 6, April 10, June 26, 1875. Report on Beale and Baker, January 1875 entry Dun and Bradstreet Collection. Crowe, *Men of El Tejon*, 81.

34. Grant to Beale, August 5, 1874. DHP, LC. Jane A. Burch, "A Historic Maryland Estate," manuscript enclosure; Jane A. Burch to Gerald Thompson, April 30, 1977, author's files.

35. Grant to Beale, September 8, 1875, April 12, 1876, DHP, LC.

36. San Francisco *Alta California*, September 14, 1875.

37. White, *Standard Oil*, 32–36.

38. Ibid., 36–38.

39. "On National Grounds—General Beale's Suggestions Regarding Grant's Resting Place," 1885, undated newspaper clippings, DHP, LC.

Chapter 12

1. Cameron to Beale, March 22, 1876, DHP, LC. Allan Nevins, *Hamilton Fish; The Innter History of the Grant Administration* (New York: Dodd, Mead & Company, 1936), 862n.

2. San Francisco *Alta California*, May 26, 1876, reproduced Nordhoff's biographical sketch from the New York *World*. *New York Times*, May 25, 1876.

3. San Francisco *News Letter* [June 1876], undated clipping, DHP, LC.

4. San Francisco *Bulletin*, May 25, 27, 1876; *New York Times*, June 5, 1876.

5. San Francisco *Alta California*, June 2, 1876. Beale to Truxton Beale, June 28, 1876, DHP, LC.

6. Thompson to Beale, May 25, 1876; Taylor to Beale, May 25, 1876, DHP, LC. Hamilton Fish to Beale, June 6, 7, 1876, Diplomatic Instructions of the Department of State, 1801–1906 [DIDS], M-77, Roll 14, General Records of the Department of State, RG 59, NA.

7. Fish to Beale, June 7, 1876, DIDS, M-77, Roll 14.

8. Beale to Fish, August 11, 1876, Dispatches from United States Ministers to Austria, 1836–1907 [DUSMA], T-157, Roll 24, General Records of the Department of State, RG 59, NA. M. S. Anderson, *The Eastern Question*,

1774–1923 (New York: St. Martin's Press, 1966), 178–220; Anatol Murad, *Franz Joseph I of Austria and His Empire* (New York: Twayne Publishers, 1968).

9. Beale to Fish, August 11, 1876, DUSMA, T-157, Roll 24.

10. Bonsal, *Edward Fitgerald Beale*, 297–99.

11. Beale to Fish, August 14, 1876, in *Foreign Relations* (Washington, D.C.: Government Printing Office, 1877), 14–15.

12. Beale to Fish, August 18, 1876, DUSMA, T-157, Roll 24.

13. Beale to Fish, September 8, 1876, DUSMA, T-157, Roll 24.

14. Beale to Fish, August 12, September 4, October 26, 1876, DUSMA, T-157, Roll 24. Fish to Beale, November 22, 1876, DIDS, M-77, Roll 14.

15. Beale to Fish, September 27, November 4, 1876, DUSMA, T-157, Roll 24, Anderson, *Eastern Question*, 188–91.

16. Beale to Fish, September 4, 1876, DUSMA, T-157, Roll 24. San Francisco *Alta California*, October 19, 1876. Mary (Mamie) Beale to Cameron, February 8, 1877, Container 14, Cameron Papers, LC.

17. Beale, *Decatur House and Its Inhabitants*, 108. Julius Andrassy to Beale, January 23, 1877, DHP, LC.

18. Beale to Fish, December 14, 1876, DUSMA, T-157, Roll 24. Fish to Beale, January 12, 1877, DIDS, M-77, Roll 14.

19. Beale to Fish, January 27, 1877, DUSMA, T-157, Roll 24.

20. Beale to Fish, January 30, 1877, DUSMA, T-157, Roll 24.

21. Mary (Mamie) Beale to Cameron, February 8, 1877, Container 14, Cameron Papers, LC.

22. Beale to Cameron, February 15, 1877, Container 14, Cameron Papers, LC. Beale to Fish, December 15, 1876, DUSMA, T-157, Roll 24. Fish to Beale, January 12, 1877, DIDS, M-77, Roll 14.

23. Beale to Fish, March 6, DUSMA, T-157, Roll 24.

24. Beale to Grant, undated [ca. March 1877], DHP, LC.

25. Beale to Evarts, April 6, 19, 1877, DUSMA, T-157, Roll 24.

26. Beale to Evarts, April 21, 1877, DUSMA, T-157, Roll 24.

27. Delaplaine to Evarts, April 21, August 1, 1877, T-157, Roll 24. *New York Times*, May 20, 1877. On August 1, John A. Kassan arrived in Vienna as the new American minister. As Beale predicted, Russia and Turkey went to war in the late spring of 1877. But the grand conflagration involving all major European powers, also predicted by Beale, did not occur. Instead, an unstable peace based on several weak, independent Balkan states emerged. Turkish control was severely weakened, but the Eastern question in its new, altered form remained unresolved. The old fears, rivalries, and competing ambitions did not fulfill Beale's dire forecast until the summer of 1914.

Chapter 13

1. "Beale Statement," 11, B-UC. White, *Standard Oil*, 52–53; Bakersfield *Southern Californian*, June 7, 1877.

2. Beale to Baker, November 8, 1877, January 4, 1878, Baker Papers, White, *Standard Oil*, 53. Grant to Beale, March 6, 1878, DHP, LC. Early March found General Grant in Constantinople, writing Beale about his recent visits to Egypt, the Middle East, Greece, and Turkey. The sultan of Turkey had insisted that

Grant take as gifts two beautiful Arabian horses. Grant asked Beale to care for the horses at Ash Hill. The general also briefly criticized the silver bill, which he felt would prove destructive to the country's interests.

3. White, *Standard Oil*, 54–56.

4. John Y. Simon (ed.), *Personal Memoirs of Julia D. Grant* (New York: G. P. Putnam's Sons, 1975), 244. Grant to Beale, May 20, July 7, 1878; and undated newspaper clipping (August 1885), DHP, LC. Grant to Beale, July 7, 1878, DHP, LC. In early July, Grant wrote to Beale and touched upon the possibility of a third term as president. Beale had mentioned that Grant's prospects looked good for 1880, but Grant said that he had received all the honors he desired and wished to avoid the "vexation of political life for the future." Abuse from slandering opponents did not bother him, but he worried about the impact of a mud-slinging campaign on his children and grandchildren.

5. Beale to Baker, September 11, 1878, January 1, 1879, Baker Papers.

6. Grant to Beale, December 6, 1878, DHP, LC.

7. Beale to Baker, March 27, 1879, Baker Papers. Henry George, Jr., *The Life of Henry George* (New York: Robert Schalkenbach Foundation, 1960), 324–25; Rolle, *California*, 425–26.

8. Beale to Baker, April 12, June 9, 1870, Baker Papers. White, *Standard Oil*, 67–68, 211–12.

9. Earl Crowe, *General Beale's Sheep Odyssey* (Bakersfield: Kern County Historical Society, 1960), 1–7. Beale to Baker, June 9, 1879, Baker Papers.

10. Crowe, *Beale's Sheep Odyssey*, 7–22. Beale to Baker, August 3, 1870, Baker Papers.

11. Grant to Beale, October 24, November 16, 1879, DHP, LC.

12. Ammen, *Old Navy*, 421–22, 463, 474–78; David M. Pletcher, *The Awkward Years: American Foreign Relations Under Garfield and Arthur* (Columbia: University of Missouri Press, 1962), 23–24.

13. Ammen, *Old Navy*, 476–79. Grant to Ammen, September 28, November 16, 1879, in *Old Navy*, 548–49. Lindley M. Keasbey, *The Nicaragua Canal and the Monroe Doctrine* (New York: G. P. Putnam's Sons, 1896), 364–65.

14. Grant to Beale, November 27, 1879, DHP, LC.

15. Washington *Evening Star*, December 29, 30, 31, 1879. Grant to Rutherford B. Hayes, November 30, 1879, Hayes Papers, Rutherford B. Hayes Library, Fremont, Ohio. Undated newspaper clippings [December 1879–January 1880], DHP, LC.

16. Clarence W. Gordon, "Report on Cattle, Sheep, and Swine, Supplementary to the Enumeration of Livestock on Farms in 1880," in *Report on Production of Agriculture: Tenth Census, 1880* (Washington, D.C.: Government Printing Office, 1883), 78; Erwin Gudde (comp.), *California Place Names* (Berkeley and Los Angeles: University of California Press, 1969), 23. Bealville File, Bakersfield Public Library.

17. Bakersfield *Kern County Californian*, February 19, 1880. Undated newspaper clipping [1880], DHP, LC.

18. Ibid. San Jose *Pioneer*, March 27, 1880.

19. Ammen, *Old Navy*, 478–87, 551. Grant to Beale, May 16, 1880, DHP, LC. "James B. Eads," *DAB*, V, 587–89. Grant to Ammen, October 17, 1880, in Ammen, *Old Navy*, 477–79. Sidney T. Matthews, "The Nicaragua Canal

Controversy: The Struggle for an American-constructed and controlled Trans-itway" (Ph.D. dissertation, Johns Hopkins University, 1947), 32–49; "Nicaragua Canal," *House Report 1698*, 40 Cong., 1 Sess. (Serial 2070), 1–6.

20. Grant to Beale, September 3 and October 22, 1880, DHP, LC.

21. Beale to Appleton P. Clark, November 19, 1880, published letter, DHP, LC.

22. Undated newspaper clipping [1881]; Grant to Beale, November 25, 1880; February 28, 1881, DHP, LC. Beale to Cameron, December 6, 1880, Con-tainer 15, Cameron Papers, LC.

23. Ernest Samuels, *Henry Adams: The Middle Years* (Cambridge, Mass.: Belknap Press of Harvard University Press, 1958), 91, 94; Henry Adams, *Democracy and Esther: Two Novels by Henry Adams* (Glouchester, Mass.: Peter Smith, 1965), 205.

24. Marian Adams to Robert W. Hooper, November 12, 21, 1880; January 16, February 16, 1881; January 1, 1882, in Ward Thoron (ed.), *The Letters of Mrs. Henry Adams, 1863–1883* (Boston: Little, Brown and Company, 1936), 233, 234, 255–56, 263, 316–19. Roscoe Conkling to Beale, October 28, 1881, DHP, LC.

25. Ray Ginger, *Age of Excess: The United States from 1877 to 1914* (New York: Macmillan Company, 1965), 101–4; Bonsal, *Edward Fitzgerald Beale*, 301. Grant to Chester Arthur, October 8, 1881, Arthur Papers, Roll 1, LC.

26. Marian Adams to R. W. Hooper, November 6, 20, 1881; January 1, 1882, in Thoron, *Mrs. Adams.*, 295–98; 301–5, 316–19, respectively. Un-dated newspaper clippings [December 1881–January 1882], DHP, LC.

27. Beale, "Common Sense About the Navy—A Talk with Gen. Edward F. Beale," printed interview, January 3, 1882, DHP, LC.

28. George F. Howe, *Chester A. Arthur—A Quarter Century of Machine Poli-tics* (New York: Frederick Ungar Publishing Co., 1957), 162–63; Grant to Beale [1882], DHP, LC.

29. Newsome, "From Chester to Asia Minor," 1–2. As Beale sold off city lots, he recorded approximately thirty-five mortgages. Mortgage Records 1878–85, Office of the Public Recorder, Delaware County Court House, Media, Penn. Copies in author's files.

30. Chester *Delaware County Republican*, May 27, 1882, Clipping; Grant to Beale, June 24, November 3, December 6, 28, 1882, DHP, LC. Beale to Baker, December 7, 28, 1882, Baker Papers, Huntington Library.

31. Undated newspaper clippings [January 1883], DHP, LC. M. Adams to R. W. Hooper, January 7, 1883, in Thoron, *Mrs. Adams*, 413. Worthington C. Ford (ed.), *The Letters of Henry Adams* (2 vols., Boston: Houghton Mifflin Company, 1930), I, 437.

32. Undated newspaper clippings [January 1883]; Will of Edward F. Beale, January 10, 1883, DHP, LC.

33. New York *Herald*, April 14, 1883. "Remarks of General Beale at the Banquet in Honor of General Diaz . . .," April 13, 1883, printed copy, DHP, LC.

34. Grant to Beale, October 17, 22, 1883; January 20, March 18, 1884; Undated newspaper clippings (January–June 1884), DHP, LC. Simon, *Personal Memoirs of Julia Grant*, 327.

35. Keasbey, *Nicaragua Canal*, 422–23; Thomas M. Pitkin, *The Captain Departs: Ulysses S. Grant's Last Campaign* (Carbondale: Southern Illinois University Press, 1973), 1–10.

36. Grant to Beale, June 26, 1884, DHP, LC. Pitkin, *Grant's Last Campaign*, 10.

37. *New York Times*, October 8, 1884. Undated newspaper clipping (October 1884), DHP, LC.

38. Bonsal, *Edward Fitzgerald Beale*, 302–3; "John R. McLean," *National Cyclopaedia of American Biography*, I, 444; Samuels, *Adams: Middle Years*, 246.

39. Grant to Beale, October 8, 13, 19, 1884, DHP, LC. Pitkin, *Grant's Last Campaign*, 24–25.

40. Grant to Beale, December 16, 1884, DHP, LC. Pitkin, *Grant's Last Campaign*, 7, 25; *New York Times*, December 29, 1884. Beale, *Decatur House and Its Inhabitants*, 106–7. Truxtun Beale remembered vividly Grant's visits to the Decatur House. "It seemed that Grant liked late hours and would sit up smoking and drinking endless tankards of ale," stated Beale's son.

41. Undated newspaper clipping [December 1884], DHP, LC.

42. Pitkin, *Grant's Last Campaign*, 7. Cyrus W. Field to Beale, telegrams, January 6, 7, 1885; Grant to Beale, January 25, 1885, DHP, LC.

43. Undated newspaper clipping [May 23, 1885], DHP, LC.

44. Simon, *Personal Memoirs of Julia Grant*, 330–31.

45. Undated newspaper clipping [July 22, 23, 1885], DHP, LC.

46. Fred Grant to Beale, telegram, July 23, 1885; and undated newspaper clippings [July–August 1885], DHP, LC. Pitkin, *Grant's Last Campaign* 95–96.

47. Fred Grant to Beale, August 6, 1885, DHP, LC. *New York Times*, August 9, 1885; Bakersfield *Kern County Californian*, December 26, 1891.

48. Beale's Eulogy on Grant, August 8, 1885; and undated newspaper clipping [1885], DHP, LC.

Chapter 14

1. Thomas F. Bayard to Beale, January 13, 1886, Special Collections, University of California at Los Angeles.

2. Undated newspaper clipping [January 1886]; Jessie B. Fremont to M. E. Beale, August 8, 1886, DHP, LC. Beale, Mexican War Pension [granted May 28, 1887], Beale's Pension File, RG 15, NA.

3. Beale to M. E. Beale, October 7, 17, 1886, DHP, LC.

4. Beale to M. E. Beale, October 20, 1886, DHP, LC.

5. Chicago *Tribune*, December 27, 1886; Mary Logan to Beale, December 25, 1886; Beale to George C. Gorham, April 30, 1887, undated newspaper clipping, DHP, LC.

6. Beale to M. E. Beale, April 8, 1888; Resolutions of the Citizens of Bakersfield, April 17, 1888; Beale to Charles P. Peake, May 14, 1888; undated newspaper clipping [May 1888], DHP, LC. Bakersfield *Kern County Californian*, April 1, 1888.

7. Burch, "A Historic Maryland Estate," 1–3, unpublished manuscript, author's files. George A. Armes, *Ups and Downs of an Army Officer* (Washington, D.C.: privately printed, 1900), 581.

8. Undated newspaper clippings on the National Republican League [December 1887–April 1888], DHP, LC. Washington *Evening Star*, March 4, June 25, 1888.

9. "Gen. E. F. Beale," December 2, 1888, undated newspaper clipping; John Sherman to Beale, December 28, 1888; Ida Grant to M. E. Beale, December 26, 1888; A. T. Britton to Beale, January 31, 1889, DHP, LC.

10. U. S. Grant, Jr. to Beale, January 1, 1889; Beale, Property Memorandum, 1889, DHP, LC.

11. Beale, Property Memorandum, 1889; Beale to Nordhoff, April 18, 1889, DHP, LC.

12. Beale to Nordhoff, April 28, 1889, DHP, LC.

13. Miles P. DuVal, Jr., *Cadiz to Cathay: The Story of the Long Diplomatic Struggle for the Panama Canal* (Stanford University Press, 1947), 80; *United States Statutes at Large*, XXV, 673–75; *Congressional Record*, 50 Cong., 2 Sess., XX, Part 1, 83, 260; Mathews, "Nicaragua Canal Controversy," 52; "Report . . . on the Maritime Canal Company," *Senate Report 1944*, 51 Cong., 2 Sess. (Serial 2826), 14–20; "Report . . . on shareholders, Maritime Canal Company," *Senate Report 2234*, 51 Cong., 2 Sess. (Serial 2827), 1–5.

14. Ammen to Beale, March 12, 1889, DHP, LC.

15. "Truxtun Beale," *National Cyclopaedia of American Biography*, XXVII, 407; undated newspaper clippings on career of T. Beale, 1889–92, DHP, LC. Washington *Evening Star*, April 26, 1889; Evalyn Walsh McLean, *Father Struck It Rich* (Boston: Little, Brown and Company, 1936), 127; *New York Times*, June 10, 1916.

16. Donald P. Ringler, "Mary Austin: Kern County Days, 1868–1892," *Southern California Quarterly*, XVI (March 1963), 25–63. Tejon Notebook, Box 24 (c), Item D-1, Mary Austin Papers, Huntington Library.

17. Beale to Benjamin Harrison, January 27, 1891, Series J, Reel 100; and February 6, 1892, Series 2, Reel 80; Benjamin Harrison Papers microfilm, LC. Mary Harrison to Beale, March 23, 1891, DHP, LC. *New York Times*, July 22, 1892.

18. Beale to M. E. Beale, April 21, 1892; "Death of H. B. Edwards," undated newspaper clipping, DHP, LC. Mathews, "Nicaragua Canal Controversy," 96–99; Howard A. Rasp, "United States Relations with Nicaragua Concerning an Interoceanic Canal, 1850–1903" (M. A. thesis, University of Arizona, 1969), 123.

19. Washington *Post*, April 23, 1893. Truxtun Beale to Beale, February 28, 1893, DHP, LC.

20. Beale, Counsels to wife—dictated to C. W. Kerlin, April, 1893, DHP, LC.

21. Beale to Truxtun Beale, April [?], 1893, DHP, LC, reprinted in Bullock and Morton, *Decatur House*, 79. Washington *Post*, April 23, 1893.

22. Washington *Post*, April 27, 28, 29, 1893.

23. "An Urn Full of Ashes," April 29, 1893, newspaper clipping, DHP, LC.

24. Quotations from Beale to M. E. Beale, January 25, 1859; undated newspaper clipping April–May 1893, DHP, LC.

BIBLIOGRAPHY

Primary Sources

Manuscript Collections:
Arizona Historical Society, Tucson, Ariz.
 Camels in Western America Collection
Bakersfield Public Library, Bakersfield, Cal.
 Allen, Mrs. Douglas (comp.) "San Emidgio Ranch." Undated. Vertical File.
Bancroft Library, University of California, Berkeley, Cal.
 Beale, Edward F. "Statement from Gen. E. F. Beale for Mr. Hubert Howe
 Bancroft." Undated (ca. 1888).
 Connor, John W. "Connor's Early California; Statement of a Few Recol-
 lections." 1878.
 Placido Vega Papers
California Historical Society, San Francisco, Cal.
 Milton S. Latham Papers
California State Archives, Sacramento, Cal.
 California State Land Commission Records
 Indian Wars File
 Records of the Board of Swamp Land Commissioners
Cornell University Records, Media, Penn.
 Bayard Taylor Papers
Delaware County Records, Media, Penn.
 Records of the County Recorder's Office
 Records of the Probate Court
 Delaware County Historical Society, Chester, Penn.
 Beale Miscellaneous File
Eleutherian Mills Historical Library, Greenville, Wilmington, Del.

Samuel F. Du Pont Papers
Federal Records Center, Laguna Niguel, Cal.
    Records of the Los Angeles District Land Office
Harvard University, Cambridge, Mass.
    Charles Sumner Papers
    Dun and Bradstreet Collection
Historical Society of Dauphin County, Harrisburg, Penn.
    Simon Cameron Papers
Historical Society of Pennsylvania, Philadelphia, Penn.
    James Buchanan Papers
Huntington Library, San Marino, Cal.
    Abel Stearns Papers
    Benjamin D. Wilson Papers
    Mary Austin Papers
    Robert S. Baker Papers
Jane A. Burch Private Collection, Hyattsville, Md.
    Burch, Jane A. "A Historic Maryland Estate." Undated.
Library of Congress, Washington, D. C.
    Abraham Lincoln Papers
    Ambrose W. Thompson Papers
    Benjamin Harrison Papers
    Decatur House papers
    James K. Polk Papers
    John M. Clayton Papers
    Simon Cameron Papers
Los Angeles County Archives and Records, Los Angeles, Cal.
    Records of the Recorder's Office
    Records of the Superior Court
National Archives, Washington, D.C.
    Department of Commerce. Records of the Bureau of the Census. Record Group 29.
    Department of the Interior. Records of the Bureau of Indian Affairs. Record Group 75. Records of the Bureau of Land Management. Record Group 49. Records of the Office of the Secretary of the Interior. Record Group 48.
    Department of the Navy. Records of the Bureau of Naval Personnel. Record Group 24. Records Collection of the Office of Naval Records and Library. Record Group 45. Records of the United States Naval Academy. Record Group 405.
    Department of State. General Records of the Department of State. Record Group 59.
    Department of War. Records of the Office of the Adjutant General. Record Group 94. Records of the Office of the Secretary of War. Record Group 107. Records of the Quartermaster General. Record Group 92.
    Records of the District Courts of the United States. Record Group 21.
    Records of the Government of the District of Columbia. Record Group 351.
    Records of the United States Senate. Record Group 46.
    Records of the Veteran's Administration. Record Group 15.

New York Public Library, New York City
    Albert Tracy Papers
Occidental College, Los Angeles, Cal.
    Rolle-Cook Collection
Princeton University, Princeton, N.J.
    Robert F. Stockton Papers
Rutherford B. Hayes Library, Fremont, Ohio
    Rutherford B. Hayes Papers
Society of California Pioneers, San Francisco, Cal.
    Jacob R. Snyder Papers
Stanford University, Stanford, Cal.
    Stephen J. White Papers

Government Publications
"Annual Report of the Commissioner of the General Land Office, 1861." *Senate Executive Document 1,* 37 Congress, 2 Session (Serial 1117).
"Annual Report of the Commissioner of the General Land Office, 1862." *House Executive Document 1,* 37 Congress, 3 Session (Serial 1157).
"Annual Report of the Commissioner of the General Land Office, 1863." *House Executive Document 1,* 38 Congress, 1 Session (Serial 1182).
"Annual Report of the Commissioner of Indian Affairs, 1853." *Senate Executive Document 1,* 33 Congress, 1 Session (Serial 690).
"Annual Report of the Commissioner of Indian Affairs, 1854." *House Executive Document 1,* 33 Congress, 2 Session (Serial 777).
"Annual Report of the Commissioner of Indian Affairs, 1863." *House Executive Document 1,* 38 Congress, 1 Session (Serial 1182).
"Annual Report of the Commissioner of Indian Affairs, 1864," *House Executive Document 1,* 38 Congress, 2 Session (Serial 1220).
"Annual Report of the Secretary of the Navy, 1837." *Senate Executive Document 1,* 25 Congress, 2 Session (Serial 314).
"Annual Report of the Secretary of the Navy, 1840." *House Executive Document 2,* 26 Congress, 2 Session (Serial 382).
"Annual Report of the Secretary of the Navy, 1841." *House Executive Document 2,* 27 Congress, 2 Session (Serial 401).
Beale, Edward F. "Wagon Road—Fort Smith to Colorado River." *House Executive Document 42,* 36 Congress, 1 Session (Serial 1048).
Beale, Edward F. "Wagon Road from Fort Defiance to the Colorado River." *House Executive Document 124,* 35 Congress, 1 Session (Serial 959).
Benton, Thomas Hart. "Speech on the Nominaton of General Kearny." *Congressional Globe,* 30 Congress, 1 Session, XIX.
Congressional Globe, 1847–58.
Congressional Record, 1888–89.
"Court Martial of John C. Fremont." *Senate Executive Document 33,* 30 Congress, 1 Session (Serial 507).
Emory, William. "Notes of a Military Reconnaisance from Fort Leavenworth, in Missouri, to San Diego, in California." *House Executive Document 41,* 30 Congress, 1 Session (Serial 517).
Foreign Relations. Washington, D.C.: Government Printing Office, 1877.

Heitman, Francis B. (comp.). *Historical Register and Dictionary of the United States Army*. 2 vols. Washington, D.C.: Government Printing Office, 1903.

"Letter from the Secretary of the Interior, Communicating the Report of Edward F. Beale, . . ., respecting the condition of Indian Affairs." *Senate Executive Document 57*, 32 Congress, 2 Session (Serial 665).

"Letter from the Secretary of War . . . in relation to a recent attempt to send arms . . . to Mexico." *Senate Executive Document 15*, 38 Congress, 2 Session (Serial 1209).

"Message from the President . . . relating to the case of Edward F. Beale." *Senate Executive Document 69*, 34 Congress, 3 Session (Serial 881).

"Message from the President of the United States, with Copies of the Correspondence in Relation to the Boundaries of Texas. . . ." Senate Executive Document 24, 31 Congress, 1 Session (Serial 554).

"Message on Accounts of J. C. Fremont." *Senate Executive Document 109*, 34 Congress, 1 Session (Serial 825).

"Nicaragua Canal." *House Report 1698*, 40 Congress, 1 Session (Serial 2070).

"Report . . . on the Maritime Canal Company." *Senate Report 1944*, 51 Congress, 2 Session (Serial 2826).

Report on the Production of Agriculture: Tenth Census, 1880. Washington, D.C.: Government Printing Office, 1883.

"Report of the Secretary of the Interior, Communicating . . . the correspondence between the Department of the Interior and the Indian Agents and Commissioners in California." *Senate Executive Document 4*, 33 Congress, Special Session (Serial 688).

"Report of the Secretary of War . . . Respecting the Purchase of Camels." *Senate Executive Document 62*, 34 Congress, 3 Session (Serial 881).

"Report . . . on shareholders, Maritime Canal Company." *Senate Report 2234*, 51 Congress, 2 Session (Serial 2827).

"Statement of the Names, Age, Tonnage, and Number of Guns of Each Vessel. . . ." *House Executive Document 132*, 27 Congress, 3 Session (Serial 421).

"Testimony Taken by the United States Pacific Railway Commission. . . ." *Senate Executive Document 51*, 50 Congress, 1 Session (serial 2507).

United States Statutes at Large, X, XXV.

The War of the Rebellion: The Official Records of the Union and Confederate Armies. 139 vols. Washington, D.C.: Government Printing Office, 1891–96.

Books:

Ammen, Daniel. *The Old Navy and the New*. Philadelphia: J. B. Lippincott Company, 1891.

Armes, George A. *Ups and Downs of an Army Officer*. Washington, D.C.; privately printed, 1900.

Atlantic and Pacific Railroad, Route to the Ocean on the 35th Parallel. Extracts from Reports of E. F. Beale, Esq., and Lieut. Whipple. . . . New York: Stockholders Job Printing Office, 1867.

Beale, Edward F. *The Presidency, Speech of Lieut. E. F. Beale*. Chester, Penn.: privately printed, 1864.

Bibliography

Beale, Edward F. *The Enfranchisement of the Colored Race.* Chester, Penn.: privately printed, 1865.

Beale, Edward F. *Address Delivered Before the Grant and Colfax Club of Chester.* Chester, Penn.: Y. S. Walter, Printer, 1868.

Booth, Edmund. *Edmund Booth—Forty-niner.* Stockton: San Joaquin Pioneer and Historical Society, 1953.

Browne, Lina F. (ed.). *J. Ross Browne: His Letters, Journals and Writings.* Albuquerque: University of New Mexico Press, 1969.

Clark, Dwight L. (ed.). *The Original Journals of Henry Smith Turner—With Stephen Watts Kearny to New Mexico and California, 1846–1847.* Norman: University of Oklahoma Press, 1966.

Colton, Walter. *Three Years in California.* New York: A. S. Barnes and Company, 1851.

Colton, Walter. *Deck and Port: Or, Incidents of a Cruise in the United States Frigate Congress to California.* New York: A. S. Barnes and Burr, 1860.

Davis, William H. *Sixty Years in California.* San Francisco: A. J. Leary, 1889.

Du Pont, Samuel F. *Extracts from the Private Journal Letters of Captain S. F. Du Pont.* Wilmington: privately printed, 1885.

Farquhar, Francis P. (ed.). *Up and Down California in 1860–1864: The Journal of William H. Brewer.* Berkeley and Los Angeles: University of California Press, 1974.

Ford, Worthington C. (ed.). *The Letters of Henry Adams.* 2 vols. Boston: Houghton Mifflin Company, 1930.

Fremont, Jessie Benton. *A Year of American Travel: A Narrative of Personal Experience.* San Francisco: Book Club of California, 1960.

Fremont, John C. *Memoirs of My Life.* 2 vols. Chicago: Belford, Clarke, 1887.

George, Henry, Jr. *The Life of Henry George.* New York: Robert Schalkenbach Foundation, 1960.

Hafen, LeRoy R., and Ann W. Hafen (eds.). *Fremont's Fourth Expedition.* Glendale, Cal.: Arthur H. Clark Company, 1960.

Hamilton, James. *Life in Earnest.* New York: Robert Carter, 1848.

Haskins, C. W. (comp.). *The Argonauts of California.* New York: Fords, Howard and Hulbert, 1890.

Heap, Gwin Harris. *Central Route to the Pacific.* Glendale, Cal.: Arthur H. Clark Company, 1957.

Knower, Daniel. *The Adventures of a Forty-Niner.* Albany: Weeds-Parsons Printing Company, 1894.

Langley, Henry G. (comp.). *San Francisco Directory for the Year Commencing October 1863.* San Francisco: Excelsior Steam Presses, 1863.

Lewis, Lesley B. (ed.). *Uncle Sam's Camels.* New Edition. Glorieta, N.M.: Rio Grande Press, 1970.

McLean, Evalyn Walsh. *Father Struck It Rich.* Boston: Little, Brown and Co., 1936.

Newmark, Harris. *Sixty Years in Southern California, 1853–1913.* 4th ed. Los Angeles: Teitlin & Van Brugge, 1970.

Nordhoff, Charles. *California: For Health, Pleasure, and Residence.* New York: Harper and Brothers, 1872.

Nunis, Doyce B. (ed.). *The San Francisco Vigilance Committee of 1856: Three Views.* Los Angeles: Los Angeles Westerners, 1971.

O'Meara, James. *The Vigilance Committee of 1856.* San Francisco: James H. Barry, Publisher, 1887.

Quaife, Milo M. (ed.). *The Diary of James K. Polk, During His Presidency, 1845 to 1849.* 4 vols. Chicago: A. C. McClurg, 1910.

Rogers, Cameron (ed.). *A County Judge in Arcady: Selected Private Papers of Charles Fernald, Pioneer California Jurist.* Glendale, Cal.: Arthur H. Clark Company, 1954.

Rogers, Fred B. *Filings from an Old Saw.* San Francisco: John Howell, 1956.

San Francisco Directory for the Year 1852–3. San Francisco: James M. Parker, 1852.

San Francisco Directory for the Year Commencing 1863. San Francisco: Excelsior Steam Presses, 1863.

Simon, John Y. (ed.). *Personal Memoirs of Julia D. Grant.* New York: G. P. Putnam's Sons, 1975.

Spence, Mary Lee, and Donald Jackson (eds.). *The Expeditions of John C. Fremont.* 5 vols. Urbana: University of Illinois Press, 1970–76.

Taylor, Bayard. *Eldorado, or Adventures in the Path of Empire.* 2 vols. New York: G. P. Putnam, 1850.

Taylor, Bayard. *The Echo Club.* New Edition. Upper Saddle River, N.J.: Literature House, 1970.

Thoron, Ward (ed.). *The Letters of Mrs. Henry Adams, 1863–1883.* Boston: Little, Brown and Company, 1936.

Udell, John. *Journal of John Udell . . . , 1858.* New Haven: Yale University Library, 1952.

Williams, Mary F. (ed.). *Papers of the San Francisco Committee of Vigilance of 1851. III. Minutes and Miscellaneous Papers.* Berkeley and Los Angeles: University of California Press, 1919.

Young, James Russell. *Around the World with General Grant.* 2 vols. New York: American News Co., 1879.

Articles:

Ames, George W., Jr. (ed.). "A Doctor Comes to California: Part II." *California Historical Society Quarterly,* XXI (December 1942), 333–57.

Dillon, Richard H. (ed.). " 'Rejoice Ye Thieves and Harlots': The Vigilance Editorials of the San Francisco Journalist James King of William." *California Historical Society Quarterly,* XXXVII (June 1958), 137–69.

Ellison, William H. (ed.). "Memoirs of the Hon. William M. Gwin: Part II." *California Historical Society Quarterly,* XIX (June 1940), 1957–84.

Florcken, Herbert G. (ed.). "The Law and Order View of the San Francisco Vigilance Committee of 1856: Part IV." *California Historical Society Quarterly,* XV (September 1936), 247–65.

[Jones, William C.] "A Ride Across Mexico." *Littell's Living Age,* XIX (October 21, 1848), 130–32.

Miller, Joaquin. "Kit Carson's Ride," *Harper's Weekly,* XV (August 5, 1871), 713–14.

Peckham, S. F. "On the Supposed Falsification of samples of California Petroleum.: *American Journal of Science and Arts*, Second Series, XLIII (May 1867), 345–51.
Robinson, Edgar E. (ed.). "The Day Journal of Milton S. Latham." *California Historical Society Quarterly*, XI (March 1932), 3–28.

Periodicals
Bakersfield *Southern Californian*, 1875–91.
Bakersfield *Kern County Weekly Courier* (California), 1870–75.
Chester *Delaware County Republican* (Pennsylvania), 1865–74.
Harper's Weekly, 1871, 1876.
Havilah *Weekly Courier* (California), 1866–71.
Los Angeles *News*, 1860–1868.
Los Angeles *Southern California*, 1855.
Los Angeles *Southern Vineyard*, 1858–59.
Los Angeles *Star*, 1851–79.
New Orleans *Picayune*, 1847–49, 1857–60.
New York *Herald*, 1847–61, 1875–78.
New York Times, 1851–93, 1916.
New York *Tribune*, 1847–71.
Philadelphia *North American*, 1848.
Philadelphia *Press*, 1861.
Sacramento *Union*, 1851–77.
Sacramento *Transcript*, 1850–51.
San Francisco *Alta California*, 1849–78.
San Francisco *Bulletin*, 1855–76.
San Francisco *Call*, 1893.
San Francisco *Examiner*, 1870.
San Francisco *Herald*, 1850–63.
San Francisco *Mining and Scientific Press*, 1860–76.
San Francisco *News Letter*, 1893.
San Francisco *Town Talk*, 1854–57.
San Jose *Pioneer*, 1877–95.
Santa Fe *Weekly Gazette*, 1853–60.
Santa Fe Weekly *Republican*, 1847–49.
Tubac *Weekly Arizonian*, 1859.
Washington *National Intelligencer*, 1845–60.
Washington *Post*, 1877–93.
Washington *Evening Star*, 1852–89.
Washington *Union*, 1845–59.

Secondary Sources

Books:
Adams, Henry. *Democracy and Esther: Two Novels by Henry Adams*. Glouchester, Mass.: Peter Smith, 1965.
Anderson, M. S. *The Eastern Question, 1774–1923*. New York: St. Martin's Press, 1966.

Ashmead, Henry Graham. *History of Delaware County, Pennsylvania*. Philadelphia: L. A. Everts & Company, 1884.

Atherton, Gertrude. *The Splendid Idle Forties: Stories of Old California*. New York: Frederick A. Stokes Company, 1902.

Bain, Naomi E. *The Story of Colonel Thomas Baker and the Founding of Bakersfield*. Bakersfield: Kern County Historical Society, 1944.

Bancroft, Hubert Howe. *Popular Tribunals*. 2 vols. San Francisco: History Company, 1887.

Barry, Louise. *The Beginning of the West: Annals of the Kansas Gateway to the American West, 1540–1854*. Topeka: Kansas State Historical Society, 1972.

Bauer, K. Jack. *Surfboats and Horse Marines: U.S. Naval Operations in the Mexican War, 1846–48*. Annapolis: U.S. Naval Institute, 1969.

Bauer, K. Jack. *The Mexican War, 1846–1848*. New York: Macmillan Company, 1974.

Bayard, Samuel J. *Sktech of the Life of Com. Robert F. Stockton*. New York: Derby & Jackson, 1856.

Beale, Marie [Oge]. *Decatur House and Its Inhabitants*. Washington, D.C.: National Trust for Historic Preservation, 1954.

Bearss, Ed, and Arrell M. Gibson. *Fort Smith: Little Gibraltar on the Arkansas*. Norman: University of Oklahoma Press, 1969.

Bonsal, Stephen. *Edward Fitzgerald Beale: A Pioneer in the Path of Empire, 1822–1903*. New York: G. P. Putnam's Sons, 1912.

Boyd, William Harland. *A California Middle Border: The Kern River County, 1772–1880*. Richardson, Tex.: Havilah Press, 1972.

Brown, Dee. *Bury My Heart at Wounded Knee*. New York: Holt, Rinehart and Winston, 1971.

Bullock, Helen D., and Terry B. Morton (eds.). *Decatur House*. Washington, D.C.: National Trust for Historic Preservation, 1967.

Burr, Henry L. *Education in the Early Navy*. Philadelphia: privately printed, 1939.

Carroll, John A. (ed.). *Reflections of Western Historians*. Tucson: University of Arizona Press, 1969.

Carter, Harvey Lewis. *"Dear Old Kit," the Historical Kit Carson*. Norman: University of Oklahoma Press, 1968.

Casebier, Dennis G. *Fort Pah-Ute, California*. Norco, Cal.: Tales of the Mojave Road Publishing Co., 1974.

Casebier, Dennis G. *The Mojave Road*. Norco, Cal.: Tales of the Mojave Road Publishing Co., 1975.

Caughey, John W. *Gold Is the Cornerstone*. Berkeley and Los Angeles: University of California Press, 1948.

Chance, Maria Scott Beale. *Chronicle of the Family of Edward F. Beale of Philadelphia*. Haerford, Penn.: privately printed, 1943.

Chaput, Donald. *Francois X. Aubry: Trader, Trailmaker, and Voyageur in the Southwest, 1846–1854*. Glendale, Cal.: Arthur H. Clark Company, 1975.

Cook, Sheburne F. *The Conflict Between the California Indians and White Civilization*. Berkeley and Los Angeles: University of California Press, 1943.

Crowe, Earl. *Men of El Tejon: Empire in the Tehachapis*. Los Angeles: Ward Ritchie Press, 1957.

Bibliography

Crowe, Earl. *General Beale's Sheep Odyssey*. Bakersfield: Kern County Historical Society, 1960.

Cullimore, Clarence. *Old Adobes of Forgotten Fort Tejon*. Bakersfield: Kern County Historical Society, 1949.

Daley, John M. *Georgetown University: Origin and Early Years*. Washington, D.C.: Georgetown University Press, 1957.

DuVal, Miles P., Jr. *Cadiz to Cathay: The Story of the Long Diplomatic Struggle for the Panama Canal*. Stanford: Stanford University Press, 1947.

Ellison, William H. *A Self-governing Dominion: California, 1849–1860*. Berkeley and Los Angeles: University of California Press, 1950.

Faulk, Odie B. *The U.S. Camel Corps: An Army Experiment*. New York: Oxford University Press, 1976.

Ferguson, Eugene S. *Truxtun of the Constellation: The Life of Commodore Thomas Truxtun, U.S. Navy, 1755–1922*. Baltimore: Johns Hopkins Press, 1956.

Fowler, Harlan. *Camels to California: A Chapter in Western Transportation*. Stanford: Stanford University Press, 1950.

Ginger, Ray. *Age of Excess: The United States from 1877 to 1914*. New York: MacMillan Company, 1965.

Goetzmann, William H. *Army Exploration in the American West, 1803–1863*. New Haven: Yale University Press, 1959.

Goodman, David M. *A Western Panorama, 1849–1875: The Travels, Writings, and Influence of J. Ross Browne*. Glendale, Cal.: Arthur H. Clark Company, 1966.

Greenly, Albert H. *Camels in America*. New York: Bibliographical Society of America, 1952.

Gudde, Erwin (comp.). *California Place Names*. New Edition. Berkeley and Los Angeles: University of California Press, 1969.

Hamilton, Holman. *Prologue to Conflict: The Crisis and Compromise of 1850*. New York: W. W. Norton & Company, 1966.

Harte, Bret. *The Complete Poetical Works of Bret Harte*. Boston: Houghton Mifflin Company, 1910.

Hervey, John. *The American Trotter*. New York: Coward-McCann, 1947.

History of Amador County, California. Oakland: Thompson and West, 1881.

History of San Luis Obispo County, California, With Illustrations and Biographical Sketches of its Prominent Men and Pioneers. Oakland, Cal.: Thompson and West, 1883.

Hodges, Frances B. S. *The Beale Family of Virginia*. Ann Arbor: Edwards Brothers, Inc., 1956.

Hopkins, Henry W. (comp.). *Atlas of Delaware County, Pennsylvania*. Philadelphia: G. M. Hopkins, Publisher, 1870.

Howe, George F. *Chester A. Arthur: A Quarter Century of Machine Politics*. New York: Frederick Ungar Publishing Co., 1957.

Hutchinson, W. H. *Oil, Land, and Politics: The California Career of Thomas Robert Bard*. 2 vols. Norman: University of Oklahoma Press, 1965.

Jackson, W. Turrentine. *Wagon Roads West: A Study of Federal Road Surveys and Construction in the Trans-Mississippi West, 1846–1869*. Berkeley and Los Angeles: University of California Press, 1952.

285

Johnson, Allen, and Dumas Malone (ed.). *The Dictionary of American Biography*, 20 vols. New York: Charles Scribner's Sons, 1935.

Keasbey, Lindley M. *The Nicaragua Canal and the Monroe Doctrine*. New York: G. P. Putnam's Sons, 1896.

Latta, Frank F. *Saga of Rancho El Tejon*. Santa Cruz, Cal.: Bear State Books, 1976.

Lavender, David. *Bent's Fort*. New York: Doubleday, 1954.

McNitt, Frank. *Navajo Wars: Military Campaigns, Slave Raids, and Reprisals*. Albuquerque: University of New Mexico Press, 1972.

Miller, Robert Ryal. *Arms Across the Border: United States Aid to Juarez During the French Intervention in Mexico*. Philadelphia: American Philosophical Society, 1973.

Miner, H. Craig. *The St. Louis-San Francisco Transcontinental Railroad: The Thirty-Fifth Parallel Project, 1853–1890*. Lawrence: University Press of Kansas, 1972.

Murad, Anatol. *Franz Joseph I of Austria and His Empire*. New York: Twayne Publishers, 1968.

Murray, Keith A. *The Modocs and Their War*. Norman: University of Oklahoma Press, 1959.

Myers, John M. *San Francisco's Reign of Terror*. New York: Doubleday, 1966.

National Cyclopedia of American Biography. 56 vols. New York: James T. White and Company, 1898.

Nevins, Allan. *Hamilton Fish: The Inner History of the Grant Administration*. New York: Dodd, Mead & Company, 1936.

Nevins, Allan. *Fremont: Pathmarker of the West*. New York: Appleton Century, Co., 1939.

Parrish, William E. *David Rice Atchison of Missouri, Border Politician*. Columbia: University of Missouri Press, 1961.

Paul Rodman W. *California Gold: The Beginning of Mining in the Far West*. New Edition. Lincoln: University of Nebraska Press, 1965.

Pitkin, Thomas M. *The Captain Departs: Ulysses S. Grant's Last Campaign*. Carbondale: Southern Illinois University Press, 1973.

Plan of the City of Washington . . . [map, 1792]. Ithaca: Historical Urban Plans, 1964.

Pletcher, David M. *The Awkward Years: American Foreign Relations Under Garfield and Arthur*. Columbia: University of Missouri Press, 1962.

Price, Glenn. *Origins of the War with Mexico: The Polk-Stockton Intrigue*. Austin: University of Texas Press, 1967.

Rolle, Andrew. *California: A History*. New Edition. New York: Thomas Y. Crowell Company, 1969.

Samuels, Ernest. *Henry Adams: The Middle Years*. Cambridge: Belknap Press of Harvard University Press, 1958.

Smith, Alexander. *Poems*. Boston: Ticknor and Fields, 1853.

Smith, Justin. *Annexation of Texas*. New York: Baker and Taylor, Co., 1911.

Stewart, George R. *Committee of Vigilance: Revolution in San Francisco, 1851*. Boston: Houghton Mifflin Company, 1964.

Taylor, Bayard. *The Poems of Bayard Taylor*. Boston: Ticknor and Fields, 1866.

Bibliography

Taylor, Frank J., and Earl M. Welty. *Black Bonanza: How an Oil Hunt Grew into the Union Oil Company of California.* New York: McGraw-Hill, 1950.

Thomas, Lately. *Between Two Empires: The Story of California's First Senator—William McKendree Gwin.* Boston: Houghton Mifflin Company, 1969.

White, Gerald T. *Formative Years in the Far West: A History of Standard Oil Company and Predecessors Through 1919.* New York: Appleton-Century-Crofts, 1962.

Williams, David A. *David C. Broderick: A Political Portrait.* San Marino: Huntington Library, 1969.

Woodward, Arthur. *Lances at San Pascual.* San Francisco: California Historical Society, 1948.

Young, James S. *The Washington Community, 1800–1828.* New York: Harcourt, Brace and World, 1966.

Articles:

Ames, George W., Jr. "Gillespie and the Conquest of California: Part III." *California Historical Society Quarterly,* XVII (December 1938), 325–50.

Bieber, Ralph P. "California Gold Mania." *Mississippi Valley Historical Review,* XXXV (June 1948), 3–28.

"Colorado Place Names (C)." *Colorado Magazine,* XVII (July 1940), 125–43.

Crouter, Richard E., and Andrew F. Rolle. "Edward F. Beale and the Indian Peace Commissioners in California, 1851–1854." Historical Society of Southern California *Quarterly,* XLII (June 1960), 107–31.

Dillon, Richard H. "Faith to Move Mountains." *Montana, The Magazine of Western History,* XXI (Autumn 1971), 61–66.

Gates, Paul W. "Carpetbaggers Join the Rush for California Land." *California Historical Society Quarterly,* LVI (Summer 1977), 98–127.

Lesley, Lewis B. "The International Boundary Survey, 1849–50." *California Historical Society Quarterly,* IX (March 1930), 3–15.

Mills, James (comp.). "Historical Landmarks of San Diego County." *Journal of San Diego History,* V (January 1959), 1–27.

Newsome, Samuel A. "From Chester to Asia Minor to Texas to California Before the Civil War." Delaware County Historical Society *Bulletin,* XXI (January–February 1970), 1–4.

Perkins, Arthur B. "Mining Camps of the Soledad: Part I." Historical Society of Southern California *Quarterly,* XL (June 1958), 149–73.

Ringler, Donald P. "Mary Austin: Kern County Days, 1888–1892." *Southern California Quarterly,* XVI (March 1963), 25–63.

Ripley, Vienette S. "The San Francisco Pass and the Pioneer Traffic that Went Over It: Part IV." Historical Society of Southern California *Quarterly,* XXX (June 1948), 111–35.

Shutes, Milton H. "Abraham Lincoln and the New Almaden Mine." *California Historical Society Quarterly,* XV (March 1936), 3–20.

Theses:

Crampton, C. Gregory. "The Opening of the Mariposa Mining Region, 1849–1859, with particular reference to the Mexican Land Grant of John Charles Fremont." Ph.D. dissertation, University of California, 1941.

Ellison, William H. "Federal Indian Policy in California, 1846–1860." Ph.D. dissertation, University of California, 1919.

Johns, Sally C. "The Battle of San Pasqual." M.A. thesis, University of San Diego, 1972.

Hussey, John A. "The United States and the Bear Flag Revolt." Ph.D. dissertation, University of California, 1941.

Leonard, Charles. "Federal Indian Policy in the San Joaquin Valley, Its Application and Results." Ph.D. dissertation, University of California, 1928.

Mathews, Sidney T. "Nicaragua Canal Controversy: The Struggle for an American-constructed and controlled Transitway." Ph.D. dissertation, Johns Hopkins University, 1947.

Rasp, Howard A. "United States Relations with Nicaragua Concerning an Interoceanic Canal, 1850–1903." M.A. thesis, University of Arizona, 1969.

Scharf, Thomas. "Amiel Weeks Whipple: Boundary and Railroad Surveys in the Southwest, 1849–1854." M.A. thesis, University of San Diego, 1973.

Stanley, Gerald. "The Republican Party in California, 1856–1868." Ph.D. dissertation, University of Arizona, 1973.

Letters:

Burch, Jane A., to author, April 30, 1977.

Glancey, Lee A., to author, December 15, 1976.

Snell, Joseph W., to author, May 13, 1975.

I N D E X

Compiled by Stephanie Sardelis

and Surveyor-General's Office,
126, 138–39
Law and Order Party, *89–96*
Lea, Luke, and California Indian
affairs, *49–64*
Leaming, Charles, *174, 198*
Lecompton Democrats, *129*
Lee, Robert E., *148*
Leopard (Arabian horse), *221, 231*
Leroux, Antoine, *60*
Lincoln, Abraham, noted, *175,
239, 264 n 16, 266 n 31*; and
Surveyor-General's Office,
125–31, 137, 147–66, 169
Lincoln Hall (Chester,
Pennsylvania), *179*
Linden Tree (Arabian horse), *231*
Lindrum, John H., *53*
Littel's Living Age (Boston,
Massachusetts), *32*
Little Axe (Indian scout), *112*
Little Colorado River (Arizona),
117
Livingston, Edward, *195*
Livingston, LaRhett L., *95*
Lizardo, Anton (Mexico), *31*
Lodge, Henry Cabot, *236*
Loeser, Lucien, *249 n 6*
Logan, John A., *222, 230*
Logan, H. C., *53, 224*
Lone Mountain Cemetery (San
Francisco, California), *91*
Long Branch (New Jersey), Beale
vacations at, *191–92, 197, 221*
Lopez, Chico, *230*
Lopez, J. J., *214, 230, 234*
Los Angeles (California), noted,
*29, 130, 134, 174, 196, 212,
234*; and Mexican War, *16–17,
22*; and Indian affairs, *46,
54–55, 62–68, 73–77*; camels
and wagon road expedition,
110, 115, 118–22; land
problems in, *142–44, 148,
153–54, 165*

Los Angeles Petroleum Refining
Company, *198*
Los Angeles *Semi-Weekly News,
177*
Los Angeles *Southern News, 134*
Los Angeles *Southern Vineyard,
121*
Los Angeles *Star*, noted, *134, 148,
153, 165, 167*; opinions on
wagon road, *121–22*; supports
Beale's reservation, *71–72*
Loudon Park Cemetery (Maryland),
236
Louisville (Kentucky), *105*
Lyon, Sanford, *94, 174, 177, 198*
Lyon's Station (California), *198*

McAllister, Hall, *93, 147*
McClellan, George B., *215*
McClelland, Robert, as Interior
Secretary, *58–61, 70–73, 256 n
22*
McClure, David, *7*
McCorkle, Joseph W., *47*
McDougall, James A., *67, 100*
Machado, Raphael, *18*
McKee, Redick, noted, *94*; as
Indian agent in California,
46–59, 65–67
McKeever, Isaac, *7*
McKnight, John, *24*
McLean, Edward Beale, *229*
McLean, Emily Beale (daughter of
E. F. Beale), noted, *158, 204,
213*; receives letter from her
father, *171–72*; in Washington
society, *219–24, 229, 234*
McLean, John R., marriage to
Emily Beale, *223–24*
McNulty, C. A., *98*
MacVeagh, Wayne, *187*
Mammoth Claim (California),
177
Mammoth Company, *174, 177*
Manchester, William R., *17*